Novell® Linux Desktop 9
User's Handbook

JOE HABRAKEN

Novell
PRESS™
Novell®

Published by Pearson Education, Inc.
800 East 96th Street, Indianapolis, Indiana 46240 USA

Novell® Linux Desktop 9 User's Handbook

Copyright © 2006 by Novell, Inc.

All rights reserved. No part of this book shall be reproduced, stored in a retrieval system, or transmitted by any means, electronic, mechanical, photocopying, recording, or otherwise, without written permission from the publisher. No patent liability is assumed with respect to the use of the information contained herein. Although every precaution has been taken in the preparation of this book, the publisher and author assume no responsibility for errors or omissions. Nor is any liability assumed for damages resulting from the use of the information contained herein.

International Standard Book Number: 0-672-32729-5

Library of Congress Catalog Card Number: 2004095994

Printed in the United States of America

First Printing: October 2005

08 07 06 05   4 3 2 1

Trademarks

All terms mentioned in this book that are known to be trademarks or service marks have been appropriately capitalized. Novell Press cannot attest to the accuracy of this information. Use of a term in this book should not be regarded as affecting the validity of any trademark or service mark.

Novell is a registered trademark; Novell Press and the Novell Press logo are trademarks of Novell, Inc. in the United States and other countries. All brand names and product names used in this book are trade names, service marks, trademarks, or registered trademarks of their respective owners.

Warning and Disclaimer

Every effort has been made to make this book as complete and as accurate as possible, but no warranty or fitness is implied. The information provided is on an "as is" basis. The author and the publisher shall have neither liability nor responsibility to any person or entity with respect to any loss or damages arising from the information contained in this book or from the use of the CD or programs accompanying it.

Special and Bulk Sales

Pearson offers excellent discounts on this book when ordered in quantity for bulk purchases or special sales. For more information, please contact

U.S. Corporate and Government Sales
1-800-382-3419
corpsales@pearsontechgroup.com

For sales outside of the U.S., please contact

International Sales
international@pearsoned.com

Acquisitions Editor
Jenny Watson

Development Editor
Scott Meyers

Managing Editor
Charlotte Clapp

Project Editor
Mandie Frank

Copy Editor
Geneil Breeze

Indexer
Chris Barrick

Proofreader
Elizabeth Scott

Technical Editor
Don Vosburg

Publishing Coordinator
Vanessa Evans

Multimedia Developer
Dan Scherf

Book Designer
Gary Adair

Page Layout
Brad Chinn

Novell Press is the exclusive publisher of trade computer technology books that have been authorized by Novell, Inc. Novell Press books are written and reviewed by the world's leading authorities on Novell and related technologies, and are edited, produced, and distributed by the Que/Sams Publishing group of Pearson Education, the worldwide leader in integrated education and computer technology publishing. For more information on Novell Press and Novell Press books, please go to www.novellpress.com.

Associate Publisher
Mark Taber

Program Manager, Novell, Inc.
Darrin Vandenbos

Marketing Manager
Doug Ingersoll

Contents at a Glance

PART I   **Novell Linux Desktop Basics**

CHAPTER 1:	Start Here	3
CHAPTER 2:	Starting Novell Linux Desktop	19
CHAPTER 3:	Working on the NLD Desktop	31
CHAPTER 4:	Modifying the NLD Desktop	57
CHAPTER 5:	Configure NLD Hardware and System Settings	87
CHAPTER 6:	Managing Files	119
CHAPTER 7:	Adding and Managing Software Applications and Tools in NLD	153

PART II   **Using the Internet and Multimedia Tools**

CHAPTER 8:	Browsing the World Wide Web with Mozilla Firefox	173
CHAPTER 9:	Using Other Internet Tools	199

PART III   **Using Productivity and Collaboration Software**

CHAPTER 10:	Working with OpenOffice.org Applications	219
CHAPTER 11:	Creating Documents with OpenOffice.org Writer	237
CHAPTER 12:	Creating Spreadsheets with OpenOffice.org Calc	273
CHAPTER 13:	Creating Presentations with OpenOffice.org Impress	301
CHAPTER 14:	Managing Email and Contacts with Novell Evolution	331
CHAPTER 15:	Staying Organized with Novell Evolution	367
CHAPTER 16:	Using Novell iFolder	391
INDEX		403

Table of Contents

Part I **Novell Linux Desktop Basics**

    CHAPTER 1: Start Here — 3

    CHAPTER 2: Starting Novell Linux Desktop — 19
- **1** About Booting the NLD System and Logon Options — 20
- **2** Log On to the System — 24
- **3** About Logoff Options — 25
- **4** Log Off the System from the Desktop — 26
- **5** Shut Down the System from the Logon Manager — 28

    CHAPTER 3: Working on the NLD Desktop — 31
- **6** About the GNOME Desktop — 32
- **7** Navigate the GNOME Desktop — 34
- **8** Use the Menu System — 36
- **9** Manage Virtual Desktops — 37
- **10** Change the System Date and Time Settings — 39
- **11** Get Help on the GNOME Desktop — 42
- **12** Run a Program from the Run Application Dialog — 45
- **13** Access the Command Line — 47
- **14** About File Commands — 50
- **15** Use File Commands — 51
- **16** About System Commands — 53
- **17** Use System Commands — 54

    CHAPTER 4: Modifying the NLD Desktop — 57
- **18** About Modifying GNOME — 58
- **19** Create Desktop Icons — 59
- **20** Add an Item to a Panel — 62
- **21** Add an Item to a Menu — 63

22	About GNOME Personal Settings	65
23	Change Personal Settings	67
24	Change the Desktop's Background	70
25	Change Fonts	73
26	Select a Screensaver	76
27	Use the Lock Screen Tool	78
28	About Desktop Themes	79
29	Change the Current Desktop Theme	81
30	Add Themes to GNOME	82
31	Change Window Preferences	85

CHAPTER 5: Configuring NLD Hardware and System Settings **87**

32	About Configuring Hardware and System Settings in NLD	88
33	Change Keyboard Settings	91
34	Change Mouse Settings	94
35	About Printing and NLD	96
36	Add and Configure a Printer	98
37	Print to a Printer	102
38	Manage Print Jobs	104
39	Delete a Printer	106
40	Configure Sound Settings	107
41	Change the Screen Resolution	110
42	Change Session Settings	112
43	Change Other System Settings	114

CHAPTER 6: Managing Files **119**

44	About the Linux File Structure and Nautilus File Manager	120
45	Configure Nautilus Preferences	122
46	Use Nautilus to Manage Folders	126
47	Browse and Open Files	129
48	Find Files	131

49	Delete Files	134
50	Copy and Move Files	136
51	Access Recent Files	137
52	Access and Save Files to a USB Memory Stick	138
53	Burn Files on a CD or DVD	140
54	About Archiving Files	144
55	Archive Files with File Roller	145
56	About Backing Up and Restoring Files	148
57	Back Up Files	149
58	Restore Files	151

CHAPTER 7: Adding and Managing Software Applications and Tools in NLD — **153**

59	About Updating and Adding Applications to NLD	154
60	About Updating Applications Using Red Carpet	156
61	Run Red Carpet to Update NLD Applications	158
62	About RPMs	160
63	Find Applications Using Red Carpet	162
64	Install Applications Using Red Carpet	164
65	Install and Remove Applications Using YaST	165
66	About Installing Applications from Other Archive Types	168

Part II Using the Internet and Multimedia Tools

CHAPTER 8: Browsing the World Wide Web with Mozilla Firefox — **173**

67	About Mozilla Firefox	174
68	Browse Web Pages	176
69	Use Tabbed Browsing	178
70	Print a Web Page	180
71	Control Pop-ups in Firefox	182
72	Access the Browsing History	185

73	Create a Bookmark	187
74	About Managing Bookmarks	188
75	Move and Edit Bookmarks	189
76	Sort Bookmarks	191
77	About Cookies and Firefox	192
78	Accept and Reject Cookies	194
79	Manage Cookies	196

CHAPTER 9: Using Other Internet Tools — 199

80	About Internet Email Accounts	200
81	Configure an Email Client	202
82	About Instant Messaging	206
83	Configure Gaim Instant Messenger	207
84	Use Gaim Instant Messenger	208
85	About Internet Usenet Newsgroups	210
86	Configure the Pan News Reader	210
87	Use the Pan News Reader	212
88	About Other NLD Internet Communication Tools	215

Part III Using Productivity and Collarboration Software

CHAPTER 10: Working with OpenOffice.org Applications — 219

89	About OpenOffice.org	220
90	Start OpenOffice.org Applications	221
91	Configure OpenOffice.org Global Options	223
92	About Sharing Documents with Microsoft Office Users	227
93	Start a New File	228
94	Save a Document	230
95	Open an Existing Document	232
96	Get Help in OpenOffice.org	233

CHAPTER 11: Creating Documents with OpenOffice.org Writer — **237**

97	About OpenOffice.org Writer	238
98	Use the AutoPilot to Create a Document	240
99	Format Characters	243
100	Format Paragraphs	245
101	About Writer Styles	247
102	Use the Stylist	249
103	Create a Paragraph Style	250
104	Insert Headers, Footers, and Page Numbers	252
105	Use Format Page Options	254
106	Move Text	257
107	Insert a Table	258
108	Insert a Text Frame	261
109	Place Graphics in a Document	263
110	Do a Mail Merge	266
111	About Printing in Writer	269
112	Print a Document	270

CHAPTER 12: Creating Spreadsheets with OpenOffice.org Calc — **273**

113	About OpenOffice.org Calc	274
114	Enter Text and Data	275
115	Enter Dates	279
116	About Creating Formulas	280
117	Create a Formula	281
118	About Calc Functions	282
119	Use the Function AutoPilot	283
120	Select and Format Spreadsheet Cells	285
121	Insert and Delete Columns	286
122	Insert and Delete Rows	288
123	Insert, Name, and Delete Sheets	289
124	Sort and Filter Data	291

125	About Calc Charts	293
126	Insert and Format a Chart	294
127	Print a Spreadsheet	297

CHAPTER 13: Creating Presentations with OpenOffice.org Impress — 301

128	About OpenOffice.org Impress	302
129	Create a New Presentation	303
130	Insert a New Slide	306
131	Add Text to a Slide	307
132	Modify Slide Layout	309
133	Change Slide Design	311
134	Use the Object Bar	313
135	Insert Graphics and Other Objects	315
136	Select a Slide Transition	317
137	Add Slide Animation Effects	319
138	Change the Workspace View	321
139	Rehearse Slide Show Timings	323
140	Change Slide Show Settings	325
141	Run the Slide Show	327
142	Print Slides, Notes, and Handouts	328

CHAPTER 14: Managing Email and Contacts with Novell Evolution — 331

143	About Novell Evolution	332
144	Add an Email Account to Evolution	334
145	About Email and Evolution	336
146	Compose and Send Email	338
147	Send an Email with an Attachment	340
148	Receive and Reply to Email	341
149	Work with Received Email Attachments	343
150	Read, Sort, and Search Your Email	345
151	Organize Your Email	348

152	Use the Junk Mail Filter	351
153	Create Virtual Folders	353
154	About the Evolution Address Book	356
155	Create a New Contact	357
156	Edit an Existing Contact	359
157	Create Contact Lists	360
158	Search for Contacts	361
159	Use Categories to Group Contacts	362
160	Import Contacts	363

CHAPTER 15: Staying Organized with Novell Evolution — 367

161	About the Evolution Calendar	368
162	Create Appointments	369
163	Send a Meeting Invitation	372
164	Manage Appointments and Meetings	375
165	Create Tasks	377
166	Create Assigned Tasks	379
167	Create Task Lists	381
168	Use Calendar Views	382
169	Set Evolution Preferences	383
170	About Synchronizing a Handheld Device with Evolution	384
171	Delete Evolution Items	387

CHAPTER 16: Using Novell iFolder — 391

172	About Novell iFolder	392
173	Start the iFolder Client	392
174	Access iFolder from the Desktop	395
175	Access Your iFolder from a Web Browser	396
176	About Synchronizing Files	398
177	Manually Synchronize Files	399
178	View Files in the iFolder Conflict Bin	400
179	Set iFolder Preferences	401

INDEX — **403**

About the Author

Joe Habraken is a best-selling author and information technology professional who has written more than 20 books on networking, desktop operating systems, and software applications. Joe serves as an assistant professor at the University of New England where he teaches a variety of information technology and communication courses. His recent titles include the *Absolute Beginner's Guide to Networking* (Fourth Edition) and *Skinning Microsoft Windows XP*.

Dedication

To Big Man the cat and all the users of Novell Linux Desktop.

Acknowledgments

It definitely takes a team to create a book, and I have a number of people to thank. I would like to thank all the folks at Novell Press who had a hand in creating this book. A big thanks to my longtime (at least it seems like a long time) acquisitions editor, Jenny Watson, who pulled the editorial team together for this book and managed the book creation process from initial idea to published manuscript. I would also like to thank Don Vosburg the technical editor on the project and Scott Meyers the development editor. Also a big thanks goes out to Vanessa Evans, Mandie Frank, Geneil Breeze, and Elizabeth Scott.

We Want to Hear from You!

As the reader of this book, *you* are our most important critic and commentator. We value your opinion and want to know what we're doing right, what we could do better, what topics you'd like to see us cover, and any other words of wisdom you're willing to pass our way.

You can email or write me directly to let me know what you did or didn't like about this book—as well as what we can do to make our books better.

Please note that I cannot help you with technical problems related to the topic of this book and that due to the high volume of mail I receive I may not be able to reply to every message.

When you write, please be sure to include this book's title and author as well as your name and email address or phone number. I will carefully review your comments and share them with the author and editors who worked on the book.

Email: feedback@novellpress.com

Mail: Mark Taber
Associate Publisher
Novell Press/Pearson Education
800 East 96th Street
Indianapolis, IN 46240 USA

Reader Services

For more information about this book or others from Novell Press, visit our website at www.novellpress.com. Type the ISBN or the title of a book in the Search field to find the page you're looking for.

PART I

Novell Linux Desktop Basics

1 Start Here   3
2 Starting Novell Linux Desktop   19
3 Working on the NLD Desktop   31
4 Modifying the NLD Desktop   57
5 Configure NLD Hardware and System Settings   87
6 Managing Files   119
7 Adding and Managing Software Applications and Tools to NLD   153

CHAPTER 1: Start Here

Understanding GNU Software

The Linux kernel is an example of software licensed under GNU (GNU is an acronym that stands for GNU's not Unix). The GNU Project actually began in 1984 to develop an open source operating system, with the result being Linux. The GNU licensing strategy means that no one actually owns Linux (or more appropriately GNU/Linux), but anyone can use the source code to develop his own distributions and tools (as already discussed). The GNU Project's key sponsor is the Free Software Foundation (FSF).

GNU software is not restricted to the Linux platform. Another example of GNU licensed software is OpenOffice.org, which is a productivity suite similar to Microsoft Office. OpenOffice.org is available for the Linux platform, but it is also available for other platforms. There is actually a version that runs in the Windows environment. We will discuss OpenOffice.org in more detail in later chapters in this book.

Other tools available for the Linux environment, such as the GNOME desktop and the Mozilla Firefox web browser, are also licensed under GNU. The possibilities provided by GNU have led to the creation of many applications and other tools that are readily available to users worldwide. It has also helped to build an operating system platform that has great promise and flexibility as developers expand and fine-tune the software available for Linux systems.

> **NOTE**
>
> Because Linux and many software programs that run in the Linux environment are licensed under GNU, it appears that Linux is really freeware. But that depends on the distribution. You can download many Linux distributions for free. However, to take advantage of proprietary software tools and other services, such as easy system updates, software media (receiving the distribution on CD or DVD), and support, it is necessary to purchase a particular distribution such as NLD. For more about GNU and the Free Software Foundation see http://www.GNU.org.

The Novell Linux Desktop GUI

In terms of actual use in businesses and other institutions, network administrators have embraced Linux for a number of years, particularly in the realm of network servers. For example, the Apache web server, which runs on the Linux platform, is a popular product for hosting websites. Neither network administrators running Linux implementations nor Linux aficionados have ever really been daunted by the fact that to administer a computer running Linux, a very good grasp of the Linux shell commands (the command-line tools) is necessary.

The Novell Linux Desktop GUI

Obviously, for Linux to become popular on an end-user's desktop, the environment has to be both friendly and easy to operate. Most end-users do not want to deal with a complex set of commands run in a command-line environment. This is where the Linux Graphical User Interface (GUI) comes in. NLD uses the GNOME (GNU Network Object Model Environment) desktop by default.

NOTE

NLD provides a choice of GUIs: GNOME and KDE (K Desktop Environment). These two GUIs are similar. However, because GNOME is the default GUI for an NLD installation, this book covers GNOME. For more information on GNOME (in terms of its development) see http://www.gnome.org. For more about KDE, check out http://www.kde.org.

GNOME isn't actually a part of the NLD operating system; it is an open source GUI (GNU software as discussed in the previous section) that can be run by NLD (and other Linux distributions). GNOME provides a desktop environment that embraces all the aspects of the typical end-user GUI. Software and files can be manipulated using icons and applications, and tools are run in windows.

The GNOME desktop provides a familiar and easy-to-use graphical user interface for NLD.

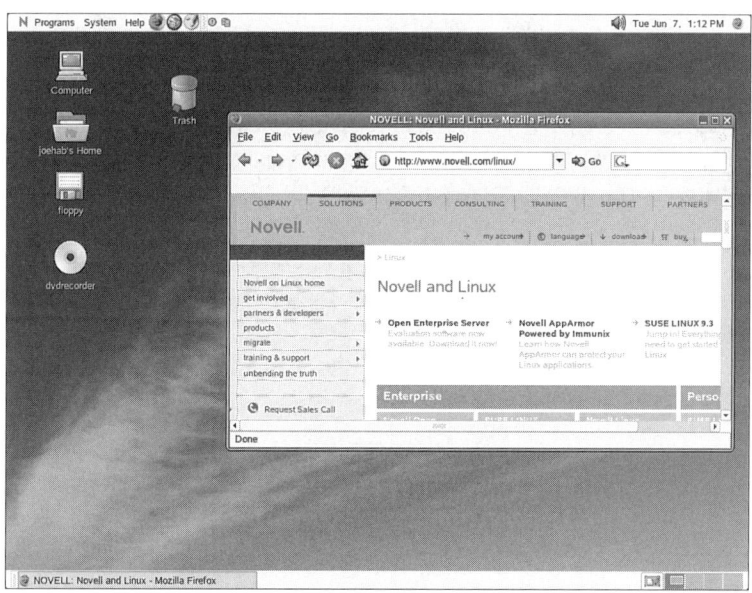

So as we discuss the ins and outs of Novell Linux Desktop in this book, GNOME will serve as the launching pad and workspace for the Linux applications and tools that you run. We will discuss GNOME in more detail in Chapter 3, "Working on the NLD Desktop," and Chapter 4, "Modifying the NLD Desktop."

Novell Linux Desktop Applications and Tools

Although each of us uses a PC for a particular purpose, every user needs a core set of applications and tools, such as a word processor, spreadsheet program, web browser, email client, calendar program, and file management tool. NLD provides all these applications and more. The great thing is that these important software packages are installed by default when you install NLD on your computer.

We will cover a number of software productivity products and tools throughout this book. Let's take a quick look at some of the most important (at least in my mind) software applications that NLD provides.

OpenOffice.org

OpenOffice.org is a productivity suite that includes Writer (a document processor), Calc (a spreadsheet program), Impress (a presentation creator), Draw (a drawing and diagram creator), and Database User Tools that allow you to connect to network databases. Each of these applications shares a common interface including menus and tools. OpenOffice.org also makes it easy to drag and drop and share information across the applications to create complex reports and other documents.

An overview of OpenOffice.org will be provided in Chapter 10, "Working with OpenOffice.org Applications." We will take a closer look at Writer, Calc, and Impress in Chapter 11, "Creating Documents with OpenOffice.org Writer"; Chapter 12, "Creating Spreadsheets with OpenOffice.org Calc"; and Chapter 13, "Creating Presentations with OpenOffice.org Impress," respectively.

NOTE

For more information on where OpenOffice.org came from and where it is going as an application suite, check out http://www.openoffice.org.

Writer is a powerful document processor and is part of the OpenOffice.org productivity suite.

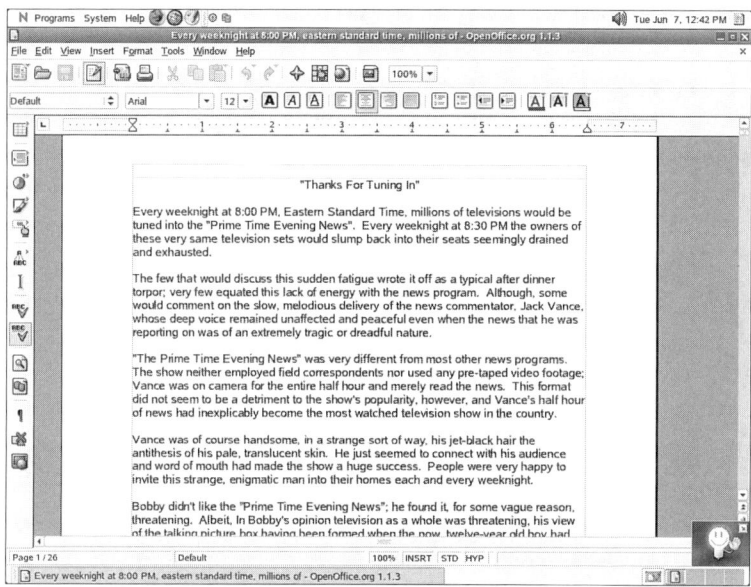

Mozilla Firefox

Whether you use the Web for business, research, or entertainment, it's important to have a web browser that minimizes the dangers of adware, pop-ups, and spyware. Your web browser also should make it easy for you to find the websites you are looking for and to save their web addresses for later reference. Mozilla Firefox fulfills all these requirements and more.

Mozilla Firefox is cross-platform (available for more than one operating system platform including Linux and Microsoft Windows) GNU software and was created by the Mozilla Foundation. Firefox provides unique features such as tabbed web browsing and a built-in pop-up blocker.

We will take a closer look at Mozilla Firefox in Chapter 8, which includes information on creating and managing bookmarks, blocking pop-ups, and using tabbed browsing.

NOTE

For general information and various reviews of Mozilla Firefox check out http://www.mozilla.org/products/firefox/.

CHAPTER 1: Start Here

The Mozilla Firefox web browser window.

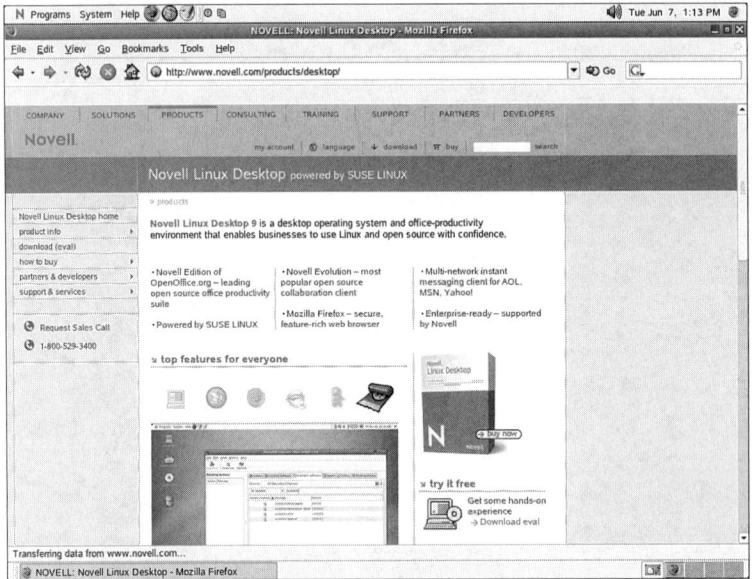

Novell Evolution

All computer users, particularly those who use the PC extensively as a business tool, strive to stay organized and maintain a list of appointments, contacts, and emails. Novell Evolution is a groupware product that pulls together important business tools into one software package. Novell Evolution allows you to manage your email, calendar, contacts, and tasks. It also provides compatibility with network groupware servers such as Novell GroupWise and Microsoft Exchange. Chapter 14, "Managing Email and Contacts with Novell Evolution," and Chapter 15, "Staying Organized with Novell Evolution," provide more detailed information on how to use Novell Evolution.

KEY TERM

Groupware—Client communication software that allows collaboration with other users and is designed to connect to a communication server product.

Keep track of your appointments using Novell Evolution's Calendar.

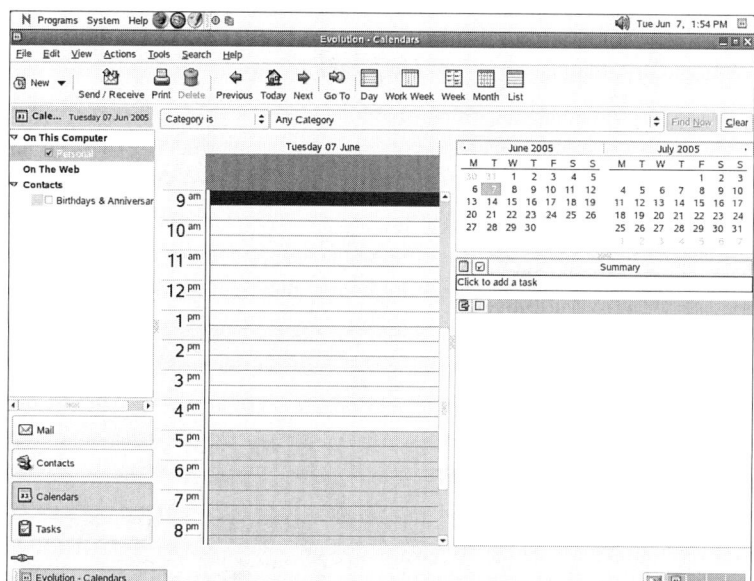

Other NLD Tools

NLD also provides a number of other tools—for example, a calculator, dictionary, and file manager (the Nautilus File Manager, covered in Chapter 6, "Managing Files"). Each of these tools can be opened via the Accessories submenu on the NLD Programs menu.

NOTE

NLD includes a lot of other software. You can play and burn CDs, watch a DVD movie (if your PC has a DVD drive), and even play a number of preinstalled games.

CHAPTER 1: Start Here

Tools such as a file manager, dictionary, and calculator are readily available from the Accessories submenu.

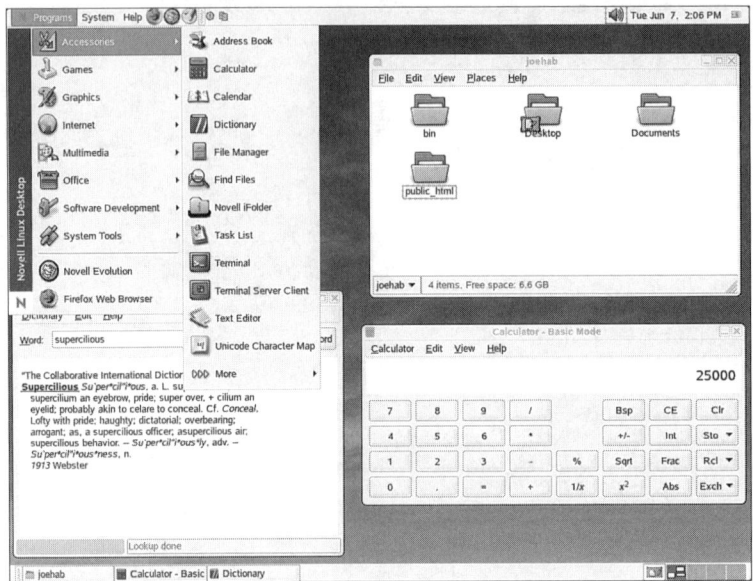

Novell Linux Desktop Installation Considerations

Before you can take advantage of all the possibilities that NLD provides, you need to install the operating system on your computer. In most business settings your computer support personnel have probably already taken care of the installation. But in case you are installing NLD yourself, this section provides some general information on the installation process.

NLD can be installed from CDs or DVDs, and the installation process for NLD is straightforward. The process is handled by YaST, an installation and configuration utility that walks you step-by-step through the install process (it is actually an automated version of YaST called autoYaST that handles the NLD installation).

NOTE

YaST (Yet Another Setup Tool) also serves as the configuration tool used to change administrative settings related to hardware and software. YaST requires the use of the root account. YaST is actually provided by the SUSE Linux core that drives the NLD OS.

YaST allows you to select settings such as the language to be used, the default desktop (GNOME or KDE), and the time zone. In terms of identifying hardware components on the PC, YaST can actually recognize most hardware configurations during the installation process, which means that much of the work you do is to accept YaST-determined settings and then move on to the next step in the process.

Let's take a look at the hardware requirements for the installation of NLD. We can then take a look at how Linux partitions are used to partition your computer's hard drive. We can then look at some of the highlights related to the actual installation process.

Hardware Requirements

Novell provides both minimum and recommended hardware configurations for the installation of NLD. These system requirements follow:

- Processor—Intel Pentium II or compatible running at 266 MHz minimum, with a recommended processor of Intel Pentium III or compatible running at 500 MHz.
- Memory (RAM)—256MB minimum and 500MB or more suggested.
- Video display—A video card that can display 800X600 pixels is the minimum, and a display that provides 1024X768 pixels is suggested.
- Hard drive space—A minimum of 800MB is suggested, and 2GB or more is recommended.

It is safe to say that in terms of hardware configurations more is always better. The higher the processor speed, the greater the memory, and the more fixed disk space available, the better NLD will run on your PC.

Understanding Linux Partitions

During the NLD installation process your hard drive (we will assume a single hard drive on the computer) is partitioned. A partition is actually a way to logically divide the disk space into pieces recognizable by the operating system. In Windows, these partitions are assigned drive letters, but not in Linux.

AutoYaST takes a look at your hard drive and then creates two partitions during the installation: a *swap partition* and a *root partition*. These partitions would be specified as /dev/hda1 and /dev/hda2, respectively, on an IDE hard drive (/dev/sda1 and /dev/sda2 on a computer using SCSI drives). You need both of these partitions for the system to function. The swap partition is used by the system to hold excess process and information that it can't currently copy into

CHAPTER 1: Start Here

the computer's memory. So, the swap drive is basically used to swap information in and out of the computer's memory as you use the computer. A root partition is also created and is used as the main virtual drive for the system. This drive holds the system files for the NLD installation and is required for the system to boot.

YaST configures the disk partitions although you have the option of creating your own.

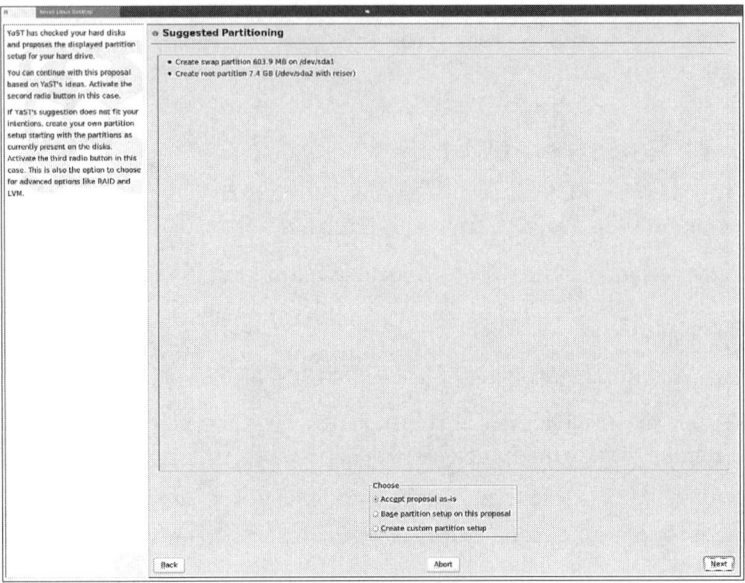

Other partitions can be created during the installation. But the process requires a working knowledge of the ins and outs of partitioning. Because data directories can be used to sequester files for different users and other purposes, it may make sense to allow YaST to perform the partitioning for you.

NOTE

If you want to attempt to install a dual-boot system that runs NLD and another operating system (such as an existing Windows installation), you might need to create your own partitions during the NLD installation. Typically, YaST looks at your hard drive and attempts to resize the existing Windows partition to create space for the swap and root NLD partitions.

Novell Linux Desktop Installation Considerations

We will take a closer look at directories and file systems in Chapter 6, which provides further insight into the naming conventions of Linux partitions and directories and how to navigate them.

Other Tips on the NLD Installation Process

Before we end our discussion of the NLD installation and then move on to actually exploring NLD and the software that it provides, a few other items should be discussed. First, in terms of the overall installation process, it is probably best to allow YaST to do its job and configure the system for you. This means that you click Accept more times than not.

When you first boot the system for the installation (your NLD CD or DVD should be in the appropriate drive), the first installation screen that appears can be a little confusing. Just press the down arrow key on the keyboard to select Installation. You can then press Enter and begin the installation process.

Press the down arrow key to select Installation and then press Enter to begin the installation process.

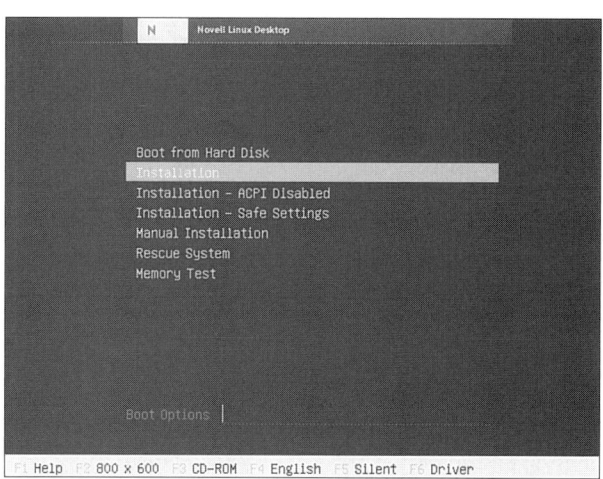

At least two accounts are created during the NLD installation: root and a user account. As already mentioned, the root account is the administrative account for the NLD system. The password created for root should be between five and eight characters and should consist of alphanumeric (both letters and numbers) characters. You can also vary the case of the characters in the password, but you have to be able to repeat the password exactly as it was created (including case). This makes a *strong password*, meaning that it is more difficult to guess.

CHAPTER 1: Start Here

During the NLD installation you enter and then repeat the password for the root account.

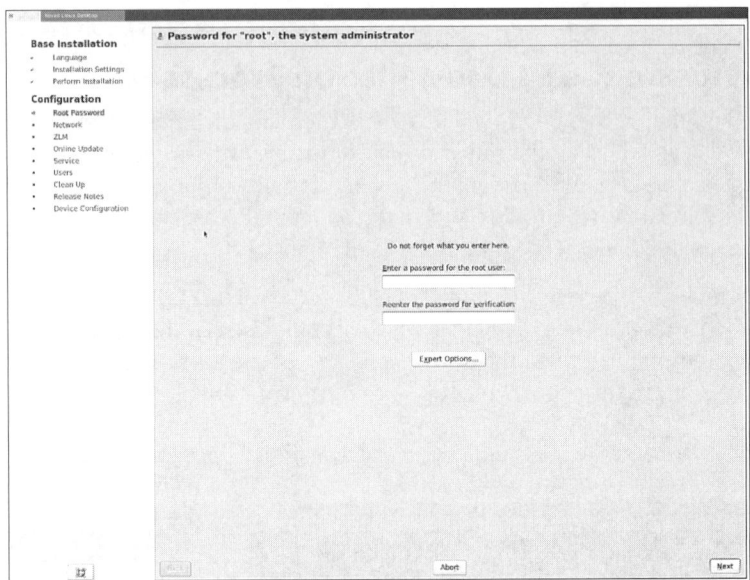

You run the root account only when the system needs to be configured or new software needs to be installed. You don't want to run as root all the time (mainly for security reasons). In some cases, you may work at a company or institution where NLD was installed on your system for you. So, you may not even have the root password for as a security precaution.

At least one user account should also be created during the installation process. This is your user account; the account you will use as you use NLD and its software. Remember that Linux is case-sensitive. Make sure that you know whether Caps Lock was on when you typed in the username and password before you move on from the installation screen that allows you to configure the root and user account.

NOTE

Additional user accounts can be created during the installation process. Click User Management on the Add a New Local User screen. They can also be created in NLD using root. NLD is actually an excellent environment for situations where a computer is shared by multiple users. Each user will have a specific working directory and can personalize the look and feel of the GNOME desktop.

TIP

You can also add user accounts from the NLD desktop after you have logged on to the system. Adding user accounts requires the root password. Administrator Settings can be reached via the System menu. You then use YaST to create users. YaST can also be used to edit user accounts; for example, you might want to change your own password. Again, however, if you don't have the root password and root privileges, you can't change settings reserved for the administrator.

After the NLD installation is complete, the system reboots. You can then log in using your username and password. We discuss the boot and logon processes in Chapter 2, "Starting Novell Linux Desktop."

CHAPTER 2

Starting Novell Linux Desktop

IN THIS CHAPTER:

1. About Booting the NLD System and Logon Options
2. Log On to the System
3. About Logoff Options
4. Log Off the System from the Desktop
5. Shut Down the System from the Logon Manager

In this chapter we take a look at booting NLD, logging on to the system, and then logging off and shutting down the system correctly. You might think that turning the computer on and then logging on to the system would be straightforward—and it is—but there are some logon options that we need to explore.

First, to log on to the system you need a valid username and password. The user could have been created by you during the NLD installation process or by your network administrator if you didn't play a part in the NLD installation on the PC.

NOTE

You only have rights to change or add user accounts if you have the root password. So, if your account has been created for you, you won't be able to add users or change settings related to the user accounts.

Logging on to the system is straightforward after the user accounts have been established (particularly the user account you will use). You might also think that logging off and then turning off the system must really be a piece of cake; however, the Linux shutdown process can actually take some time as the various system processes are terminated. Pulling the plug (meaning turning off the power) on the system before the shutdown is complete can actually lead to corruption of the system files and loss of data. Let's take a closer look at the logon screen and logon options.

1 About Booting the NLD System and Logon Options

When you boot the NLD system, your computer initializes its hardware (such as the processor). Then a boot loader, a small program that resides on the root partition of your hard drive, begins to load the Linux kernel and passes control of the system over to Linux (in this case NLD). The boot loader program actually provides a text screen that allows you to select boot options such as a regular boot (Linux) or a boot to a floppy or failsafe boot, which provides a command line only.

KEY TERM

Boot—The process where a computer system is initialized, and an operating system is loaded.

About Booting the NLD System and Logon Options

The boot loader provides options for how you want the system to boot.

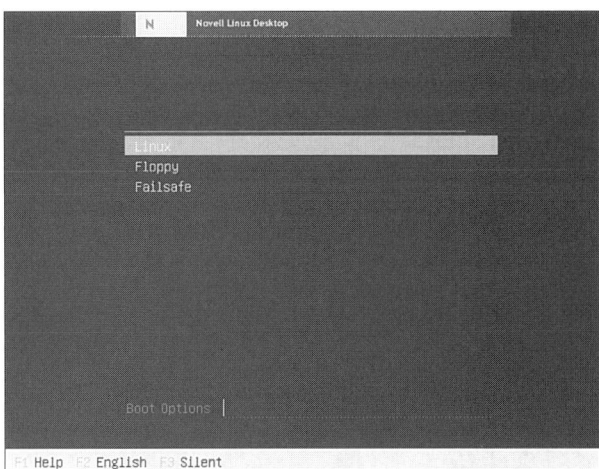

NLD then communicates with the computer's memory and other hardware components as it readies the system for use. As these events take place, the kernel writes them to the screen, so you will actually see messages related to hardware initializations and other boot events.

The NLD boot process is displayed as messages on the screen.

```
Mounting shared memory FS on /dev/shm                              done
Activating swap-devices in /etc/fstab...
Adding 1036152k swap on /dev/sda1.  Priority:42 extents:1          done
Checking root file system...
fsck 1.34 (25-Jul-2003)
Reiserfs super block in block 16 on 0x802 of format 3.6 with standard journal
Blocks (total/free): 2361552/1720721 by 4096 bytes
Filesystem is clean
Filesystem seems mounted read-only. Skipping journal replay.
Checking internal tree..finished                                   done
md: Autodetecting RAID arrays.
md: autorun ...
md: ... autorun DONE.
Activating device mapper...
device-mapper: 4.3.0-ioctl (2004-09-30) initialised: dm-devel@redhat.com
Creating /dev/mapper/control character device with major:10 minor:63.
                                                                   done
Checking file systems...
fsck 1.34 (25-Jul-2003)                                            done
Setting up                                                         done
Mounting local file systems...
proc on /proc type proc (rw)
tmpfs on /dev/shm type tmpfs (rw)
devpts on /dev/pts type devpts (rw,mode=0620,gid=5)
```

21

CHAPTER 2: Starting Novell Linux Desktop

TIP

If you even bother to watch the boot messages you will probably find that they don't make compelling entertainment. However, you actually can get troubleshooting tips from these messages if there is a problem with your system. As the kernel displays a message for a particular boot task it then adds the "done" tag. In cases where hardware fails to initialize or other problems arise, a message will be followed by the "failed" tag.

After the system is loaded, the Logon Manager appears. This is where you enter your username and password to log on to NLD.

Enter your username and password in the NLD Logon Manager.

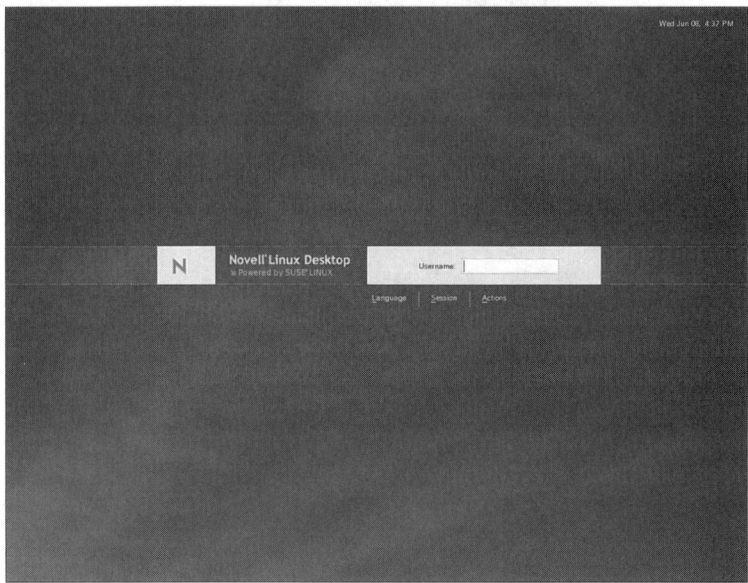

However, before walking through the actual logon process (which is only a couple of steps), let's briefly explore the options that the Logon Manager provides. These options come in the form of three menus:

- Language—This menu allows you to select the language for your NLD session. The default language will be the language selected during the NLD installation. To change the language, make a selection and then click OK.

1 About Booting the NLD System and Logon Options

- Session—This menu allows you to choose the GUI desktop that is loaded when you log on for this session. Choices include GUIs such as GNOME (the default desktop for NLD) and KDE. Two choices also are provided that can be used to troubleshoot problems with your NLD installation: Failsafe GNOME and Failsafe Terminal (the terminal provides a command shell only).

NOTE

Typically, you will want to use your default Session setting; this provides the desktop GUI you use on a regular basis (GNOME, for example).

- Actions—This menu includes options for shutting down the computer, rebooting the computer, or configuring the Logon Manager. Select the appropriate option and then click OK to proceed. The configuration possibilities revolve around the look of the Logon Manager and allow you to change the "graphical greeter" from the default greeter to other greeters such as the Happy GNOME with Browser greeter. To change the configuration (including the graphical greeter screen), you must know the root password.

Other graphical greeters can be configured for the Logon Manager such as the Happy GNOME with Browser greeter.

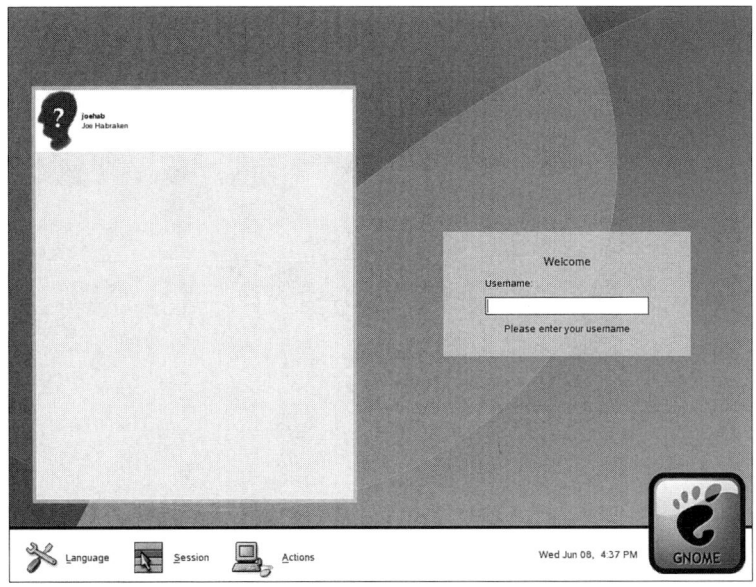

23

CHAPTER 2: Starting Novell Linux Desktop

Whether you take advantage of any of the configuration possibilities provided by the Logon Manager menus is really up to you. This book discusses NLD in terms of the installation defaults.

2 Log On to the System

After you have made changes to the Logon Manager (or stayed with the defaults), you are ready to log on to the system and begin an NLD session. A session is really just a way to describe the time between your logon and logoff.

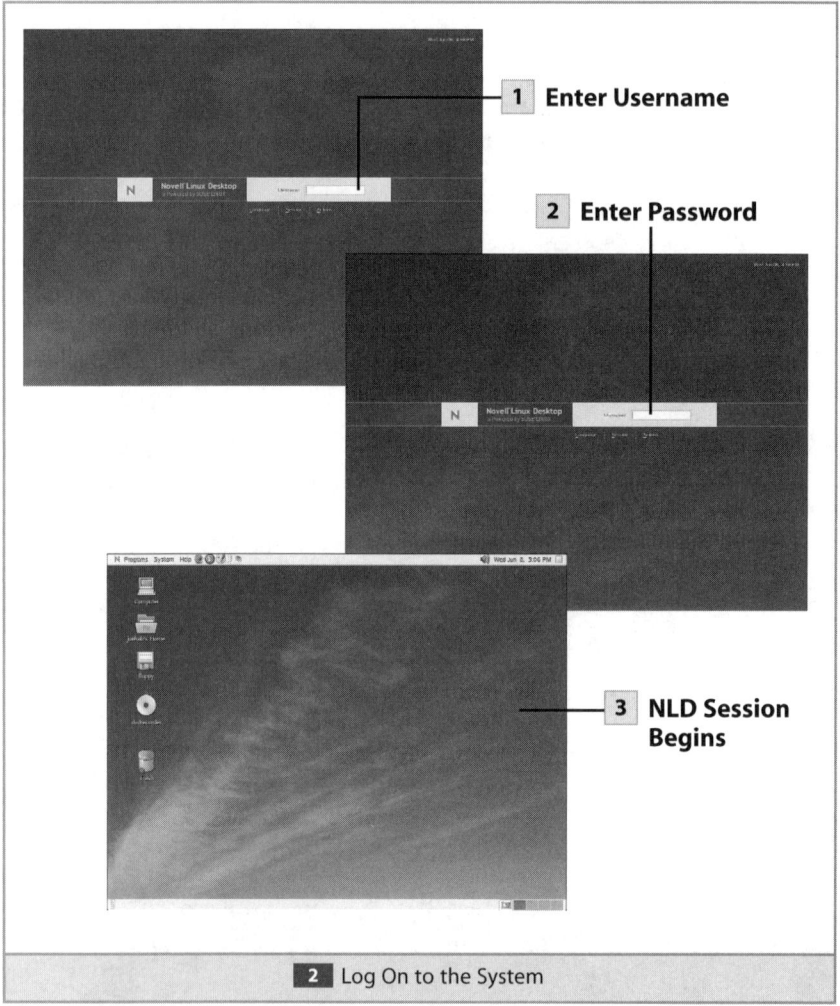

2 Log On to the System

1 Enter Username

Type your username in the Logon Manager Username box and then press **Enter**.

2 Enter Password

Type your password in the Logon Manager Password box and then press **Enter**.

3 NLD Session Begins

You are logged on to the system, and your NLD session begins. You can now take advantage of the various productivity software and tools launched via the GNOME desktop.

3 About Logoff Options

✓BEFORE YOU BEGIN

1. About Booting the NLD System and Logon Options
2. Log On to the System

After you have completed an NLD session, you will want to log off the system. What actually happens when you log off is controlled by the Logoff dialog box, accessed via the desktop System menu. The options provided are

- Logout—This option logs you off the system and returns you to the Logon Manager.
- Shutdown—This option shuts down the computer.
- Restart the Computer—This option restarts the computer and opens the Logon Manager.

TIP

The Logoff dialog box provides a Save Current Setup check box. Selecting this check box saves certain settings that you have changed for the GNOME desktop such as font settings, color settings, and other desktop appearance settings.

CHAPTER 2: Starting Novell Linux Desktop

Options are provided in the Logoff dialog box.

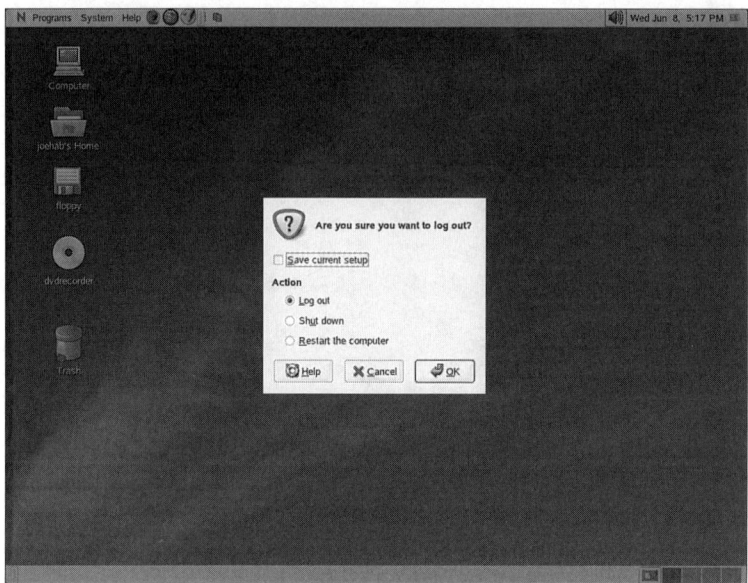

The choice that you make in the Logoff dialog box depends on how you want to end your session. If you want to log off and allow another user to log on, use the Logout option. If you want to end your session and shut down the computer, select Shutdown.

4   Log Off the System from the Desktop

✔ BEFORE YOU BEGIN

3 About Logoff Options

Logging off the system either returns you to the Logon Manager or shuts down the system. Either choice effectively ends your current NLD session.

4 Log Off the System from the Desktop

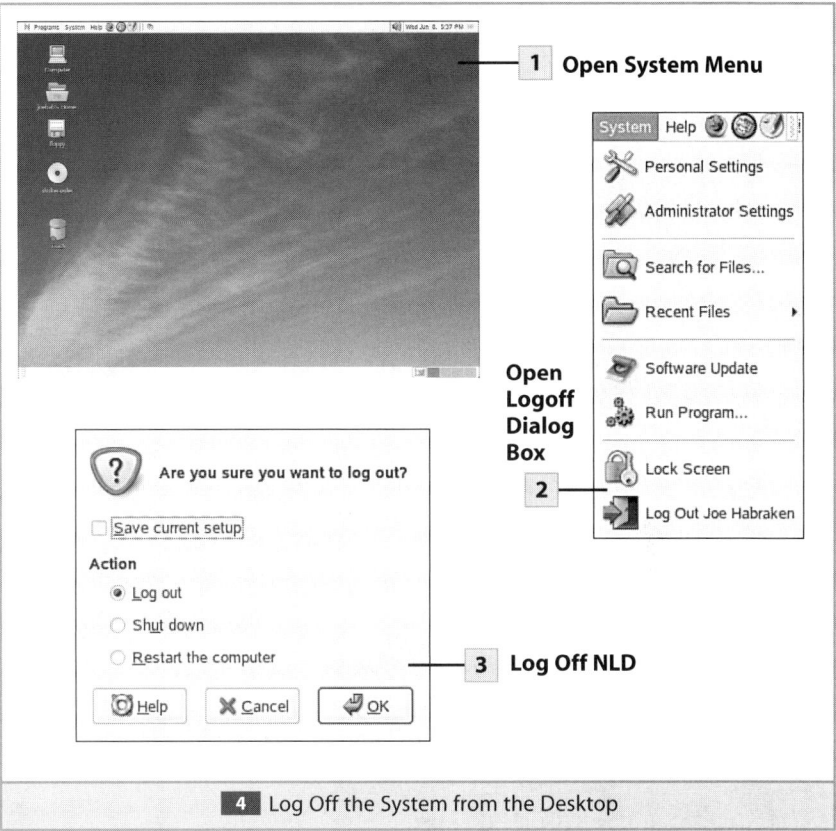

4 Log Off the System from the Desktop

1 Open System Menu

On the GNOME desktop, select the **System** menu, located between the Program and Help menus at the top of the desktop.

2 Open Logoff Dialog Box

Select the **Log Out** (username) command on the System menu.

3 Log Off NLD

The **Log Out** option is selected by default. Click **OK** to log off the system and return to the Logon Manager.

CHAPTER 2: Starting Novell Linux Desktop

TIP

If you are planning on shutting down the system, select **Shut Down** in the Logoff dialog box.

5 Shut Down the System from the Logon Manager

✔ **BEFORE YOU BEGIN**

1 About Booting the NLD System and Logon Options
3 About Logoff Options
4 Log Off the System from the Desktop

You have probably already realized that you can shut down the system as you log off by selecting the Shutdown option in the Logoff dialog box. You can also shut down the system from the Logon Manager.

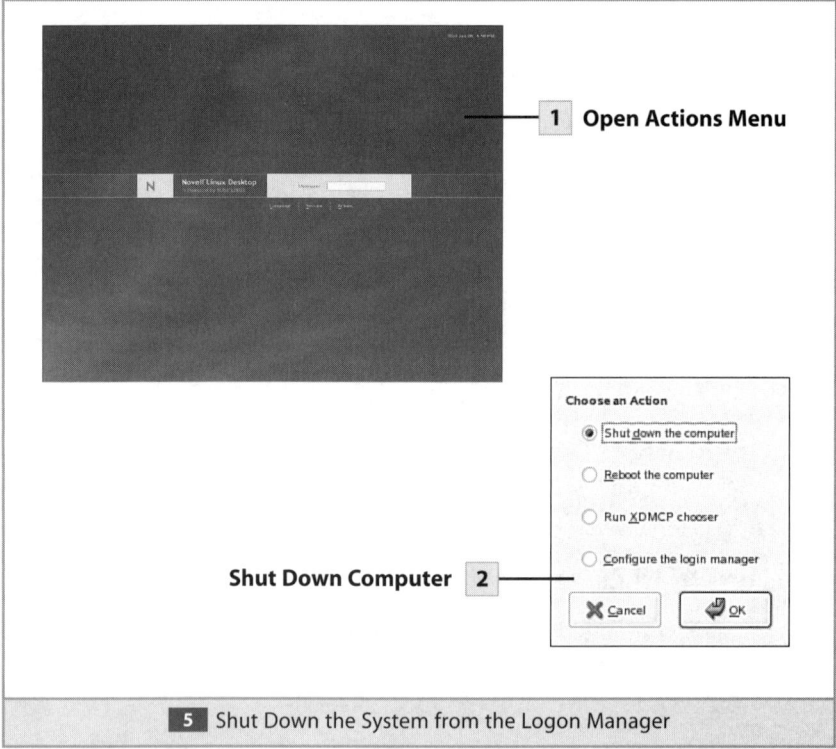

5 Shut Down the System from the Logon Manager

5 Shut Down the System from the Logon Manager

1 **Open Actions Menu**

Select the Logon Manager's **Actions** menu. The **Shut Down the Computer** option is selected by default.

2 **Shut Down Computer**

Click **OK**, and the computer shuts down.

TIP

NLD shuts down one system level at a time, and each of these levels is noted on the text screen that appears as the system goes through the shutdown process. Wait until all the NLD processes have been terminated before shutting down older computers that do not automatically shut down. Otherwise, you can lose data or corrupt the system files.

CHAPTER 3

Working on the NLD Desktop

IN THIS CHAPTER:

- 6 About the GNOME Desktop
- 7 Navigate the GNOME Desktop
- 8 Use the Menu System
- 9 Manage Virtual Desktops
- 10 Change the System Date and Time Settings
- 11 Get Help on the GNOME Desktop
- 12 Run a Program from the Run Application Dialog
- 13 Access the Command Line
- 14 About File Commands
- 15 Use File Commands
- 16 About System Commands
- 17 Use System Commands

CHAPTER 3: Working on the NLD Desktop

NLD uses the GNOME desktop (by default) to provide an easy-to-use desktop environment. In this chapter we take a look at the basics of navigating the GNOME desktop including how to use the desktop menus, work with application windows and virtual desktops, and access a command shell to execute NLD command-line tools.

First we discuss GNOME and where GNOME came from. Then we can explore the GNOME desktop in a more hands-on fashion.

6 About the GNOME Desktop

The GNOME desktop (GNOME stands for GNU Network Object Model Environment) is GNU (open source) software that can be run on a number of Linux distributions; it also runs on some UNIX implementations. GNOME is a desktop environment that provides the GUI that you see and use as you work in NLD.

GNOME was created and is updated by the GNOME Project. The GNOME community of developers is one of the first free software groups to create human interface guidelines for the GNOME desktop, which are also suggested guidelines for programmers creating applications for Linux-based systems.

WEB RESOURCE

http://www.gnome.org

See this website for more information about GNOME and the GNOME project.

The actual graphical display system that allows you to use GNOME and other desktop environments such as KDE on a Linux system (such as NLD) is the X Window System. The X Window System contains the programming code that allows the system to display items in a graphical format (rather than text only).

KEY TERM

X Window System—The graphical display system used by many Linux implementations including NLD.

When you configure items such as your monitor, graphics card, and display resolution, you are actually configuring the X Window System. Because the NLD installation process automatically configures most X Window System

6 About the GNOME Desktop

settings for you, you can work in GNOME without worrying too much about what the X Window System is up to (although when you do change display settings, you are configuring the X Window System). Because it is GNOME that we actually interface with (rather than the X Window system), we should take a closer look at GNOME's geography.

GNOME provides a desktop workspace that contains a set of default desktop icons, a top and bottom panel, and a menu system in the top panel. Let's break out and define the various areas of the GNOME desktop for clarity:

- Desktop icons—A set of default icons resides on the NLD desktop: Computer, Home, floppy (if one exists on the computer), CD or DVD (depending on the type of drive installed), and Trash. The Computer icon provides access to the computer's removable media drives (floppy and CD for example), the file system (folders on the computer), and the Network (this icon allows you to browse the local area network). The Trash icon provides quick access to the Trash folder, which holds all recently deleted files and folders.

- Top panel—The top panel provides access to the NLD menus (Program, System, Help) and quickstart icons for the Mozilla Firefox browser, Novell Evolution, and OpenOffice.org Write. Two additional quickstart icons, Network Connection and Updates, also appear on the top panel as does the Volume Control and current date/time.

- Bottom panel—The bottom panel contains the Show Desktop icon (which is used to clear the desktop by minimizing all currently open windows) and the Workspace Switcher. The Workspace Switcher allows you to work on multiple virtual desktops. Each of these separate workspaces can contain open windows and running applications.

KEY TERM

Virtual desktop—A separate workspace that can be used to run applications. Each workspace shows the GNOME desktop, but each workspace is a discrete operating space, which allows you to keep the actual desktop (within each virtual desktop) less crowded (with application windows).

As with similar graphical user interfaces (such as Windows or the Mac OS), windows on the desktop can be maximized, minimized, and dragged to new locations on the desktop. Desktop icons require a double-click to open, whereas quickstart icons on the top panel require only a single click.

33

CHAPTER 3: Working on the NLD Desktop

The GNOME desktop provides the user environment for NLD applications and tools.

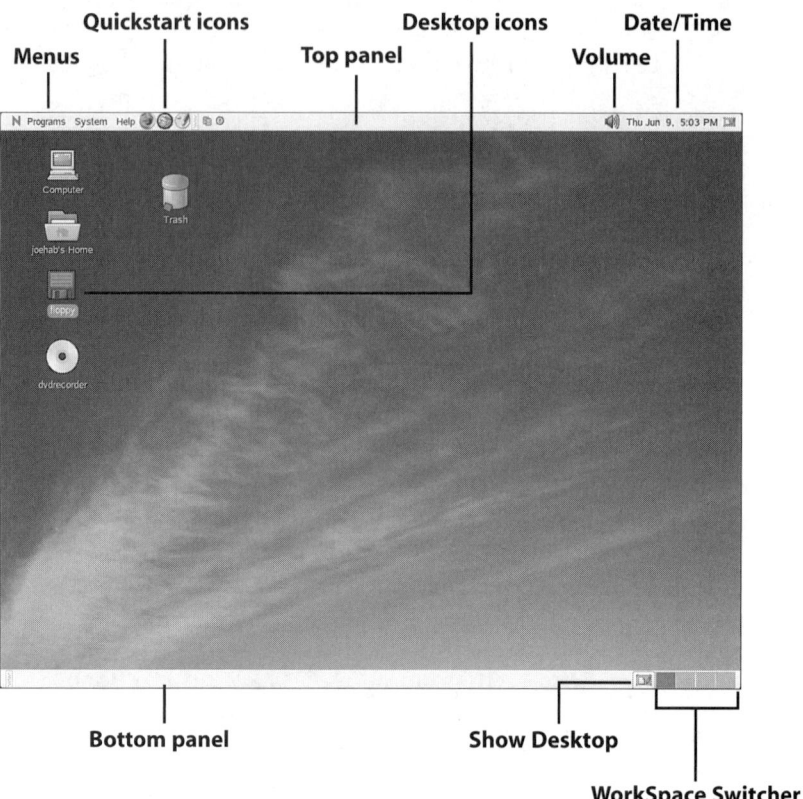

7 Navigate the GNOME Desktop

Working on the GNOME desktop is really a study in manipulating your utility and application windows, which can be opened using either the menu system or icons (either existing or desktop icons that you have created or quickstart icons that exist by default or that you have added). The default desktop icons (such as Computer and Home) are designed to allow you to locate and manage the files that you create using your various applications.

7 Navigate the GNOME Desktop

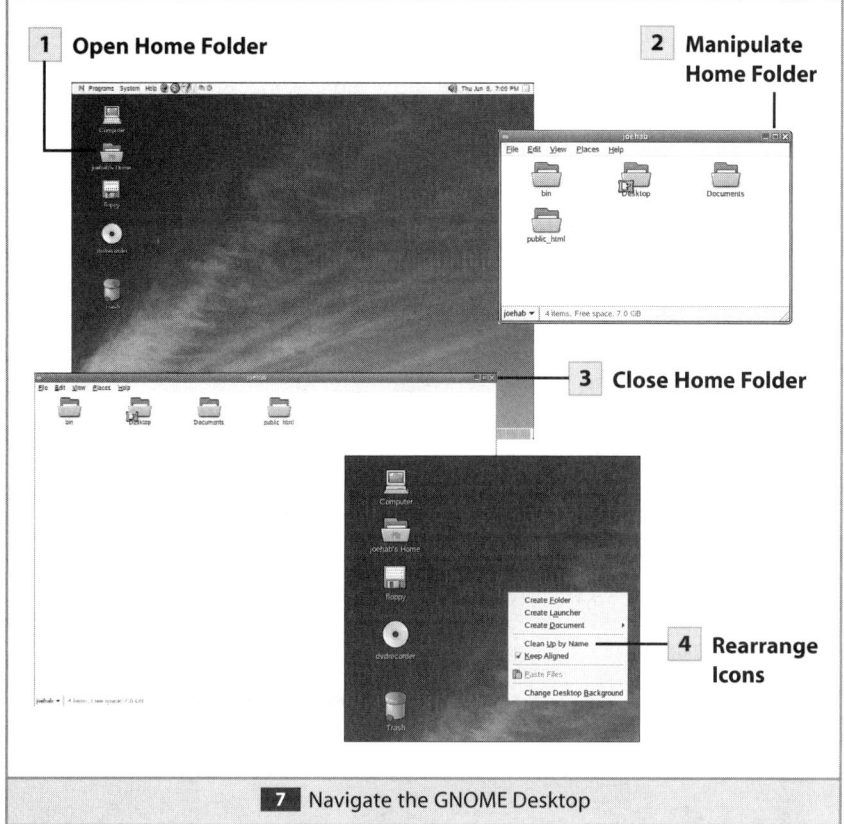

1 Open Home Folder

Double-click on the **Home** (*username* Home) icon on the desktop. Your Home folder opens.

2 Manipulate Home Folder

Click the **Maximize** button to maximize the Home folder. You can open any of the folders present in the Home folder with a double-click.

3 Close Home Folder

To close the Home folder, click the **Close** button.

4 Rearrange Icons

You can drag icons on the desktop as needed. To rearrange any icons that you have dragged on the desktop, right-click on the desktop and select **Clean Up by Name**. This aligns the icons by name.

CHAPTER 3: Working on the NLD Desktop

TIP

To view the desktop without closing a maximized application window, click on the **Minimize** button in that window. The application can be restored to the desktop by clicking its icon on the bottom panel of the desktop.

8 Use the Menu System

You can access the application and other tools provided by NLD using the menus that reside in the top panel of the desktop. The Programs menu divides the installed applications into categories such as Accessories, Graphics, and Office. Selecting a particular category provides a list of applications in that category. For example, the Accessories submenu provides access to tools such as the Calculator, Dictionary, and File Manager. The Office submenu provides access to the OpenOffice.org suite, which includes Write, Calc, and Impress.

The System menu provides access to personal and administrative settings. It also allows you to quickly search for a file and provides you with the ability to log off the system.

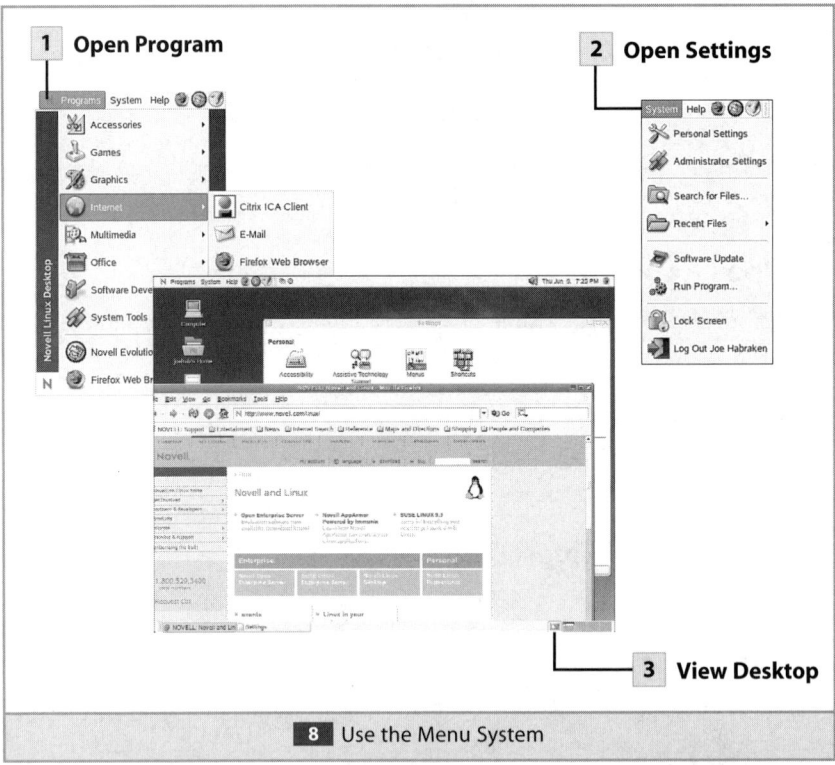

1 Open Program

Select the **Programs** menu and then select one of the program categories such as **Internet**. Then click an application icon such as **Firefox Web Browser**. The application (in this case Firefox) opens on the desktop. You can **Minimize** or **Close** the application as needed.

2 Open Settings

Select the **System** menu and then select an item on the menu such as **Personal Settings**. This opens the Settings window. You can minimize or maximize the Settings window as needed.

3 View Desktop

To minimize the application currently running on the desktop, click the **View Desktop** icon on the desktop's bottom panel. You can then restore any of the open applications to the desktop by clicking its icon on the bottom panel.

TIP

To quickly start applications such as Firefox, Evolution, and OpenOffice.org Write, click the appropriate quickstart icon on the top panel.

TIP

If you are running a multimedia application such as the CD Player or Music Player, you can quickly adjust the sound by selecting the Volume Control icon on the top panel.

9 Manage Virtual Desktops

✔ **BEFORE YOU BEGIN**

7 Navigate the GNOME Desktop

8 Use the Menu System

Multitasking environments such as NLD make it easy for you to run multiple applications on the desktop. However, the desktop can become quickly overrun with application windows. Even with some applications minimized, the bottom panel can contain any number of icons, making the process of switching between applications an annoyance. Virtual desktops allow you to place

CHAPTER 3: Working on the NLD Desktop

applications on different desktops. You can then switch between these desktops and use the running applications, without sorting through a pile of windows on one desktop only.

TIP

On the far left of the top panel is the Window Switcher icon. When you are working on a particular virtual desktop, you can quickly get a list of open application windows (and switch to particular application) by selecting the Window Switcher.

You switch between the virtual desktops using the Workspace Switcher on the right side of the bottom panel. The Workspace Switcher actually provides a thumbnail of each of the virtual desktops currently in use.

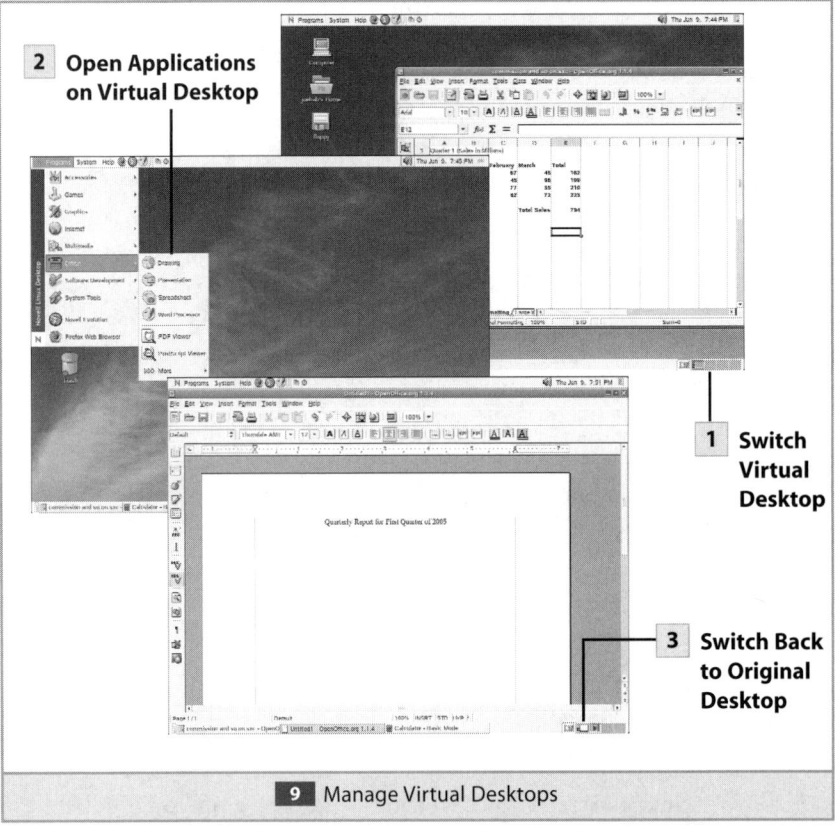

Manage Virtual Desktops

1 Switch Virtual Desktop

To switch from your current desktop (and the applications currently open on the desktop), click one of the blank virtual desktops in the Workspace Switcher. Although your applications still show as open on the bottom panel (as icons), you are provided a "fresh" desktop.

2 Open Applications on Virtual Desktop

You can now open applications as needed on the virtual desktop. For example, select **Programs**, **Office**, **Word Processor** to open the OpenOffice.org Write application.

3 Switch Back to Original Virtual Desktop

To switch back to the original virtual desktop, select the Workspace Switcher box for that desktop. To return a virtual desktop to its original state (meaning devoid of application windows), close the applications on that virtual desktop.

10 Change the System Date and Time Settings

The date and time are displayed by the Clock applet that resides on far right of the top panel of the NLD desktop. Selecting the applet displays the current month showing the current date. You can change clock preferences and even copy the time and date (and then paste it into another application) by accessing this applet.

You can also access date and time settings using the Clock applet icon; however, date and time settings are considered administrative settings. This means that you must know the root account password to change these settings.

NOTE

The date and time settings are administrative settings configured using YaST, which is the NLD configuration utility. YaST actually played an important part when you installed NLD on your system. Access to YaST, no matter what settings you are trying to edit, always requires the root password.

CHAPTER 3: Working on the NLD Desktop

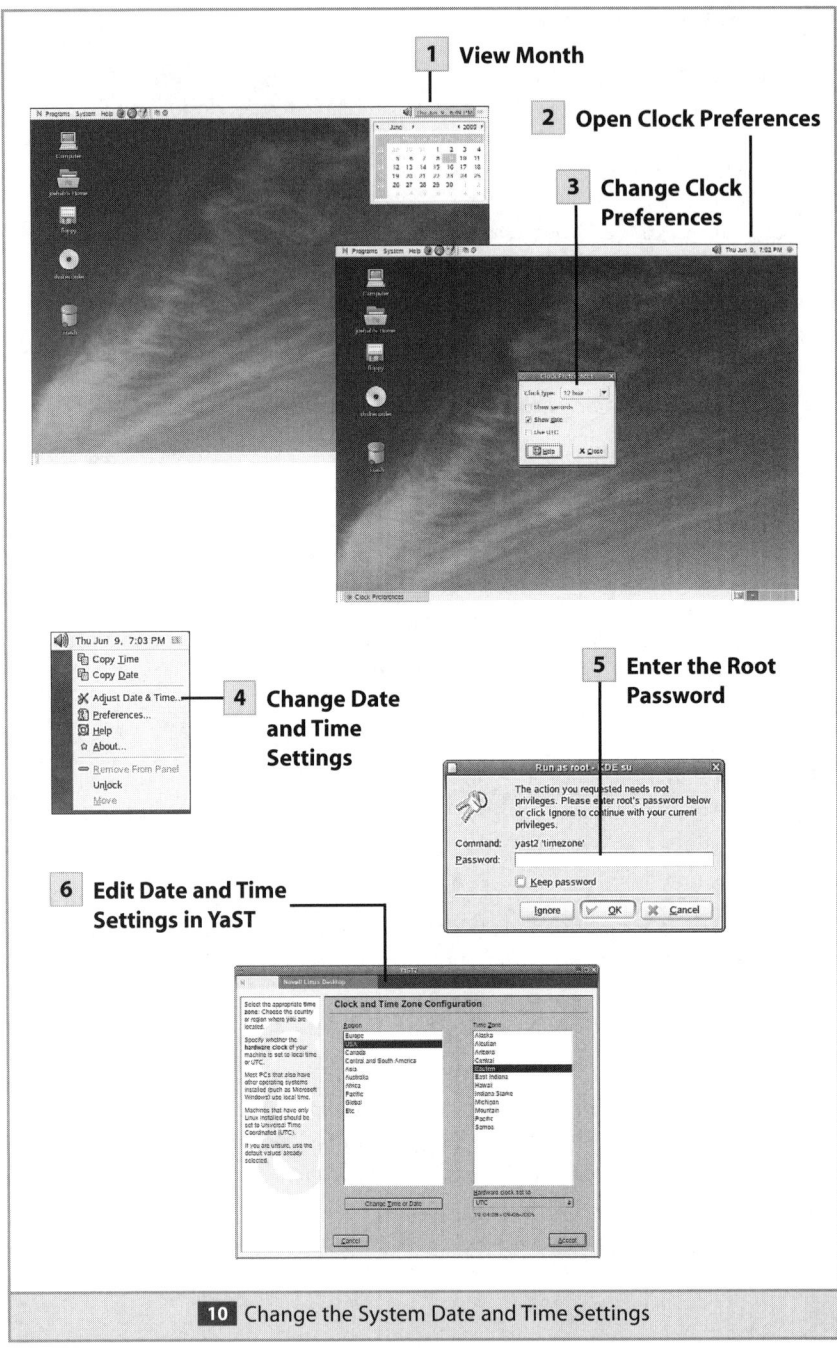

1 View Month

To view the current date in the context of the current month, select the **Clock** (showing the current date and time on the top panel). To close the month view, select the **Clock** a second time.

2 Open Clock Preferences

Right-click on the date and time and then select **Preferences** from the shortcut menu that appears. This opens the Clock Preferences dialog.

3 Change Clock Preferences

Select the **Clock Type** drop-down box to select either a 12 hour, 24 hour, UNIX time (the seconds that have elapsed since January 1, 1970; this is used primarily by developers), or Internet time (a universal time reference used all over the world) for the clock. To show seconds on the clock, select the **Show Seconds** check box. To change the clock to UTC (Universal Coordinated Time or Greenwich Mean Time), select the **Use UTC** check box. When you have completed editing the preferences, click **Close**.

4 Change Date and Time Settings

Right-click on the date and time and then select **Adjust Date and Time** from the shortcut menu. The Run as Root dialog box appears.

5 Enter the Root Password

Type the root password in the Password box and then click **OK**. The YaST window opens showing the Clock and Time Zone Configuration.

6 Edit Date and Time Settings in YaST

In the Region pane select your region. In the Time Zone pane select the appropriate region. To change the time or date, select the **Change Time or Date** button. The Change System Date and Time dialog opens. Enter the correct time in the Current Time boxes and enter the correct date in the Current Date boxes (the correct format for each entry is provided). After entering the time and date information, click **Apply**. This returns you to YaST. If you want to change the hardware clock setting to local time (the default is UTC), click the **Hardware Clock Set To** drop-down box and select **Local Time**. After changing the clock settings in YaST, click **Accept**. YaST writes a new configuration file and then closes, returning you to the NLD desktop.

NOTE

If NLD is the operating system installed on your computer, go with the default hardware clock setting, which is UTC. If you have a computer that is configured for a dual boot situation and also has Microsoft Windows installed on the computer, use local time as your hardware clock setting.

11 Get Help on the GNOME Desktop

Although the GNOME desktop is easy to navigate, there may be times when you need some extra help. You can quickly access the Novell's GNOME User's Manual from the desktop. The user manual provides basic information on GNOME and provides a section to make it easier for Windows users to switch to the GNOME desktop.

The manual also provides information on specific applications such as Firefox, Evolution, iFolder, and the OpenOffice.org suite. Additional information is provided on managing printers, and basic information is provided on administrative tasks and working in a command shell (entering commands at the command line). You can access Help content using the content links in the Navigation Area (the left frame), or you can search for content by performing either a simple search or a more complex search on the Search tab.

1 Open the Help Center

Select the **Help** menu on the top panel and then select **User's Manual**. The Help Center opens on the desktop. You can maximize the Help Center; select the **Maximize** button on the left side of the window.

2 Select Content Topics

The Help Center consists of two areas: a navigation area, which lists topics, and a view window, which shows the information contained in the selected topic. To view a particular topic found in the navigation area (when the Contents tab is selected), select that topic. To view specific information related to the selected topic, select a link in the view window (the right pane of the Help Center).

TIP

To enlarge the font for text in the View window, select the **Increase Font Sizes** button on the Help toolbar (Decrease Font Sizes decreases the text size). To go back to a previous topic page, click the **Back** button. If you want to print a topic, click the **Print** button on the toolbar.

11 Get Help on the GNOME Desktop

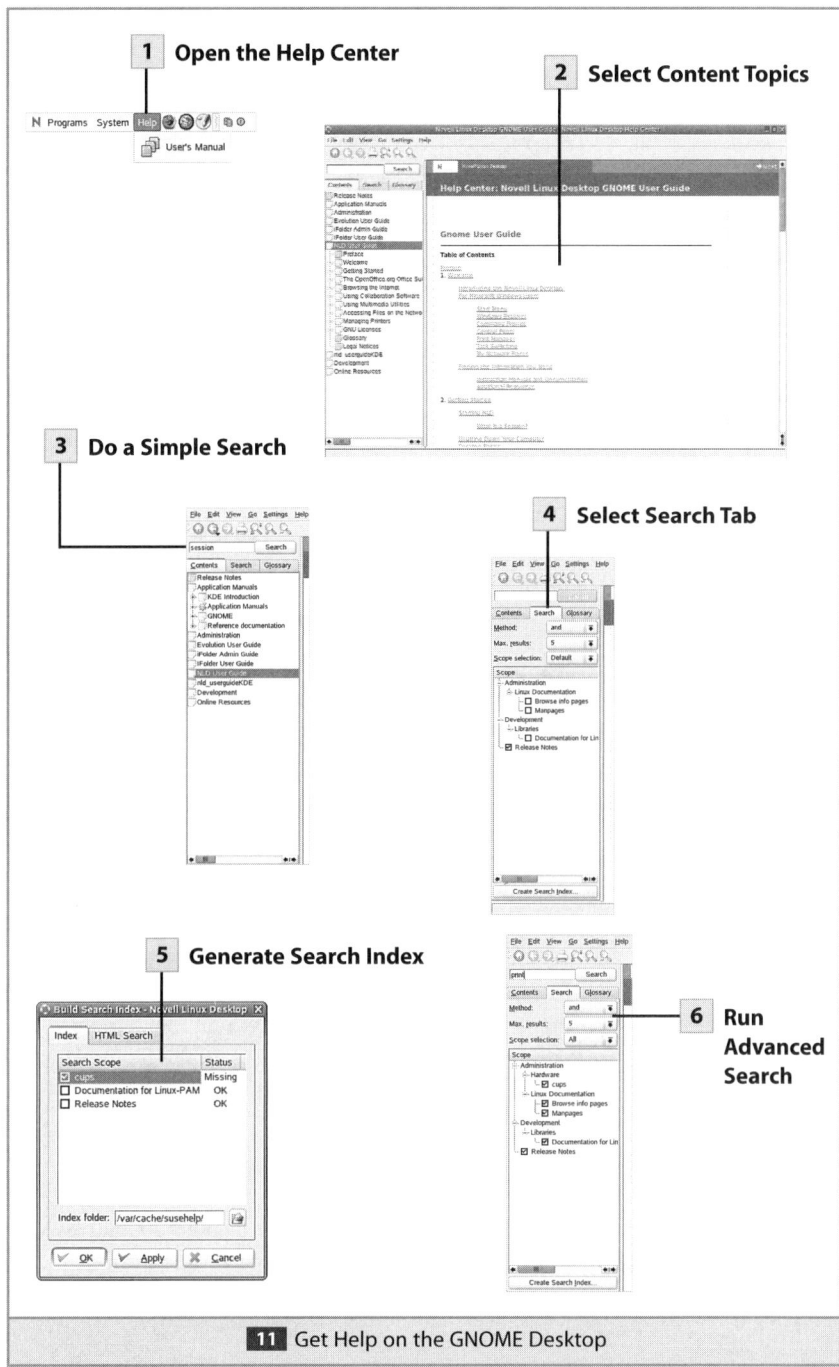

3 Do a Simple Search

To quickly search for specific Help content, enter a search term in the Search box above the navigation area; then click the **Search** button. The results of your search appear in the view window. Select specific links provided as search results to view the topic pages.

4 Select the Search Tab

You can also run a more complex search, which provides you the ability to set more parameters for the search. Select the **Search** tab of the Help navigation area. Before you run the search, you need to generate a search index for content that the Help system contains. Click the **Create Search Index** button at the bottom of the Search pane. This opens the Build Search Index dialog.

5 Generate Search Index

In the Build Search Index dialog, select check boxes of index topics that currently have a status of missing (meaning that an index has not been generated for these topic areas). Then click **OK** to generate the indexes. The Build Search Indices message box opens declaring that the index creation is complete. Click **Close** to close this message box.

6 Run Advanced Search

Enter your Search criteria in the Search box. Set the **Method** drop-down to either **and** (the default) or **or**. Use the **Max Results** drop-down box to select the number of results that you want to receive from the search. The final step is to set the scope for the search.

You can use the Scope Selection drop-down list to either select **All** or **Custom** (**None** is also a selection possibility but doesn't apply in this case). If you select Custom, you can then use the check boxes provided in the Scope area of the Search pane to select individual topic areas to include in the scope. After determining the scope, click the **Search** button. The Search results appear as links in the view window.

TIP

To view a list of Glossary terms (and access their definitions), select the **Glossary** tab of the Help navigation area. You can view the glossary alphabetically or by topic.

12 Run a Program from the Run Application Dialog

→ SEE ALSO

- **20** Add Items to a Panel
- **21** Add Items to a Menu
- **63** About Finding and Installing New Applications

GNOME provides menu icons for many of the applications and applets installed when you run the NLD installation. These menu icons are present on either the Programs or System menus. Additional applets and other useful utilities are installed with NLD that are not represented on the menu system. One way you can run these is from the Run Application dialog.

NOTE

The Run Application dialog is really one way of accessing the NLD command line. You must know the command that starts a particular application or applet to take advantage of the Run Application dialog.

The Run Application dialog is also useful if you add applications or applets to your NLD installation (you can download any number of GNU applications and applets for Linux distributions such as NLD). Seldom-used applications and applets can be run from the Run Application dialog. However, if you find that you are using an application or applet a lot, it makes sense to add that application or applet to a panel (such as the top panel) as a shortcut or add the program to a menu.

1 Open the Run Application Dialog

Select the **System** menu on the top panel and then select **Run Program**. The Run Application dialog opens. To view a list of some of the applications installed with NLD, select the Show list of known applications. This list does not list all the applications or applets available. You can view the command that actually starts one of the listed applications by selecting a particular application in the known applications list.

NOTE

Understanding file types and finding specific files, particularly those that launch applications, requires that you have an understanding of how programs are installed and then launched in NLD. See Chapter 7, "Adding and Managing Software Applications and Tools in NLD," for more information.

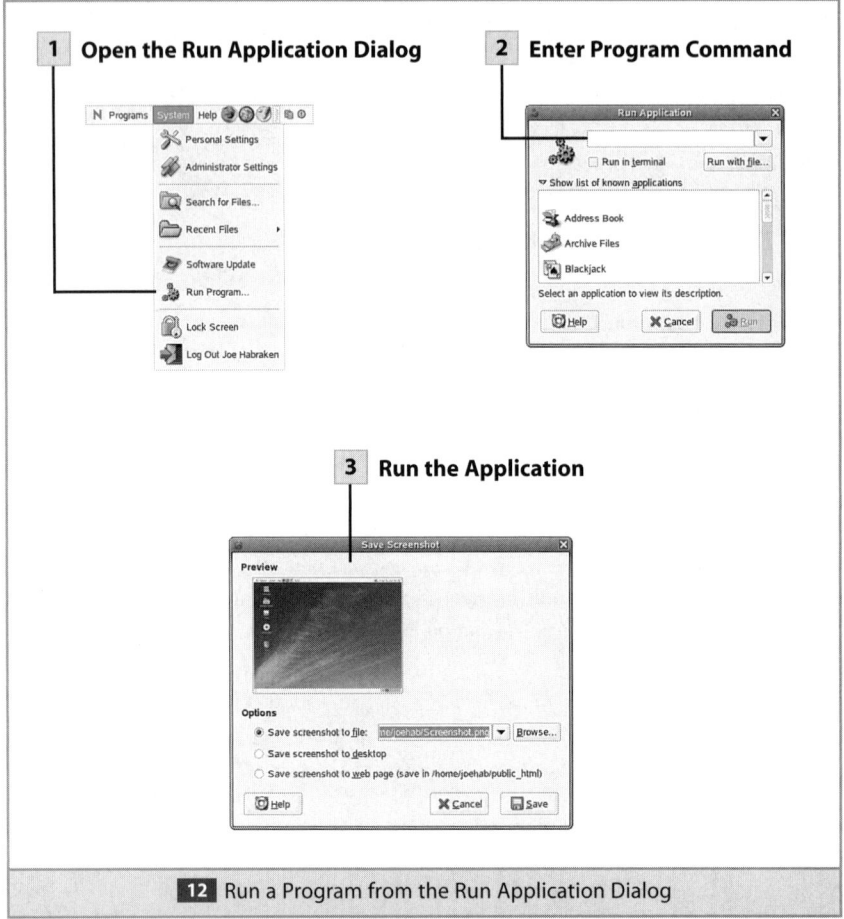

12 Run a Program from the Run Application Dialog

2 Enter Program Command

Enter the program command in the command box. As you type the command, if the command is recognized, an autocomplete feature helps you complete the command. For example, a command you might find useful is the `gnome-panel-screenshot` command that takes a screen shot of the NLD desktop. When you run the command, it opens a dialog box that allows you to specify where the screen capture file should be saved.

3 Run the Application

To run the application after entering the appropriate command, click the **Run** button. The application or applet opens in a window. In the case of the `gnome-panel-screenshot` command, a Save Screenshot dialog opens, which allows you to specify the location for the saved screen capture.

13 Access the Command Line

✔ BEFORE YOU BEGIN

- **12** Run a Program from the Run Application Dialog

→ SEE ALSO

- **14** About File Commands
- **15** Use File Commands
- **16** About System Commands
- **17** Use System Commands

Although GNOME provides easy access to applications and applets using the menu system and the Run Application dialog, there may be occasions when you need to access a command shell and work at the command line. The information provided here is not a comprehensive look at the command shell or the various commands that can be run at the command line but is a primer to provide you with an overview of the command shell.

NOTE

Shell commands consist of an actual command and optional switches, which allow for certain options with a particular command. After typing a command and any accompanying switches, press **Enter** to invoke the command.

In NLD the default terminal or shell program is GNOME Terminal. This terminal allows you to work at the command line without leaving the NLD desktop. Most shell commands really come in two flavors: commands that provide an immediate response, such as the `ls` command, which provides a list of files in the current folder, and shell commands that start a particular command-line utility. For example, the `passwd` command starts a utility that walks you through the process of changing your user password.

NOTE

You may wonder why you should even consider working with shell commands when GNOME provides desktop utilities and tools that take care of most of your day-to-day needs in terms of managing files. It is a good idea to know a few file and system commands and to be aware of the capabilities of the command shell, particularly if you decide you want to expand your knowledge of the Linux system over time (from user to "better" user).

CHAPTER 3: Working on the NLD Desktop

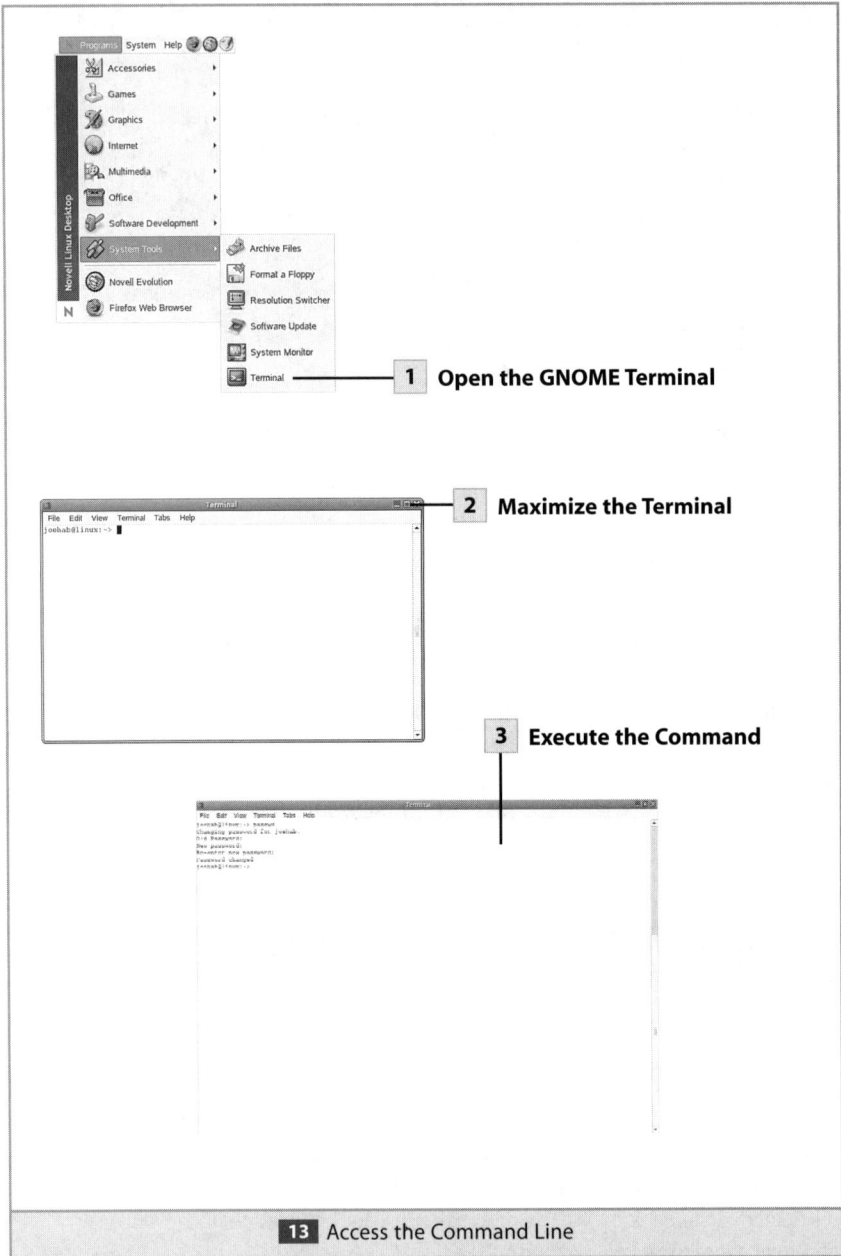

1 Open the GNOME Terminal
2 Maximize the Terminal
3 Execute the Command

13 Access the Command Line

1 Open the GNOME Terminal

Select the **Programs** menu on the top panel, select the **System Tools** submenu, and then select **Terminal**. The GNOME Terminal opens on the desktop. The command line in the terminal consists of your username@linux. You enter commands at the command line.

2 Maximize the Terminal

It is easier to view the results of shell commands if you maximize the terminal window. Click the **Maximize** button on the window. Now you are ready to enter shell commands.

3 Execute the Command

A good command utility to try out is the `passwd` command, which allows you to change your user password. At the command line type `passwd` and then press **Enter**. Type your current password and then press **Enter**. Then type your new password and press **Enter**. Reenter the new password and press **Enter**. The password has been changed.

TIP

To clear the entries currently on the terminal screen, type `clear` and then press **Enter**.

TIP

You can get help on a command by typing the command followed by `-- help` (such as `ls --help`). To view the manual information for a particular command, type the command and then type man and press **Enter**. This opens the manual for the command. You can use the up and down arrow keys to move through the manual (the spacebar moves you down one screen at a time). To exit the manual for the command (or any manual pages that you access at the command line) press the **q** key on the keyboard.

14 About File Commands

✔ BEFORE YOU BEGIN	→ SEE ALSO
13 Access the Command Line	46 Use Nautilus to Manage Folders
	47 Browse and Open Files
	48 Find Files

You can list and manipulate the files in your folders from the command line. NLD provides the Nautilus File Manager, which allows you to manage your files using a GUI utility. You will probably want to use Nautilus for most of your file work. However, it is not a bad idea to know and understand a few file management shell commands—at least some of the basic file commands. Table 3.1 lists a few file management commands that you can use in the GNOME Terminal.

TABLE 3.1 FILE MANAGEMENT COMMANDS

COMMAND	PURPOSE
ls	Lists the files in the current directory.
cd	Used to change to a particular directory folder; for example, cd Documents would move you from the current parent folder to a subfolder named Documents. The cd command would return you to the parent folder.
mkdir	Used to create a new directory. For example, mkdir joe would place a new directory (subfolder) in the current folder.
rmdir	Used to remove a directory. From the folder's parent directory, type **rmdir** followed by the folder name. For example, **rmdir joe** would remove the joe folder (the folder must be empty to be removed).
copy	Used to copy a file from one folder to another. For example, to copy a file from the current folder to another folder the syntax would be copy *filename*.
rm	Used to delete a file. The syntax is rm *filename*. Be careful with this command; it does not provide you with a second chance in terms of deleting a file.

WEB RESOURCE

http://www.linuxforum.com/shell.php

For a complete listing of Linux commands by category check out this website.

Remember that Linux commands and references are case-sensitive. So if a folder begins with a capital letter, you must type the name exactly to manipulate that folder. In terms of experimenting with folders and files at the command line, you can create new folders within your Home folder and keep documents and other files that you use in the Documents subfolder.

15 Use File Commands

✔ BEFORE YOU BEGIN

  13 Access the Command Line
  14 About File Commands

When you open the terminal window, you are in your Home directory. Within the home directory are the subfolders: bin, Desktop, Documents, and public_HTML. You can use commands such as `ls`, `cd`, and `mkdir` to view the contents of these folders and to make new subfolders.

1 Use the ls Command

In the GNOME Terminal window, type **ls** at the command line and then press **Enter**. The contents of your Home folder are listed.

2 Use the cd Command

Type `cd Documents` at the command line and press **Enter**. This changes the location to the Documents subfolder. To view whether any files are in this subfolder use the **ls** command. To return to the main Home folder, type **cd** and press **Enter**.

TIP

To recycle through your recently used commands, press the up arrow key on the keyboard.

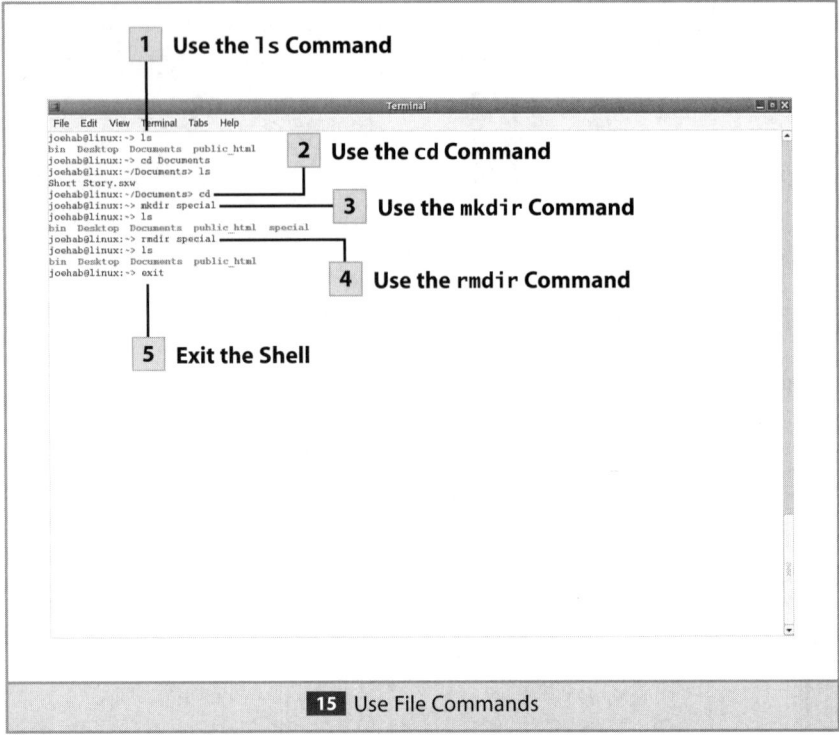

15 Use File Commands

3 Use the `mkdir` Command

You can create a new subfolder within your Home folder. Type `mkdir special` (where the new subfolder will be special) and then press **Enter**. To view the new subfolder run the `ls` command.

4 Use the `rmdir` Command

To remove a directory from the current parent folder, such as the special subfolder created in step 3, use the `rmdir` command. Type `rmdir special` and then press **Enter**. When you run the `ls` command you will see that the folder has been deleted.

NOTE

When you create a new subfolder, you typically will use it to hold files. You can copy files from any of your folders to another folder using the **copy** command.

5 Exit the Shell

When you have finished working with the shell commands in the terminal window, you can close the terminal. Type **exit** at the command line and then press **Enter**. You are returned to the NLD desktop.

16 About System Commands

✔ BEFORE YOU BEGIN

13 Access the Command Line

There are also shell commands that can quickly provide you with information related to your computer system. For example, you can use the `df` command to view statistics related to your hard drive including the total amount of disk space and the free space available. Other system shell commands can list information related to your computer's memory and swap space and provide a list of processes (programs) that are currently running. Table 3.2 provides a list of some of the shell system commands.

TABLE 3.2 SYSTEM COMMANDS

COMMAND	PURPOSE
df	Lists the total disk space, space currently in use, and the free space (*df* stands for *disk free*).
du	Shows the total amount of disk space in use in the current folder.
free	Shows statistics on current memory and swap file use.
date	Shows the current system time.
ps	Displays a list of currently running processes (programs).
kill	Used to terminate a process. This is a sort of last-ditch effort to kill a program that won't shut down. The syntax is `kill` *process ID*.

The system commands provided in Table 3.2 are used to view information about the system. The only "dangerous" command is `kill`. `kill` should be used only in cases where you cannot get an application to close in NLD after you have tried all other possibilities. To use `kill` you must find the process ID for the offending application using the `ps` command.

> **TIP**
>
> Again, you may wonder why you need to know anything about the command line. It actually provides one of your recourses for troubleshooting when you are having problems with your system. If you are still feeling squeamish about the command line and system commands, check out the System Monitor. This desktop tool allows you to view running processes and usage statistics related to the computer's memory and processor. Select Programs, System Tools, and then System Monitor.

17 Use System Commands

> **✓ BEFORE YOU BEGIN**
>
> **13** Access the Command Line
> **16** About System Commands

A number of system commands are available to the end-user such as **df** and and **du** that allow you to view the disk space currently used and the amount of disk space occupied by a particular folder, respectively. These system commands do not require you to be be logged on as root (the superuser administrator account).

1 Use the df Command

In the GNOME Terminal window, type **df** at the command line and then press **Enter**. This shows you the amount of disk space used (and the percentage used) and the amount of free space on the drive (drive meaning volume).

2 Use the du Command

Use the ls and cd commands to locate one of your folders. Type **du** and then press **Enter**. This shows the amount of disk space used in that folder.

3 Use the free Command

Type **free** at the command prompt and then press **Enter**. This shows you memory use and swap file statistics.

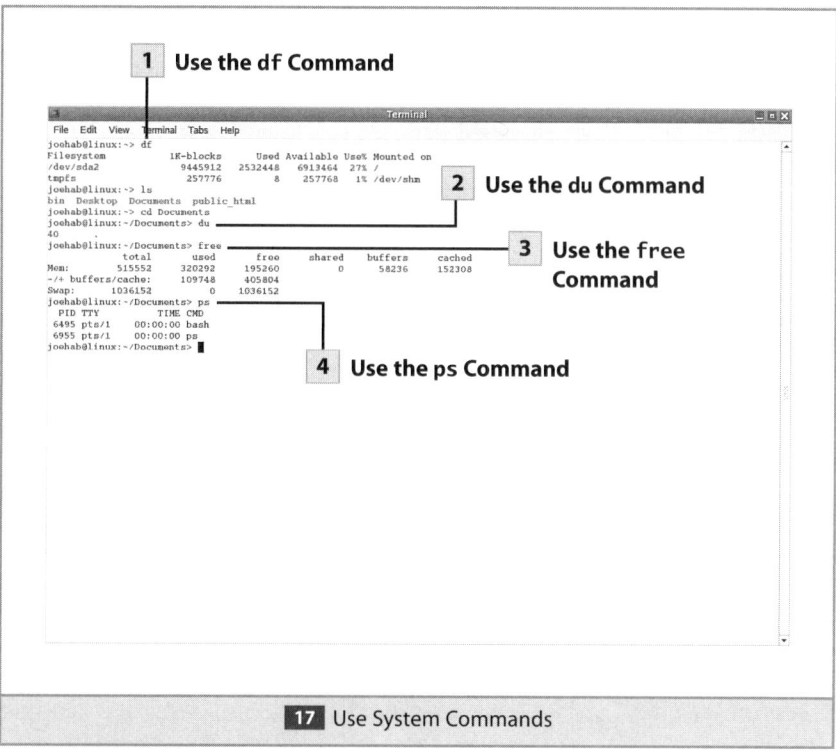

4 Use the ps Command

To view currently running processes, type **ps** at the command line and press **Enter**. The number of processes listed depends on what you were running on the NLD desktop before initiating the **ps** command. Note that a pid or process id is supplied for each running process (process really being synonymous with program). You would use the pid with the `kill` command to terminate an errant process.

After you have worked with some of the system commands, you can close the terminal window. Type **exit** and then press **Enter** to return to the NLD desktop.

> **NOTE**
>
> The root account (the administrator account) has been mentioned in this chapter and the fact that some NLD settings can be changed only when you know the root password. You can also administer NLD from the command shell, and there are a large number of commands and command utilities available to root. To access the root account at the command line, type **su** and then press **Enter**. Type the root password and then press **Enter** again. If you are really interested in more of the administrative possibilities related to NLD, you may want to check out the book *Novell Linux Desktop 9 Administrator's Handbook* by Emmett Dulaney.

CHAPTER 4

Modifying the NLD Desktop

IN THIS CHAPTER:

- 18 About Modifying GNOME
- 19 Create Desktop Icons
- 20 Add an Item to a Panel
- 21 Add an Item to a Menu
- 22 About GNOME Personal Settings
- 23 Change Personal Settings
- 24 Change the Desktop's Background
- 25 Change Fonts
- 26 Select a Screensaver
- 27 Use the Lock Screen Tool
- 28 About Desktop Themes
- 29 Change the Current Desktop Theme
- 30 Add Themes to GNOME
- 31 Change Window Preferences

CHAPTER 4: Modifying the NLD Desktop

The GNOME desktop not only provides a GUI launch pad for your productivity software tools and utilities, but it also provides NLD (and you) a highly customizable user environment. Think about the kind of desktop personalization that other operating systems provide for their desktop GUIs, and you will be in the same league with GNOME.

You can control and personalize the desktop background, the items available on the menus and desktop panels, and you can control personal settings for both software and hardware items including the mouse and your printers. This chapter begins with an overview of personalizing the NLD desktop.

18 About Modifying GNOME

GNOME provides you with the ability to add desktop icons and shortcut icons to the panels on the desktop. You can also add new items to the menu system. In terms of modifying and personalizing the desktop, you can control the desktop background, change the desktop fonts, and select the screensaver that you want to use.

The number of changes that you can make to the NLD desktop at the user level (without using the root password) are limited to the look and feel of the desktop, meaning how you perceive the desktop environment (colors, backgrounds, and so on). An item that controls a number of look-and-feel elements is a theme. A *theme* is a set of coordinated settings that control how the various parts of your application and applet windows look including the window frame and controls. A theme also controls the look of certain desktop icons and some icons on the panels. To create a unified look for the NLD desktop, you can use themes and desktop backgrounds that complement each other.

NLD provides several themes that you can choose from. You can also download and install additional themes.

KEY TERM

Theme—Settings that affect the look of program and utility windows including the frame and controls. Themes also control the look of certain desktop and panel icons.

In terms of the hardware settings you can modify, you will find the appropriate utilities in the Settings dialog box, which is launched via the System menu. You can modify settings related to the keyboard, mouse, and printers and even change the screen resolution. Most of the settings related to personalizing the desktop environment are found in the Settings dialog box.

19 Create Desktop Icons

One of the easiest ways to personalize the NLD desktop is to add icons to the desktop, panels, and menus that make it easier for you to run your applications. Let's begin our discussion of modifying the NLD desktop with a look at adding icons to the desktop.

19 Create Desktop Icons

You can create desktop icons for applications, applets, folders, and files. You can quickly drag icons from the menus to make a desktop icon or use the Create Launcher dialog box to create icons for programs, folders, and icons.

✔ BEFORE YOU BEGIN	→ SEE ALSO
6 About the GNOME Desktop	**46** Use Nautilus to Manage Folders
7 Navigate the GNOME Desktop	**47** Browse and Open Files
18 About Modifying GNOME	

1 Drag Icon from Menu

To quickly create a desktop icon from a menu item, open the menu and submenu that contains the icon. Then drag the icon onto the desktop. To use the icon to launch the program, double-click the icon.

2 Open Create Launcher Dialog

Right-click on the desktop and select **Create Launcher**. The Create Launcher dialog box opens. This dialog box allows you to create program, folder, and file icons on the desktop.

3 Create Program Icon

To create a program icon enter a name (which appears on the icon) and a command (the command that launches the program). To select an icon for the program (a generic icon is used otherwise), select the **No Icon** box. The Browse Icons dialog box appears. Select an icon and then click **OK** to return to the Create Launcher dialog. Click **OK** to create the new program icon on the desktop.

CHAPTER 4: Modifying the NLD Desktop

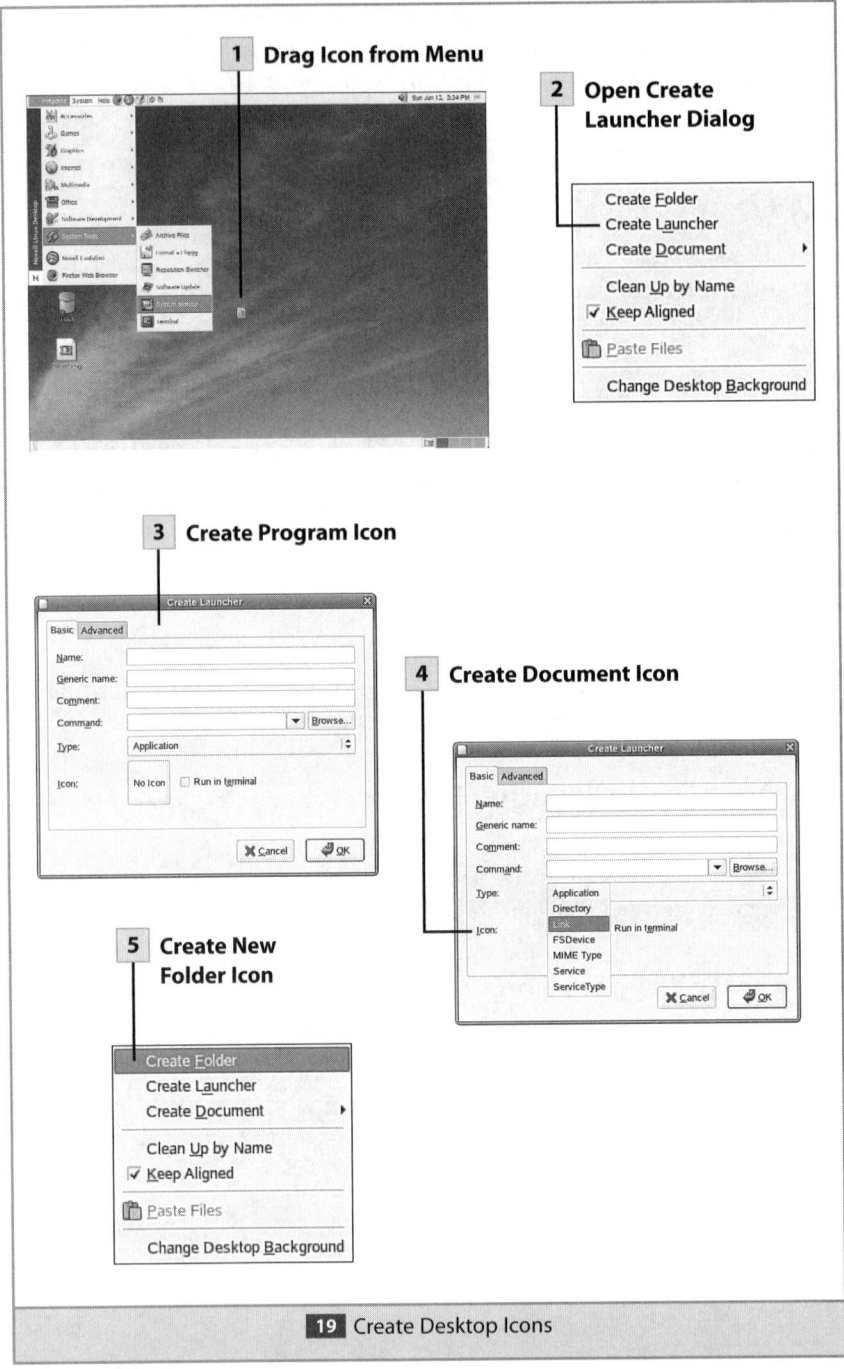

19 Create Desktop Icons

19 Create Desktop Icons

4 Create Document Icon

You can also place document icons on the desktop that allow you to quickly access a particular application file such as a document or spreadsheet. In the Create Launcher dialog box select the **Type** drop-down box and select **Link**. You can use the **Browse** button to locate the file that you want to create the icon for. If you want to use a special icon for the document, click the **No Icon** box and select an icon. To place the icon on the desktop click **OK**.

NOTE

The path to the file is actually placed in the URL box of the Create Launcher dialog box (when you select Link in the drop-down list, the Command box changes to the URL box). Interestingly, URLs can point to local files or to external websites, which we most often think of in terms of URLs.

5 Create New Folder Icon

To quickly create a new folder on the desktop right-click on the desktop and select **Create Folder** from the shortcut menu. The new folder appears on the desktop. Type a name for the new folder. To open the new (and empty folder) double-click the icon.

NOTE

Folders that you create on the desktop are actually there to hold documents and subfolders. They differ from the desktop icons that you create, which are merely pointers to applications, applets, or other items.

TIP

To arrange the desktop icons (including any new icons that you have created), right-click on the desktop and select **Clean Up by Name**.

TIP

Removing icons from the desktop is simple. Select the icon and then press **Delete**. The icon is moved to the Trash.

CHAPTER 4: Modifying the NLD Desktop

20 Add an Item to a Panel

You can also add quickstart icons to the desktop panels. This allows you to quickly access any number of programs without cluttering the desktop with additional icons. You can add quickstart icons to either the top or bottom panel.

✔ BEFORE YOU BEGIN

- 6 About the GNOME Desktop
- 7 Navigate the GNOME Desktop
- 19 Create Desktop Icons

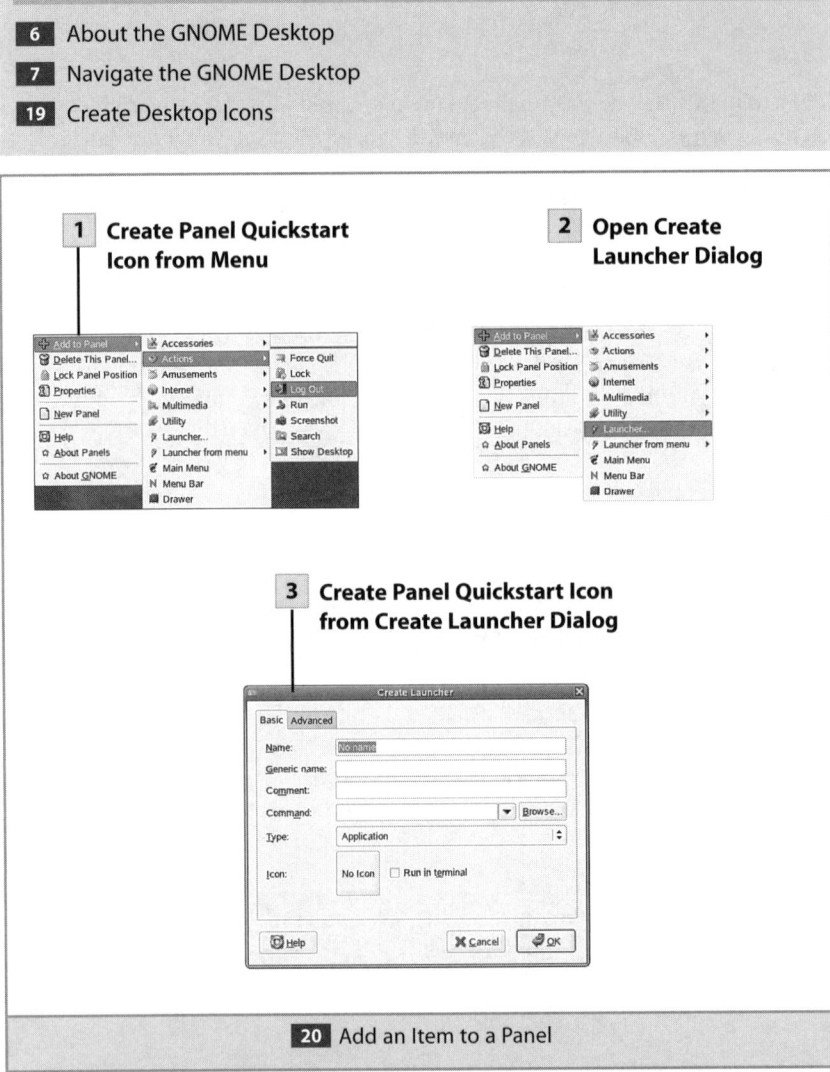

62

1 Create Panel Quickstart Icon from Menu

Place the mouse pointer on either the top or bottom panel. Right-click and select **Add to Panel**. A submenu appears that provides a series of categories (Accessories, Actions, Amusements, and so on). Each category contains a set of applets and utilities. Select a category and then a specific applet. A quickstart icon for that applet is placed on the panel.

2 Open Create Launcher Dialog

You can also create quickstart icons for the panels using the Create Launcher dialog box. Right-click on a panel, select **Add to Panel**, and then select **Launcher**. The Create Launcher dialog box opens.

3 Create Panel Quickstart Icon from Create Launcher Dialog

Enter a program, document, or other item name and then enter the appropriate information in the Type box (select the **Type** from the drop-down box). After entering the appropriate information, click **OK** to create the panel icon.

TIP

You can remove any quickstart icons that you add to your panels. Right-click on the icon and select **Remove from Panel**.

TIP

You can add additional panels to the desktop if you want and then populate them with quickstart icons. Right-click on an existing panel and select **New Panel**. A new vertical panel is added on the right side of the desktop. You can add icons to this new panel as needed. If you want to remove an added panel, right-click on the panel and select **Delete This Panel**.

21 Add an Item to a Menu

You can add items to the Programs menu (items cannot be added to the System menu). In particular, you can add programs or applets not currently present on the main Programs menu or its submenus. The procedure is similar to creating program icons for the desktop and the desktop panels; you use the Create Launcher dialog box to enter the information for the program icon.

CHAPTER 4: Modifying the NLD Desktop

✓ **BEFORE YOU BEGIN**

- **6** About the GNOME Desktop
- **8** Use the Menu System
- **20** Add an Item to a Panel

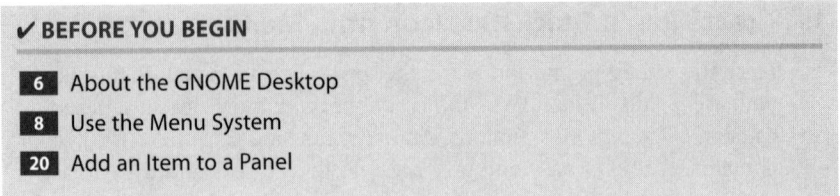

1 Select Submenu for New Icon

2 Open Create Launcher Dialog

3 Enter Information in Create Launcher Dialog

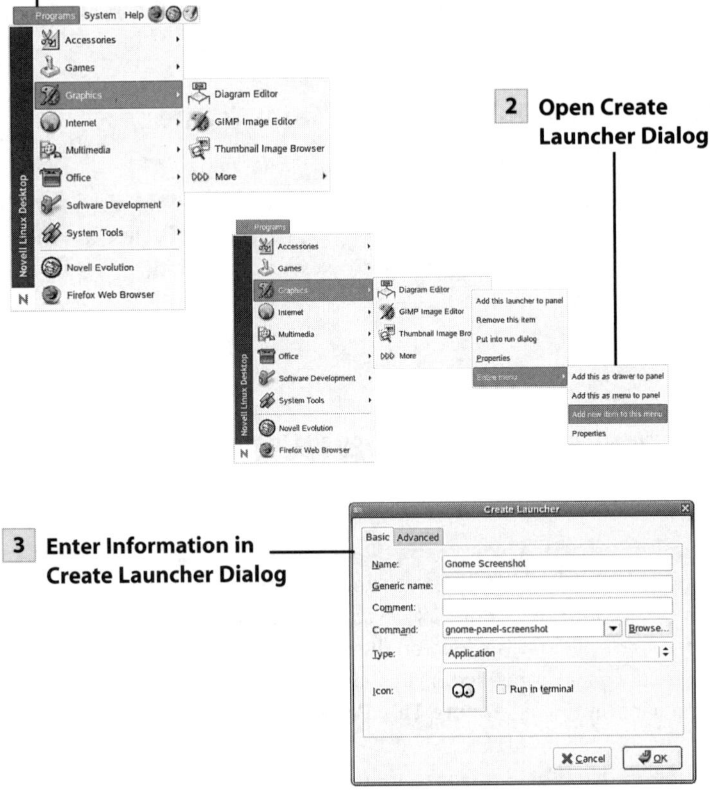

21 Add an Item to a Menu

64

1 Select Submenu for New Icon

Open the **Programs** menu and then select the submenu where you want to place the new icon.

2 Open Create Launcher Dialog

Right-click on the submenu. Select **Entire Menu** on the shortcut menu that appears and then select **Add New Item to This Menu**. The Create Launcher dialog box opens.

3 Enter Information in Create Launcher Dialog

Enter the appropriate information in the Create Launcher dialog box (the program name and program command). Select an icon for the program (select the **No Icon** box). To create the new menu item, click **OK**. You can now access the program on the appropriate submenu using the new icon.

TIP

You may have to log out and then log in to see the changes that you have made (such as the adding of icons) to the NLD menu system.

22 About GNOME Personal Settings

✔ **BEFORE YOU BEGIN**

6 About the GNOME Desktop

The NLD personal settings provide control over special accessibility features, appearance settings, hardware settings, and system settings. For example, if you want to set up a screensaver or add a new printer, you are dealing with personal settings. The various user settings are accessed via the Settings dialog box, which is a set of icons divided into categories.

These four setting categories are

- Personal—These settings relate to accessibility features that can be enabled on the keyboard and tools that can be used to better view the desktop (in cases where the user needs special abilities related to viewing the desktop). Two of the four icons available under Personal settings that control accessibility features are Accessibility and Assistive Technology Support. The Menus icon allows you to modify the group submenus currently shown on the Programs menu. The Shortcuts icon allows you to add or edit the keyboard shortcut keys for GNOME actions such as menu and icon access.

Many of your personal desktop settings are accessed using the Settings dialog box.

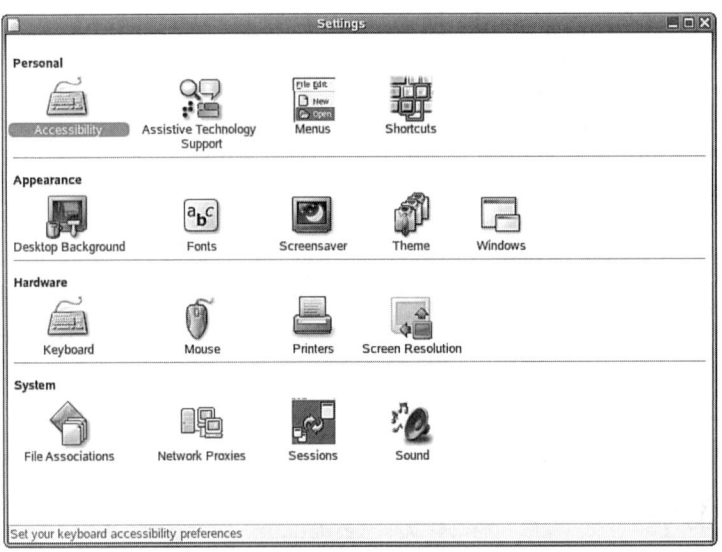

- Appearance—The Appearance settings group includes icons that allow you to control the desktop background, desktop fonts, the screensaver, current theme (the overall look of the NLD desktop), and the look and feel of your application and applet windows.
- Hardware—The hardware settings available in the Settings dialog box include keyboard settings and settings for the mouse, your printers, and the screen resolution.
- System—System settings that you can adjust include file associations, network proxies, sessions, and sound.

NOTE

We take a look at the Personal and Appearance settings in this chapter. Hardware and System settings are discussed in Chapter 5, "Configuring NLD Hardware and System Settings."

Remember that all the configuration possibilities available to you in the Settings dialog box are user settings. This means that you can change these settings without requiring the root password. More complex settings (those that require administrative privileges) are accessed via the Administrator Settings command on the Systems menu.

23 Change Personal Settings

The first group of icons in the Settings dialog box is categorized as Personal settings. These settings relate to special accessibility features and also provide control over the items on the Programs menus and the settings for keyboard shortcuts.

✔ BEFORE YOU BEGIN

22 About GNOME Personal Settings

WEB RESOURCE

http://www.novell.com/documentation/nld/index.html

Go to this website to access documentation provided by Novell for NLD.

1 Open Settings Dialog Box

To open the Settings dialog box select the **System** menu and then select **Personal Settings**.

2 Open Personal Settings

To open one of the Personal Settings dialog boxes, double-click the appropriate icon.

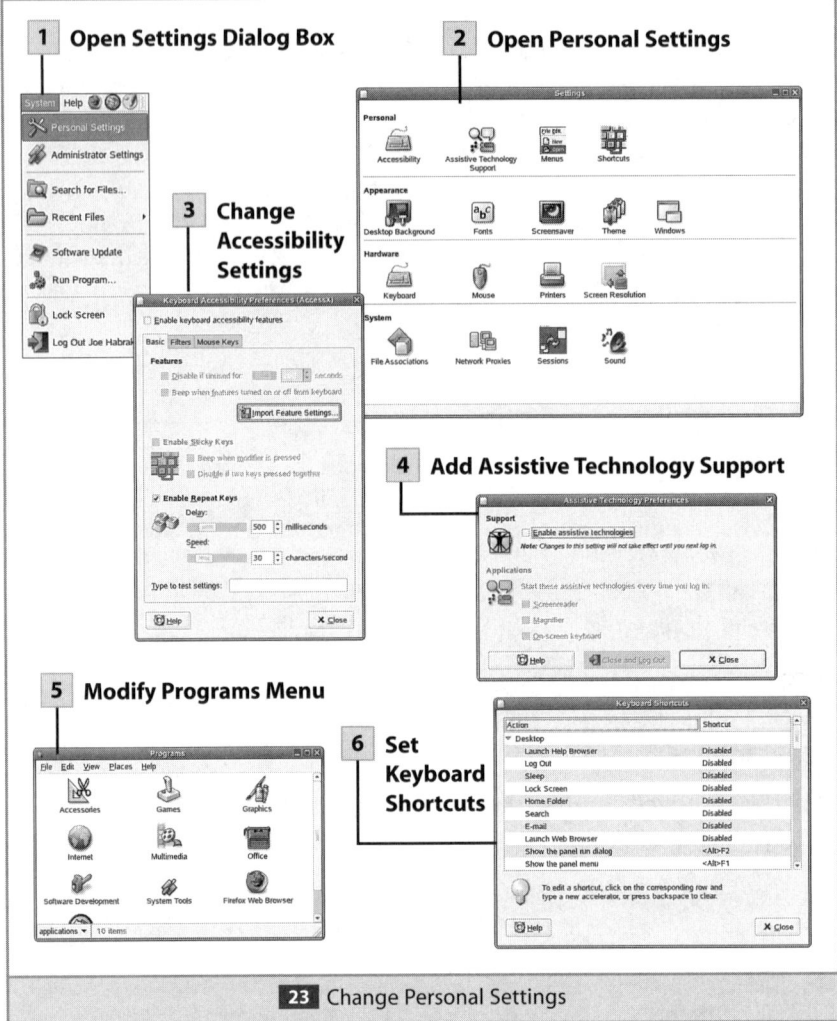

23 Change Personal Settings

3 Change Accessibility Settings

If you do not want to configure keyboard accessibility settings, you can skip this step. Double-click the **Accessibility** icon to open the Accessibility dialog. On the Basic tab, select **Enable Keyboard Accessibility Features** (to enable accessibility). You can then enable sticky keys (helper keys such as Alt and Ctrl that only have to be tapped rather than held down when used for shortcuts) and repeat keys (the delay set for a key before it repeats) on this tab.

Select the **Filters** tab. On this tab you can configure slow keys (key must be pressed for certain duration) and bounce keys (prevents double typing by setting a time limit for consecutive uses of a single key).

Select the **Mouse Keys** tab. This tab allows you to configure the arrow keys on the number as a keyboard mouse. You can configure items such as the speed and acceleration for the keyboard mouse. After you have finished configuring the Accessibility settings select **Close** to close the dialog box.

TIP

If you want to use the Assistive Technology Support features, which provide onscreen keyboard support and special screen magnifiers, you must install four additional packages (which are not installed as part of the typical NLD installation): dasher, gok, gnopernicus, and gnome-mag. You can install these packages if you have access to the root password. These packages are available on either CD 2 of the NLD CD set or on the DVD. Open the **Administrator Settings** dialog (from the **System** menu). Then select **Install and Remove Software**. On the Filter drop-down list, select **Selections**. Then click the **Accessibility** check box. The four accessibility packages should be selected on the right of the YaST window. Place the appropriate CD or DVD in your drive. Then click **Accept** to install these packages.

4 Add Assistive Technology Support

If you do not want to take advantage of the Assistive Technology Support features, skip this step. Double-click the **Assistive Technology Support** icon in the Settings dialog. Select the **Enable Assistive Technologies** check box. Then select the settings you want to use: Screenreader, Magnifier, On-screen Keyboard. To enable the settings, you must log off the system. Click the **Close and Log Out** button.

When you log on to the system, the assistive tools that you selected will be enabled. The screenreader/magnifier divides the screen into two sections: The normal desktop is on the left, and on the right is a magnified version of the mouse pointer's position on the desktop. The onscreen keyboard (GOK) allows you to use the mouse to launch programs, manipulate windows, and compose from a keyboard using the mouse.

CHAPTER 4: Modifying the NLD Desktop

TIP

To close the screenreader/magnifier, close the Gnopernicus window (which allows you to configure the screenreader/magnifier). You can relaunch any of your assistive tools using the **Accessories** submenu on the **Programs** menu. To deactivate all the assistive tools, return to the Assistive Technologies Preferences dialog and clear the **Enable Assistive Technologies** check box.

5 Modify Programs Menu

You can modify the Programs menu by adding new folders and program launcher icons. Double-click the **Menus** icon in the Settings dialog. To create a new folder on the Programs menu or in any of the subfolders (double-click a subfolder to open it), select **File** and then select **New Folder**. Type a name for the new folder.

To add a program icon, Select **File** and then select **Create Launcher**. In the Create Launcher dialog provide a name and a command that starts the program (you can also browse for the program command). Click **OK** to create the launcher icon. After you have finished adding items to the Programs menu (or submenus), close the Programs window.

6 Set Keyboard Shortcuts

Keyboard shortcuts (a combination of a helper key such as Alt or Shift and another keystroke) allow you to quickly perform a particular task such as open your web browser, log out, or change the system sound volume. Double-click the **Shortcuts** icon to open the Keyboard Shortcuts dialog box. To set the shortcut for a particular action, select that action in the Action list (actions without shortcuts are marked disabled). To create the shortcut, press the key combination on the keyboard. The shortcut key combination appears in the Shortcut list to the left of the selected action. After you have completed setting your keyboard shortcuts, select **Close**.

24 Change the Desktop's Background

The background or wallpaper covers the largest part of the desktop, providing the backdrop for the working environment. You can personalize the desktop by selecting your own background. You can select from a list of existing backgrounds, or you can download additional backgrounds. The file format for backgrounds is the jpeg graphic format. Any file that you download as a jpeg or any photo that you save as a jpeg can be used as the desktop.

24 Change the Desktop's Background

✔ **BEFORE YOU BEGIN**

22 About GNOME Personal Settings

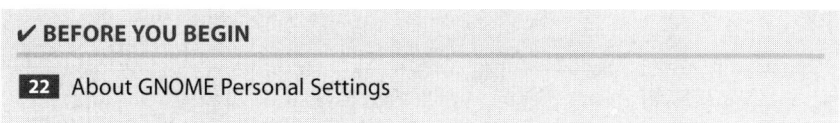

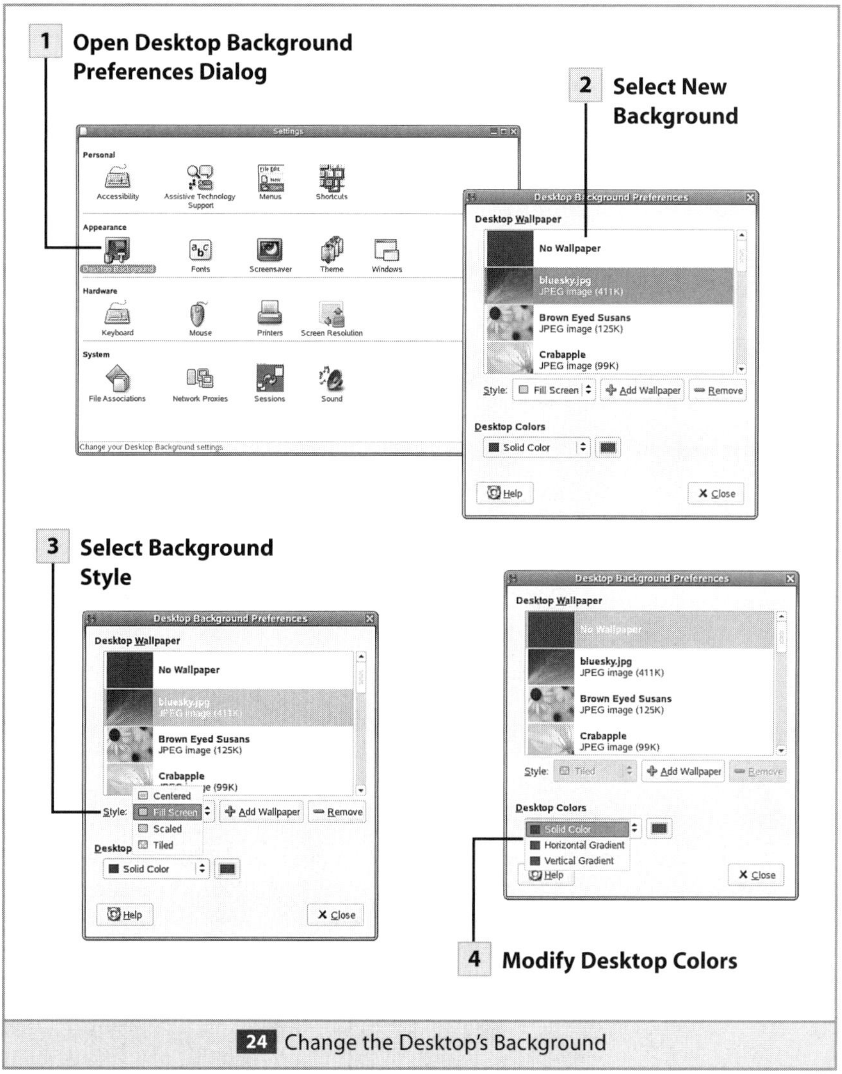

1 Open Desktop Background Preferences Dialog

2 Select New Background

3 Select Background Style

4 Modify Desktop Colors

24 Change the Desktop's Background

WEB RESOURCE

http://www.gnome.org

Go to this website to download additional backgrounds for the GNOME desktop.

71

> **TIP**
>
> If you want to create your own background using drawing software or by taking advantage of digital photos that you have taken, save the final jpeg in an appropriate size so that it covers the desktop without being distorted. For example, if you run NLD desktop at 800X600 pixels, save your images and photos in the 800X600 size. This makes the files ideal as the background for your desktop.

1. Open Desktop Background Preferences Dialog

In the Settings dialog box (in the Appearance pane), double click the **Desktop Background** icon.

2. Select New Background

To select from the list of backgrounds, scroll through the **Desktop Wallpaper** list and then select a new background.

3. Select Background Style

There are four settings in terms of placing the background on the desktop:

- Centered—Places the background in the center of the desktop. (This option does not necessarily cover the entire desktop with the background depending on the image dimensions.)
- Fill Screen—This option stretches the background to cover the entire desktop; however, it does maintain the height/width ratio of the image to minimize distortion.
- Scaled—Stretches the image to the edges of the screen and maintains the height/width ratio of the image to minimize distortion.
- Tiled—Depending on the size of the file (and your desktop resolution), the image will be repeated as tiles on the desktop. Most of the default background files actually appear scaled (because of the image size) when you select one of them.

Select the placement setting you want to use from the Style drop-down list.

4 Modify Desktop Colors

If you want to forgo a background image, you can select the **No Wallpaper** setting in the Desktop Wallpaper list. You can then select either Solid Color (one-color desktop), Horizontal Gradient (creates a gradient from left to right using two selected colors), or Vertical Gradient (creates a gradient from top to bottom using two selected colors) in the Desktop Colors drop-down list.

To select the color (or colors for a gradient), select the **Color** button (or buttons) next to the Desktop Colors drop-down list. The Pick a Color palette opens. Select a color from the color wheel and then click **OK**. Repeat the process if you are creating a gradient. After you have completed your changes to the desktop background settings, click the **Close** button.

TIP
You can quickly change the desktop background by right-clicking on the desktop and selecting **Change Desktop Background** from the shortcut menu.

TIP
To add a new background file (background files are in the jpeg graphics format, so any jpeg can be used—even photos), select the **Add Wallpaper** button in the Desktop Background Preferences dialog. An Add Wallpapers window opens. You can browse for the image file (jpeg) that you want to add to the background list. Select the new background file and then select **Open**. The background is added to your list of backgrounds.

25 Change Fonts

You also have control over the fonts used for your applications, the desktop, window titles, and your terminal sessions. These options are available in the Font Preferences dialog box.

✔ **BEFORE YOU BEGIN**
  22 About GNOME Personal Settings

CHAPTER 4: Modifying the NLD Desktop

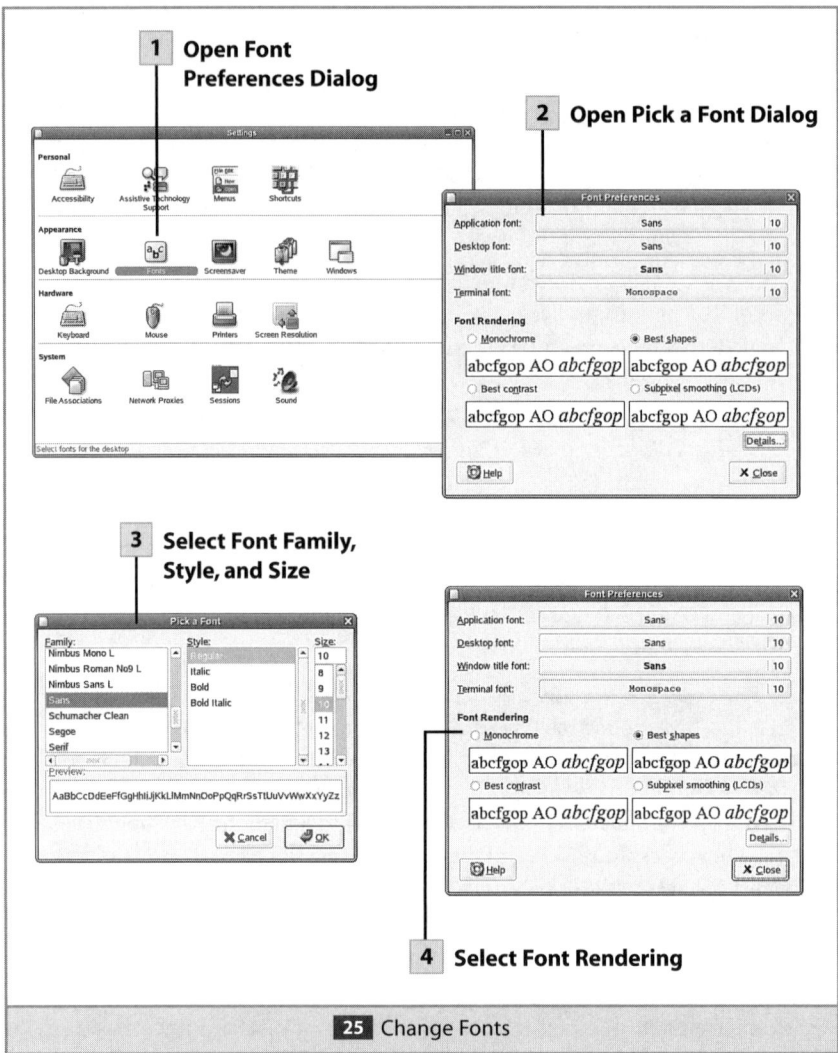

25 Change Fonts

1 Open Font Preferences Dialog

In the Settings dialog box (in the Appearance pane), double-click the **Fonts** icon. This opens the Font Preferences dialog box. Font changes can be made for applications, the desktop, window titles, or the terminal by clicking on the appropriate choice.

2 Open Pick a Font Dialog

Select one of the font change boxes (such as Application font). This opens the Pick a Font dialog box.

TIP

You can add TrueType fonts to your system as needed. Use Firefox to locate websites that provide font downloads. Download the fonts to a folder that you create on your desktop (right-click on the font download link and select **Save Target** to specify the appropriate folder). Open the folder on the desktop that you use to store the downloaded fonts. Open your Home folder on the desktop. In the Home window, select **File** and then select **Open Location**. In the dialog that opens, type **fonts:///** and then click **Open**. This opens the Font folder for the system. Drag fonts from the folder that you created to hold downloaded fonts to the Font system folder. You now have access to the added fonts.

3 Select Font Family, Style, and Size

In the Pick a Font dialog box, select a new font family from the Family list. If you want to change the font style, select a new style in the Style list box. Finally, to change the font size, make a selection in the Size list. Click **OK** to return to the Font Preferences dialog box.

4 Select Font Rendering

By default fonts are rendered using the Best Shapes option. This option smoothes the edges of the fonts and is typically the best setting for standard monitors. You can also select Monochrome (fonts are shown in black and white, but edges are not smoothed), Best Contrast (sharpens the contrast and smoothes font edges; setting is designed to make screen easier to read), and Subpixel Smoothing (LCDs). The Subpixel Smoothing option is designed to get the best performance out of LCD (laptops) and flat-screen monitors. After making your font rendering selection, click **Close** to exit the dialog box.

NOTE

Changing the fonts and other options for your applications only affects your GNOME applications, which is fine because GNOME is the default GUI for NLD. However, if you switch to the KDE desktop, you will find that your font changes are not applied to your applications and applets.

CHAPTER 4: Modifying the NLD Desktop

TIP

You can specify additional settings related to how fonts are rendered on your monitor. Select the **Details** button to fine-tune settings for smoothing and hinting.

26 Select a Screensaver

Screensavers were originally developed to protect computer screens (we're talking about those old amber and monochrome monitors) from having a static image burned onto the screen during long periods of screen inactivity. The monitors that we now use do not have the same burn-in problems, and most are energy-compliant devices that shut down after a period of inactivity. So screensavers are really mostly for fun and also provide you with the ability to lock your screen when you are away from your computer.

✔ BEFORE YOU BEGIN	→ SEE ALSO
22 About GNOME Personal Settings	27 Use the Lock Screen Tool

1 Open Screensaver Preferences Dialog

In the Settings dialog box (in the Appearance pane), double-click the **Screensaver** icon. This opens the Screensaver Preferences dialog box.

2 Select Screen Saver Mode

Select the **Mode** list to select one of the following: Only One Screen Saver, Random Screen Saver (allows you to select a list of screensavers for random selection), Blank Screen Only (screen blanks, but a screensaver is not used) or Disable Screen Saver (the screensaver feature is not used).

3 Select Screensaver

If you select the Only One Screen Saver mode, select a screensaver from the list of screensavers provided. If you select Random Screen Saver, check boxes are placed next to the screensavers in the list. Enable or clear check boxes as needed to select the screensavers that will be used.

26 Select a Screensaver

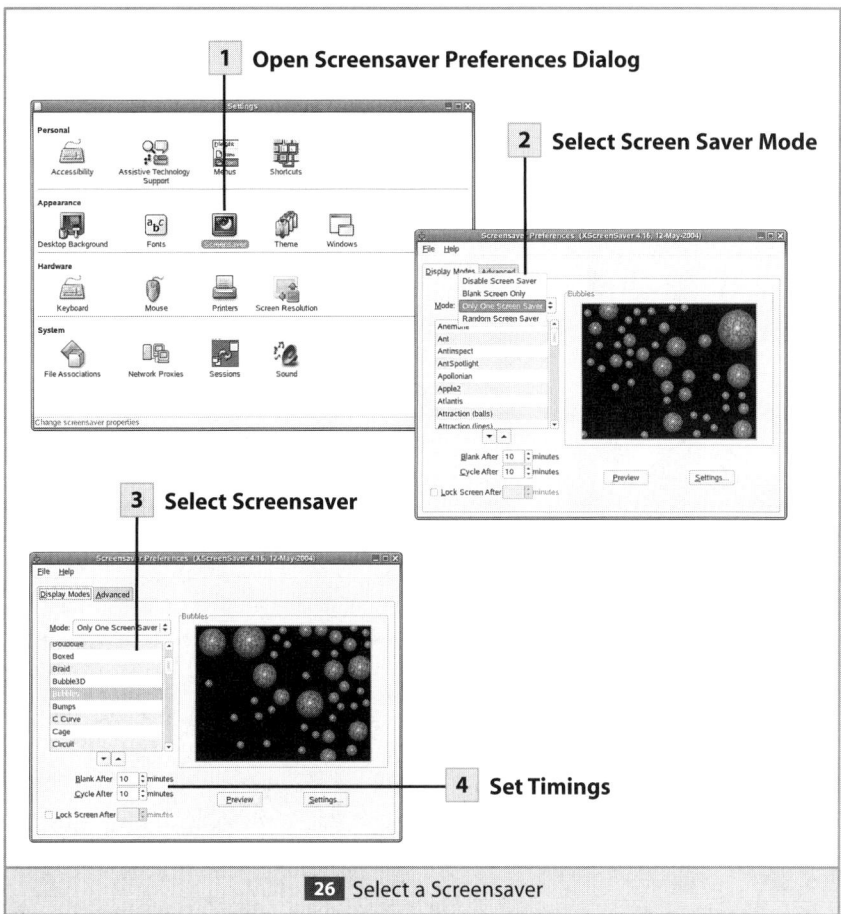

26 Select a Screensaver

TIP

To see a full-screen preview of a screensaver, select the screensaver in the list and then select **Preview**. Also, be advised that some of the screensavers available require a lot of computer resources to run. If you have a newer system with a lot of power, feel free to run any screensaver. On older systems, you may want to stick with some of the simpler screensaver choices.

77

CHAPTER 4: Modifying the NLD Desktop

[4] Set Timings

You can also set timings for how long the screensaver should run before the screen is blanked and how often the screensavers should be cycled if you chose to use the Random Screen Saver mode. Set the **Blank After** and **Cycle After** time settings as needed. If you also want to lock the screen and require your password to reenter the system, select the **Lock Screen After** check box and set a timing (for the Lock Screen tool). After completing the settings in the Screensaver Preferences dialog box, close the dialog box.

TIP

If you want to set Display Power Management for a compliant monitor (such as the timing for the monitor to use when it goes into standby), select the **Advanced** tab of the Screensaver Preferences dialog box. The Advanced tab also provides settings for image manipulation where you can set up a screensaver to use image files that you have stored in a folder.

[27] Use the Lock Screen Tool

The screen can be locked by setting a timing in the Screensaver Preferences dialog box when you configure your screensaver. In cases where you want to lock the screen when you are ready to step away from your computer, you can use the Lock Screen command on the System menu. After you have locked the screen, the screensaver starts after a short period provided to unlock the screen using your user password.

✔ **BEFORE YOU BEGIN**

[22] About GNOME Personal Settings

[26] Select a Screensaver

[1] Lock Screen

Select the **System** menu and then select **Lock Screen**. The XScreenSaver lock dialog appears. You can now go about your business and step away from your computer.

28 About Desktop Themes

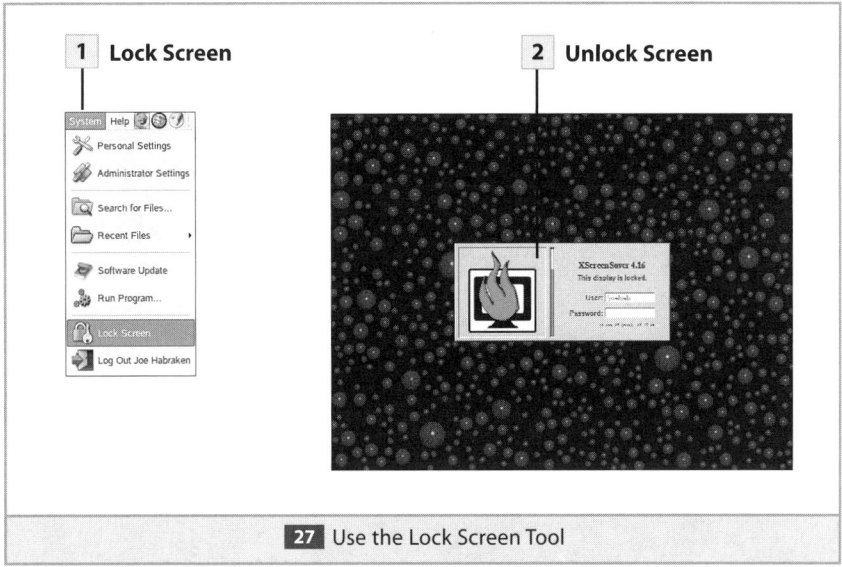

27 Use the Lock Screen Tool

2 Unlock Screen

When you return to your computer, your screensaver will be running; move the mouse or tap a key on the keyboard. The lock dialog reopens. Your username will already be entered. Enter your password and press **Enter** to unlock your computer.

28 About Desktop Themes

> ✔ **BEFORE YOU BEGIN**
>
> **18** About Modifying GNOME
> **24** Change the Desktop's Background

In terms of refining and personalizing the look and feel of the GNOME environment, your best bet is to use desktop themes. Although the desktop background sets the main image that you see on the NLD desktop, theme elements can be used to provide a custom look for how the windows that you open actually look on the desktop.

CHAPTER 4: Modifying the NLD Desktop

So, a theme gives your windows a makeover. Each theme actually consists of three subthemes: Controls, Window Border, and Icons. Each of these subthemes stored in a particular theme can be viewed for the themes provided with NLD desktop using the Theme Details dialog box.

Themes actually consist of three subthemes: one for controls; one for the window borders; and one for the desktop icons.

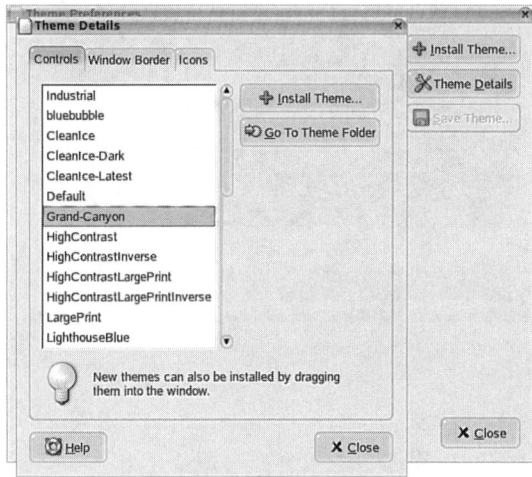

You can actually mix and match the subthemes provided and create your own themes. Matching your desktop background with the colors and overall style provided by a theme allows you to actually create a custom and unified desktop environment for your NLD desktop.

You can download additional themes and subthemes and add them to your theme settings. This increases the material that you have to work with as you design your own NLD desktop themes.

TIP

You can download subthemes from the Web using Firefox. A good place to start is http://www.gnome.org. On the GNOME home page, select the **Art and Themes** link to access the page that provides themes for downloading. When you are ready to download a theme (these are typically subthemes for controls or window frames), right-click on the download link and use the **Target Save As** option to save the theme to a folder on your desktop. This makes it easy to add these theme elements to existing themes or new themes that you create.

29 Change the Current Desktop Theme

Choose a theme and desktop background that are complementary and provide a unified look for your NLD desktop.

29 **Change the Current Desktop Theme**

Theme selection is made in the Theme Preferences dialog box. This dialog box is opened via the Theme icon in the Settings dialog box.

✔ **BEFORE YOU BEGIN**

22 About GNOME Personal Settings

28 About Desktop Themes

1 **Open Theme Preferences Dialog**

From the Settings dialog box, double-click the **Theme** icon. This opens the Theme Preferences dialog box.

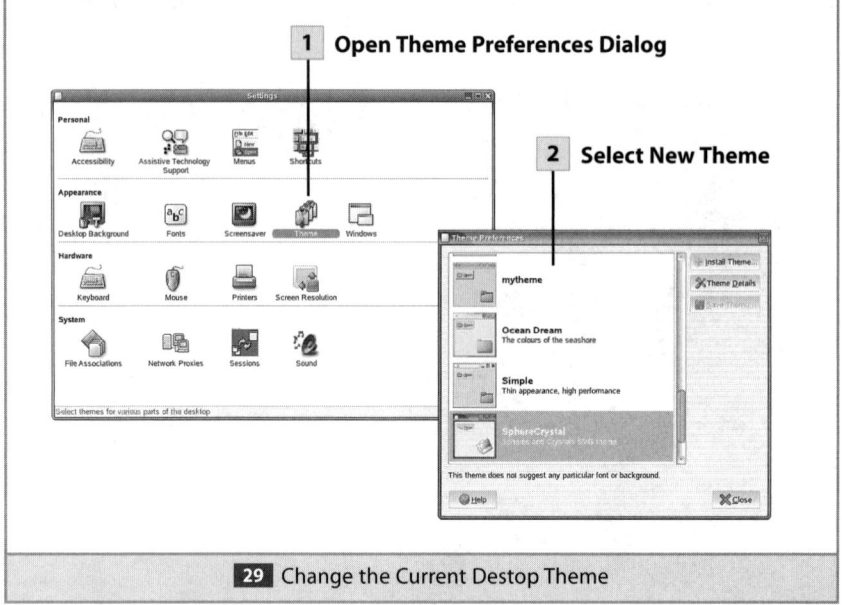

29 Change the Current Destop Theme

2 Select a New Theme

In the Theme Preferences dialog box select a new theme from the theme list. The changes that the theme makes to the window controls and borders are applied to your currently open windows (including the Theme Preferences dialog box). You can then close the Theme Preferences dialog box; select **Close**.

30 Add Themes to GNOME

There are two ways to add themes to GNOME. You can create your own themes and save them under new names, or you can download themes and theme elements from the Web and add them to the Theme Preferences dialog box, making them available for selection.

Creating a new theme is just a matter of modifying the subtheme settings (controls or window frame elements) and then saving the theme under a new name. Theme elements that have been downloaded can be dragged from a folder on your desktop directly to the subtheme tabs (Controls, Window Borders, Icons) provided on the Theme Details dialog box.

30 Add Themes to GNOME

✓ BEFORE YOU BEGIN

- **22** About GNOME Personal Settings
- **28** About Desktop Themes
- **29** Change the Current Desktop Theme

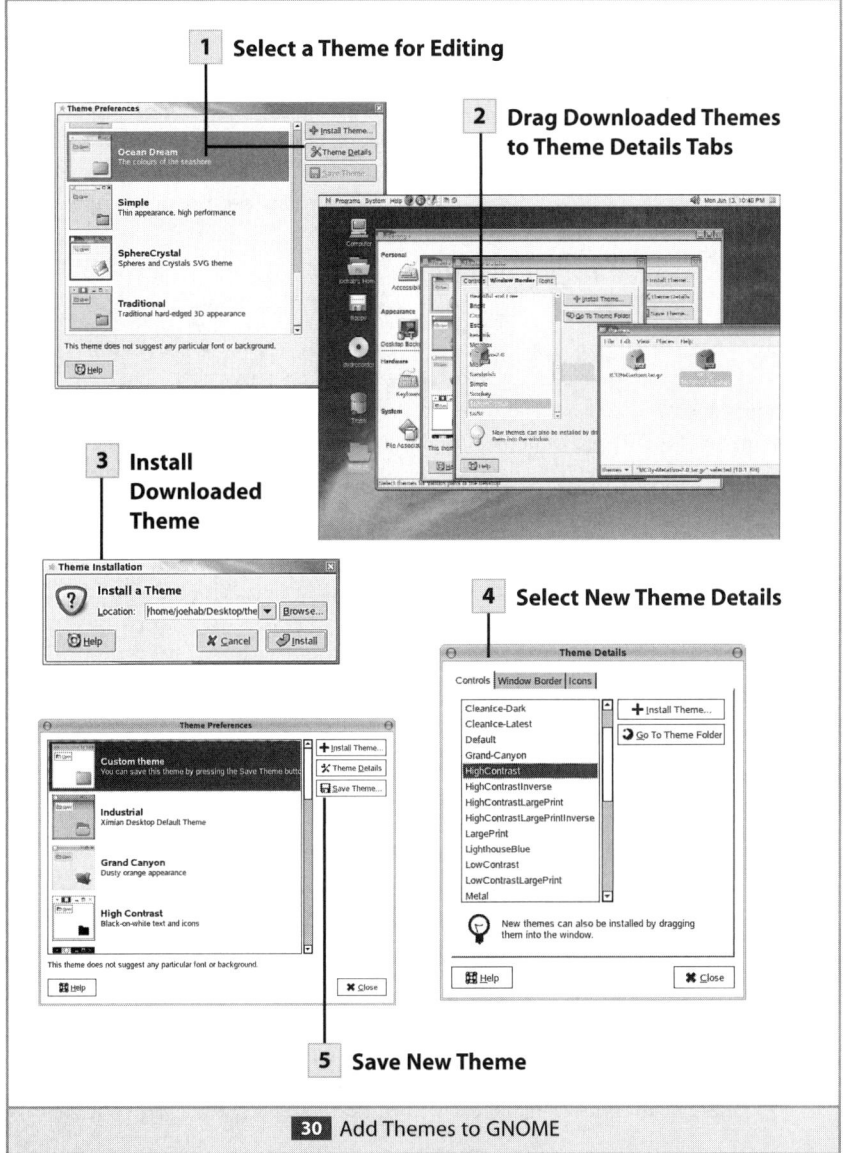

1. Select a Theme for Editing
2. Drag Downloaded Themes to Theme Details Tabs
3. Install Downloaded Theme
4. Select New Theme Details
5. Save New Theme

30 Add Themes to GNOME

1 Select a Theme for Editing

In the Theme Preferences dialog box select a theme to edit. Select a theme that has some attributes that you may use in the theme that you are creating (such as the controls or icons). Then select the **Theme Details** button to open the Theme Details dialog box.

2 Drag Downloaded Themes to Theme Details Tabs

This step is optional. If you have downloaded theme elements from the Web, you can add them to the Theme Details tabs. For example, if you have downloaded a Window Border theme (themes and theme elements are downloaded as file archives in the format *filename*.tar.gz), you can add it to the Window Border tab. Select the **Window Border tab** and drag the downloaded file to the tab. When you release the file, the Theme Installation dialog opens.

NOTE

Theme files that you download have the tar.gz extension. This means that they are archived files. You do not have to unarchive the files to use them. The archived theme files can be dragged directly onto the Theme Details tabs and installed.

3 Install Downloaded Theme

This step is optional and requires step 2. In the Theme Installation dialog box, select the **Install** button. The new theme element is added to the appropriate tab (the tab that you dragged the theme file onto). You can add other downloaded theme elements to the appropriate tabs by repeating steps 2 and 3.

4 Select New Theme Details

Now you can select the subthemes for the new theme on the Controls, Window Border, and Icons tab. After selecting the new elements, select the **Close** button in the Theme Details dialog box. You are returned to the Theme Preferences dialog box.

5 Save New Theme

A new theme appears at the top of the Theme list in the Theme Preferences dialog box named Custom theme. Select the **Save Theme** button. The Save Theme dialog box opens. Provide a name for the new theme and optional comments. Then select **Save**. The new theme appears in the Theme list. The new theme will be selected as the current theme. To close the Theme Preferences dialog box, select **Close**.

 Change Window Preferences

The Settings dialog box also provides you with the ability to control the behavior of windows on the desktop when you move the mouse over them or double-click the title bar. In terms of double-clicking on the title bar, you can select from two different behaviors. You can have the window either maximize or roll up. When you select roll up, only the title bar remains, clearing the bulk of the window from the desktop.

✔ **BEFORE YOU BEGIN**

22 About GNOME Personal Settings

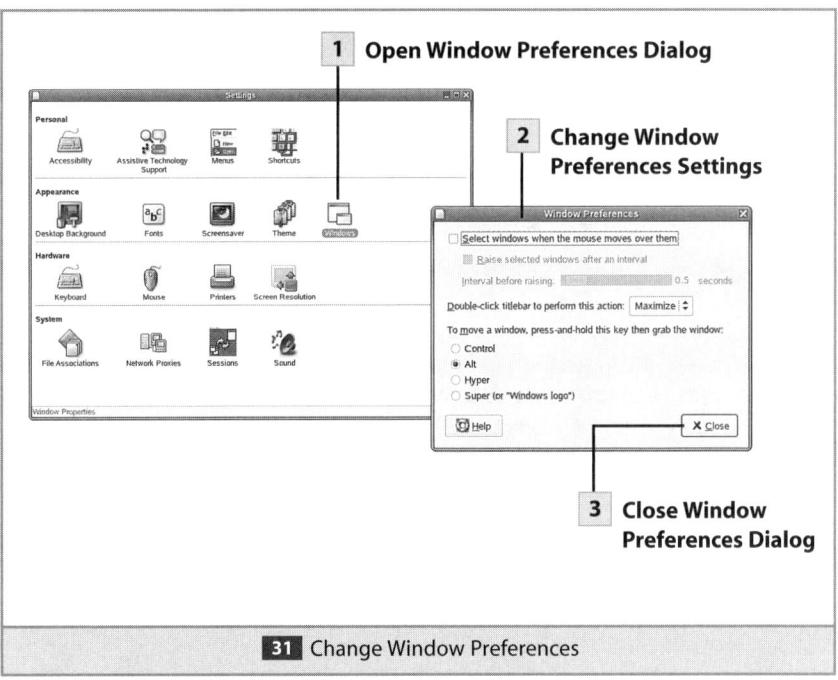

CHAPTER 4: Modifying the NLD Desktop

1   Open Window Preferences Dialog

In the Settings dialog box, double-click the **Windows** icon in the Appearance pane of the dialog box. The Window Preferences dialog box opens.

2   Change Window Preferences Settings

In the Window Preferences dialog select the **Select Windows When the Mouse Moves Over Them** check box if you want to activate windows by rolling the mouse over them. You can also set the interval of time that must be met before the window gains focus. Select the **Raise Selected Windows After an Interval** check box and then set the interval time.

If you want to change the behavior of windows when the title bar is double-clicked (the default is Maximize), select the **Double-Click Titlebar to Perform This Action** box and select **Roll Up**. Windows now roll up when you double click the title bar.

You can also select the helper key used when you want to drag that window (by default no helper key is required, and the default is the Alt key). Select an option box such as **Control**, **Hyper**, or **Super (or "Windows logo")** to change the key selection.

3   Close Window Preferences Dialog

After making your changes to the settings in the Window Preferences dialog box, select the **Close** button to close the dialog box and return to the Settings dialog box.

NOTE

Other than the ability to focus on a window by rolling the mouse over it and the ability to roll up a window with a double-click on the title bar, the other options in the Window Preferences dialog are probably best left at the defaults.

CHAPTER 5

Configuring NLD Hardware and System Settings

IN THIS CHAPTER:

- **32** About Configuring Hardware and System Settings in NLD
- **33** Change Keyboard Settings
- **34** Change Mouse Settings
- **35** About Printing and NLD
- **36** Add and Configure a Printer
- **37** Print to a Printer
- **38** Manage Print Jobs
- **39** Delete a Printer
- **40** Configure Sound Settings
- **41** Change the Screen Resolution
- **42** Change Session Settings
- **43** Change Other System Settings

CHAPTER 5: Configuring NLD Hardware and System Settings

It's important when working in a GUI environment such as NLD to have the ability to configure hardware settings for input and output devices such as the keyboard, mouse, monitor, and sound card. GNOME provides a set of easy-to-use tools that allow you to control the settings for these various devices.

Every user needs to print her work, and NLD provides you with the ability to configure printers and then manage your print jobs. This chapter looks at how to configure these various hardware items such as the keyboard, the mouse, and a printer. We also look at other settings, including session and system settings such as file associations. We begin our discussion with an overview of the tools that GNOME provides the user for configuring various hardware settings.

32 About Configuring Hardware and System Settings in NLD

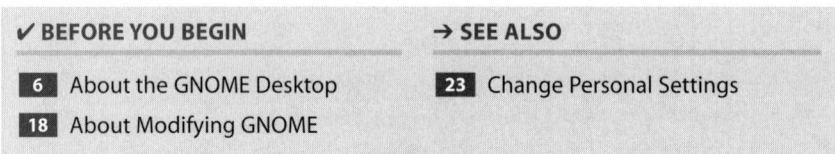

✔ BEFORE YOU BEGIN	→ SEE ALSO
6 About the GNOME Desktop	23 Change Personal Settings
18 About Modifying GNOME	

The NLD hardware and system settings that can be configured by a user (as opposed to an administrator who knows the root password) are available in the Settings dialog box.

User hardware and system settings are accessed using the Settings dialog box.

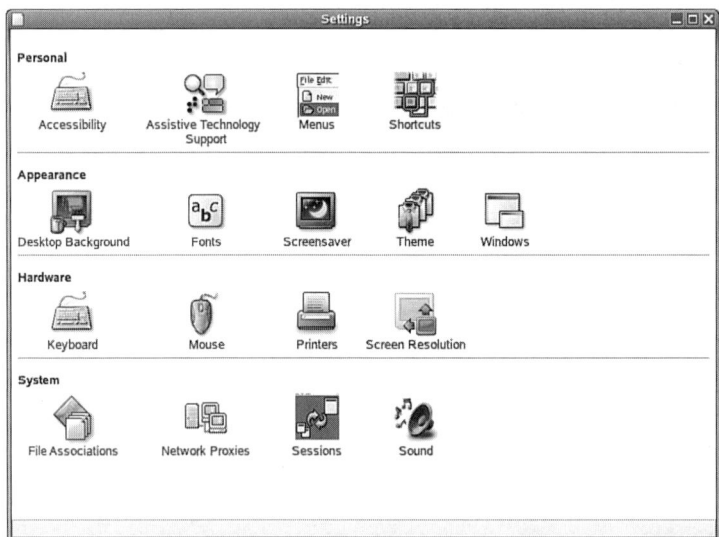

32 About Configuring Hardware and System Settings in NLD

NOTE

Although other operating systems (particularly those designed for home and small office use), provide a user with greater abilities in terms of changing hardware and system settings, NLD is designed for network environments, although it can certainly function as a standalone OS on a home PC. NLD provides much more security in terms of hardware and system settings, with many requiring the root password. This actually limits the number of "user error" configuration problems because only a basic subset of all the possible hardware and system settings are available to the typical end-user.

The hardware settings available are

- Keyboard—Settings available include repeat key delay and speed, cursor blinking speed, and keyboard layout. You can also configure the typing break feature, which actually locks the screen after a specific amount of time, requiring you to take a break from the keyboard (which can help avoid repetitive motion injuries).

- Mouse—Settings available include the mouse orientation (left or right-handed), double-click timeout, cursor sizes, and mouse speed and sensitivity.

- Printers—The features accessed via the Settings dialog's Printers options include the ability to add printers (if you have access to the root account, meaning the root password), set printer properties (such as paper type, layout, and paper source), and also open the printer's job queue and manage your active print jobs.

- Screen Resolution—Access is provided to the Screen Resolution Preferences dialog box, which allows you to control the resolution and refresh rate.

KEY TERM

Refresh rate—The refresh rate is basically the number of times that a monitor screen is redrawn in a second. Refresh rates are measured in Hz (hertz). For example, an 80Hz refresh rate would translate to the screen being refreshed 80 times per second.

Sound settings actually are not grouped with the other hardware settings discussed in the previous list. To access sound settings, double-click the Sound icon in the System panel of the Settings dialog box. The System settings also provide you with the ability to configure file associations, network proxies, and sessions settings. More details on the System settings follow:

- File Associations—The File Types and Programs allows you to control the types of files included in file categories such as Audio, Documents, and Images. You can also associate different applications and services with a particular file category. Most file types are readily identified by GNOME using the file extensions, so the use of the File Types and Programs configuration tool is only really necessary when you are working with a file that is not recognized as a particular file type by the system.
- Network Proxies—You can configure the proxy settings for your Internet connection. In most cases the proxy settings are defined during the NLD installation. However, you can use the Network Proxy Configuration dialog box to configure your own proxy settings. A proxy server sits between your computer (and other computers on the network) and handles transactions between your computer and servers and other computers on the Internet.

KEY TERM

Proxy server—Proxy servers are used to provide security for networked computers that connect to the Internet. The proxy server sits between your network and the Internet and handles outgoing and incoming information that is passed between the internal network and the Internet. Only the proxy server is really "visible" to computers outside the internal network, which protects your computer and others on the internal network from external attacks.

TIP

Proxy settings are usually configured during the NLD installation. Do not change proxy settings unless you are sure that it is required for you to connect to the Internet.

- Sessions—Each time that you log on to NLD, you are working in a session. The Sessions dialog box allows you to configure settings such as automatically saving changes that you have made to NLD during the current session. It also allows you to view (and remove) programs currently running and specify programs that should start when you log on and begin a new session.
- Sound—The Sound Preferences dialog allows you to specify whether sound files should play when certain events take place on the system. These events include user interface events such as choosing a menu and other events such as when new mail is received or you log off the system.

33 Change Keyboard Settings

Your keyboard is identified during the NLD installation. However, you can change keyboard settings in the Keyboard Preferences dialog box.

✔ **BEFORE YOU BEGIN**

23 Change Personal Settings

32 About Configuring Hardware and System Settings in NLD

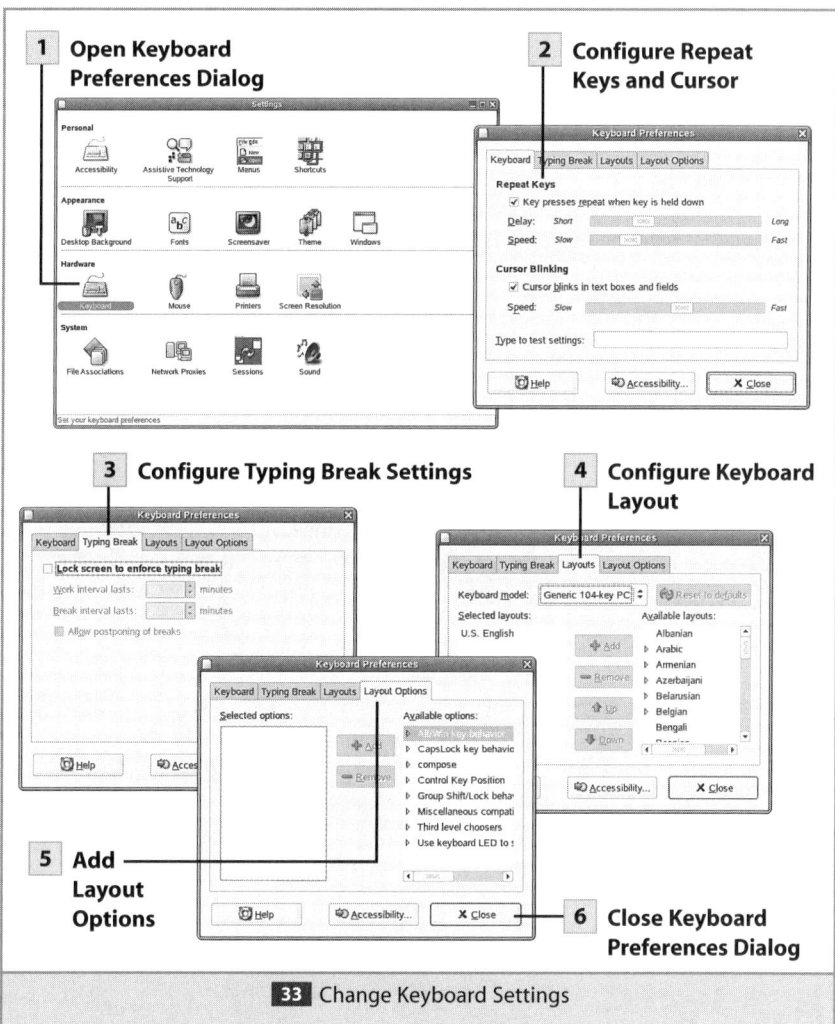

1 Open Keyboard Preferences Dialog
2 Configure Repeat Keys and Cursor
3 Configure Typing Break Settings
4 Configure Keyboard Layout
5 Add Layout Options
6 Close Keyboard Preferences Dialog

33 Change Keyboard Settings

CHAPTER 5: Configuring NLD Hardware and System Settings

1 Open Keyboard Preferences Dialog

In the Settings dialog box (select **System, Personal Settings**) double-click the **Keyboard** icon.

2 Configure Repeat Keys and Cursor

On the **Keyboard** tab of the Keyboard Preferences dialog box, use the **Delay** and **Speed** slider bars below the Repeat Keys check box to set the time delay for when a key should repeat (for example, how long it takes for the letter *d* to repeat when you hold down the *d* key) and the speed (how fast the action is repeated) of repetition, respectively. To set the cursor blind speed (how rapidly it blinks), use the **Cursor Blinking Speed** slide bar.

TIP

After you change repeat key and cursor blink settings on the Keyboard tab, use the Type to Test Settings box to enter some sample text and test the new settings.

3 Configure Typing Break Settings

Select the **Typing Break** tab of the Keyboard Preferences dialog box. This tab allows you to set typing breaks. A typing break is designed to force you to take a break from the keyboard and so is an optional setting. To configure typing breaks, select the **Lock Screen to Enforce Typing Break** check box. Then enter the time settings in the **Work Interval Lasts** and the **Break Interval Lasts** spinner boxes. If you want to have the ability to postpone a "forced" break, select the **Allow Postponing of Breaks** check box.

TIP

If you enable typing breaks, a red timer appears on the top panel. Place the mouse on it to see how much time is left until the next break. When the break begins a Take a Break dialog box opens and shows the amount of time left in the break. To postpone the current break (you must enable the Allow Postponing of Breaks check box), select the **Postpone Break** button that appears in the lower left of the "frozen" desktop.

NOTE

The keyboard type that you are using is identified during the NLD installation. You may want to tread lightly in terms of reconfiguring your keyboard layout, particularly changing the keyboard model.

4 Configure Keyboard Layout

Select the **Layouts** tab of the Keyboard Preferences dialog box. To change the keyboard model, select the **Keyboard Model** list and choose your model from the list (make sure that your keyboard and the model on the list match correctly). To add layouts to the current keyboard configuration, scroll through the **Available Layouts** list and select a layout on the list; then click the **Add** button. Layouts can also be removed from the Selected Layouts list. Select a layout and then click the **Remove** button. Use the **Up** and **Down** buttons to reorder layouts in the Selected Layouts list.

TIP

If you want to restore the keyboard layout settings to the default, select the **Reset to Defaults** button on the Layouts tab.

5 Add Layout Options

You can also add configuration options to your keyboard layout that control the behavior of certain keys and key combinations. Select the **Layout Options** tab. A list of layout options is provided on the right side of the dialog box. Select the expand arrow for any option category to view specific options. For example, expand the **Alt/Win Key Behavior** category to view options such as the Add Standard Behavior to Menu Key (the Window key). Select a particular option from the list and then select the **Add** button to add the selected option to the Selected Options list. Add options as needed. If you want to remove an option, select the option and then select the **Remove** button.

6 Close Keyboard Preferences Dialog

When you have finished setting options and preferences for the keyboard, click the **Close** button to close the Keyboard Preferences dialog box and return to the Settings dialog box.

CHAPTER 5: Configuring NLD Hardware and System Settings

34 Change Mouse Settings

You can set your mouse in either a right-handed (the default) or left-handed mode. You can also control other mouse settings such as the cursor (mouse pointer) size and the speed and sensitivity of the mouse.

✔ BEFORE YOU BEGIN

  23 Change Personal Settings
  32 About Configuring Hardware and System Settings in NLD

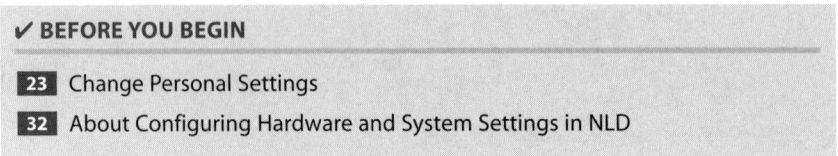

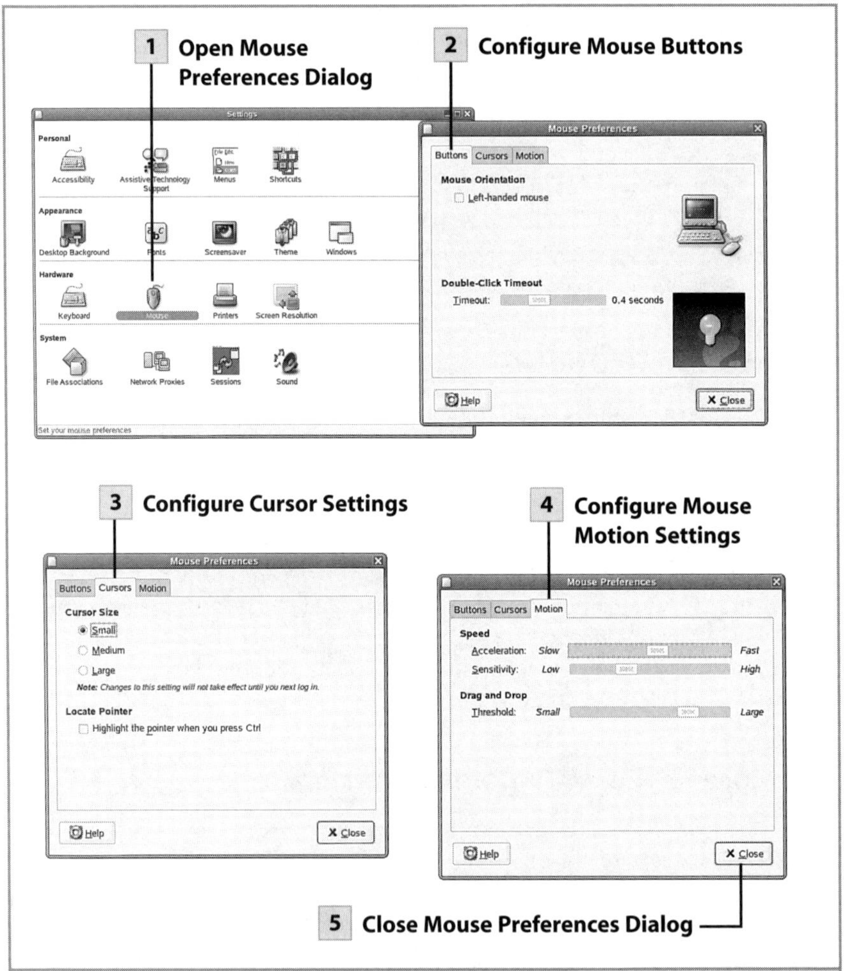

1 Open Mouse Preferences Dialog

2 Configure Mouse Buttons

3 Configure Cursor Settings

4 Configure Mouse Motion Settings

5 Close Mouse Preferences Dialog

34 Change Mouse Settings

34 Change Mouse Settings

1 Open Mouse Preferences Dialog

In the Settings dialog box (select **System**, **Personal Settings**) double-click the **Mouse** icon.

2 Configure Mouse Buttons

On the Buttons tab, to switch the mouse for left-handed use, select the **Left-Handed Mouse** check box. To set the Double-Click Timeout, use the slider bar. The Timeout is the time interval that must be met for two subsequent clicks of the mouse to be interpreted as an actual double-click.

TIP
Remember that the default Timeout for a double-click is .4 seconds. If you adjust your Timeout setting, try out the new setting by working with desktop icons or other GNOME objects that require a double-click.

3 Configure Cursor Settings

Select the **Cursors** tab. This tab allows you to adjust the size of the mouse pointer. You can change from the default (Small) to Medium or Large; select the appropriate option button. An additional option that can be used to quickly locate the mouse pointer (this can be useful on older LCD screens) is the Locate Pointer option. Select the **Highlight the Pointer When You Press Ctrl** check box to enable this option.

TIP
Some settings changes, such as the mouse cursor size change, require that you log off and then log back on to the system to put the new configuration settings into effect. Use the Systems menu to log off when necessary; you can then log back on from the Logon Manager.

4 Configure Mouse Motion Settings

Select the **Motion** tab. To change the mouse acceleration, slide the **Acceleration** slider in the appropriate direction. To change the mouse sensitivity, use the **Sensitivity** slider. To set the distance (in terms of a small or large distance) that an object must be dragged before the action is seen as a drag-and-drop function, adjust the **Threshold** slider as needed.

5 Close Mouse Preferences Dialog

After you have completed your changes to the mouse configuration, you can close the Mouse Preferences dialog; click the **Close** button.

35 About Printing and NLD

NLD makes it easy for you to configure printers and manage your print jobs. This includes adding and removing printers (adding or removing printers requires the root password) and selecting paper size and paper tray options. You can also view and manage print jobs on the desktop.

Most printers (directly connected to the PC) are automatically installed during the NLD installation. You can change the configuration of an installed printer at any time, and you can add new printers as needed.

To be honest, printing from Linux/UNIX systems has not always been a picnic. However, NLD takes advantage of a printing system known as CUPS (Common UNIX Print System). CUPS makes it easy to add and configure printers that are attached directly to your computer or are made available to you by other computers on a network, such as other computers running NLD (or other flavors of Linux).

NOTE

CUPS is a portable print system, meaning that it isn't part of the operating system. It is designed to work "with" your operating system including NLD and other Linux distributions. (CUPS is also being developed for the Windows environment.) CUPS actually provides the software drivers for the printers that you want to use. For more information about CUPS and the CUPS printer driver download library, check out http://www.cups.org.

CUPS also makes it possible to connect to printers attached directly to the network using HP Directjet technology (the printer basically has its own network interface card). And if you work in an environment where you can share printers with Microsoft Windows users, you can take advantage of SAMBA (a protocol that allows Linux systems to share files and printers with Windows systems). You certainly don't have to know much about SAMBA to take advantage of it. The GNOME Add a Printer utility makes it easy for you to select a printer on a Windows workgroup or network and then helps you to configure the basic SAMBA settings to attach to the printer.

35 About Printing and NLD

> **NOTE**
>
> HP DirectJet technology is only one of the possible hardware solutions for directly connecting a printer to a network. However, it is the industry leader in terms of large network implementations. Other possibilities for smaller networks include the USB Fast Ethernet Print Server from D-link and Netgear's USB Mini Print Server.

> **KEY TERM**
>
> ***CUPS***—Short for Common UNIX Print System, CUPS provides the set of print drivers and the printing architecture that make it easy to configure printers and to print from Linux (such as NLD) and UNIX systems.

> **KEY TERM**
>
> ***SAMBA***—An open source protocol that duplicates the capability of Microsoft's SMB (Server Message Block) protocol. In simpler terms, SAMBA provides the bridge that allows Linux systems such as NLD to talk to computers running Microsoft Windows (and SMB). This means that Linux systems can share files and printers transparently.

When you add a printer that is remote to your system (meaning on another computer on the network), you need certain information to complete the installation. In the case of CUPS printers (attached to other NLD or Linux computers), you need to know the URI (Uniform Resource Identification) for the printer. You can enter this information in two formats:

   http://hostname:631/ipp/

or

   ipp://hostname/ipp/

The hostname is the name given to the computer during installation. You need the hostname of the remote computer that is serving as the connection for the remote printer. You can quickly find the hostname of your computer or another NLD (Linux) computer by opening a terminal window (select **Programs**, **System Tools**, **Terminal**). The prompt in the terminal shows your *username@hostname*. Where the *hostname* is the name of the computer.

> **NOTE**
>
> Unless you have a small office or home network of NLD or other systems and serve as the network administrator, you really need to talk to your network administrator and get some help setting up connections to remote printers on the network. The network administrator can even do this for you, saving you time and headaches.

CHAPTER 5: Configuring NLD Hardware and System Settings

In cases where you want to take advantage of a printer hosted by a Microsoft Windows-based computer on a small office or home network, you need to know the name of the Windows computer and the name of the workgroup that the Windows computer is a member of. You also need to know a username and password that has been set up on the Windows computer so that you can establish the connection to the remote printer.

You can add and configure printers (both local and remote) using the GNOME Add a Printer utility, which is accessed using the New Printer icon in the Printers window (which is opened using the Printers icon in the Settings dialog box). The GNOME Add a Printer utility actually walks you through the steps of setting up a printer.

> **NOTE**
>
> Printers identified during the NLD installation should be "preinstalled" on the system in most cases.

You do have the option of adding and deleting printers using the YaST configuration utility, available through the Administrator Settings. We will assume, however, in the printer installation information that follows, that you are a typical user with access to the root password and will use the GNOME Add a Printer utility to connect to a printer.

One last thing about printers: You can set up a local or network printer. A local printer is attached directly to your computer (by a cable). The printer can be attached as a parallel port (historically, the "typical" printing port on personal computers), a serial port (a communications port that can be used for other devices such as external modems), or a USB port (most computers have multiple USB ports). Many new printers make it possible to connect it to your computer only via a USB port.

Make sure that you have the printer physically connected to the computer before you add the printer to the NLD configuration. Having the printer ready to go after it is set up via CUPS also allows you to immediately check your printer installation by printing a test page.

36 Add and Configure a Printer

The Settings dialog provides access to the Printers window, which is launched using the Printer icon in the Hardware pane. The Printers window allows you to add a printer, change a printer's settings, and open a printer's queue to view pending print jobs.

36 Add and Configure a Printer

✔ BEFORE YOU BEGIN

32 About Configuring Hardware and System Settings in NLD

35 About Printing and NLD

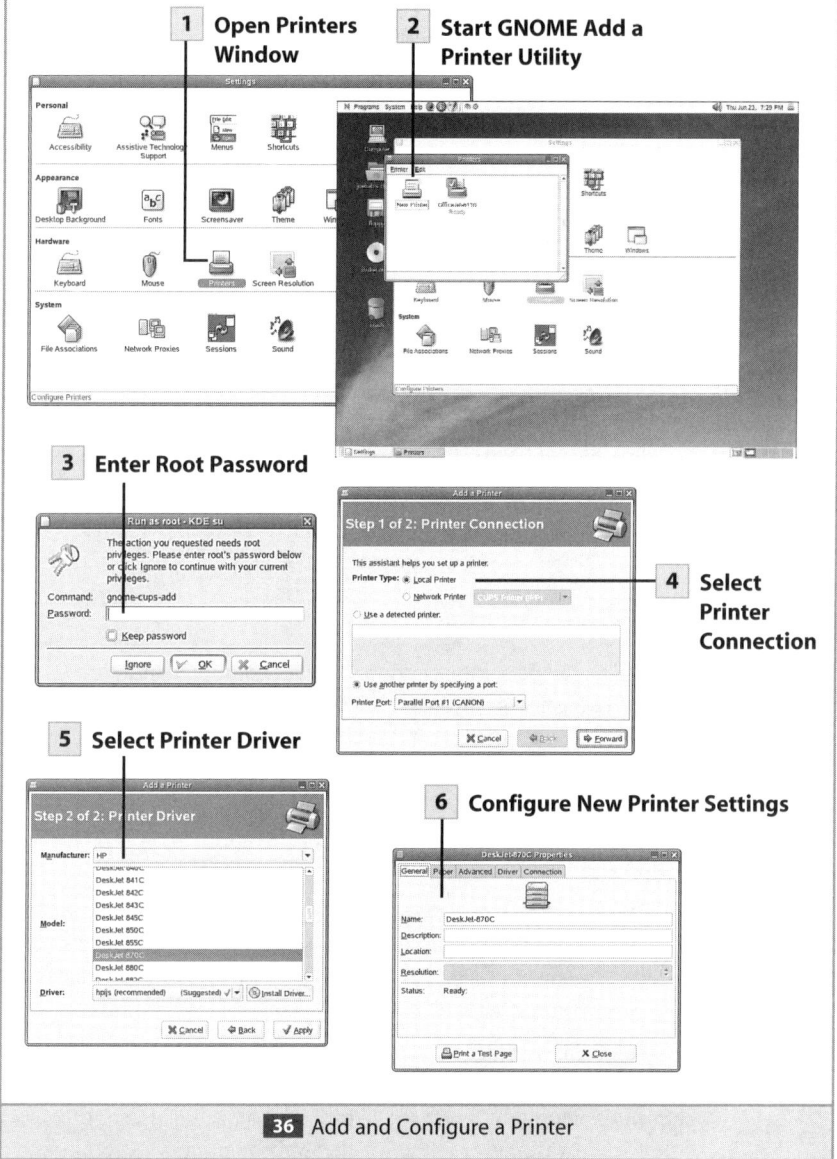

1 Open Printers Window

2 Start GNOME Add a Printer Utility

3 Enter Root Password

4 Select Printer Connection

5 Select Printer Driver

6 Configure New Printer Settings

36 Add and Configure a Printer

1 Open Printers Window

In the Settings dialog box (select **System, Personal Settings**) double-click the **Printers** icon. The Printer window opens.

2 Start GNOME Add a Printer Utility

The Printers window shows currently installed printers. To add a printer with the GNOME Add a Printer Utility, double-click the New Printer icon.

3 Enter Root Password

The Run as Root dialog box opens. Enter the root password and then click **OK**. The GNOME Add a Printer utility opens.

4 Select Printer Connection

On the Step 1 screen specify the connection for the printer. If the printer is a local printer, use the **Printer Port** drop-down list to choose the port type (parallel, serial, or USB).

In cases where you have just attached a new printer and the printer is listed in the detected printer list, select the **Use a Detected Printer** option button and then select the printer in the list.

TIP

If you just connected a new plug-and-play printer to your computer and you don't see it listed in the detected printer list, try rebooting the system and see whether the printer shows up on the list after rebooting.

If you are installing a network printer, select the **Network Printer** option button. Then use the drop-down list to select the connection type for the network printer:

- CUPS Printer (IPP)—Use this connection for network printers connected to other NLD or Linux systems on the network. If you select this connection type, you need the URI for the computer hosting the printer.

- Windows Printer (SMB)—Use this connection for network printers attached to PCs (or servers) running the Microsoft Windows operating system. You need the Windows computer name, the workgroup (or domain) name for the computer, and a username and password configured on the Windows computer.

36 Add and Configure a Printer

- Unix Printer (LPD)—Use this connection to connect to UNIX systems or Linux systems on a network that is using the TCP/IP protocol stack (nearly every network you can think of). You connect to the remote printer via the hostname (or the IP address) and print queue name (of the remote system).

- HP JetDirect Printer—Most HP Laserjet printers designed for network printing use a HP DirectJet card that allows them to be directly connected to the network. To use this connection type, you need to know the hostname or IP address of the printer.

After selecting the connection type and providing any other information required, click the **Forward** button.

5 Select Printer Driver

On the Step 2 screen, select the **Manufacturer** drop-down list and select the manufacturer of your printer. Then scroll through the **Model** list and select your printer's model. The driver for the printer appears in the Driver box. Click the **Apply** button to accept the print driver.

TIP

If you don't see your printer on the Printer Driver list, you can download new print drivers from http://www.cups.org. You can then install them from your hard drive or removable media using the Install Driver button on the Step 2 screen of the Add a Printer utility.

6 Configure New Printer Settings

The Properties dialog box opens for your newly installed printer. It contains five tabs: General, Paper, Advanced, Driver, and Connection.

On the General tab, change the name of the printer, add a description, or add a location for the printer. On the Paper tab, select the paper size, paper type, and source. On the Advanced tab, set the printout mode. On the Driver tab, select a different driver for the printer. On the Connection tab, modify the connection information (for a network printer).

TIP

You can print a test page from the printer's Properties dialog box. It is probably a good idea to print a test page before changing any of the default properties. If the test page does not print, check the driver information on the Driver tab and the connection information (that you supplied during the installation), which appears on the Connection tab.

When you have completed viewing and configuring the printer's settings, select **Close**. This returns you to the Printers window. Your printer is now ready for use.

> **TIP**
>
> You can access the properties of any installed printer. In the Printers window, right-click on the printer and select **Properties** from the menu. You will have access to the General, Paper, and Advanced tabs of any printer as a regular user. If you want to access the Driver and Connection tabs for the printer, select the **Become Administrator** button and enter the root password. The Driver and Connection tabs are added to the printer's properties dialog.

37 Print to a Printer

After you have a printer installed on your system, you can, of course, print. All the applications and applets that have the capability to print can access the installed printer or printers.

In many cases, a print icon on a toolbar allows you to send the current document or other item directly to the printer. In cases where you want more control over the printout, you can access a Print dialog box. The actual settings available in an application's or applet's Print dialog box vary from program to program.

✔ BEFORE YOU BEGIN	→ SEE ALSO
32 About Configuring Hardware and System Settings in NLD	111 About Printing in Writer
35 About Printing and NLD	112 Print a Document
	127 Print a Spreadsheet
	142 Print Slides, Notes, and Handouts

1 Open an Application or Applet

Select the **Programs** menu, a submenu (such as **Accessories**), and then an application or applet icon to open an application. Type a document or create an item, such as a drawing.

2 Open Print Dialog

In most applications and applets, select **File**, **Print** to open the Print dialog box.

37 Print to a Printer

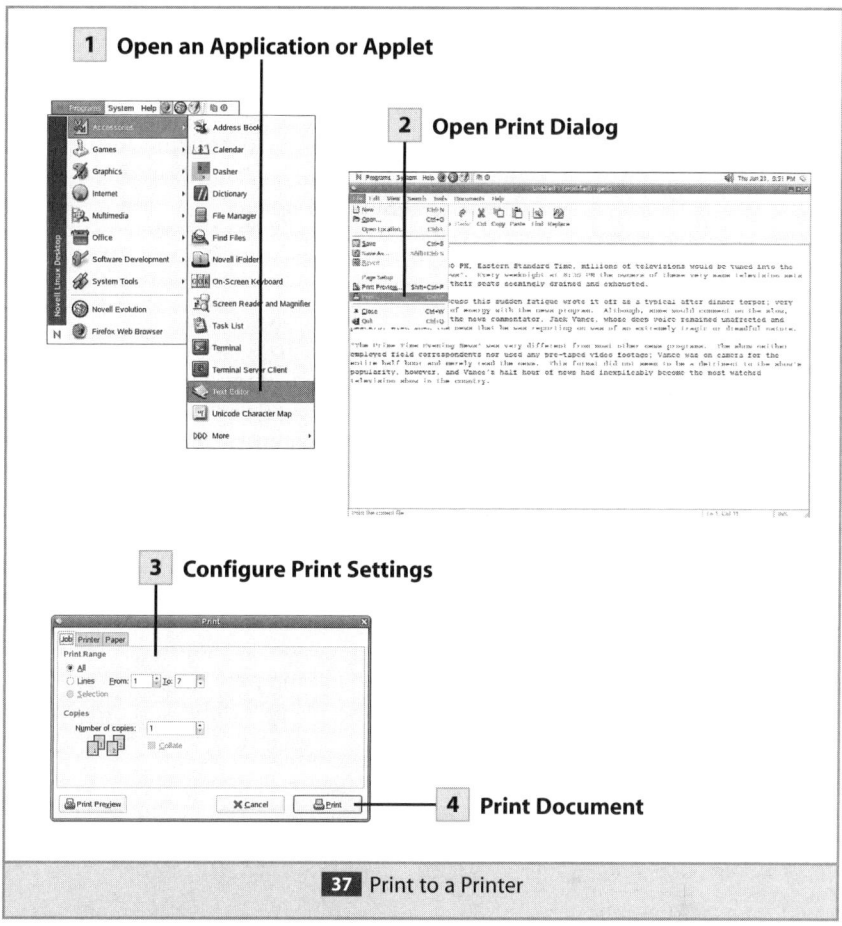

3 Configure Print Settings

Each Print dialog box varies depending on the program you are running. In the GNOME Text Editor's Print dialog box, you are provided three tabs: Job, Printer, and Paper. The features provided on these tabs are available in most applications.

On the Job tab, you can set the number of lines to print (in other applications this is pages you want to print) and the number of copies you want to print. On the Printer tab, you can select the printer that you want to use and configure the printer for duplex printing (among other settings). On the Paper tab, you can set the paper type, orientation (portrait or landscape), and the paper tray to be used.

4 Print Document

After you have configured the print settings, you are ready to print. If you want to view the printout onscreen as a preview, select the **Print Preview** button (the location of this button varies depending on the application you are using). When you are ready to print your document, click the **Print** button to send the item to the printer.

> **NOTE**
>
> NLD provides you with the ability to print your documents and other items directly to PDF files. PDF files are the standard for documents used on websites, and they also preserve the "published" look of documents that you create. PDF documents are read using the Adobe Acrobat Reader (which is a free utility from Adobe). This is a big deal because most other operating systems require that you purchase add-on software to create PDF documents this easily.

38 Manage Print Jobs

You can manage the print jobs currently waiting in the print queue. You can pause the printer (pausing all jobs) or pause specific print jobs. You can also cancel a selected job if necessary.

✓ **BEFORE YOU BEGIN**

- 32 About Configuring Hardware and System Settings in NLD
- 35 About Printing and NLD
- 37 Print to a Printer

1 Open Printers Window

You access a printer's queue from the Printers window, which displays all your installed Printers. In the Settings dialog box (select **System, Personal Settings**), double-click the **Printers** icon.

2 Open Printer Queue Dialog

To open the queue dialog for a specific printer, double-click the printer icon in the Printers window.

38 Manage Print Jobs

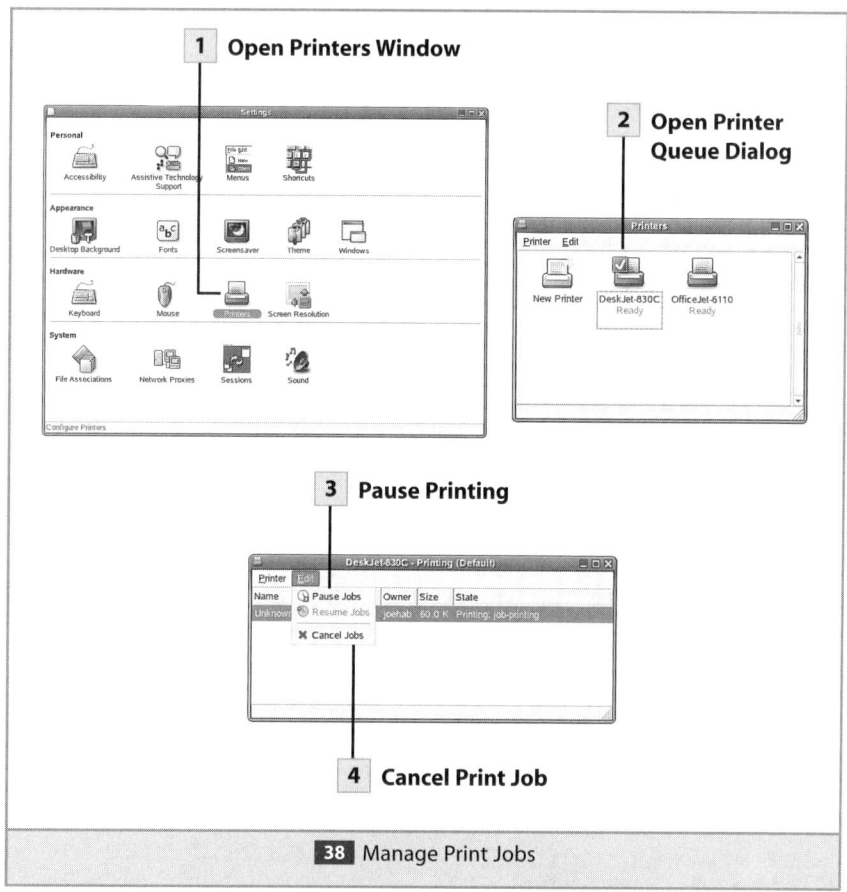

3 Pause Printing

Select the print job you want to pause and then select **Edit**, **Pause Jobs**. To resume a paused job, select the job and then Select **Edit**, **Resume Jobs**.

TIP

To pause all the print jobs listed, select **Printer**, **Pause Printer**. This is a lifesaver in cases where you have run out of paper or have a printer jam.

4 Cancel Print Job

To cancel a print job, select the print job in the list and then select **Edit**, **Cancel Jobs**. This removes the print job from the list. When you have finished working with a printer's queue dialog, click the **Close** button in the upper right of the window.

CHAPTER 5: Configuring NLD Hardware and System Settings

TIP

You can also pause and cancel print jobs by right-clicking on a print job in the queue and selecting **Pause** or **Cancel** from the shortcut menu.

39 Delete a Printer

You can also delete printers from your NLD system. Deleting printers requires the root password. Printers can be deleted from the Printers window.

✓ BEFORE YOU BEGIN

- 35 About Printing and NLD
- 36 Add and Configure a Printer
- 37 Print to a Printer
- 38 Manage Print Jobs

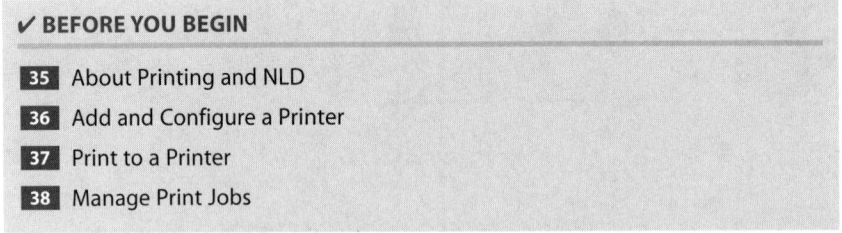

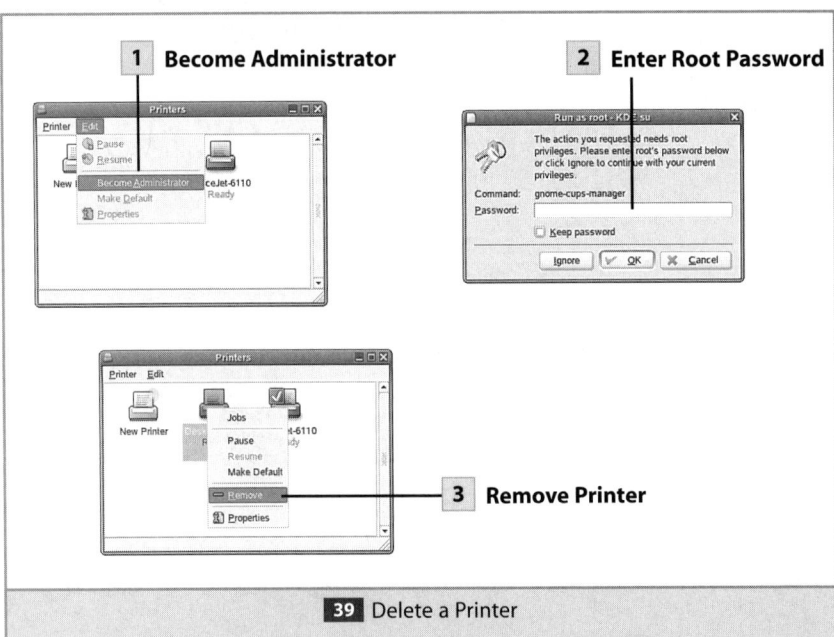

39 Delete a Printer

1 Become Administrator

You remove printers in the Printers window; to become an administrator, select **Edit**, **Become Administrator**. The Run as Root dialog box opens.

2 Enter Root Password

Enter the root password in the Run as Root dialog and then click **OK**.

3 Remove Printer

Right-click on the printer that you want to remove (in the Printers window) and select **Remove** from the shortcut menu. The printer is removed from the Printers window (and deleted from your system).

40 Configure Sound Settings

Your sound card should be identified and configured during the NLD installation. The audio functionality is provided by Advanced Linux Sound Architecture (ALSA), which is licensed under GNU.

> **NOTE**
>
> ALSA supports most sound cards. However, some new sound cards or even existing sound cards (from more obscure vendors) may not be supported. You can attempt to fine-tune the settings for an unsupported card and manually choose the driver for the card. In terms of supporting new hardware, sound cards included, it is important that you update your NLD system using Red Carpet whenever the Updates Available notification icon appears in the top panel of the desktop.

When you boot NLD, sound on your NLD system is initiated by the sound server. As a user, you can enable system sound events and select the sounds for specific events. Of course, you also have control over the sound volume and settings for specific devices such as a microphone, the CD drive, and video sound.

107

CHAPTER 5: Configuring NLD Hardware and System Settings

NOTE

Advanced sound settings related to adding or configuring a sound card can be accessed via the Administrator Settings (select **Hardware** and then **Sound**), but you need to know the root password to perform actions in YaST. Because the sound card is set up at installation, the use of YaST to configure the sound card will probably require little attention from you.

✔ BEFORE YOU BEGIN

23 Change Personal Settings
32 About Configuring Hardware and System Settings in NLD

1 Open Sound Preferences

From the Settings dialog (select **System**, **Personal Settings**), double-click the **Sound** icon in the System pane. The Sound Preferences dialog opens. By default the Enable Sound Server Startup and Sounds for Events options are enabled.

2 Set Sound Events

To set Sounds Events, select the **Sound Events** tab on the Sound Preferences dialog. To view (and listen to) a sound assigned to a current event, select an event in the Event list. If you want to listen to the sound file, select the **Play** button.

TIP

The sound files used by the NLD events are in the .wav format. You can search the Web and download any number of .wav files and assign them to events to personalize your NLD system. Your sound scheme can actually be matched to the desktop background and the theme that you assign to NLD.

To change the sound for an event or assign a sound to an event, select the event and then use the **Browse** button to locate the sound file.

3 Enable System Bell

To change the system bell settings, select the **System Bell** tab. The bell is enabled by default. If you also want to add visual feedback when the system bell sounds, select the **Visual Feedback** check box on the System Bell tab. After you have completed working in the Sound Preferences dialog, click **Close**.

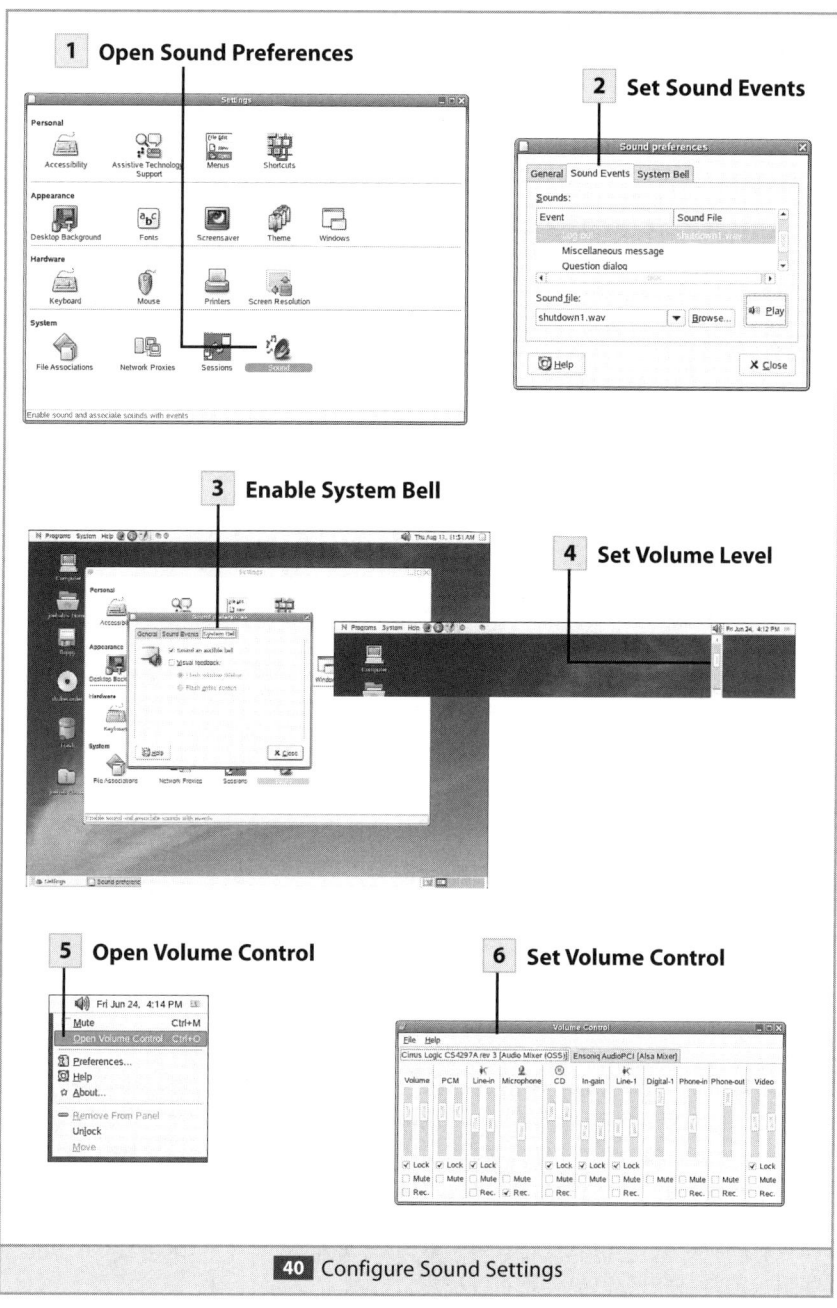

4 Set Volume Level

To quickly set the volume level, select the **Volume Control** icon on the right side of the upper panel. Use the slider bar to set the general sound level.

5 Open Volume Control

To set individual volume controls, you need to open the Volume Control dialog box; right-click on the **Volume Control** icon and select **Open Volume Control**.

6 Set Volume Control

Use the slider bars and check boxes to control the volume and input/output for the sound devices on your system. When you have finished changing the settings, select **Close** to close the dialog box.

> **NOTE**
>
> The appearance of the Volume Control dialog box and the settings available depend on the capabilities of the sound card that you have installed on your PC.

41 Change the Screen Resolution

As a user, you can quickly change the screen resolution for your desktop. The screen resolutions available depend on the video card installed on your system (and the capabilities of your monitor). The video card and the monitor are both configured automatically during the NLD installation.

> **NOTE**
>
> More advanced settings related to your video adapter and screen are set via the Administrator Settings. To open YaST and configure video settings, you need to know the root password. The graphic cards settings are opened via the Hardware and then the Graphics Card and Monitor icons. Because your video card and monitor are configured during installation, you should access these settings only if you are installing a new sound card or are not getting the appropriate performance from the current sound card settings.

41 Change the Screen Resolution

✔ **BEFORE YOU BEGIN**

23 Change Personal Settings
32 About Configuring Hardware and System Settings in NLD

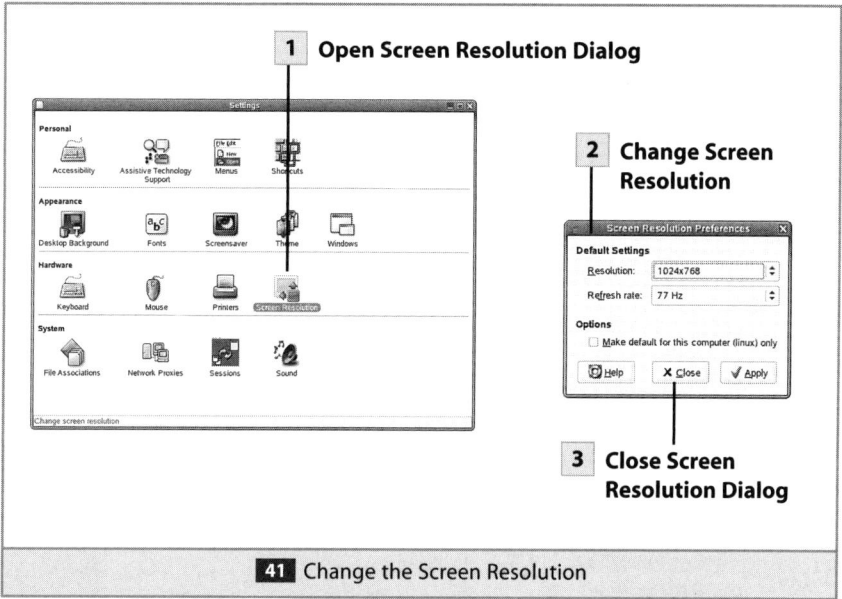

41 Change the Screen Resolution

1 Open Screen Resolution Dialog

From the Settings dialog (select **System**, **Personal Settings**), double-click the **Screen Resolution** icon in the Hardware pane. The Screen Resolution dialog box opens.

2 Change Screen Resolution

To change the screen resolution select the **Resolution** drop-down list and select a new resolution. The refresh rate changes automatically for each resolution selected. To view the changes on the desktop, select the **Apply** button.

3 Close Screen Resolution Dialog

When you have completed your changes to the screen resolution, select the **Close** button.

42 Change Session Settings

A session, which loads your GUI environment, begins when you log on and ends when you log off. In the Sessions dialog box, you can control session settings such as the display of a confirmation box when you end a session (by logging out) and whether changes to a particular session are automatically saved. These changes would be in the form of changes to the GNOME desktop (icons, colors, fonts, and so on) and application and applet windows left open (or minimized) on the desktop.

When you save the changes to your current session, any applications open on the desktop will start automatically the next time you log on to the session. This means that you can park commonly used applications (and a particular document or spreadsheet) and get right back to work the next time you log on.

Not all programs automatically reload when you log back on to your session. These are referred to as *nonsession managed applications* (as opposed to *session managed applications* such as OpenOffice.org, Firefox, and most all the NLD applications).

An example of a nonsession managed application would be a utility or tool that must be run from a terminal window. If you want to run nonsession managed applications upon logging on to a session, you can add them to the Startup Programs tab of the Sessions dialog box.

✔ **BEFORE YOU BEGIN**

- **1** About Booting the NLD System and Logon Options
- **23** Change Personal Settings
- **32** About Configuring Hardware and System Settings in NLD

---

1 Open Sessions Dialog

From the Settings dialog (select **System**, **Personal Settings**), double-click the **Sessions** icon in the System pane. The Sessions dialog box opens.

2 Set Session Options

By default the session options are configured to show a splash screen at logon (that is, the NLD splash screen you see as GNOME is loaded) and prompt you to save changes to your session at logout. If you want changes to your current session saved automatically when logging off, select the **Automatically Save Changes to Session** check box.

42 Change Session Settings

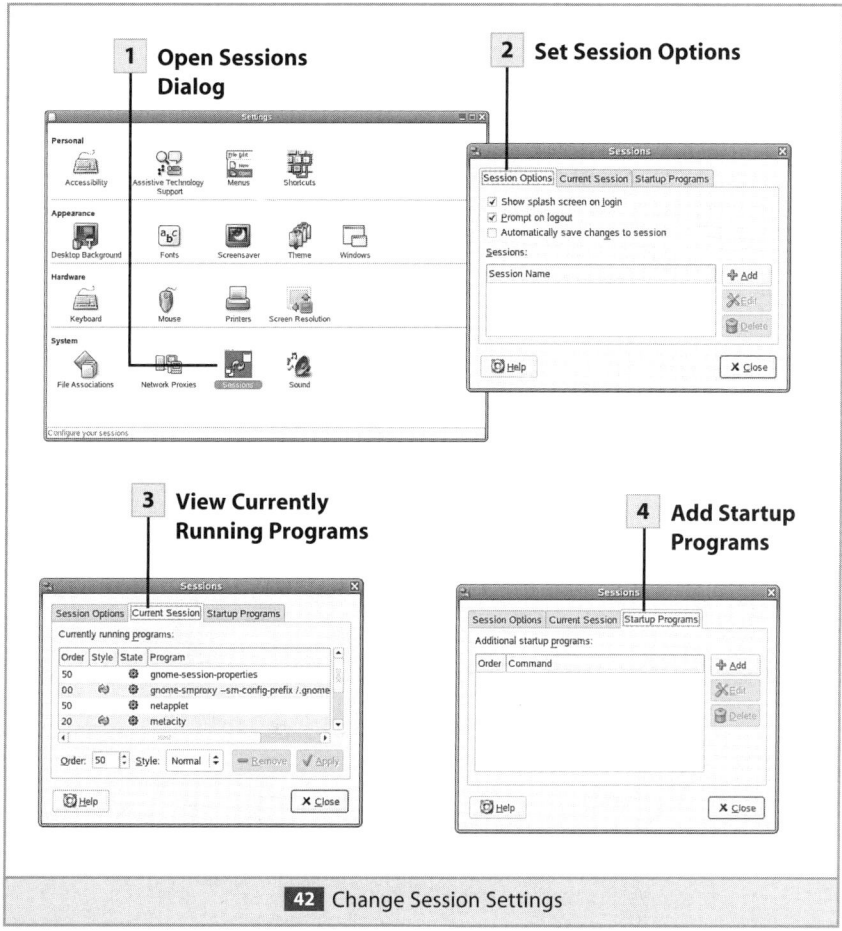

42 Change Session Settings

NOTE

The Session Options tab also provides you with the ability to create sessions and save them under a particular name. This feature would be extremely useful if there was a quick and easy way to switch between the sessions or easily load them at startup. You do have the ability to load your last session at startup (which is the default option on the Logon Manager). A command-line tool, gnome-session, can be used to load a particular session at startup, but you would have to load NLD from a command line or special script. The GNOME documentation (http://www.gnome.org) promises some sort of session switcher utility in future versions of GNOME.

113

3 View Currently Running Programs

Select the **Current Session** tab. This tab provides a list of applications and applets that are running during the session that are session managed applications, meaning their state can be saved during the session and reloaded the next time you start the session. You can change the order that the application is started; select the **Order** spinner box and input a new order number. If you want to change the Style for an application (how it is treated during session loading), click the **Style** drop-down list. The Normal style starts the application when you log on to the NLD system. The Restart style restarts the application whenever you close it. The Trash style is selected when you do not want the application to start. Any changes to this tab must be confirmed; select **Apply**.

> **NOTE**
>
> Unless you fully understand the issues related to application load order and style (found on the Current Session tab), you may want to leave all these settings at the defaults.

4 Add Startup Programs

Select the **Startup Programs** tab. To add an applet or application to the startup list (it starts automatically when the session is started), select the **Add** button. In the Add Startup Program dialog that appears, provide the command that starts the application or use the **Browse** button to locate the application. Click **OK** to close the Add Startup Program dialog.

After you have finished working in the Sessions dialog box, click the **Close** button.

43 Change Other System Settings

Two other system settings that you should be aware of (but won't necessarily need to configure) are File Associations and Network Proxies. Both of these settings can be reached via the appropriate icon in the System panel of the Settings dialog box.

File Associations settings (opened by double-clicking on the **File Associations** icon in the Settings dialog box) allow you to add a particular file type to a file category and associate applications and services to these file types. This is an

43 Change Other System Settings

advanced feature, so you may want to forgo changing any of the file associations or services. (In fact, some of the file association settings such as selecting the program to run are not even available in this GNOME release.)

> **NOTE**
>
> Most file associations are configured automatically when you add applications to your NLD configuration. So, you typically do not have to set file associations or add services to your setup manually. Configuring file associations requires information such as MIME type (how file types are represented to your email and web browser programs) and requires you to specify the application to handle the file type. Again, you probably don't want to edit file type settings unless you are an advanced user. Advanced users may want to take the next step in NLD literacy by referring to Emmett Dulaney's *Novell Linux Desktop 9 Administrator's Handbook*.

Network Proxies settings relate to how you connect to the Internet though a proxy server. In most cases, your proxy server settings should have been configured during the NLD installation; however, there may be cases where you need to configure these settings on-the-fly, particularly when you are using a laptop where you connect to the Internet a certain way at work and then a different way at home.

> ✔ **BEFORE YOU BEGIN**
>
> **23** Change Personal Settings
> **32** About Configuring Hardware and System Settings in NLD

1 **Open Network Proxy Configuration Dialog**

From the Settings dialog (select **System**, **Personal Settings**), double-click the **Network Proxies** icon in the System pane. The Network Proxy Configuration dialog box opens.

2 **Set Proxy Settings**

By default the proxy settings are configured to use the system's proxy configuration (determined during the NLD installation). To override proxy settings and connect directly to the Internet, select the **Direct Internet Connection** option.

115

CHAPTER 5: Configuring NLD Hardware and System Settings

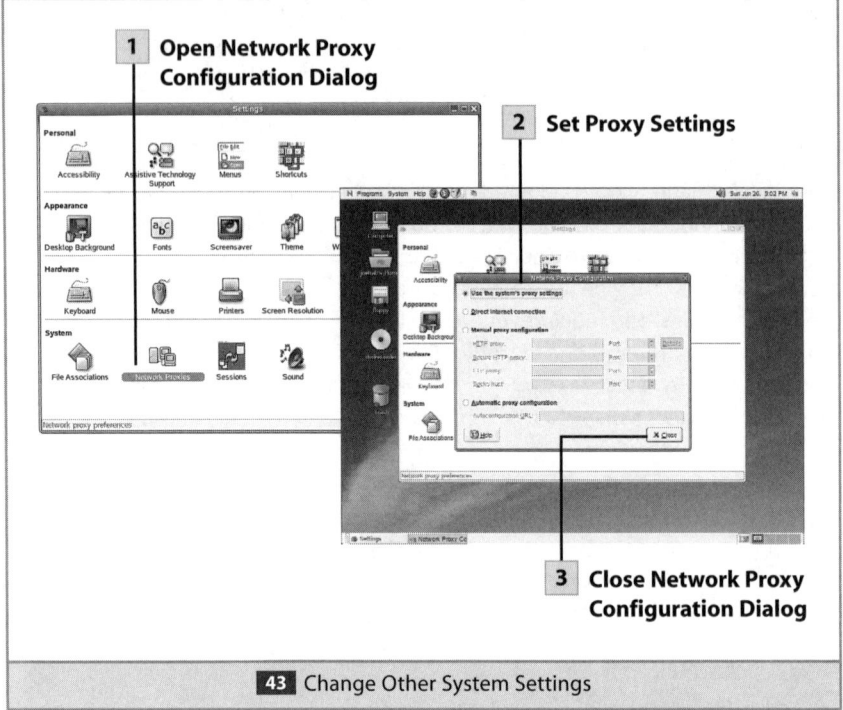

43 Change Other System Settings

NOTE

To manually configure proxy settings, you need to know the DNS name (the "friendly" domain name) for your proxy server and the port number used to communicate with the proxy servers when you request web pages. Port numbers are communication pipelines (in essence) that allow an application on your computer, such as your web browser, to communicate with software on the proxy server. Don't change your proxy settings unless you have all the information necessary to correctly set up the proxy configuration.

To set manual proxy settings, select **Manual Proxy Configuration** and then provide the following:

- HTTP Proxy—Provide the DNS name for the proxy server (or the IP address) for HTTP transactions, meaning web browsing related transactions.

- Secure HTTP Proxy—In some cases a secure connection is used to the proxy server. If so, you must enter the DNS name or IP address for the proxy server when secure transactions take place.

- FTP Proxy—You actually download and upload files from your web browser in many cases using FTP (File Transfer Protocol). To use the FTP service, provide the DNS name or IP address of the proxy server for FTP.

- Socks Host—Socks is a protocol used by the proxy server to handle incoming and outgoing traffic. You need to enter the DNS name or the IP address of the Socks Host (which in most cases is the same as the HTTP proxy).

- Automatic Proxy Configuration—If you want to automatically configure your proxy settings, and a configuration file has been supplied to you and is available on your computer (or can be loaded remotely from a URL), select the **Automatic Proxy Configuration** option.

- Autoconfiguration URL—Enter the URL (which can be a path on your local computer) that supplies the location of the auto-configuration file for the proxy settings.

3 Close Network Proxy Configuration Dialog

After you have completed entering the settings for the proxy configuration, select **Close**.

CHAPTER 6

Managing Files

IN THIS CHAPTER:

- **44** About the Linux File Structure and Nautilus File Manager
- **45** Configure Nautilus Preferences
- **46** Use Nautilus to Manage Folders
- **47** Browse and Open Files
- **48** Find Files
- **49** Delete Files
- **50** Copy and Move Files
- **51** Access Recent Files
- **52** Access and Save Files to a USB Memory Stick
- **53** Burn Files on a CD or DVD
- **54** About Archiving Files
- **55** Archive Files with File Roller
- **56** About Backing Up and Restoring Files
- **57** Back Up Files
- **58** Restore Files

It is important to be able to manage the files that you create using the various productivity tools provided by NLD. You need to be able to create folders (directories) to store your files and be able to locate, copy, move, and delete files when necessary.

In this chapter we take a look at managing files using Nautilus, NLD's GUI file manager. We look at how you access or save files to portable media such as a USB stick (drive) and burn files on CDs or DVDs. We also look at how to archive files and back up and restore files.

44 About the Linux File Structure and Nautilus File Manager

Before we put the Nautilus File Manager to the test in terms of working with files, we should take a look at the Linux file structure. Linux uses a hierarchical, diverging file system. You can think of each folder (or *directory*, if you prefer the term over folder) as a container. The top of the file system and the hierarchical start of the system is the root, which is designated by a slash (/). Every other folder branches off the root, and each folder can contain subfolders increasing the number of sub-branches in the hierarchy. So in a simple representation of the Linux file structure that you will deal with when using NLD, the root (/) would be on the left of the diagram, and all the main folders (often referred to as *standard folders* or *directories*) would branch to the right. Any subfolders in the main folder would provide further sub-branches.

NOTE

Root is the / container at the top of the file system hierarchy. There is also a folder called root, which contains folders and files for the root user (administrator). It is the root user's home folder and cannot be opened unless you are logged on as root. The other root (/) is the logical top of the file system.

You can access the file system using Nautilus (which is also often referred to as the File Manager in the NLD Help documents) and view all the main folders contained in the root. To view the contents of a particular folder (subfolders or files), double-click on that folder.

44 About the Linux File Structure and Nautilus File Manager

The Linux file system is hierarchical with root at the top of the system.

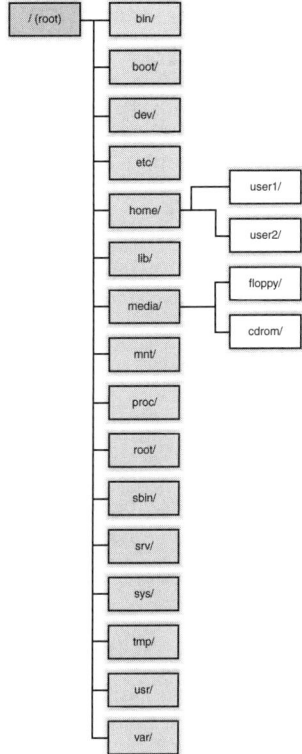

You can use Nautilus to view the file system structure.

CHAPTER 6: Managing Files

Each standard folder in the hierarchy holds a particular set of files. You normally really should not mess around with these folders; for example, the /etc folder contains configuration files. The /lib folder contain library code used by NLD programs.

Other folders that you may want to be aware of are /media, which contains the mountable removable media drives that are on your system (such as a floppy, CDROM, DVD, and so on), and /tmp, which is used by programs that need to create temporary files as they are used.

As a "regular" user there are not that many folders that you need to be concerned with. When your user account was created (during installation or after using the root account), a home folder was created for you. This home folder can easily be opened from the Home icon provided on your NLD desktop. This is the best folder for saving the files that you create. You can create subfolders in your home folder as needed.

The Nautilus File Manager provides you with the ability to manage files locally, on your hard drive, and on other media drives, and it allows you to browse for files on the network. You can use Nautilus to access files on a Linux network or on a Windows network. Nautilus really provides one-stop shopping in terms of managing and locating the files that you need to get your work done.

NOTE

If you have configured your NLD installation to use a printer that is shared by a Windows computer in a workgroup, your computer has also been configured to access files on that same workgroup. You can easily access any files shared by Windows computers in the workgroup.

45 Configure Nautilus Preferences

Nautilus makes it easy for you to configure preferences related to how folders and files are viewed and accessed. The Nautilus preferences are accessed via the Preferences command on the Edit menu.

1 Open Nautilus

Select the **Programs** menu and then **Accessories**; then select **File Manager**. Nautilus opens showing your home folder.

45 Configure Nautilus Preferences

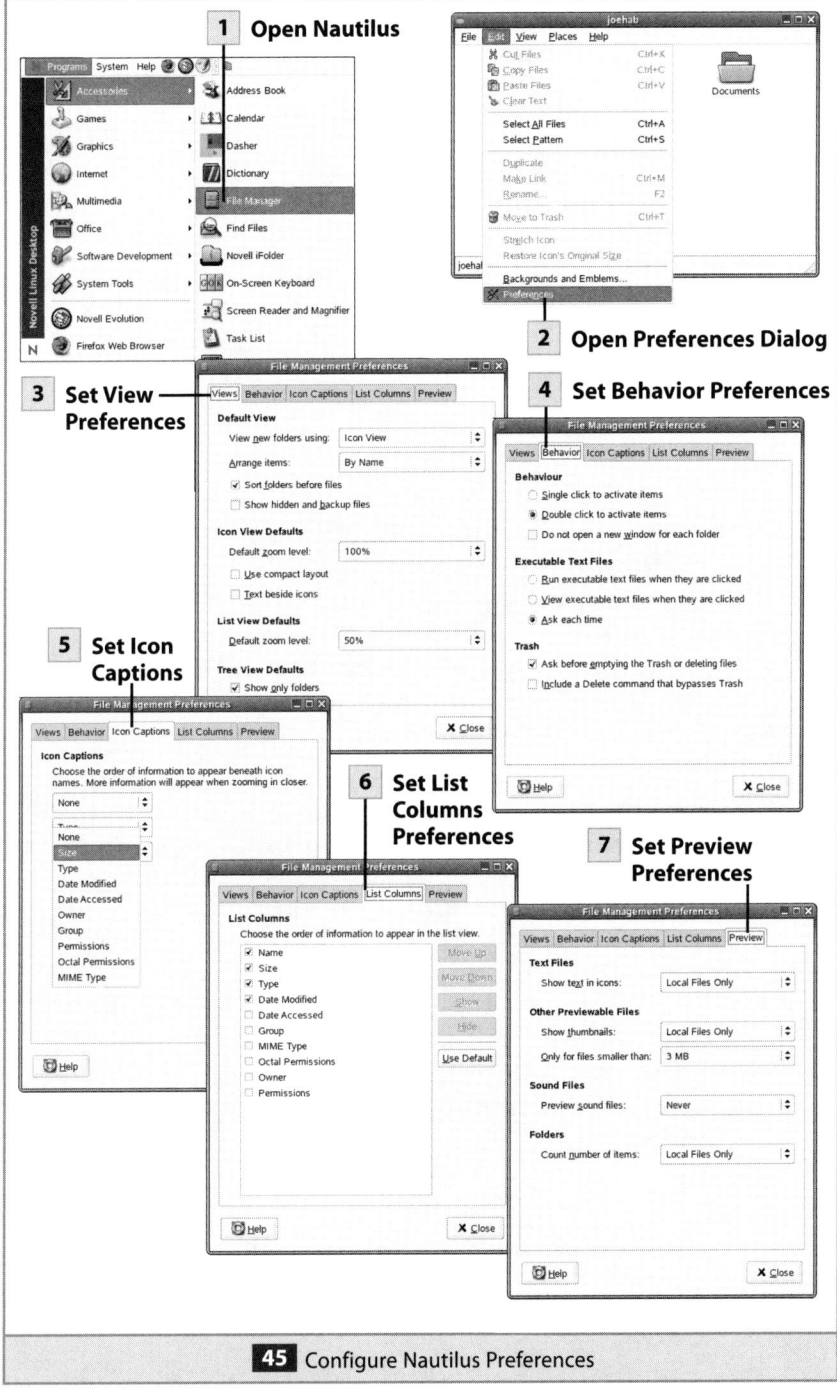

CHAPTER 6: Managing Files

TIP

You can also quickly open Nautilus by double-clicking your Home icon, which shows your home folder; the Computer icon, which provides access to the file system; or the desktop icons present for any of your removable media drives such as a floppy or CD drive.

2 Open Preferences Dialog

Select **Edit** and then **Preferences** to open the Nautilus Preferences dialog box.

3 Set View Preferences

On the Views tab, you can set how folders and files are viewed and the preferences for the view you select. To select the view type, select the **View New Folders Using** drop-down list and select Icon View (the default) or List View (items are placed in a list of smaller icons).

Select **Arrange Items** and then select By Name (default), By Size (file size), By Type (file type), By Modification Date, or By Emblems. If you are using the Icon view, you can select the **Use Compact Layout** check box to pack the icons tighter in the Nautilus window or select **Text Beside Icons** to place the text next to the icon rather than below the icon.

TIP

Emblems are special pseudo-icons that can be used to categorize folder and file icons in Nautilus. For example there is an Urgent emblem, a New emblem, and a host of other emblem types. Open the Backgrounds and Emblems dialog box (in Nautilus, select **Edit, Backgrounds and Emblems**). Drag an emblem from the Backgrounds and Emblems dialog onto a folder in Nautilus to categorize it with the emblem.

You can also change the zoom level for either the Icon view or the List view. Select the appropriate **Default Zoom Level** drop-down list and select your zoom level.

TIP

If you want to view system or hidden files, select the **Show Hidden and Backup Files** check box on the Views tab. In most cases, it makes sense to let these file types remain hidden to avoid the possibility of accidentally moving or deleting them.

4 **Set Behavior Preferences**

Select the **Behavior** tab. To activate items with a single click, select the **Single Click to Activate Items** option button. To view the contents of a folder in the current window, select the **Do Not Open a New Window for Each Folder** check box.

To start executable text files with a single click, select the **Run Executable Text Files When They Are Clicked** option button. If you would rather view these files, select the **View Executable Text Files When They Are Clicked** option button.

TIP

If you don't like emptying the trash, you can clear the **Ask Before Emptying the Trash or Deleting Files** check box. If you want to have access to a delete command that bypasses the trash completely, select the **Include a Delete Command That Bypasses Trash** check box.

TIP

By default the Nautilus File Manager opens a new window each time you open a folder. If you want to view the contents of a drive or folder in the current window (and not open a new window), select the **Do Not Open a New Window for Each Folder** check box on the Behavior tab.

5 **Set Icon Captions**

Select the **Icon Captions** tab. Each of the three drop-down lists allows you to display information under a folder or file icon. Set the first drop-down list to one of the selections such as Date Modified, Type, or Size. Set the other drop-down lists as needed. When you click on the Nautilus View menu and then zoom in on a file icon, the information is shown as set on the Icon Captions tab.

6 **Set List Columns Preferences**

Select the **List Columns** tab. Check the boxes for the information that you want to appear for a file when viewed in the list view. If you want to move an information type up or down in the list, select the information type and then use the **Move Up** or **Move Down** button as needed.

7 Set Preview Preferences

Select the **Preview** tab. This tab allows you to view text in file icons, show thumbnails for files such as image files, or automatically preview sound files. All the settings allow you to select either Always, Never, or Local Files Only (because getting a thumbnail of a remote file may take time or a network). You can also set the file size threshold for files shown as thumbnails. Select the options as preferred.

After you have finished setting the Nautilus preferences, select **Close** to close the dialog box. You are returned to the Nautilus window.

46 Use Nautilus to Manage Folders

Nautilus makes it easy to create, delete, move, and copy folders and their contents. You can also add emblems to folders, which is a way of categorizing a folder so that you can act on the folder contents in terms of follow-up, deletion, and so on. You can also record notes related to a folder to help you keep organized.

> ✔ **BEFORE YOU BEGIN**
>
> 7 Navigate the GNOME Desktop
> 14 About File Commands
> 15 Use File Commands

1 Create a Folder

In Nautilus (select **Programs, Accessories, File Manager**) navigate to a particular location where you want to create a new folder. Right-click in the location (in the Nautilus window) and select **Create Folder** from the shortcut menu. A new folder icon appears. Type a name for the new folder.

TIP

To rename a folder, right-click on the folder and choose **Rename** from the menu. Type your new name and then press **Enter**.

46 Use Nautilus to Manage Folders

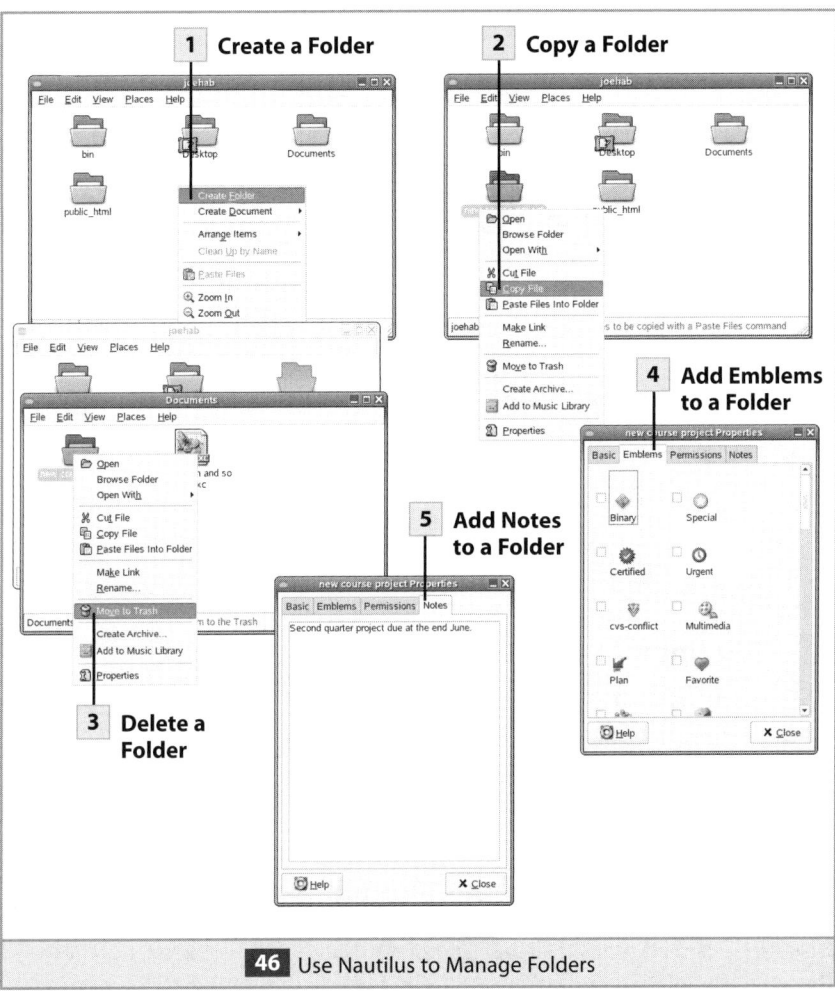

46 Use Nautilus to Manage Folders

2 Copy a Folder

To copy a folder, right-click on the folder and select **Copy File** from the shortcut menu. Navigate to the location where you want to place the copy of the folder. On the Nautilus menu system, select **Edit**, **Paste Files** to place a copy of the folder in the current location.

TIP

To move a folder, drag the folder from its current location to the new location. You can drag a folder from one Nautilus window to another as needed.

3 Delete a Folder

To delete a folder, right-click on the folder and select **Move to Trash**. This places the folder in the Trash.

TIP

To empty the trash, right-click on the desktop Trash icon and select **Empty Trash**. You are asked whether you are sure you want to empty the trash; click the **Empty** button to proceed.

4 Add Emblems to a Folder

Right-click on a folder and select **Properties** to open the Properties dialog box for that folder. Then select the **Emblems** tab. To add visual cues to a folder that help you keep track of how important a folder is or what you plan to do with a particular folder, you can use emblems. Select an emblem or emblems by clicking on the appropriate check box.

5 Add Notes to a Folder

Select the **Notes** tab. You can enter descriptive or other text on the folder's Notes tab. This helps you keep track of the contents of the folder.

After you have finished working in the folder's Properties dialog box, click **Close**. This returns you to the Nautilus File Manager window.

NOTE

Every folder and file that you create (and all the folders and files that are part of the NLD installation) is assigned permissions. These permissions grant rights to a file or folder, and these rights provide different levels of access; the permission levels are read, write, and execute. Certain rights (read, write, and execute) are assigned to you as the owner of a file or folder. Other rights (read and execute) are assigned to the user group that you belong to. You can change the permissions for any file or folder that you create on the Permissions tab of that item's Properties dialog box. Permissions become important when you work in a networked environment or share your computer with multiple users.

47 Browse and Open Files

47 Browse and Open Files

Nautilus provides the perfect visual utility for quickly browsing available folders and then opening a file that you need to work with. Double-clicking on a file opens the file in the applications used to create it.

> ✔ **BEFORE YOU BEGIN**
>
> **14** About File Commands
> **15** Use File Commands
> **46** Use Nautilus to Manage Folders

1 Open Computer Window

Double-click the **Computer** icon on the desktop. This opens Nautilus and provides access to your removable media drives, the file system, and the network.

TIP

If you are using best practices for file storage, you are storing your files in your home directory or subfolders within your home directory. The fastest way to get to your home directory is to double-click the Home directory icon on the desktop.

2 Open File System

To open the file system (the root and all its subfolders), double-click the **FileSystem** icon in the Nautilus window.

TIP

You can quickly switch from the standard Nautilus view to a browser mode that makes it easy for you to type a folder or file location into the Nautilus browser window. Right-click on any folder and select **Browse Folder** on the shortcut menu. The Browse view for Nautilus makes it easy to switch between the Icon and List views and zoom in and out on folder and file icons. You can make this the default view for Nautilus; select the **Do Not Open a New Window for Each Folder** check box on the Behavior tab.

129

CHAPTER 6: Managing Files

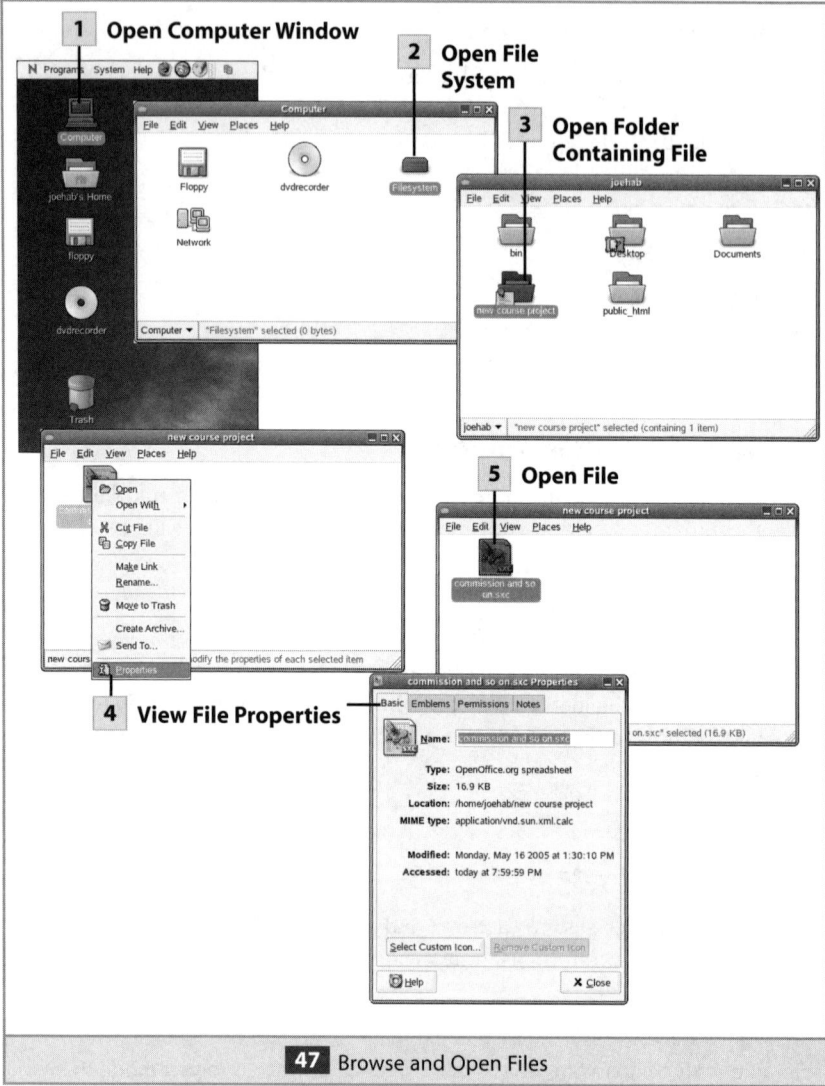

47 Browse and Open Files

3 Open Folder Containing File

To open a particular folder, double-click that folder. Each time you open a folder, a new window opens for that folder.

4 View File Properties

To view the file properties, right-click on the file icon and select **Properties** from the shortcut menu. This opens the Properties dialog box for that particular file. On the **Basic** tab, the file size and when the file was last modified and accessed are provided. If you want to view permissions for the file, select the **Permissions** tab. After you have finished viewing the file properties, select **Close**.

TIP

You can attach emblems to your files by using the Emblems tab and enter comments for the file on the Notes tab. If you want to select a custom icon for the file, select the **Select Custom Icon** button. The Select an Icon dialog box appears. Select a new icon and then click **OK**.

5 Open File

You can quickly open the file in the application that it was created in. Double-click on the file, and the application window opens. You can now edit and then save any changes that you have made to the file. After you have finished working in the application, close its window, and you are returned to the Nautilus window containing the file icon.

48 Find Files

NLD provides a quick search tool that makes it easy to find files on your computer anywhere in the file system. You can search by filename and a number of other parameters, such as the text the file contains, the date the file was last modified, and/or the size of the file.

✔ **BEFORE YOU BEGIN**

- 14 About File Commands
- 15 Use File Commands
- 46 Use Nautilus to Manage Folders
- 47 Browse and Open Files

CHAPTER 6: Managing Files

48 Find Files

1 Open Search Window

Select the **System** menu and then select **Search for Files**. The Search for Files window opens.

2 Enter Search Name and Path

In the **Name Contains** box, enter all or part of the filename (wildcards such as * are not necessary). In the **Look In Folder** box, type the path for the folder you want to search. You can also locate the folder; click the **Browse** button.

TIP

When you open the Browse window with the Browse button, you are provided icons for the desktop, your home folder, and your removable media drives. To add a location to the Browse window, right-click in the right pane of the window and select **Open Location** from the shortcut menu. You can type in the path. The easiest way to see all the available folders is to type a slash (/) for the root and all the folders contained in the file system appear. Click on the one you want to add. You can now use this location as the start for your search.

3 Show More Search Options

To access more search options, select the **Show More Options** switch in the Search for Files window.

4 Enter Additional Search Options

Select the **Available Options** drop-down list and select one of the options listed:

- Contains the Text—Enter any text contained in the file.
- Date Modified Less Than—Enter the number of days that the modification date must be less than.
- Date Modified More Than—Enter the number of days that the modification date must be greater than.
- Size At Least—Enter the "at least" file size in kilobytes.
- Size At Most—Enter the "at most" file size in kilobytes.
- File Is Empty—Looks for empty files (you will use this rarely because anything you create in an application is essentially "not empty").
- Owned By User—Enter the user who owns the file.
- Owned By Group—Enter the group that owns the file.
- Owner Is Unrecognized—Allows you to search for files where the owner cannot be recognized by the system.
- Name Does Not Contain—Enter a character string not contained in the filename. This allows you to "rule out" certain files that would contain the character string in the name.
- Name Matches Regular Expression—Regular expressions are special search strings that you can create using a text editor. Using regular expressions is certainly an advanced way to search but requires a fair amount of knowledge to create.

CHAPTER 6: Managing Files

WEB RESOURCE

http://www.regular-expressions.info

If you are just dying to learn more about regular expressions and how to create them for searches, check out this website. It provides tutorials and advice related to creating regular expressions for searches.

After selecting an option, click **Add**. A new box opens for the option that you selected, and you can enter the search criteria in the box. For example, if you selected Contains the Text, enter the text that you want to use in the search in the box.

5 Run Search

After you have entered all your search parameters, click the **Find** button. The results of your search appear in the Search for Files window.

TIP

When you run the search, watch the Search Results list. When you see the file appear in the list (the one you are looking for), you can click **Stop** to end the search.

6 Open File in Search Results List

To open a file listed in the search results, double-click on the file. The file opens in the appropriate application. At this point, you can close the Search for Files window or run another search.

49 Delete Files

You can delete files from the Nautilus window by opening the appropriate location. You can also delete files that you find in the Search for Files window.

✔ **BEFORE YOU BEGIN**

- 14 About File Commands
- 15 Use File Commands
- 46 Use Nautilus to Manage Folders
- 47 Browse and Open Files
- 48 Find Files

49 Delete Files

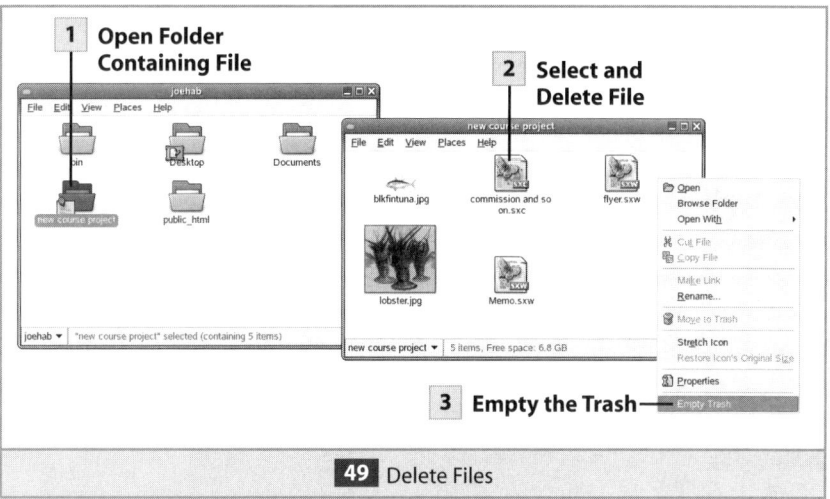

49 Delete Files

1 Open Folder Containing File

In the Nautilus window locate the folder that contains the file or files, you want to delete. Then open the folder.

2 Select and Delete File

Select the file you want to delete. If you want to select multiple files, select the first file and then hold down the Ctrl key as you select subsequent files. Press the **Delete** key. The file or files will be removed and placed in the trash.

TIP

To select all the files in a folder, from the Nautilus menu, select **Edit, Select All Files**. You can also use the mouse to drag a selection area around files in the Nautilus window to select them.

3 Empty the Trash

Right-click on the **Trash** icon and select **Empty Trash**. In the warning dialog box that appears, select **Empty** to remove the file from your system.

TIP

If you inadvertently delete a file or files, open the Trash and drag the file back to its folder of origin.

50 Copy and Move Files

You can quickly copy or move files from location to location in the Nautilus window. Moving a file is particularly easy because Nautilus by default opens multiple windows for opened folders, allowing you to drag a file or files to a new location as needed.

> ✔ **BEFORE YOU BEGIN**
>
> **14** About File Commands
> **15** Use File Commands
> **46** Use Nautilus to Manage Folders
> **47** Browse and Open Files
> **48** Find Files
> **49** Delete Files

1 Open Folder Containing File

In the Nautilus window locate the folder that contains the file or files, you want to copy. Then open the folder.

2 Copy File

Right-click on the file you want to copy and select **Copy File**.

TIP

To copy multiple files, select the files by using the mouse to draw a frame around the files that you want to select. If you want to select all the files in a particular folder, choose **Select All Files** from the Nautilus menu. Then select **Edit**, **Copy Files** to copy the selected files. You can also use the shortcut key Ctrl+C to copy a file or selected files.

3 Paste File

Navigate to the folder that you will copy the file into. Select the **Edit**, **Paste Files** from the menu.

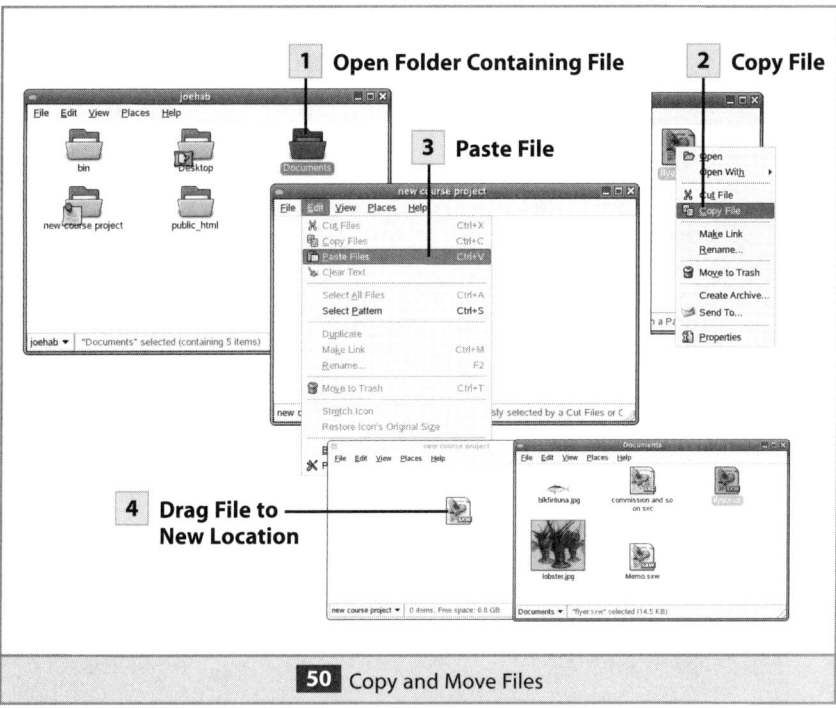

4 Drag File to New Location

To move a file, open the source folder and the destination folder on the desktop. Drag the file (or selected files) to the destination folder.

TIP

If you don't like dragging files from folder to folder, select **Edit**, **Cut** from the menu and then paste the file or files into the destination folder.

51 Access Recent Files

You can quickly access your recently opened files from the System menu. This allows you to quickly get back to work on your most recent documents and other files.

✔ **BEFORE YOU BEGIN**

47 Browse and Open Files
48 Find Files

CHAPTER 6: Managing Files

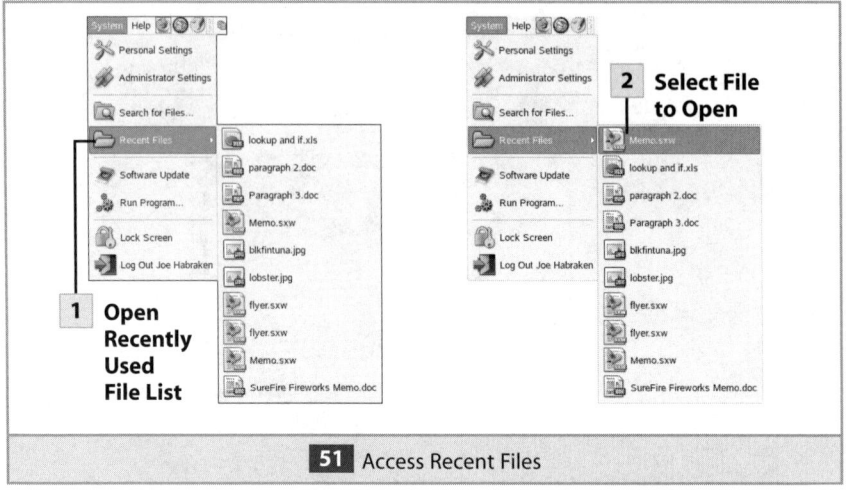

51 Access Recent Files

1 **Open Recently Used File List**

From the NLD desktop, select **System**, **Recent Files**. A list of recently used files appears.

2 **Select File to Open**

Select the file that you want to open from the list. The file opens in its parent application.

---

52 **Access and Save Files to a USB Memory Stick**

You can access files from portable media such as USB memory stick drives. When the drive is attached to your computer, it acts the same as any other drive, and you can save, copy, move, and delete files on the drive.

When the drive is attached to the system, it is mounted by the system, so you can find it anytime that you need it in the /media folder in the file system.

✔ **BEFORE YOU BEGIN**

14 About File Commands **47** Browse and Open Files
15 Use File Commands **48** Find Files
46 Use Nautilus to Manage Folders **49** Delete Files

52 Access and Save Files to a USB Memory Stick

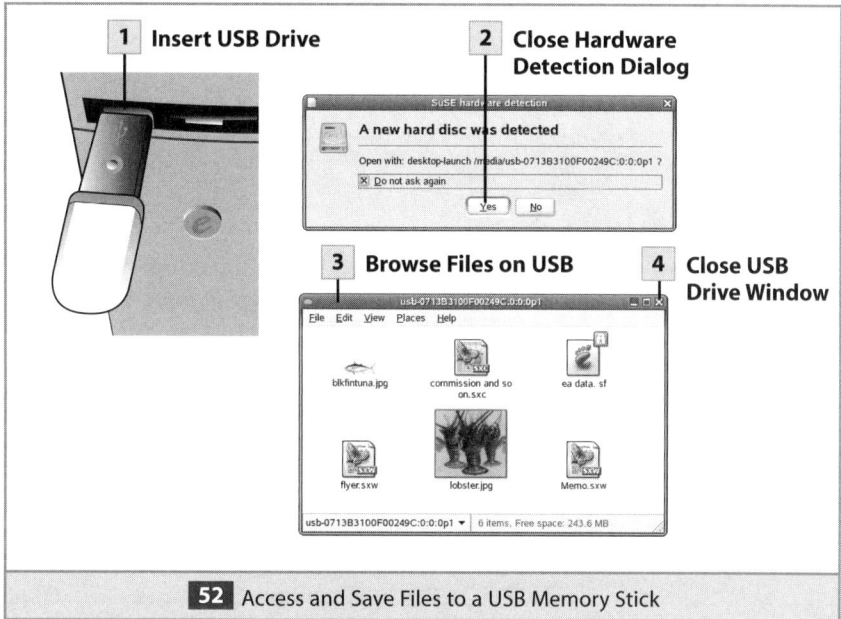

52 Access and Save Files to a USB Memory Stick

1 Insert USB Drive

Insert the USB drive into a USB port on your computer. A hardware detection dialog opens. If you want this dialog box to open each time you insert the USB drive, clear the **Do Not Ask Again** check box.

TIP

To remove the USB drive, make sure that you close all applications and applets accessing the drive. You can then remove the drive. If this makes you queasy, open a terminal window, type su, and then press **Enter**. Type the root password (and press **Enter**). Type umount /media/usb* and press **Enter**. You can type exit and then press **Enter** to exit as root, and then type exit and press **Enter** again to close the terminal. In some cases, the light on the USB drive will still be blinking, but you can now remove it. If you still don't want to just yank out the drive, power down the system and then remove the USB drive.

2 Close Hardware Detection Dialog

Select **Yes** on the Hardware Detection dialog box to open the USB drive.

139

3 Browse Files on USB

The USB drive window opens. You can browse the files and folders on the USB drive as needed. You can open another File Manager window if you want to copy or move files from the USB drive.

4 Close USB Drive Window

After you have finished working with the files and folders on the USB drive, select the **Close** button to close the window.

TIP

If you close the USB drive's Nautilus window, you can reopen it at any time. Open the Computer window (double-click on the **Computer** icon on the desktop) and then open the **Filesystem**. Open the /media folder, and the USB drive appears as an icon. Double-click the icon to open the drive.

53 Burn Files on a CD or DVD

You can burn folders and files to a CD or DVD (depending on the drive types installed on your computer) using the K3b burning software. You can create data CDs (or DVDs), create music CDs, or copy a CD. Now here's the bad news: Linux systems are set up to protect direct access to devices by users other than the root account. So, you can log on as root, burn your CDs or DVDs, and then log off; no questions asked.

If you want to configure your system so that a "regular" user can access the burn drives and configure K3b so that it works correctly (and its core executables such as cdrecord have proper access), you are talking about several tweaks and changes to file attributes and configuration files.

Commands such as **chown** and **chmod** are involved, and you have to do a fair amount of work at the command line as the root user to get things working properly. Going through all the possibilities is certainly beyond the scope of this book, and applying the "fixes" incorrectly can have dire consequences for your system. If you really have NLD administration in mind, you might want to consult NLD and Linux administration books such as Emmett Dulaney's *Novell Linux Desktop 9 Administrator's Handbook* (as well as some of his other publications).

53 Burn Files on a CD or DVD

✔ **BEFORE YOU BEGIN**

14 About File Commands

15 Use File Commands

46 Use Nautilus to Manage Folders

47 Browse and Open Files

48 Find Files

49 Delete Files

1 Open K3b

From the desktop, select **Programs**, **Multimedia**, **CD Burner**. The K3b program window opens. A Tip of the Day window also opens. Select **Close** to close the tip window.

NOTE

When you use insert a burnable CD or DVD in the burner drive, a hardware detection window opens. Click **Yes** to start K3b. This allows you to forgo starting K3b from the menu.

2 Start a Project

To start a new project, select one of the project options in the lower pane of the K3b window. For example, to burn data files to a CD, select **New Data CD Project**.

NOTE

All the project types available in K3b are similar in terms of operation; you select the project and then select the files that will be burned to the writable media (CD or DVD). In the case of music CDs, you can burn a number of audio file types including wav and MP3 files. When you select to copy a CD, the process is really just a matter of identifying the source CD and then the drive that will be used to burn the copy onto the destination CD.

CHAPTER 6: Managing Files

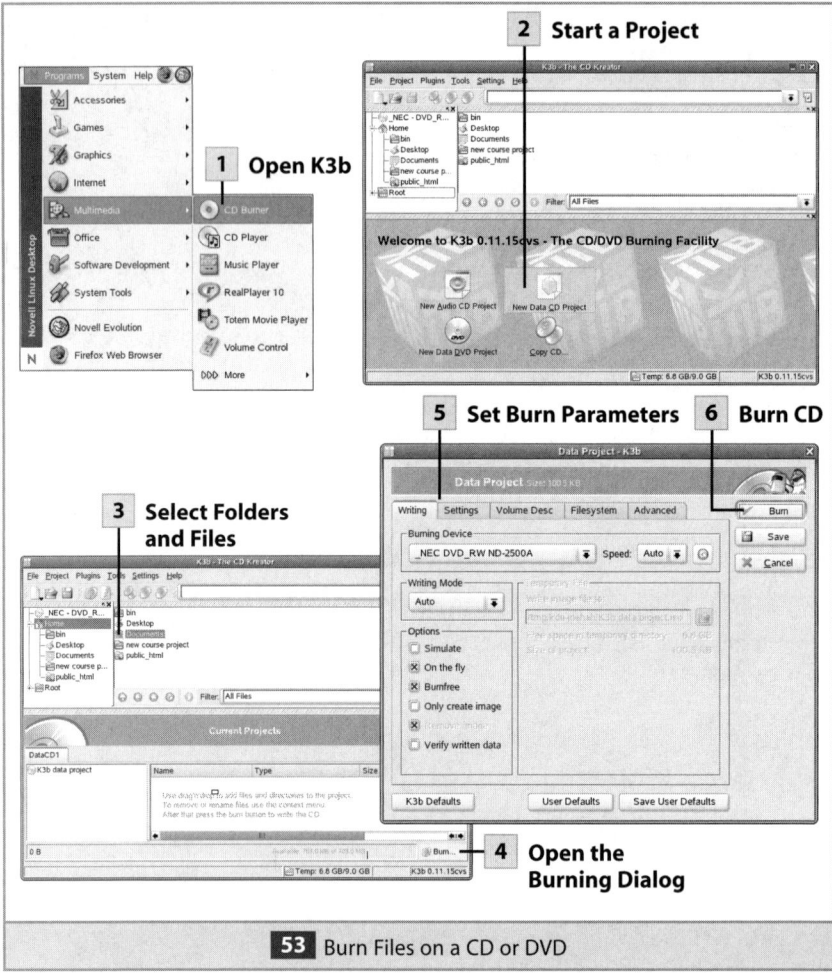

53 Burn Files on a CD or DVD

3 Select Folders and Files

You select the folders and/or files that will be burned to the CD using the two panes in the top of the K3b window. Use the left pane to locate the folder that contains the files. Select a folder in the left pane to view its contents in the right pane. After you have located a folder or file, drag the item to the lower panel. Repeat the process as needed until you have added all the items to the lower panel that you want to burn onto the CD (or DVD).

53 Burn Files on a CD or DVD

> **NOTE**
>
> A space counter in the lower panel tells you the amount of space still available on the CD or DVD as you drag items onto it.

4 Open the Burning Dialog

To open the Burning dialog box (the place where you set the burn parameters), select the **Burn** button in the lower right of the K3b window.

5 Set Burn Parameters

On the Writing tab of the Data Project dialog box, make sure that the correct burning device is selected (if you have multiple burners). You can also choose the writing mode, which is set by default to Auto. Select the **Writing Mode** drop-down list and select DAO (data at once), TAO (track at once), or RAW (raw data).

To select the speed for the burn, select the **Speed** drop-down list and select a burn speed. You also have options that can be set: On the Fly allows you to burn the data directly to the CD without a copy being made on the hard drive. The Only Create Image option burns an ISO image to your hard drive, which can be used to create a CD at a later time.

You may also want to enter descriptive information for the newly created CD including the volume name. Select the **Volume Desc** tab of the project's dialog box. Enter a volume name in the **Volume Name** box. Enter other descriptive information as required.

> **TIP**
>
> Burning CDs and DVDs can sometimes be more of an art than a science. You many want to simulate the burn process to test your settings (select the **Simulate** option on the Writing tab). In some cases, you may also have to burn through a couple of CDs or DVDs just to determine the best settings for your particular CD burning device (fortunately, CDs are relatively cheap and CD-RWs can be erased). Sometimes you are just dealing with trial and error to determine your own best settings. After you establish the settings that work best for you, save them by selecting **Save User Defaults**.

CHAPTER 6: Managing Files

6 Burn CD

When you are ready to burn the CD (or DVD) select the **Burn** button on the right of the project's dialog box. The files are burned to the CD. The Writing Data dialog box shows the progress of the burn process. When the process is complete, you can close this dialog box. When you close K3b, you are given the option of saving the parameters from the CD creation session.

TIP

There is also a quick but less elegant way to burn CDs directly from the Nautilus window. Select **Go** and then **CD Creator**. Drag folders and files that you want to place on the CD onto the CD Creator window that appears. Then select **File**, **Write to CD**.

TIP

When you use removable media such as CDs, right-click on the device's icon and select **Eject** before removing the media. This allows the Linux system to "unmount" the media before removal. Do the same for floppies; right-click on the icon and remove them from the file system before ejecting the disk.

54 About Archiving Files

You can take files and folders and archive them into a single, compressed file. This is useful in cases where you want to carry a bunch of files on removable media with limited disk space, want to prepare older files for backup, or want to send files via email or upload to a website.

Archive files are created with the File Roller application. File Roller also has the capability to extract files from archives, which can be useful in cases where you download Linux applets or other items from the Web that have been saved as an archive. Any number of folders and files can be saved in an archive file.

File Roller allows you to create (and open) archives in different formats. Some of the common (more are supported) file formats are

- arj—A compressed file type (.arj) using the ARJ32 archive program.
- java—A java compressed file format (.jar) created using the `jar` command.
- lha—A compressed archive format (.lha) created using the LHA archive command.

55 Archive Files with File Roller

File Roller can create new archive files and open existing archive files to be extracted.

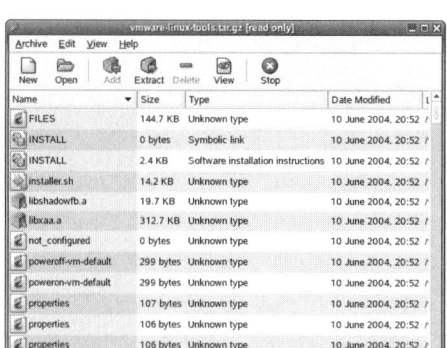

- tar—An archive file type (.tar) created and unwrapped using the UNIX **tar** command.

- tar compressed—tar files can be compressed and are found in file formats such as tar.bz, tar.gz, and tar.tzo depending on the compression tool used to compress the tar archive.

- zip—A compressed file format that can be saved as a .zip file or as an unzipping executable file. This is a popular archive file format in the DOS/Windows environment.

The most common file archive that you will run up against is probably the tar.gz file format. It is commonly used to archive and compress Linux applets and utilities that can be downloaded and installed on your system. It is also a good bet when creating your own archive files because it provides a good amount of compression for the archive file itself.

TIP

You can quickly create a tar.gz archive from the Nautilus window. Select folders and files and then select **Edit, Create Archive**. Name the archive and then click **Create**.

55 Archive Files with File Roller

File Roller basically provides a GUI environment where you can "gather up" a group of folders and files and then save them in a single file in the form of a compressed archive. This is a great way to store files that you aren't using that often.

CHAPTER 6: Managing Files

> ✔ **BEFORE YOU BEGIN**
>
> | 14 | About File Commands |
> | 15 | Use File Commands |
> | 46 | Use Nautilus to Manage Folders |
> | 47 | Browse and Open Files |
> | 54 | About Archiving Files |

1 Open File Roller

From the desktop select **Programs**, **System Tools** and then select **Archive Files**. The File Roller program window opens.

2 Open New Archive

In the File Roller window, select the **New** button. The New dialog box opens.

3 Enter Archive Name and File Type

Type a name for the archive in the **Name** box. Use the **Save in Folder** drop-down box to select a folder or to select another folder or device (remember devices such as USB, CD, and floppy drives are in the /media folder). Select the **Browse for Other Folders** toggle link and then browse to specify the location for the archive. To specify the file type for the archive, select the **Archive Type** drop-down list and select a file type (such as tar compressed with gzip, which is a pretty good choice).

Click the **New** button. You are returned to the File Roller window, and your filename appears on the title frame of the window. Select the **Add** button.

4 Add Folders and Files

In the Add dialog box browse folders as needed and then select the folders and/or files you want to include in the archive and drag them to the File Roller window (the File Roller window displaying the name you gave your archive). After you have finished adding items to the archive window, select **Close** to close the Add dialog box.

55 Archive Files with File Roller

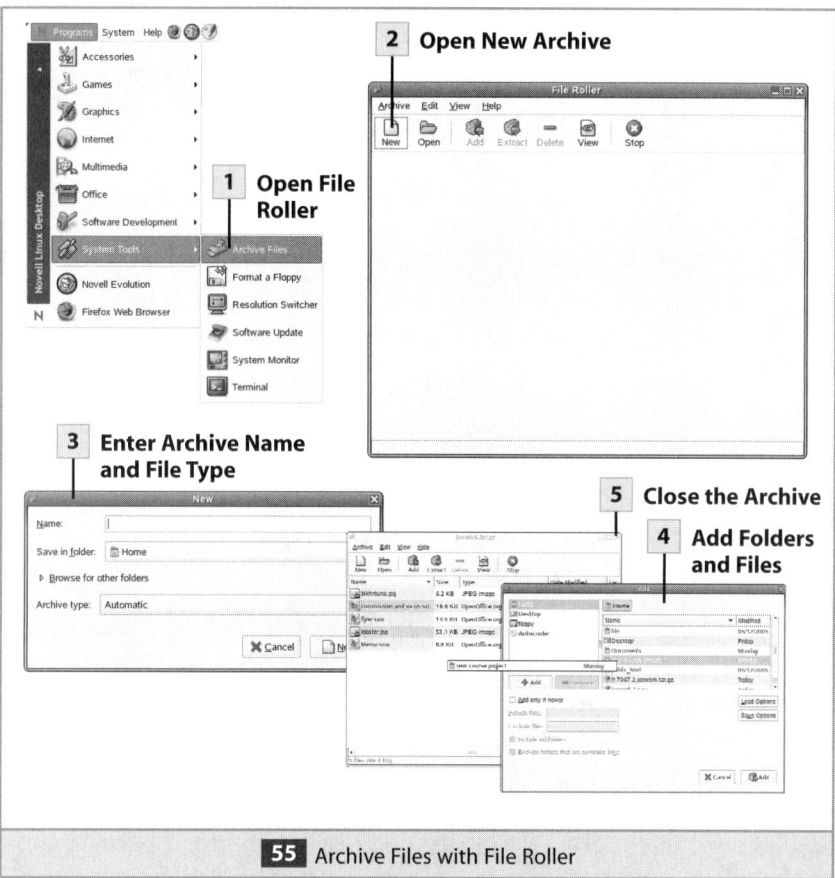

55 Archive Files with File Roller

TIP

You can also drag files or folders from a Nautilus window into the File Roller archive window to add files and folders to your archive.

5 **Close the Archive**

The files that you have added to the archive will be listed in the archive window. Select **Close**.

CHAPTER 6: Managing Files

TIP

You may wonder what happened to the folders you added to the archive. Only the files are listed. When you open the archive (open it in a Nautilus window) and then extract the files in File Roller to a destination, the original folders are re-created for you.

TIP

If you work a lot with Microsoft Windows users, you might want to archive your files as zip files. It is easy for Windows users to open and create archives in the zip file format.

56 About Backing Up and Restoring Files

When the concept of backing up and restoring data is discussed, we typically think of a single GUI program or command-line utility that allows us to back up files to some sort of compressed format and then, if disaster strikes, restore them to a computer. System administrators deal with fairly sophisticated hardware and software to back up files and can often be heard discussing such things as incremental and full backups. But I'm basically looking at the backup of important files in terms of the things that you create on the computer: your letters, databases, and spreadsheets.

NLD provides both a System Backup and a Restore System utility. You can back up important system files (it can be done automatically without you even choosing) and then, if there is a problem, you can use the Restore System utility. This type of backup protects program and system files. Both these utilities must be run by root because you can't open YaST without the root password.

NLD provides administrative utilities to back up the system.

57 Back Up Files

But system software can be reinstalled if there is a major catastrophe. Program files can be reinstalled as well. You might lose some configuration files, but your job isn't really to protect the system but to use NLD as a productivity tool.

As a user, you generate important documents and store important information on your computer related to contacts, your schedule, and a host of other things. It is important that things you can't afford to lose are "backed up" using some sort of system.

The Linux environment offers a number of command-line tools that can be used to make elegant backups of your data, including pax, tar, dd, dump, and others. But why not combine features that you already understand such as creating archives and then placing them on a removable USB drive or on a network drive, or burning them to a CD. This combines your abilities with File Roller and removable media drives and provides an easy-to-use system to back up your work.

TIP

pax and dump are just two of a number of command-line backup and restore utilities. Both pax and dump are available as Red Carpet Available Software for installation. You can view other backup utilities by searching for backup in the Red Carpet window. We discuss Red Carpet and installing files in Chapter 7, "Adding and Managing Software Applications and Tools in NLD."

57 Back Up Files

The backup phase consists of creating an archive file. You can create an archive using File Roller. However, there is a shortcut that you can use to quickly create a compressed tar archive in the Nautilus window. Then you can place the archive in a safe place and burn it to a CD, stick it on a USB drive, or even place it on a network drive if available.

✔ BEFORE YOU BEGIN

- **46** Use Nautilus to Manage Folders
- **47** Browse and Open Files
- **54** About Archiving Files
- **55** Archive Files with File Roller
- **56** About Backing Up and Restoring Files

CHAPTER 6: Managing Files

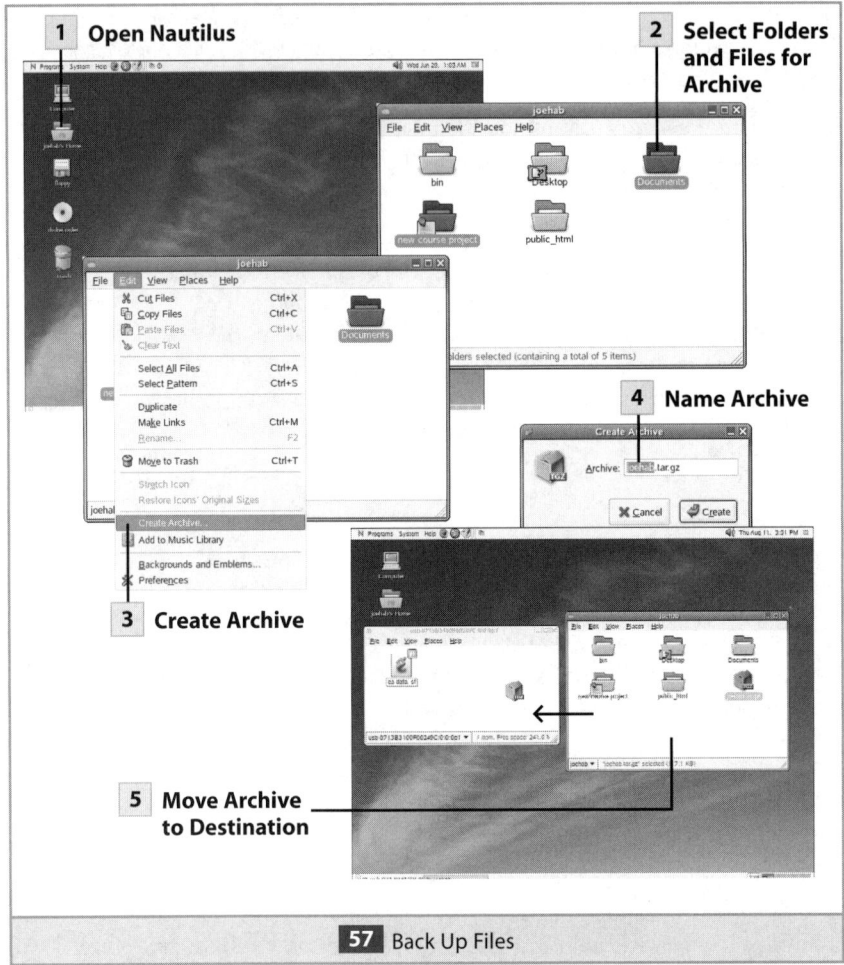

57 Back Up Files

1 Open Nautilus

On the desktop double-click your Home icon.

2 Select Folders and Files for Archive

Select the folders and files that you want to place in the archive.

3 Create Archive

In Nautilus, select **Edit**, **Create Archive**. A Create Archive dialog box opens.

58 Restore Files

4 Name Archive

Type a name for the archive in the Create Archive dialog box. The file is saved as a tar.gz file. Click **Create** to end the creation process.

5 Move Archive to Destination

Open a USB drive or other location in a second Nautilus window and drag the archive file to its new location while holding down the Alt key. When you release the archive file in the destination window, click **Move Here** on the shortcut menu. You have archived and backed up your important files.

---

58 Restore Files

Restoring your important files is just a matter of locating the archive that you created as a backup. You can then use File Roller to extract the files so that you can use them.

✔ **BEFORE YOU BEGIN**

55 Archive Files with File Roller
56 About Backing Up and Restoring Files
57 Back Up Files

1 Open Archive Location

Use Nautilus to locate the folder, CD, USB drive, or network drive where you stored your archive file.

TIP

To open network locations, double-click the **Computer** icon and then double-click the **Network** icon. Browse your network as needed to find the folder location.

2 Open Archive File

Double-click the archive file, and the File Roller window opens showing the contents of the archive.

CHAPTER 6: Managing Files

58 Restore Files

3 Specify Destination Location

In the File Roller window, select the **Extract** button. In the Extract dialog box that appears, select the folder (the location) where you want to extract the file. Folders will be re-created for the extracted files by default.

4 Extract Files

In the Extract dialog box, click the **Extract** button. The files are extracted to the location that you chose, and folders will be re-created. **Close** the File Roller window. Use Nautilus to open the location and view the extracted files and folders.

CHAPTER 7

Adding and Managing Software Applications and Tools in NLD

IN THIS CHAPTER:

- 59 About Updating and Adding Applications to NLD
- 60 About Updating Applications Using Red Carpet
- 61 Run Red Carpet to Update NLD Applications
- 62 About RPMs
- 63 Find Applications Using Red Carpet
- 64 Install Applications Using Red Carpet
- 65 Install and Remove Applications Using YaST
- 66 About Installing Applications from Other Archive Types

CHAPTER 7: Adding and Managing Software Applications and Tools in NLD

After you become comfortable with the NLD environment, you will probably consider adding additional applications and applets to your system. You will also want to keep your NLD installation files up-to-date. NLD makes it easy for you to install and update software.

In this chapter we explore different ways to update the software on your computer and add new software. We take a look at program archive types and become familiar with YaST and Red Carpet.

59 About Updating and Adding Applications to NLD

NLD provides two different GUI tools that make it easy for you to update programs, add software, and remove software. YaST, the NLD administrative configuration tool, allows you to add and remove software from your NLD installation (add software using the NLD installation disks or updates) and also makes it easy for you to run a system update and apply patches to your system.

Three icons in the YaST GUI window (when Software is selected in the left pane) are of particular interest:

- Install and Remove Software—This tool allows you to view the software installed on your system from a particular installation CD or DVD. You can also use this tool to remove software from the system.
- System Update—This tool allows you to connect to Novell's update servers and update your system software.
- Patch CD Update—This tool allows you to install patches to your system from a patch CD or DVD.

KEY TERM

Patch—A **patch** is a software update to a particular system or software file that resolves issues or tightens security.

To access YaST you must know the root password. This makes sense because even though YaST makes it easy to add and remove or update software, there is always a level of risk involved related to maintaining the integrity of your system. Think carefully before adding and removing software.

Another tool that makes it easy to quickly update your NLD software and search for other software packages on the Novell software update servers is Red Carpet. Red Carpet provides a GUI window where you can view available updates, view software installed on your system, and search for available uninstalled software on the NLD update servers. To use Red Carpet you need to know the root password.

59 About Updating and Adding Applications to NLD

YaST provides easy access to software installation and system update tools.

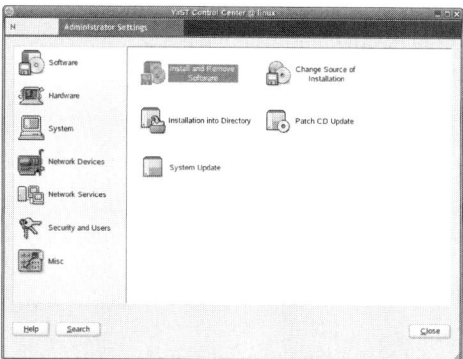

Red Carpet makes it easy to update your system from online software resources.

NOTE

If you are running a free or "sample" version of NLD, you typically get updates for only a limited period of time. A "full-blown" purchased version of NLD provides a much longer time frame for updating the system software, software applications, and applets. In either case, you must activate the updates for your system for Red Carpet to work properly.

One other thing that we need to discuss before looking at Red Carpet and then YaST is the issue of dependencies. Let's say that you want to install program A, but there is a dependency for program B. This typically means that program B must also be installed on the system for program A to actually function after you install it. In some few cases, programs have negative dependencies, meaning that you can't install both the programs on the system if you want either one to run.

CHAPTER 7: Adding and Managing Software Applications and Tools in NLD

KEY TERM

Dependency—A necessary software module for a program to run on the Linux system. Linux applications and applets require other software modules and files to be installed before the application or applet will run.

Dependencies for a software package must be met for it to run after installation.

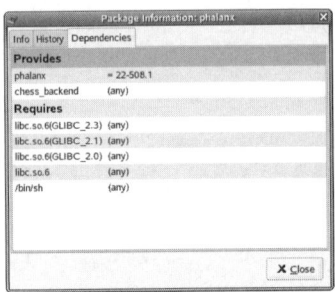

So the question arises: When should you use YaST and when should you use Red Carpet to install and update software? They both share some of the same capabilities.

YaST works best for adding software and patches to your system from CDs and DVDs. YaST actually has a better tool than Red Carpet to check whether all the dependencies are met for a package you want to install without having to view a list of dependencies.

Red Carpet is easy to deal with in terms of performing system updates because an indicator appears on the top panel when system updates are available. Red Carpet (at least in my opinion) also makes it easier to quickly view all the software installed on your system, and with just a couple of clicks you can remove or add a package.

60 About Updating Applications Using Red Carpet

Red Carpet provides you with the ability to quickly do a system software update, including updates for installed applications and applets. Red Carpet updates are provided by servers set up to support NLD. These are called *services*. The services supply update channels that you can subscribe to (for example, the NLD channel), meaning that you need to be connected to the Internet to run the Red Carpet update.

You have the option of installing all the available updates or selecting individual updates for specific applications or applets. In terms of updating the NLD

60 About Updating Applications Using Red Carpet

software, Red Carpet is quick and painless, particularly if you don't overthink the whole update process and allow Red Carpet to install all the updates that are located.

You can select to install all available updates or install individual updates.

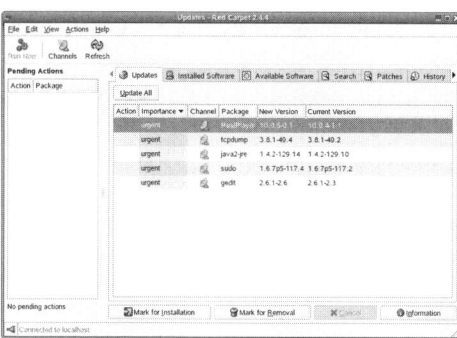

Red Carpet's capabilities don't end with easy updates. You can also quickly view the software installed on your system. This makes it easy to view the information for a particular package. You also have the option of removing packages if you want.

Installed packages can be reviewed and removed.

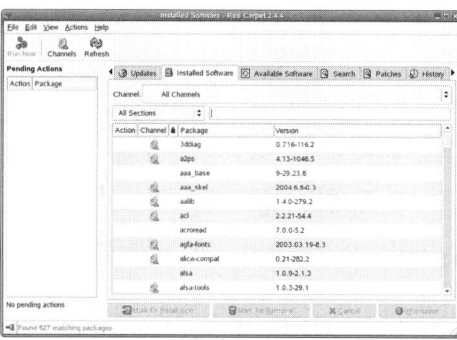

NOTE

Red Carpet is easy to deal with because your subscribed channels provide the update list and allow you to view software available on the channels. You don't have to deal with CDs or DVDs; everything is handled online.

When you are perusing installed software packages, you might find the complete list rather long and imposing. You can use the Sections drop-down list to

CHAPTER 7: Adding and Managing Software Applications and Tools in NLD

view subsets of installed and available software. For example, if you just want to see the productivity tools installed, you can select **Productivity** on the All Sections drop-down list.

Viewing software by the various sections (such as Productivity, Games, Multimedia, and Internet) also makes it easier to then look at the information related to a specific package because you know what type of package it is. To view the information for a specific package, select the package and then select the **Information** button. The Information dialog for the package provides package information and also allows you to view the dependencies for the package.

You can view the information for a specific package.

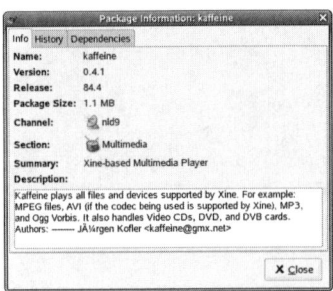

Red Carpet is an intuitive tool in terms of working with updates and adding other available packages or removing installed packages. The History tab in the Red Carpet window allows you to peruse a date and time list of updates including the new and replaced version of the updated package.

61 Run Red Carpet to Update NLD Applications

In terms of stability and usability (updated software often provides interface enhancements), you want to keep your NLD software up-to-date. It makes sense to update your system when you are alerted that updates are available.

✔ **BEFORE YOU BEGIN**

60 About Updating Applications Using Red Carpet

61 Run Red Carpet to Update NLD Applications

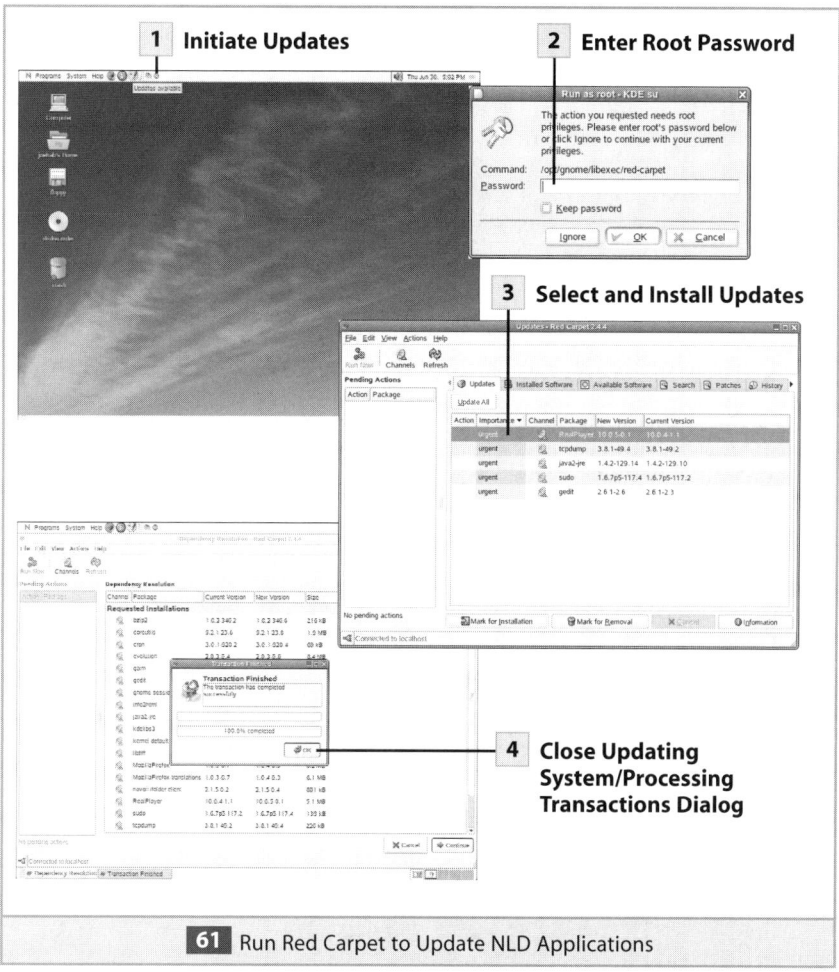

1 Initiate Updates

From NLD, select the **Updates Available** icon in the top panel. The Run as Root dialog box opens.

2 Enter Root Password

Enter the root password in the Run as Root dialog box and then click **OK**. The Red Carpet window opens.

3 Select and Install Updates

To install all the available updates, select **Update All**. Then select the **Continue** button.

TIP
If you want to select individual updates, double-click on the software update in the list. To run that update or other selected updates, select the **Run Now** button on the Red Carpet toolbar.

4 Close Updating System/Processing Transactions Dialog

The Updating System/Processing Transactions dialog box shows you the status of the installation. When the transaction, the installation of updates, is complete, click **OK**. You are returned to the Red Carpet window, which notifies you that the system is up-to-date.

62 About RPMs

✔ BEFORE YOU BEGIN

- 12 Run a Program from the Run Application Dialog
- 21 Add an Item to a Menu
- 60 About Updating Applications Using Red Carpet

→ SEE ALSO

- 66 About Installing Applications from Other Archive Types

Programs that you install on your system come as archive files. The most common and the easiest to deal with is the RPM file. *RPM* stands for *RedHat Package Manager*, which was developed originally for RedHat Linux. Other implementations of Linux including NLD and SUSE have embraced the RPM format because the program contained in the archive (the RPM) has been compiled and is ready to install.

KEY TERM
RPM—An archived, compressed, and compiled software application, code library, or help file. RPM stands for RedHat Package Manager.

62 About RPMs

RPM files can be downloaded from the Web and then installed to your system from a Nautilus window. All you have to do is download the file to a folder on your computer. Then locate the downloaded file using Nautilus.

Locate the downloaded RPM using Nautilus.

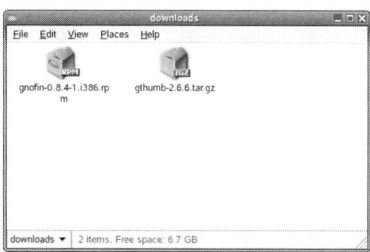

WEB RESOURCE

http://www.linux.org

This website is a good place to begin your search for Linux software not available through your NLD subscription channels (and Red Carpet). This site provides a listing of software by category (such as Games). You can read about a particular program before downloading. Remember that you want to look at the license type for these files because not all are GPL or GNU (meaning open source). Try to find an RPM compatible with NLD. Generally, RPMs designed for SUSE Linux Professional will work with NLD.

When you double-click on the file, you are asked to provide the root password. Red Carpet then opens, ready to install the application. The great thing is that Red Carpet also lists and installs any required files needed for the new application to run (taking care of the dependencies).

You can then run the newly installed program from a Run Application window (select **System**, **Run Program**). All you need to do is type the name of the application in the window and press **Enter**. You can also add the application to the Programs menu for easy access.

NOTE

It is certainly not required that you spend a lot of time searching for new software packages on the Web. Your subscribed channels will provide you with most of the software that you need (using Red Carpet). However, on occasion you may need to look elsewhere for something special. Be advised that even software listed on high-profile Linux websites such as linux.org isn't always available. Many of the links dry up over time (the sites don't exist anymore). Remember that most

Linux software is GNU (open source), and so developers create a new application with much excitement, but the excitement dies down over time. Some applications never go through a revision cycle or are dropped by the developer altogether. The Red Carpet support for NLD is guaranteed to be there for five years from the release date, so you know that software will be there.

63 Find Applications Using Red Carpet

Red Carpet can quickly provide you a list of all the software available on your subscribed channels. You can also search for software by category (section) and keywords.

> ✓ **BEFORE YOU BEGIN**
>
> 60 About Updating Applications Using Red Carpet

1 Open Red Carpet

From the NLD desktop, select the **System** menu and then select **Software Update**.

2 Enter Root Password

Enter the root password in the Run as Root dialog box and then click **OK**. The Red Carpet window opens.

3 Select Search and Software Section

To begin the search process, click the **Search** tab in the Red Carpet window. To select a particular software section (category) such as Productivity, Games, or Multimedia, select the **All Sections** drop-down list. To view only uninstalled software, select the **All Packages** drop-down list and select **Uninstalled Packages**.

4 Enter Keywords

To search for software by keyword, enter keywords in the text box provided.

63 Find Applications Using Red Carpet

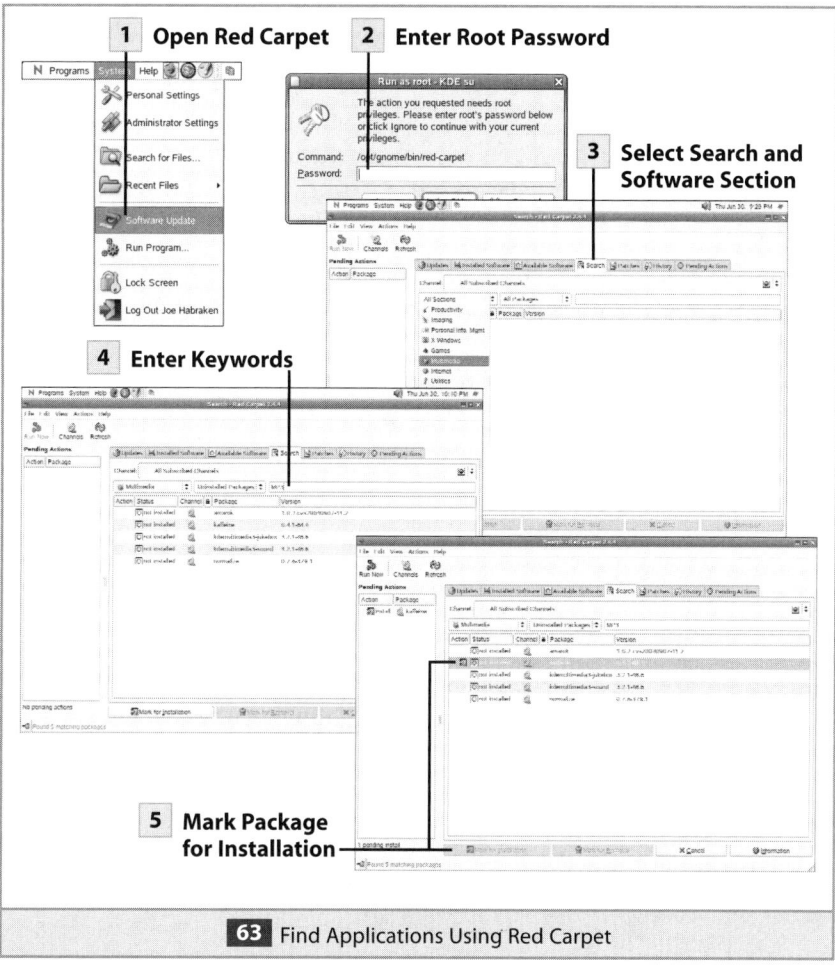

63 Find Applications Using Red Carpet

5 Mark Package for Installation

The results of your search appear in the Red Carpet window. If you want to mark a package for installation, select a package in the Search Results list. Then select the **Mark for Installation** button. The package is added to the Pending Actions list.

At this point you can redefine your search parameters and do a new search. Add any packages you want to install to the Pending Actions list.

TIP

To read about a particular package, select the package in the list and then select the **Information** button.

64 Install Applications Using Red Carpet

✔ BEFORE YOU BEGIN

- 60 About Updating Applications Using Red Carpet
- 63 Find Applications Using Red Carpet

1 Select Package to Install

In the **Pending Actions** list select the packages or packages you want to install.

TIP

Select multiple packages in the Pending Actions list by selecting the first one and then holding down the Ctrl key as you select subsequent packages. If you want to remove packages from the list, right-click on a package and select **Cancel** from the shortcut menu.

2 Run Installation

After selecting the package or packages, select the **Run Now** button. The package will be queued for installation.

3 Complete Installation

Select the **Continue** button. The Updating System dialog box opens, showing you the installation process. When the installation is complete, click **OK**. You can also close the Red Carpet window at this point.

4 Run Application

You can now run the application in the Run Application dialog box (select **System, Run Program**). Enter the program name in the Run Application dialog and then select **Run**. The program opens on the NLD desktop.

65 Install and Remove Applications Using YaST

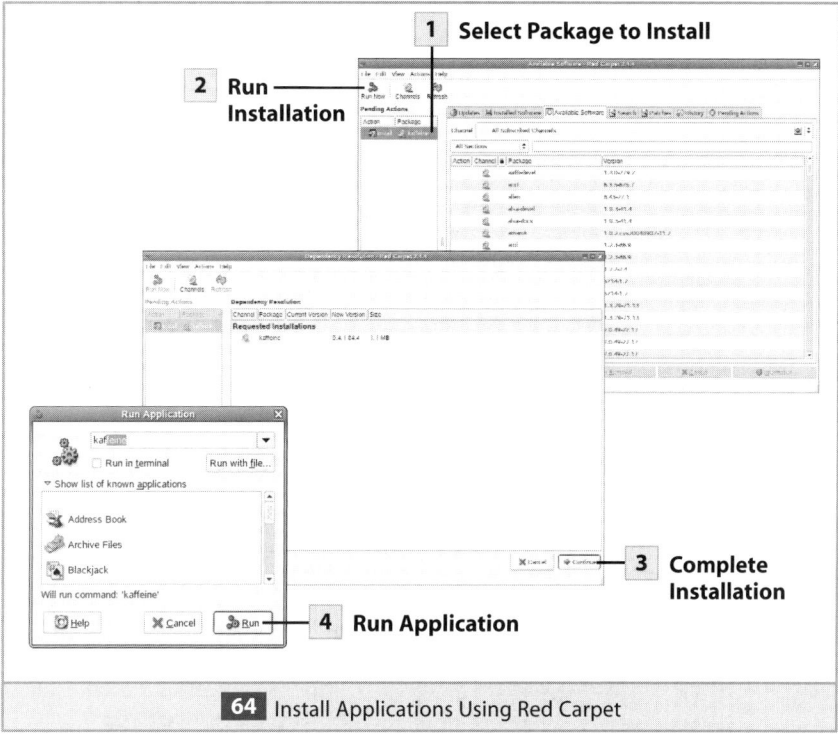

64 Install Applications Using Red Carpet

NOTE

The process is the same to add RPMs that you download from other sites using your web browser. Double-click on a downloaded RPM in a Nautilus window and then install the package as outlined here.

65 Install and Remove Applications Using YaST

You can view the applications installed on your system using YaST. YaST also provides you with the ability to add applications from installation and update CDs or DVDs. You need to have your installation or update CDs (or DVD) available to install applications to the system.

✔ **BEFORE YOU BEGIN**

59 About Updating and Adding Applications to NLD

165

CHAPTER 7: Adding and Managing Software Applications and Tools in NLD

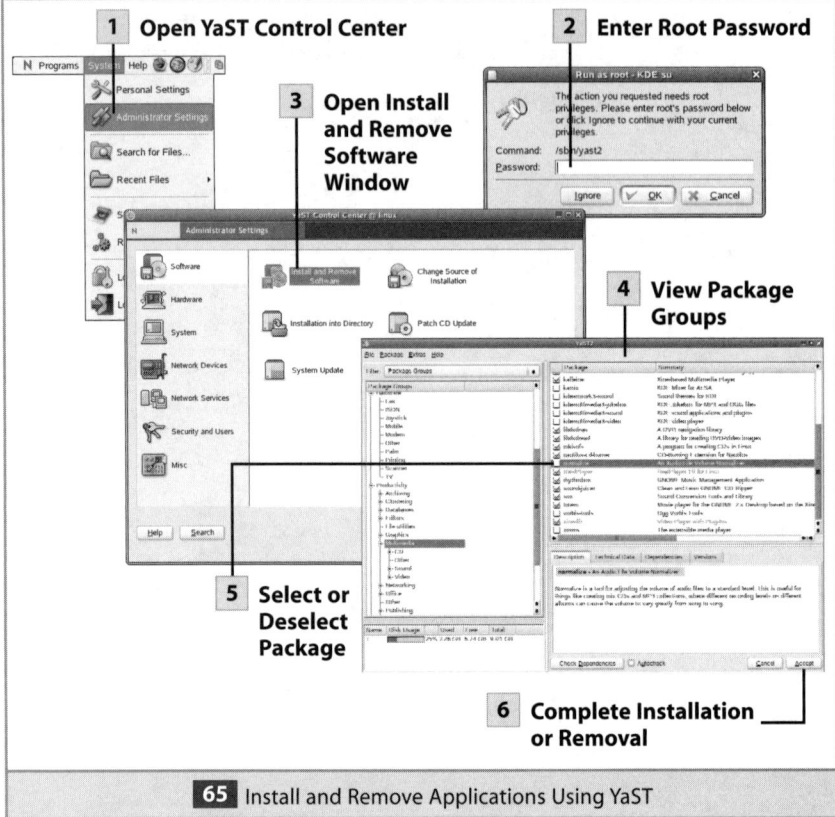

65 Install and Remove Applications Using YaST

1 Open YaST Control Center

From the desktop, select **System**, **Administrator Settings**. The Run as Root dialog box opens.

2 Enter Root Password

Enter the root password in the Run as Root dialog box and then click **OK**. The YaST Control Center opens.

3 Open Install and Remove Software Window

Select (click once) the **Install and Remove Software** icon in the YaST window. (YaST requires only one click on icons to activate the module.)

65 Install and Remove Applications Using YaST

4   View Package Groups

To view the software packages by group, click the **Filter** list and select **Package Groups**. Expand a particular group listing. To view the information about a particular package, select that package in the list.

NOTE

Installed packages are marked with a check mark. Uninstalled packages have an empty check box.

TIP

To quickly check whether the dependencies for a particular package are met before installing, select the **Check Dependencies** button. A message box opens and tells you whether all dependencies are met. If you want to autocheck dependencies, select the **Autocheck** option button at the bottom of the YaST window.

5   Select or Deselect Package

To remove a package from installation, click the check box for that package until a trash can icon appears, marking the package for deletion. To include a package for installation, select the empty check box (this places a check mark in the box).

NOTE

You can add packages as needed, but I would caution you in terms of removing packages. Remember the importance of dependencies. Removing one package could disable other packages on the system.

6   Complete Installation or Removal

When you are ready to complete the process, click the **Accept** button. The packages are installed (or uninstalled), and you are returned to the YaST Control Center.

TIP

Make sure that you place the appropriate installation or update CD (or DVD) in the CD (or DVD) drive you used for the NLD installation. If you do not have the appropriate CD in the drive, you are prompted for the correct one.

> **NOTE**
>
> The YaST Add and Remove Software module also allows you to mark installed packages for update. Right-click on the check box for the package and select **Update**. For packages that you have installed in the past and then removed because they didn't work correctly or caused system problems, you can mark them as taboo (meaning don't ever install). Right-click on the package's check box and select **Taboo—Never Install**.

66 About Installing Applications from Other Archive Types

✔ **BEFORE YOU BEGIN**

55 Archive Files with File Roller
62 About RPMs

As you become more comfortable with NLD and its various applications and tools, you may find yourself on the lookout for new applications and applets that serve specific purposes (okay, so it might even be a game that you are dying to play).

We have already discussed how you can add RPM software packages to your NLD installation either through channels or by downloading packages from a website. However, there may be occasions when you find a program that you want to install and it is available only in another file archive type, the most common being the compressed tar file: tar.gz.

Installing tar.gz files to your system is a little more difficult than RPMs. The first thing you should do after you download the file is use Nautilus to locate the downloaded package. If you double-click on the package, File Roller opens, and you can view the package contents.

You are looking for an Install or readme text file in the package contents. You can double-click to open the installation or readme file to get information on how you install the package. This is a multistep process because the program must be compiled and then run to install the package. Here is a quick run-through of the process, but the final steps depend on the package you are dealing with.

66 About Installing Applications from Other Archive Types

You can view the files in the tar archive using File Roller.

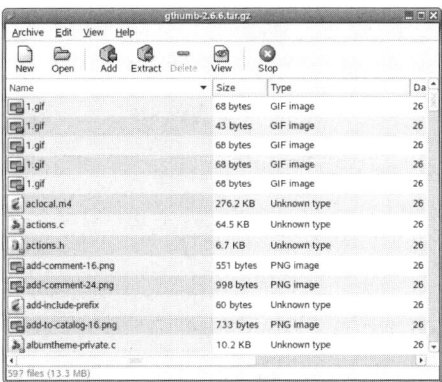

After you create a new folder to hold the files and open the package in File Roller, you can extract the package to a folder using File Roller. Select all the files in the package and then select **Extract**. A specific folder may be created for the package files when you extract the files.

After the files are in a folder, you should have read and printed out the install text file included with the package. Now comes the hard part.

NOTE

Installing tar packages is tricky. In many cases you need a C compiler installed on your system. Use Red Carpet to install the GCC compiler on your system. Also make sure that the following are installed on your system: make and automake. These are both development tools that can be installed using YaST from your installation CDs. You may want to install other development tools as needed.

Open a terminal window. Type **su** at the command prompt and then enter the root password. You have to be logged in as root in the terminal window to install software. Use the **cd** (change directory) command to navigate to the folder that holds the files for the package.

Type **./configure** at the command prompt and press **Enter**. This configures the package for your system. Now you can compile the package.

Type **make** and then press **Enter**. This compiles the installation for the software. Now you can type **make install** and press **Enter**. This installs the software.

You should now be able to run the program from the Run Program window. If the program works, you can add it to a menu or panel.

CHAPTER 7: Adding and Managing Software Applications and Tools in NLD

Don't be upset if this process doesn't work the first time. You may need to do a little research on the software that you are trying to install because some packages require more than just the **configure**, **make**, and **make install** commands (see whether there is a website for the package). In some cases, you may have downloaded a bad archive package.

As a final word related to software installation, it makes sense to use RPMs that have been specifically designed for NLD. When dealing with tarballs, do not install from a tarball unless you are absolutely sure that you need a program that is available only as a tar.gz file (and is not available as an RPM). I would also suggest that you do not install a file that doesn't have a support website or hasn't had a revision for some time. Be sure that you know from where the files you install come, and what impact they will have on your system.

PART II

Using the Internet and Multimedia Tools

8 Browsing the World Wide Web with Mozilla Firefox 173

9 Using Other Internet Tools 199

CHAPTER 8

Browsing the World Wide Web with Mozilla Firefox

IN THIS CHAPTER:

- **67** About Mozilla Firefox
- **68** Browse Web Pages
- **69** Use Tabbed Browsing
- **70** Print a Web Page
- **71** Control Pop-ups in Firefox
- **72** Access the Browsing History
- **73** Create a Bookmark
- **74** About Managing Bookmarks
- **75** Move and Edit Bookmarks
- **76** Sort Bookmarks
- **77** About Cookies and Firefox
- **78** Accept and Reject Cookies
- **79** Manage Cookies

CHAPTER 8: Browsing the World Wide Web with Mozilla Firefox

The Internet has become an increasingly important communication infrastructure for businesses and individuals. It is safe to say that one of the Internet's most popular information conduits is the World Wide Web.

In this chapter we take a look at the Mozilla Firefox web browser. This browser provides all the tools and capabilities that you expect from a web browser. It also provides added security and is easy to get up and running because it is installed by default during your NLD installation.

67 About Mozilla Firefox

The Mozilla Suite is a set of Internet-related tools including a web browser, email client, and newsreader. The various Mozilla tools are all open source.

Firefox is not the same as the standard Mozilla browser that is part of the Mozilla Internet tools but is a standalone browser created using the Mozilla browser source code. Firefox is a multiplatform web browser. It can operate on a number of operating systems including Microsoft Windows and Linux distributions such as NLD.

> **NOTE**
>
> The Mozilla project was actually launched by Netscape in 1998 when it released the source code for the Netscape web browser. Available under GPL and GNU licenses, Mozilla tools such as the Firefox browser are open source.

If you haven't been following the news related to security and web browsers, you probably haven't seen all the positive press for the Firefox browser and its capabilities for dealing with security threats, pop-ups, and cookies. Firefox is not actually part of the operating system and so doesn't open you up to threats caused by security holes in the operating system itself. Firefox also does not run certain active content types such as ActiveX controls. (ActiveX controls were developed by Microsoft to provide active content to Microsoft Internet Explorer.) ActiveX controls have been identified as a route used by hackers to invade computer systems.

Most of the security issues that Firefox protects against are really issues related to the Windows operating system and Microsoft's Internet Explorer web browser. So, you don't have to think about some of these issues at all. Remember that Linux (NLD) already provides a more secure environment from the get go; your use of Firefox as your NLD-based web browser just makes your web experience even more secure and flexible.

67 About Mozilla Firefox

Firefox provides a number of enhancements (other than security-related enhancements) that differentiate it from other web browsers that you may have used. Some of these enhancements are

- Tabbed browsing—The Firefox window can be divided into multiple tabbed windows allowing you to open multiple websites. Move from site to site by selecting the appropriate tab.
- Google search box—You can quickly conduct a Google search using the Google Search box provided at the right end of the Firefox toolbar.
- Extensions—Extensions are add-on modules that can perform all sorts of tasks. There are a number of different extensions, with new extensions becoming available, including an extension that shows weather forecasts on the toolbar, an extension that provides more control over the download of PDF files, and an extension that will allow JavaScripts to run only when you browse trusted websites.
- Download Manager—The Firefox Download Manager allows you to track and access the files that you download from sites on the Web.

Firefox also makes it easy for you to configure the various user preferences. A Preferences dialog box (select **Edit**, **Preferences**) provides access to these settings:

- General—This group of preferences includes the setting for your home page and the fonts and colors used in the browser window.
- Privacy—These settings include the length of time to keep your browsing history and cookie management preferences. You can also view the history for the download manager and you can manage the passwords that you have saved for secure websites.
- Web features—A set of options related to pop-ups and scripting types that are allowed to run on accessed sites.
- Downloads—These settings include the ability to choose the folder for downloads and whether to show the Download Manager when a file is downloaded.
- Advanced—A series of options related to accessibility, browsing, and tabbed browsing. You can also select the type of security protocols used for secure connections.

Firefox will serve you well as your web browser; there are some downsides, however. Because Firefox will not run certain content types, you may have problems with some interactive sites, particularly sites that have been created with Microsoft Internet Explorer in mind. But the enhancements and security provided by Firefox more than make up for some of the compatibility issues you may have to deal with.

68 Browse Web Pages

If you've used any web browsers in the past (Especially Netscape's old web browser or any of the recent Mozilla browsers), using Firefox should be a breeze for browsing web pages.

✔ BEFORE YOU BEGIN

67 About Mozilla Firefox

1 Start Firefox

From the NLD desktop, select the **Firefox Web Browser** icon in the top panel. The Firefox window opens.

2 Enter URL

To enter a URL (a web address that you know), select the current address; then type the URL in the Address box and press **Enter**.

3 Follow Web Link

Click a link on a web page to follow an internal link to a new page or to an external link.

TIP

You don't have to type the whole URL, meaning you can type **www.sitename.sufffix** (such as .com, .org, and so on.). You don't have to enter the HTTP://.

4 Perform a Google Search

To quickly perform a search using Google type your search terms in the Google Search box and then press **Enter**.

68 Browse Web Pages

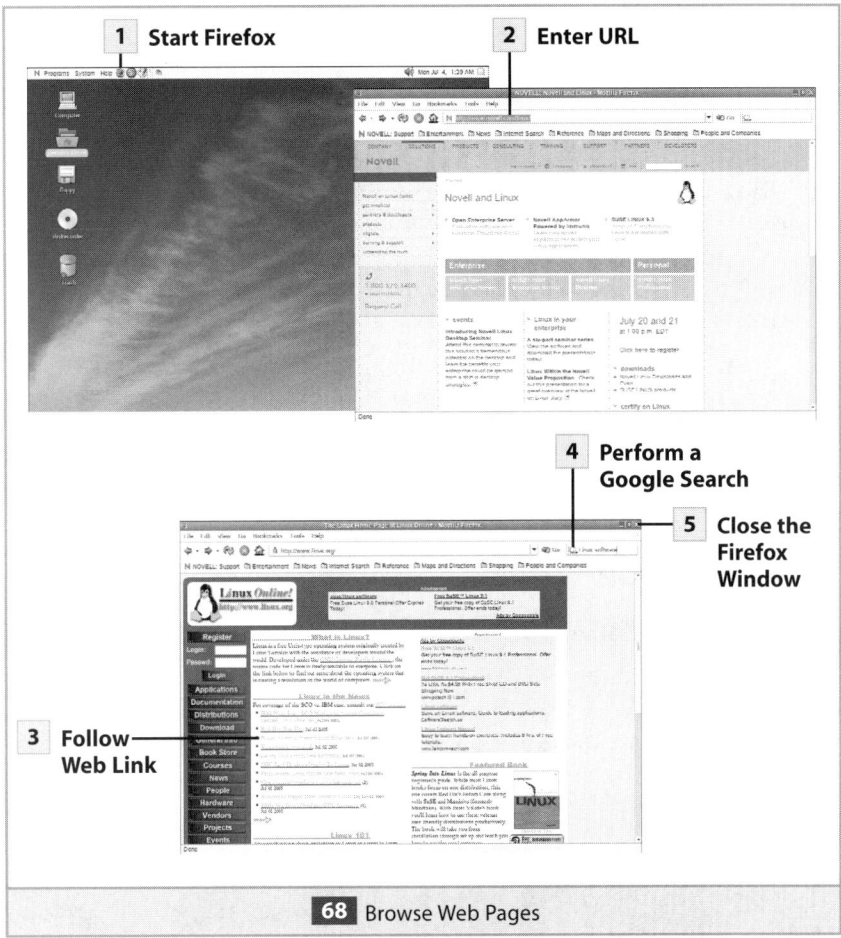

68 Browse Web Pages

TIP

You can use the Back and Forward buttons as needed when you are browsing the Web. To see a list of sites that you can go back (or forward) to, click the drop-down list button next to the **Back** or **Forward** buttons. You can also select the **Go** button to view a list of recently visited sites. Select a site in the list to go to that site.

TIP

Downloading pictures and files with Firefox is straightforward. To save a picture on a web page, right-click on the picture and select **Save Image As**; then save the image to a folder on your computer. (You can also use the Set As Wallpaper command on the shortcut menu to make the picture your desktop background.) To download a file click on the file download link and then specify a location for the downloaded file. The Download Manager window opens showing the progress of the download. To open the downloaded file (this works especially well with RPMs, because Red Carpet opens after you enter the root password), select the downloaded file in the Download Manager window and then select **Open**.

5 Close the Firefox Window

After you have finished working in the Firefox window, click the **Close** button to close the window.

69 Use Tabbed Browsing

Firefox provides you with the ability to open websites in tabbed windows. This means that you can have several websites open at the same time and switch between the sites using the various tabs. This makes browsing multiple sites much easier than the alternative of having to open a new window for each site.

✔ **BEFORE YOU BEGIN**

67 About Mozilla Firefox
68 Browse Web Pages

1 Open New Tab Window

In the Firefox window select **File**, **New Tab** from the menu. A new tab window (Untitled) opens.

TIP

You can also quickly open an new tab window by pressing **Ctrl+T** on the keyboard.

69 Use Tabbed Browsing

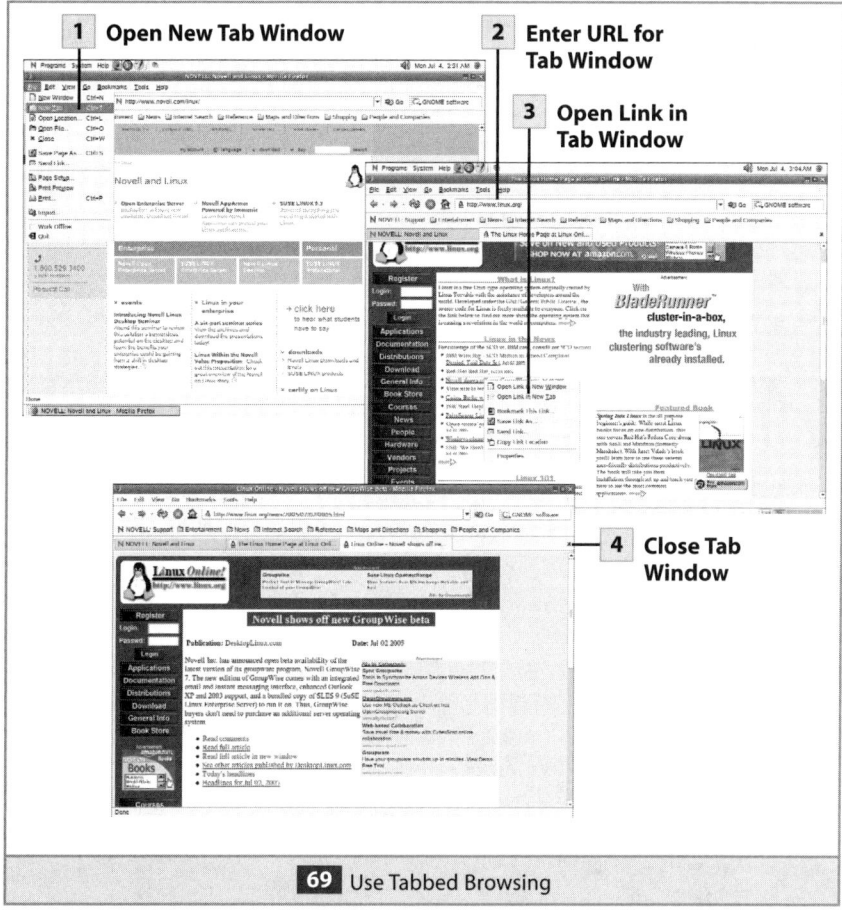

69 Use Tabbed Browsing

2 Enter URL for Tab Window

Enter a URL for the new tab window in the address box (and then press **Enter**), or use the **Go** button to select a site from your list of recently visited sites. You can also select a site from your Bookmarks list. The selected site opens in the tab window.

TIP

To open your history list and select a site from the history (to open in the tab window), press **Ctrl+H** (or select **History** on the Go list). The History pane appears on the left side of the browser window. Click a site in the history to open that site.

3 Open Link in Tab Window

To open a web link in a new tab window, right-click the link and select **Open Link in New Tab** from the shortcut menu.

TIP

You can also open a link in a new tab window by holding down the **Ctrl** key and then clicking on the link or by pressing the middle button on a three-button mouse.

4 Close Tab Window

To close the currently selected tab window, click the **Close** button to the far right of the tab. To close all the other current tab windows (precluding the one that you right-click), right-click on a tab and select **Close Other Tabs**. A Confirm Close dialog box opens. Select **Close Tabs** to close the other tabs in the Firefox window.

70 Print a Web Page

You can print web pages from the Firefox window. The Print dialog provides you the ability to select a printer, to select how to print the web page (such as print range and frames), and to specify the number of copies to be printed.

✔ **BEFORE YOU BEGIN**

- **36** Add and Configure a Printer
- **37** Print to a Printer
- **67** About Mozilla Firefox
- **68** Browse Web Pages

1 Open Print Dialog

In the Firefox window, select **File**, **Print** from the menu. The Print dialog box opens.

70 Print a Web Page

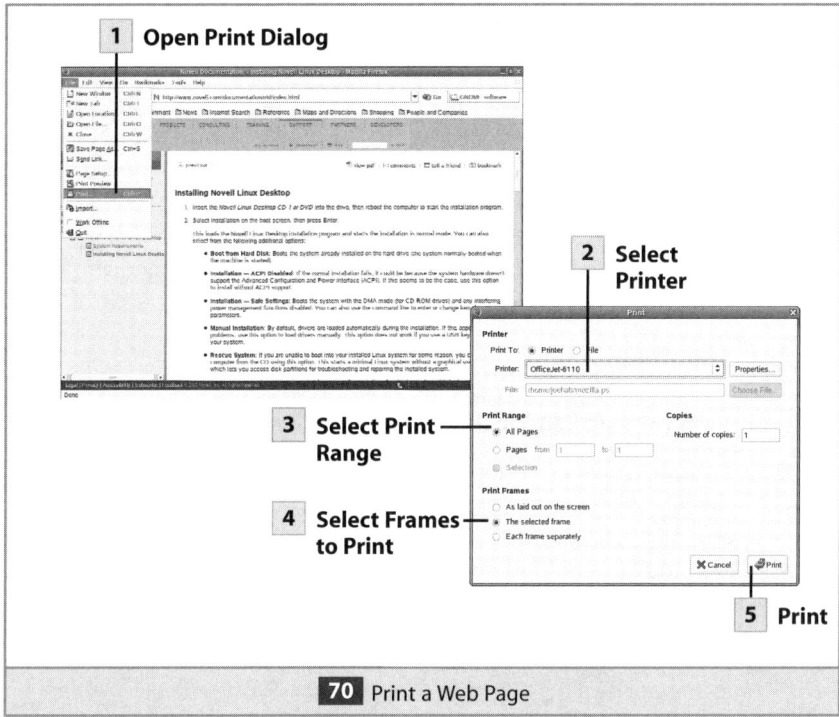

70 Print a Web Page

TIP

To view a preview of the web page printout, select **File**, **Print Preview**.

2 **Select Printer**

Select the **Printer** drop-down list to select the printer that you want to use for the print job.

3 **Select Print Range**

Use the **Pages** option button to specify a print range for the printout.

TIP

If you want to print just a selection on the web page, select the text before opening the Print dialog box and then select the **Selection** option button in the dialog box.

4 Select Frames to Print

In the Print Frames area of the Print dialog box select the appropriate option such as **The Selected Frame** or **Each Frame Separately**.

5 Print

After you have selected the appropriate options in the Print dialog box, select **Print** to send the print job to the printer. The Printing dialog box opens briefly as the job is sent to the printer's queue.

---

71 Control Pop-ups in Firefox

Pop-ups are those annoying windows that open up automatically as you are browsing the Web. Firefox is configured by default to block pop-up windows. In some cases, however, you may use websites where you want pop-ups to be allowed. You can temporarily allow pop-ups for a particular site, and you can also configure the pop-up options for Firefox in the Preferences dialog box.

> ✔ **BEFORE YOU BEGIN**
>
> 68 Browse Web Pages

1 Temporarily Allow Pop-ups

As you browse the Web a message may appear at the top of the page's window that says Firefox prevented this site from opening a pop-up window. To access pop-up options for this site, click to the right of the message. In the options menu that appears select **Allow Popups** to temporarily allow pop-ups for the site.

2 Open Preferences Dialog

You can configure the options for the Pop-up Blocker. Select **Edit**, **Preferences** from the menu. The Firefox Preferences dialog box opens.

TIP

You can also quickly open the pop-up options by selecting **Edit Popup Blocker Options** when the Firefox prevented pop-up window message appears.

71 Control Pop-ups in Firefox

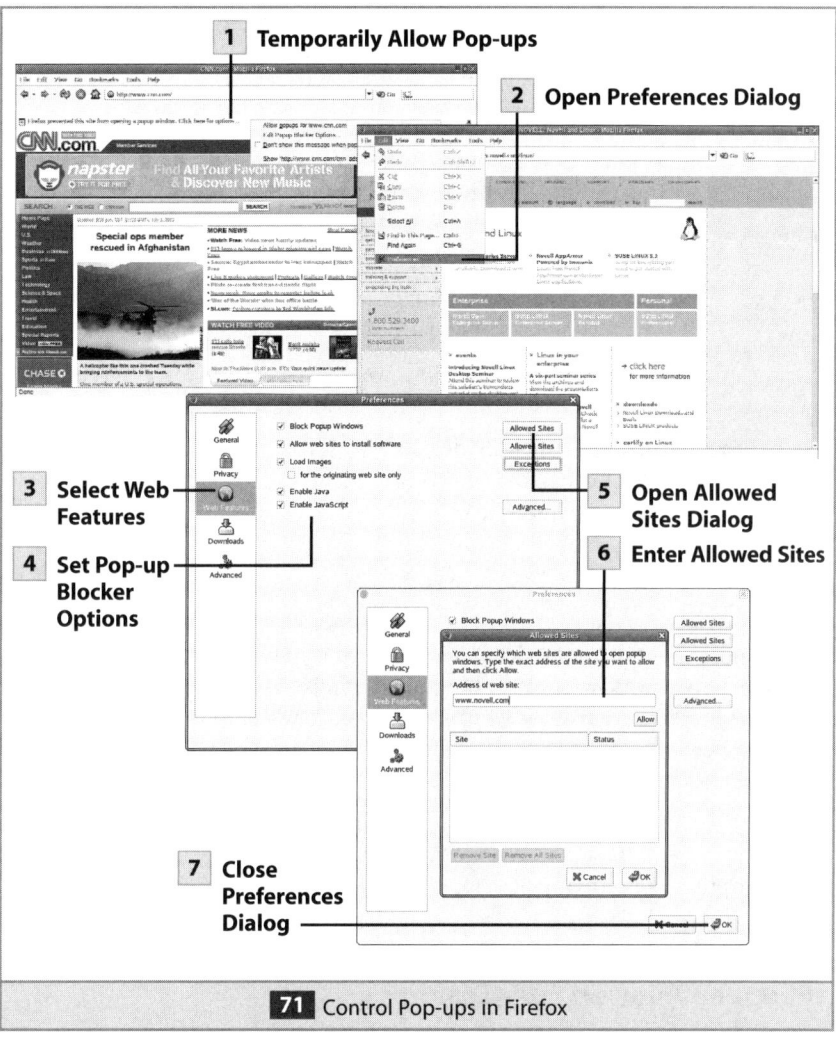

71 Control Pop-ups in Firefox

3 Select Web Features

In the Preferences dialog box select the **Web Features** icon.

4 Set Pop-up Blocker Options

You have several options available related to pop-ups and what you allow a site to do in relation to your computer:

- Block Popup Windows—You can enable (the default) or disable this option. You can also build a list of sites where pop-ups are allowed.
- Allow Web Sites to Install Software—By default, no sites are allowed to install software. You can build a list of trusted sites that can download software to your system.
- Load Images—By default, images on sites are loaded. You can disable this option if you want. You can also create a list of exceptions that specifies sites where image loading is either allowed or not allowed.
- Enable Java—By default, Java web-based applets are allowed to run. You can disable this option by clearing the check box.
- Enable JavaScript—By default, JavaScript is enabled, allowing JavaScript active content to play on all sites. You can disable this option by clearing the check box.

NOTE

You can select options for JavaScript related to what you allow the script to do to your browser. Options include hide the status bar, raise or lower windows, and change images. If you have JavaScript enabled, you may want to go with the default options set for JavaScript. As you use Firefox over time, you can fine-tune these options to meet your own needs.

Clear any of the option check boxes related to pop-ups, downloads, and scripting as needed. In most cases, you will want to keep these options enabled.

5 Open Allowed Sites Dialog

You can build an allowed site list for the pop-up and install software options. The Load Images Exceptions list is built in a similar manner but allows sites to be blocked or allowed.

Select the **Allowed Sites** button (for either the pop-up or install software options). The Allowed Sites dialog box opens.

6 Enter Allowed Sites

In the Allowed Sites dialog box enter a URL for a site that will be allowed. Then select the **Allow** button. Repeat this process for other sites. When you have finished adding sites to the list, click **OK**.

7 Close Preferences Dialog

After you have finished setting pop-up and related options, click **OK** to close the Preferences dialog box.

---

72 Access the Browsing History

As you browse the Web, you may want to return to a particular website that you have looked at in the past, but can't remember the URL and didn't bother to bookmark the site. You can access the browsing history and recall sites from the history list.

> ✔ **BEFORE YOU BEGIN**
>
> 68 Browse Web Pages

1 Open History Pane

To open the History pane in the browser window, select the **Go** menu and then **History**. The History pane opens in the browser sidebar (on the left side of the browser window).

TIP

Right-click on the Firefox Navigation toolbar and select **Customize**. You can drag additional icons to the toolbar from the Customize Toolbar dialog box. For example, you can add the History icon to the toolbar, making it easier to access your browsing history.

2 Select Time Frame

By default, the History list is arranged by date. Select a time frame such as **2 Days Ago** to view the sites visited on that day.

TIP

To change how the History list is viewed, select the **View** drop-down list at the top of the History sidebar and select one of these options: By Date and Site, By Site, By Date, By Most Visited, or By Last Visited.

CHAPTER 8: Browsing the World Wide Web with Mozilla Firefox

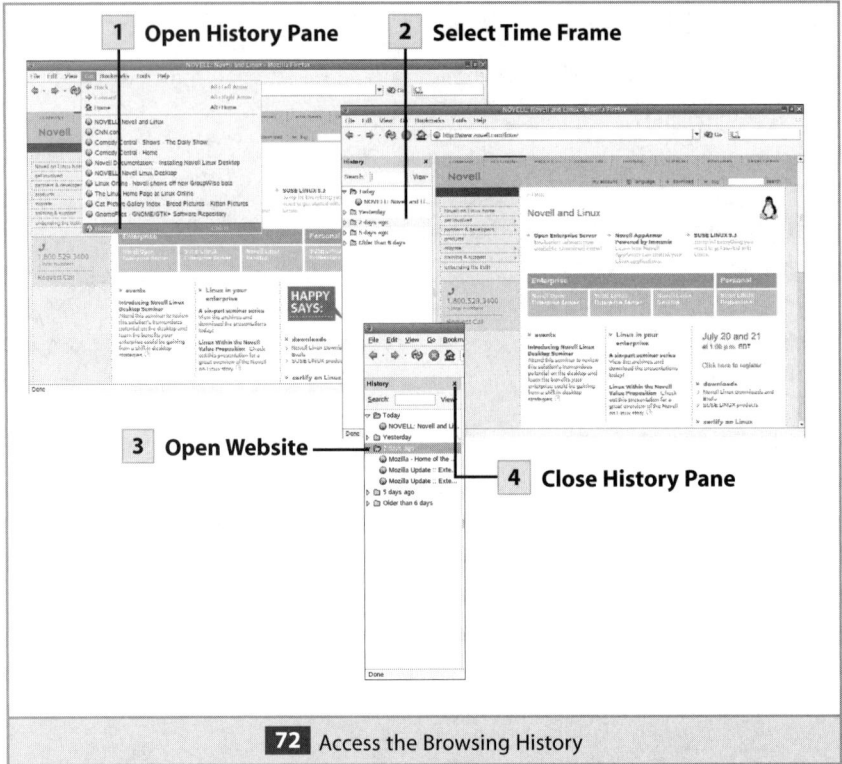

72 Access the Browsing History

3 Open Website

Select a site in the History list to open that site in the browser window.

TIP

To change the number of days remembered in the History list, select **Edit, Preferences**. Select the **Privacy** icon, and then expand the **History** options. Set the number of days as needed. If you want to clear the History list, click the **Clear** button.

4 Close History Pane

After you have finished using the History pane, select the **Close** button at the top right of the pane.

TIP

You can also search the History list, which is useful if you don't really remember when you viewed a particular site. Type a keyword or words in the History pane Search box. A list of sites that meet your search criteria appears in the History pane.

73 Create a Bookmark

Bookmarks provide a way to catalog your favorite and most useful websites. Bookmarks can be saved in the main Bookmark list or saved in folders. You can save a bookmark in one of the default folders or create a folder of your own.

✔ **BEFORE YOU BEGIN**

68 Browse Web Pages

1 Open Add Bookmark Dialog

Go to a site that you want to bookmark. From the menu, select **Bookmarks**, **Bookmark This Page**. The Add Bookmark dialog box opens.

2 Select Location for Bookmark

In the Add Bookmark dialog box, select the Bookmarks folder list (the button to the right of the Create In box). This shows the main bookmark folder and the Bookmarks Toolbar folder (click this folder to expand the list).

Select a folder for the new bookmark. If you want to create a new folder, select **New Folder**. Type a name for the folder and an optional description; then click **OK**.

NOTE

It makes sense to save your bookmarks in a series of folders that allow you to quickly find a bookmark when you need it. Create folders as needed that provide categories that make sense to you when you need to locate a particular site's bookmark.

CHAPTER 8: Browsing the World Wide Web with Mozilla Firefox

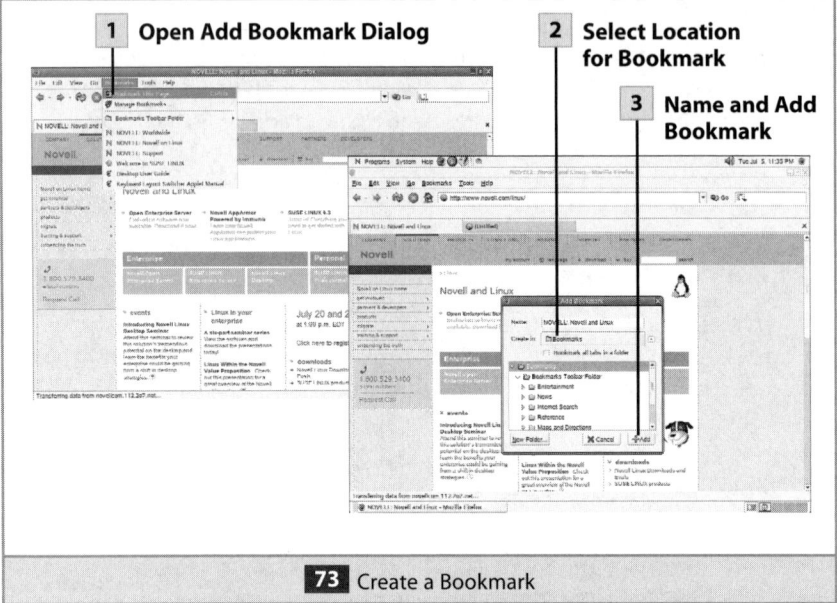

73 Create a Bookmark

3 Name and Add Bookmark

After selecting the folder for the bookmark, you can specify a name for the site (other than the URL or name provided by the site). Type the alternative name in the Name box. When you are ready to add the bookmark, select the **Add** button. You can now access the site from the Bookmarks list.

TIP

To view your bookmarks in the Firefox sidebar (the left pane), press **Ctrl+B**, and the bookmark list appears.

74 About Managing Bookmarks

✓ **BEFORE YOU BEGIN**

68 Browse Web Pages
73 Create a Bookmark

Firefox allows you to manage the bookmarks that you create. You can change link-specific information such as the name and address of the bookmark. You can also move and delete bookmarks as needed and create new folders to hold your bookmarks.

You manage your bookmarks In the Bookmarks Manager, which allows you to sort bookmarks, change bookmark properties, and perform other tasks such as moving and deleting bookmarks.

The Bookmarks Manager allows you to manage your bookmarks.

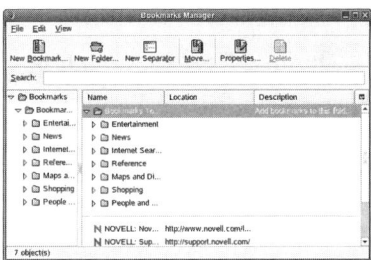

The Bookmarks Manager also allows you to import and export bookmark lists. This allows you to import the bookmarks from another computer and web browser. If you use more than one computer running NLD, you can make sure that the systems share the same bookmarks by exporting (from NLD) and then importing (from NLD) as needed. The import and export functions are available on the Bookmarks Manager's File menu.

75 Move and Edit Bookmarks

Occasionally, after you've accumulated a number of bookmarks you'll want to organize them in a way that makes them easy to find. You may want to edit the bookmarks so that their titles appear a certain way in your bookmark menu. This task will show you how to do this.

✔ **BEFORE YOU BEGIN**

73 Create a Bookmark
74 About Managing Bookmarks

CHAPTER 8: Browsing the World Wide Web with Mozilla Firefox

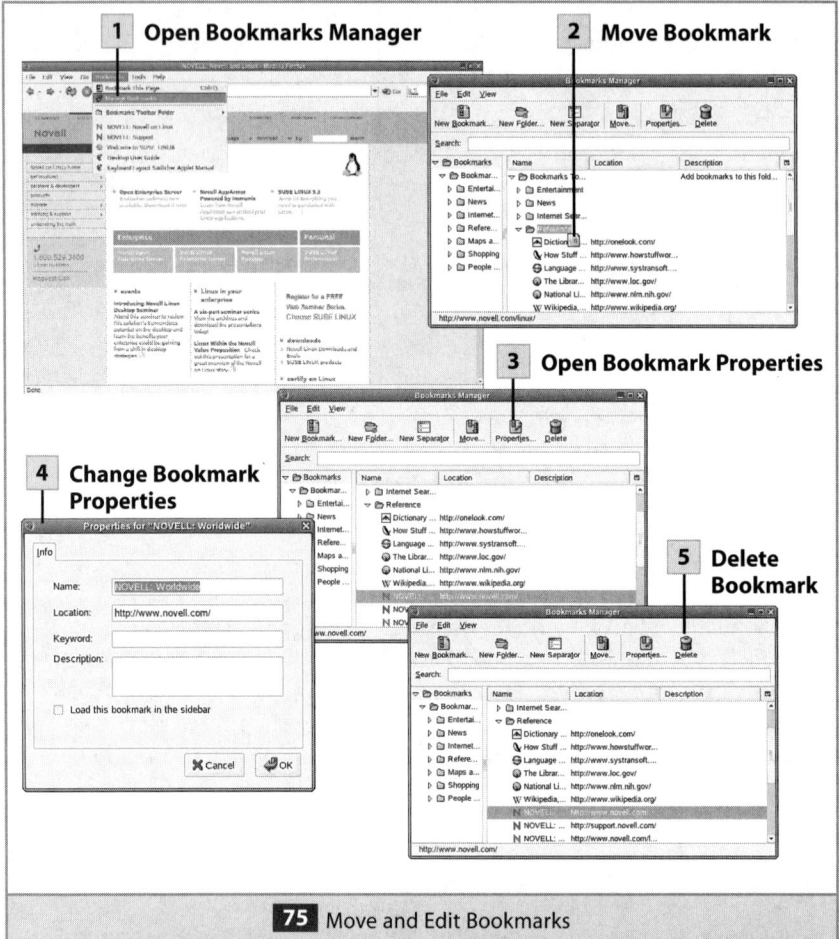

75 Move and Edit Bookmarks

1 Open Bookmarks Manager

From the Firefox window, select **Bookmarks**, **Manage Bookmarks**. The Bookmarks Manager opens.

2 Move Bookmark

Expand the Bookmarks Toolbar folder to view the "ready-made" folders provided by Firefox. To move a bookmark from the main folder to one of the toolbar folders (or from any folder to another folder), drag the bookmark to the new location.

TIP

If you don't like dragging the bookmarks around in the Bookmarks Manager window to move them, select a bookmark that you want to move and then click the **Move** button on the toolbar. The Choose Folder dialog box opens. Choose the folder that is the destination for the bookmark and then click **OK**.

3 Open Bookmark Properties

If you want to change the properties for a bookmark such as the bookmark text or the URL for the bookmark, select a bookmark and then select **Properties**. The Properties dialog box opens for that bookmark.

4 Change Bookmark Properties

Change the Name and Location information as needed. You can also enter keywords for the site and a description. After you have finished working with the bookmark's properties, click **OK**.

5 Delete Bookmark

To delete a bookmark, select the bookmark and then select the **Delete** button on the toolbar. The bookmark is removed from the list.

TIP

The Bookmarks Manager also makes it easy for you to add new separator lines between the folders and bookmarks in the Bookmarks list. Select a folder (a position) in the list and then select the **New Separator** button on the toolbar.

TIP

You can add new divider lines and folders directly to the Bookmarks list. Right-click on a bookmark and select the appropriate choice from the shortcut menu.

76 Sort Bookmarks

Depending on the number of bookmarks that you have, you might find it advantageous when you are working in the Bookmarks Manager to be able to sort the folders and bookmarks. You can sort these items alphabetically, by keyword, by description, and even by last visited. This ability to sort makes it easier to manage the bookmarks.

More importantly, you can sort bookmarks directly in the Bookmarks list when you are working in Firefox. This makes it easy to quickly find a bookmark by sorting the various folders and bookmarks alphabetically.

> **✓ BEFORE YOU BEGIN**
>
> **73** Create a Bookmark
> **74** About Managing Bookmarks
> **75** Move and Edit Bookmarks

1 Sort Items in the Bookmarks Manager

In the Bookmarks Manager select the **View** menu, then select one of the sort options such as Sorted by Name or Sorted by Last Visited. The folders and bookmarks within the folders are sorted using your sort choice. You can now manage the bookmarks as needed using the various Bookmarks Manager features. To close the Bookmarks Manager; click the **Close** button.

TIP

Sorting items in the Bookmarks Manager does not sort the bookmarks on the Bookmarks menu. You have to sort the menu items using the shortcut menu for a bookmark.

2 Sort Items on the Bookmarks Menu

When you are working in the Firefox window, select the **Bookmarks** menu; then point to a folder to open the list of bookmarks it contains. To sort the bookmarks alphabetically, right-click and select **Sort by Name**. The bookmarks in the folder are sorted by name.

77 About Cookies and Firefox

A cookie is an information file stored on your computer as a text file. Cookies can hold preference information for how you view and interact with a particular website. Cookies can also hold passwords and other personal information related to a particular website that you use.

77 About Cookies and Firefox

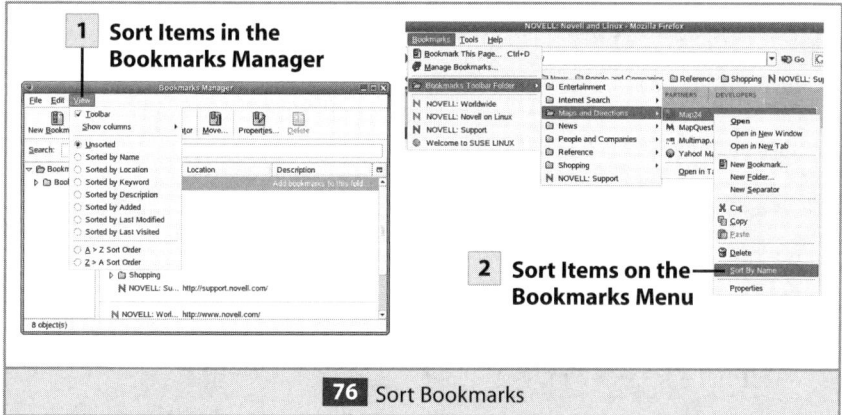

76 Sort Bookmarks

Cookies can't spread viruses or do bad things to your computer's hard drive. But some websites can use cookies to record your preferences and other information without you knowing it and then use it to show you certain advertisement content or bombard you with certain pop-ups. So, cookies can be annoying, but they certainly aren't a major threat to your system.

TIP

If you don't want to deal with nefarious cookies, you should stay off nefarious websites. The types of sites that you browse at home are one thing, but in a professional environment, stay away from sites of an unsavory nature (you'll have to decide what you consider unsavory).

In some cases a cookie is required to use a website. This is particularly true of sites that you subscribe to and that use a logon name and password to enter the site.

Firefox actually provides you with a lot of flexibility in dealing with cookies. You can create cookie rules and then accept or reject cookies on-the-fly as you browse the Web. By default Firefox is configured to accept all cookies. In some cases, blocking a cookie (or deleting a cookie from the cookie list) keeps a particular site from functioning correctly when you attempt to go to that site.

78 Accept and Reject Cookies

You can configure Firefox so that it allows you to accept and reject cookies from websites as you browse the Web. Cookie-related settings are configured in the Firefox Preferences dialog box.

> ✔ **BEFORE YOU BEGIN**
>
> 77 About Cookies and Firefox

1 Open Firefox Preferences

From the Firefox window, select **Edit, Preferences**. The Preferences dialog box opens.

2 Select Privacy Settings

In the Preferences dialog box, select the **Privacy** icon to view the cookie settings. Select the **Keep Cookies** drop-down list. To have the option to deny or select cookies as you browse, select **Ask Me Every Time**.

> **TIP**
>
> If you don't want to allow any cookies, clear the **Allow Sites to Set Cookies** check box. But be advised that disallowing cookies can make many websites, more than you would imagine, act oddly and in many cases unsatisfactorily.

3 Open Website Exceptions

If you want to negate your cookie settings for a few exceptions, click the **Exceptions** button. The Exceptions dialog box opens.

4 Enter Exceptions

Type a website URL in the Address of Web Site box and then select **Block, Allow for Session,** or **Allow**. These exceptions should be the antithesis of your main cookie settings (in the Preferences dialog), meaning that if you are blocking all cookies, some sites will be "allowed" to set cookies when you add them to the list and select **Allow**. After entering the exceptions, click **OK**.

You are returned to the Preferences dialog box. Click **OK** to save your preferences and return to the Firefox window.

78 Accept and Reject Cookies

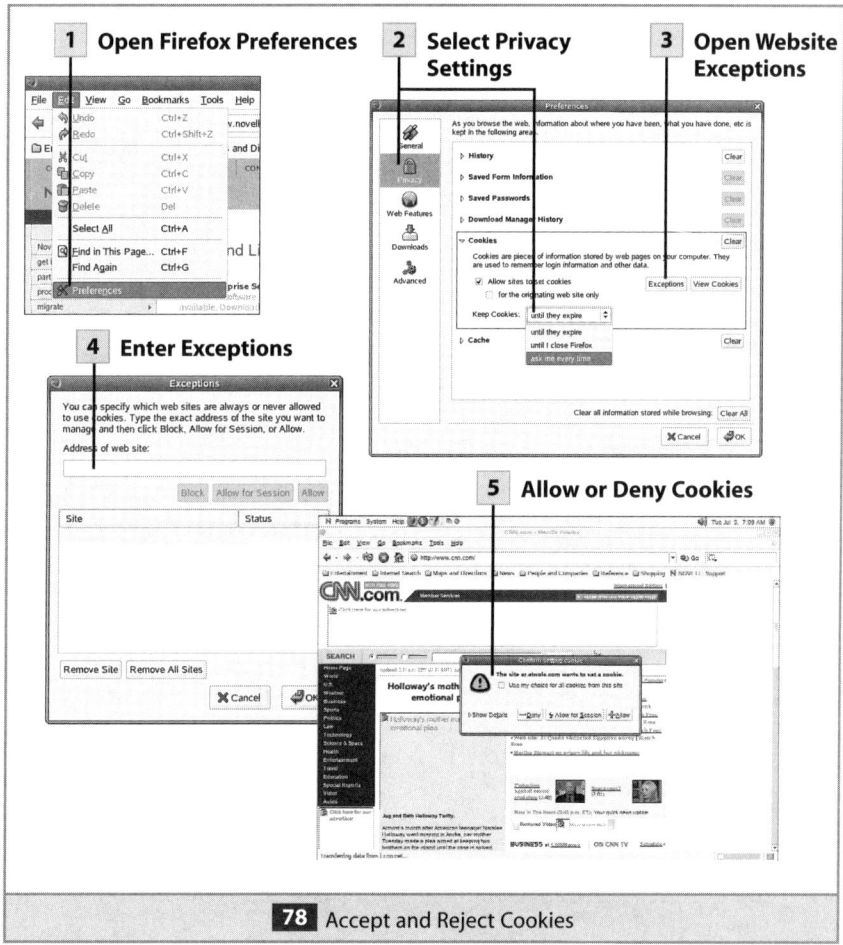

5 Allow or Deny Cookies

You can now browse the Web using your new cookie settings. If you selected the Ask Me Every Time cookie option, a Confirm Setting Cookie dialog box opens when a website attempts to set a cookie. Select either **Deny**, **Allow for Session**, or **Allow** as needed.

TIP

If you choose to be asked every time, you may find that you are clicking the Deny or Allow buttons a lot because many sites seek to set multiple cookies. Again, only block cookies if you feel (or your system administrator feels) that cookies pose a threat related to your personal or business information.

79 Manage Cookies

You can also view the cookies set on your system and delete selected cookies. If you want, you can delete all cookies and then choose to negate sites from setting cookies when you have previously deleted those sites' cookies from your system.

> ✔ **BEFORE YOU BEGIN**
>
> **77** About Cookies and Firefox
> **78** Accept and Reject Cookies

1 Open Stored Cookies Dialog

From the Privacy pane of the Firefox Preferences dialog box (select **Edit, Preferences, Privacy**), select the **View Cookies** button. The Stored Cookies dialog box opens.

2 Select and Delete Cookies

To delete a cookie, select the cookie and then select **Remove Cookie**. Repeat as necessary. If you want to remove all the cookies, select the **Remove All Cookies** button. If you want to keep sites from setting cookies after you have deleted the cookies from those sites, select the **Don't Allow Sites That Set Removed Cookies to Set Future Cookies** check box.

After you have viewed and/or deleted cookies, click **OK**. To close the Preferences dialog box, click **OK** again.

79 Manage Cookies

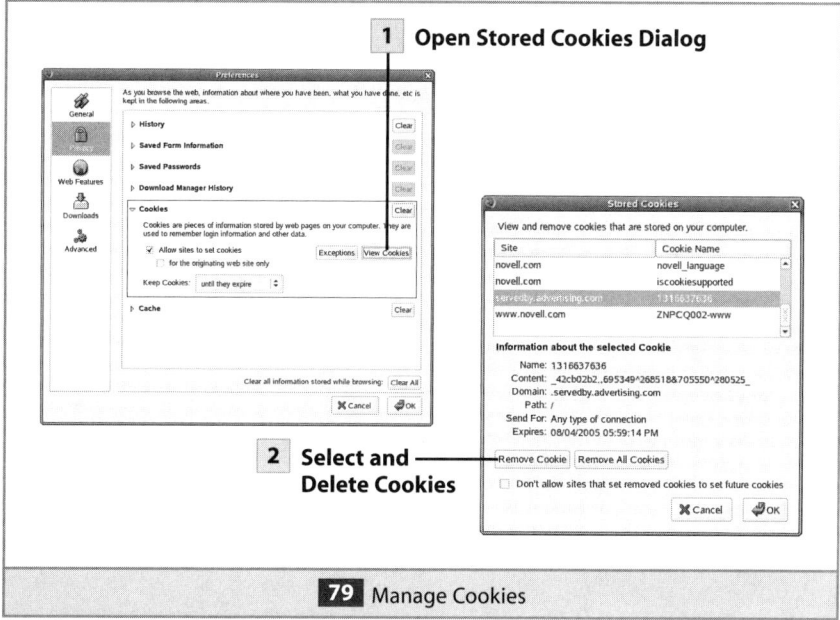

79 Manage Cookies

CHAPTER 9

Using Other Internet Tools

IN THIS CHAPTER:

- 80 About Internet Email Accounts
- 81 Configure an Email Client
- 82 About Instant Messaging
- 83 Configure Gaim Instant Messenger
- 84 Use Gaim Instant Messenger
- 85 About Internet Usenet Newsgroups
- 86 Configure the Pan News Reader
- 87 Use the Pan News Reader
- 88 About Other NLD Internet Communication Tools

CHAPTER 9: Using Other Internet Tools

The World Wide Web isn't the only communication medium that takes advantage of the Internet's infrastructure. In this chapter we look at some other strategies for communication on the Internet including email, instant messaging, and Internet newsgroups.

NLD comes with a number of Internet tools preinstalled. You can quickly get your email account up and running with Novell Evolution (a powerful email client and information manager). And NLD also offers the Gaim Instant Messenger, which can be used for instant messaging on a variety of IM platforms including AOL, ICQ, Jabber, Yahoo, and MSN. You can also take advantage of the wealth of information held in Usenet newsgroups by configuring and using the preinstalled Pan News Reader.

80 About Internet Email Accounts

→ SEE ALSO

- **144** Add an Email Account to Evolution
- **145** About Email and Evolution
- **146** Compose and Send Email

Electronic mail (email) has been available on the Internet since 1972, dating back to a time when the Internet was still called ARPAnet. Email is certainly one of the most widely used applications on the Internet.

To configure an email account you need to know certain things such as the names of the mail servers that you will use to send and receive email. And of course you need to know your email address and a password to access the email account.

If you work for an organization that maintains its own mail servers, your email account will typically be configured for you. If you are using NLD with an email only account through an Internet service provider, there are some things you need to know about to actually configure your account.

80 About Internet Email Accounts

NOTE

The type of email account that you have depends on the network environment that you work in. Home and small office users typically use Internet email accounts hosted by an Internet service provider. In a corporate environment your email account is a corporate account that also provides Internet email capabilities and is controlled by your organization; the organization typically has its own email servers (such as Novell or SUSE Linux mail servers) and system and network administrators that configure desktop computers and servers. In most corporate and institutional environments, your email account will be set up for you on your system. If you are an NLD home user or small office user, the information that you need to configure your Internet email account will be available from your Internet service provider.

The following list provides short descriptions of things you need to know to configure your own Internet email account:

- Email address—You need to know your Internet email address. Sometimes you are allowed to select this when you sign up with an Internet service provider. It takes the form of *username@company*.com. Where the *username* would be your email account username and the information that follows the "at" (@) sign is the domain name for the Internet service provider that is supplying you with the account.

- Email account password—Email is a secure service and so it is password protected. You need to know the password for your email account.

- SMTP server name—SMTP (Simple Mail Transport Protocol) allows you to send your email. So, you need to know the domain name (friendly name) of your provider's SMTP server. It is typically in a format such as *smtp-server*.mail.*company*.com.

- POP3 server name—Mail that is sent to you is held on a POP (Post Office Protocol) server, until you download the email to your computer (using your email client). You need to know the POP3 server name, which will be in a format such as *pop-server*.mail.*company*.com.

KEY TERM

SMTP server—The server that accepts your email when you send an email. The SMTP server then passes the email on to its final destination.

KEY TERM

POP3 server—The server that acts as the post office and holds your received email until you download them to your computer using your email client.

NOTE

There is also another mail server type called an IMAP (Internet Message Access Protocol) server. An IMAP server can take the place of a POP3 server as the post office for your received mail. IMAP allows you to leave mail on the server (even after you access it) and store the mail in folders on the server. This is useful for people on the go who may access their mail from different devices such as computers, handheld personal assistants, or email-ready cell phones. IMAP allows you to see all your email messages you received no matter what device you are using.

It goes without saying that you have to be connected to a corporate network that supports email or have an Internet connection to take advantage of Internet email. One thing that I did not mention that you need is an email client. NLD provides Novell Evolution as the default email client, and it is installed when NLD is installed on your computer. It is Evolution that you will configure for corporate and/or Internet email accounts.

81 Configure an Email Client

To configure an email account you must supply email account and password information. You must also enter information related to the mail servers that handle your outgoing and incoming email.

You configure your email client the first time that you start Evolution. Other email accounts can be added to Evolution as needed.

✔ BEFORE YOU BEGIN	→ SEE ALSO
80 About Internet Email Accounts	144 Add an Email Account to Evolution

1 Open the Evolution Setup Assistant

From the NLD desktop, select the **Evolution** icon in the top panel. The Evolution Setup Assistant window opens. To bypass the introductory screen of the Assistant, select **Forward**.

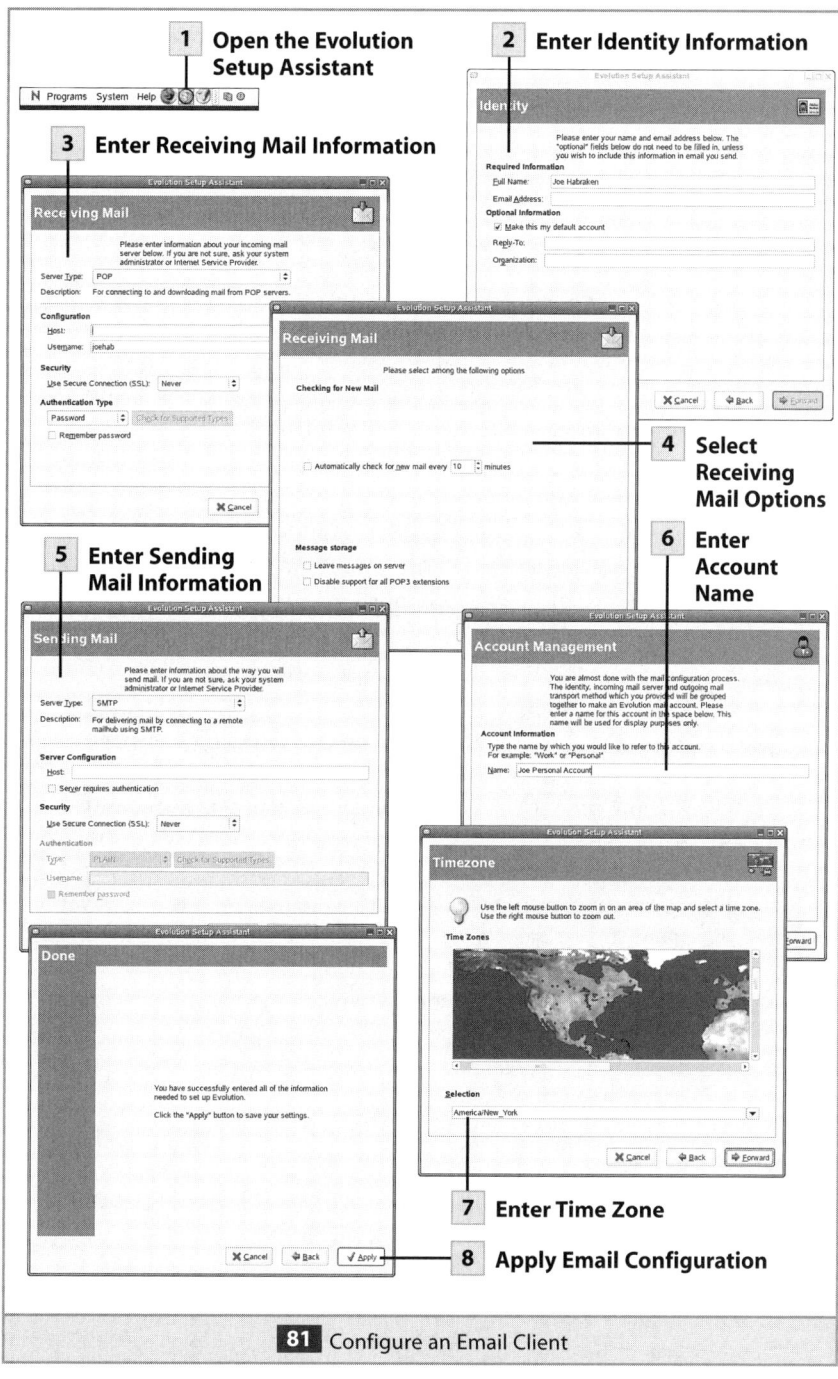

2 Enter Identity Information

On the Identify Information screen enter your name and email address. You can also enter optional reply to and company information that will be included on all your sent emails. After entering the information, select **Forward**.

3 Enter Receiving Mail Information

The next screen requires that you enter information related to receiving mail. Select the **Server Type** drop-down box and select the type of server that you use to receive mail (POP, IMAP, and so on). You also need to enter the hostname for the server (the domain name such as *pop-server*.mail.*company*.com or variation) in the Host box and your username in the Username box (this will be the name that precedes the @ sign on your email account).

To select the authentication type, use the Authentication Type drop-down box. In most cases (particularly for Internet email), this selection will be **Password**. After entering the appropriate information select **Forward** to continue.

NOTE

When you configure the Receiving Mail options for your email account, there is an optional Security drop-down box. This drop-down box allows you to select whether a secure connection should be used when you connect to your post office mail server. You can select: Always, Whenever Possible, or Never from the drop-down list. Because your account information and password are sent to the mail server, when you connect to receive your mail, you may want to take advantage of a secure connection (which makes it more difficult for someone snooping on the network to capture your account information). Check with your network administrator or Internet service provider to determine whether you can configure your email account to take advantage of this security feature.

TIP

You won't actually enter your email account password until you send email for the first time from Evolution. If you want Evolution to remember the password (after you enter it), select the **Remember Password** check box.

4 Select Receiving Mail Options

On the next screen select the **Automatically Check for New Mail** check box if you want to have Evolution periodically check for new mail. Use the minute's spinner box to set the time frame for the automatic checks. Select **Forward** to continue.

5 Enter Sending Mail Information

On the next screen you enter information related to sending mail. Select the **Server Type** drop-down list to select the server type for sending mail (SMTP being the most likely). In the Host box type the name of the server (such as *smtp-server*.mail.*company*.com; this is information you need from your network administrator or ISP). After entering the information, select **Forward** to continue.

NOTE

In some cases mail servers for sending mail will require password authentication for you to connect. Parameters for authentication can be set on the Sending Mail screen of the Evolution Setup Assistant. This is information that you must get from your network administrator or Internet service provider).

6 Enter Account Name

On the next screen enter the name that you want to use to refer to this account. This name is up to you and should be descriptive, particularly in cases where you have multiple accounts. Type the name in the Name box and then select **Forward** to continue.

7 Enter Time Zone

On the next screen you enter your time zone. Select the **Selection** drop-down list and choose your time zone. Select **Forward** to continue.

8 Apply Email Configuration

You have entered all the information necessary to configure an email account. Select **Apply**. The Assistant window closes, and Evolution opens. You can close Evolution by selecting the **Close** button.

CHAPTER 9: Using Other Internet Tools

82 About Instant Messaging

Instant messaging is becoming one of the most popular communication platforms on the Internet. It allows real-time messaging between individuals and groups of individuals.

Instant messaging is not brand new to the Internet, however. As early as the 1980s Internet Relay Chat (IRC) has been available on the Internet and provides a venue where users can conduct conversations on a predetermined channel. IRC does not provide the privacy that newer instant messaging (IM) platforms provide where you can talk to a single individual.

A number of IM platforms and client software packages are available for use on the Internet. There is AOL Instant Messenger, MSN (Microsoft) IM, ICQ, and Jabber. All these platforms function similarly. You use client software to determine whether a "buddy" is online and then you can chat with him using a text window. Some IM platforms now provide support for voice and video communication and provide the capability to transfer files between users.

NLD provides the Gaim Instant Messenger (preinstalled on your system), which is an open source IM client that can be used for AOL, MSN, ICQ, Jabber, Yahoo, and other IM accounts. To use Gaim you must have already signed up for an account on the platform you want to use. For example, if you are going to use Gaim for AOL Instant Messenger, you need to have an AOL IM account.

WEB RESOURCE

AOL IM: www.aim.com
ICQ IM: www.icq.com
MSN IM: www.msn.com
Yahoo IM: www.yahoo.com
Jabber IM: www. jabber.com (for open source software, www.jabber.org)

You need an IM account to use Gaim for instant messaging. Check out these websites to establish an account.

NOTE

Jabber is both an open source and a proprietary IM platform. An open source server and open source clients can be used to configure a Jabber communication network either on a corporate network or on the Internet. Mention Jabber to your network administrator if you want to earn a few points. It has a lot of possibilities for inexpensive and secure real-time communication within a corporation. Check out http://www.jabber.org for more information.

83 Configure Gaim Instant Messenger

Gaim is a multiplatform IM client. You need to have an IM account (or accounts) prior to configuring and using Gaim.

1 Open Gaim

From the NLD desktop, select **Programs**, **Internet**, **Instant Messenger**. The Gaim Login and Accounts window opens.

2 Open Add Account Dialog

In the Accounts window (which is empty), select the **Add** button. The Add Account dialog box opens.

TIP

If you have more than one IM account (on different platforms), you can add multiple accounts to the Gaim configuration.

3 Add Account Information

You can now add your IM account information. Select the **Protocol** drop-down list to select the IM protocol (AIM/ICQ, Jabber, Yahoo, and so on). Enter your screen name, password, and alias in the appropriate box. If you want to have Gaim remember the password select the **Remember Password** check box.

TIP

You can also configure Gaim to auto-login to your IM account when you start Gaim. Select the **Auto-login** check box when you configure the IM account. To keep your Gaim session open as you work on your desktop (without the Gaim window open), select the **Preferences** button in the Gaim window. In the Preferences dialog box, select **Plugins** and then select the **System Tray** icon. Select the **Hide New Messages Until Tray Icon Is Clicked** check box.

4 Save Account

After you have added your account information, select the Save button. You are returned to the Gaim Login and Accounts windows. If you do not need to enter any additional accounts, close the Accounts window.

CHAPTER 9: Using Other Internet Tools

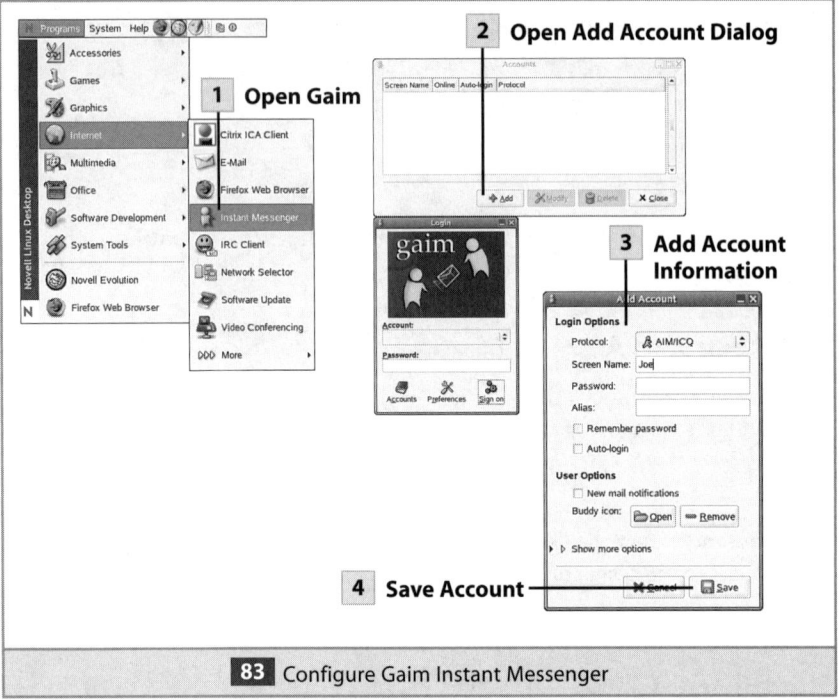

83 Configure Gaim Instant Messenger

84 Use Gaim Instant Messenger

After you have added an IM account to Gaim, you can use Gaim for instant messaging. If you added multiple IM accounts, the Gaim Login window provides a drop-down list that allows you to select the account you want to use for your IM session.

✔ **BEFORE YOU BEGIN**

83 Configure Gaim Instant Messenger

1 Log On to IM Session

In the Gaim Logon window (select **Programs**, **Internet**, **Instant Messenger**), select the **Account** drop-down list to select the account you want to use (enter password if necessary). Select **Sign On** to begin the IM session.

84 Use Gaim Instant Messenger

84 Use Gaim Instant Messenger

2 Open IM Window

After you are connected, the Buddy List appears. Select a buddy from your list and select **IM**. The IM window for that buddy opens.

TIP

To list a buddy (or buddies) in the Buddy List, select **Buddies**, **Add Buddy**. Enter the name and alias to add the buddy to the list. Repeat as necessary to build your buddy list.

3 Exchange Messages with Buddy

Type your text messages in the lower message pane and then select **Send**. Messages from you and to you from the buddy appear in the upper message pane. Exchange messages as needed. To end the session, close the Message window.

209

CHAPTER 9: Using Other Internet Tools

TIP

To add emoticons to your messages, select the **Insert Smiley** icon and select an icon to place in your current message. You can also send files to your buddy; use the **Send File** icon at the bottom of the Message window.

85 About Internet Usenet Newsgroups

Usenet newsgroups have been available on the Internet since 1979. However, they are a mystery to most Internet users, who primarily use the World Wide Web for information gathering.

Usenet is a network of news servers that allow users to post information in a variety of categories. Posts can be read using a news reader and you can also post replies to existing posts. New posts on a subject can also be created using a news reader.

NLD provides the Pan News Reader. It is an easy to configure and use news reader that also provides you with the ability to post your own news items. To use a news reader such as Pan you must have access to a news server. So, if your company does not provide access to newsgroups, you won't be able to take advantage of Pan. Most Internet service providers do provide access to a news server. To configure Pan you need the name of the news server that you will connect to.

NOTE

Usenet provides a lot of information on technical issues related to computers and software including NLD and Linux. Usenet also contains a lot of unsavory information and probably should not be used in an environment where children also have access to the computer. And I do mean "unsavory."

86 Configure the Pan News Reader

The default newsreader in NLD is the Pan Newsreader which provides a nice graphical interface for searching, browsing, and reading Usenet Newsgroups.

✔ **BEFORE YOU BEGIN**

   85 About Internet Usenet Newsgroups

86 Configure the Pan News Reader

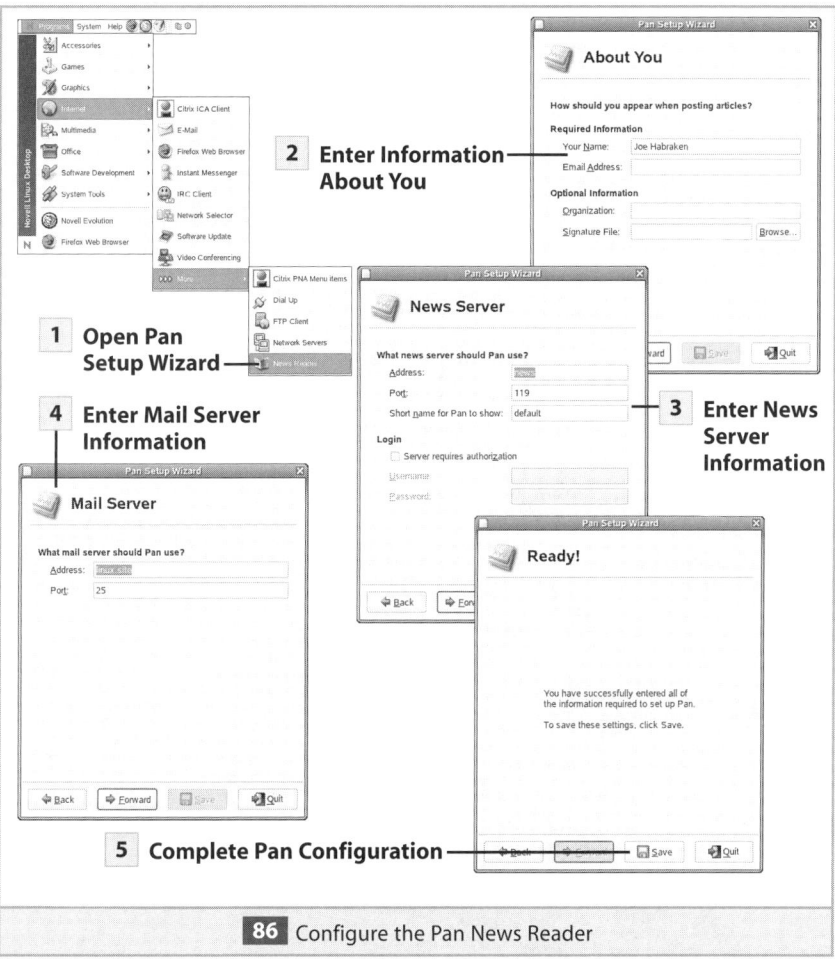

86 Configure the Pan News Reader

1 Open Pan Setup Wizard

From the NLD desktop, select **Programs**, **Internet**, **More**, and then select **News Reader**. The Pan Setup Wizard opens. Select **Forward** to bypass the initial wizard screen.

2 Enter Information About You

On the next wizard screen enter information about you including your name and email address. This information appears when you post an item to a newsgroup. If you do not want your email address to appear with posts do not enter an email address. Select **Forward** to move to the next wizard screen.

3 Enter News Server Information

On the next wizard screen enter the news server name. It will be in a format such as news-server.company.com. This is information that you must get from your network administrator or Internet service provider. If your server requires authorization (most do not) select the **Server Requires Authorization** check box and then enter the Username and Password. Select **Forward** to continue.

4 Enter Mail Server Information

On the next wizard screen enter the email server information. This would be the SMTP server information that you use to configure your Evolution email account. Select **Forward** to continue.

5 Complete Pan Configuration

The final wizard screen appears; select **Save**. The Pan News Reader window opens.

---

87 Use the Pan News Reader

After you have configured Pan, you can view posts in newsgroups. You locate posts by having Pan download a list of newsgroups on the news server. The first time Pan opens, a dialog box allows you to download a list of groups.

> ✔ **BEFORE YOU BEGIN**
>
> 85 About Internet Usenet Newsgroups
> 86 Configure the Pan News Reader

1 Download List of Newsgroups

In the Pan window (select **Programs**, **Internet**, **More**, and then **News Reader**) select the **Servers** menu and then select **Get List of all Groups**. A list of newsgroups appears on the left pane of the Pan window. If this is the first time that you have used Pan since configuring the software, click **Yes** in the download message box to download the group list.

87 Use the Pan News Reader

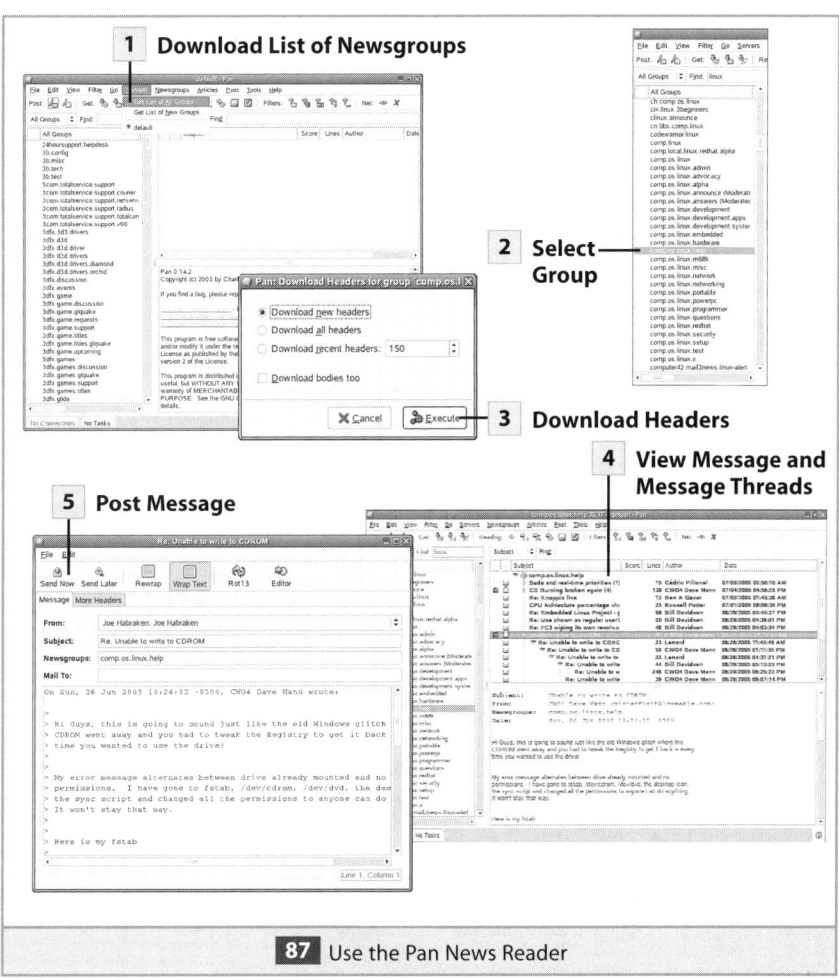

NOTE

If Pan cannot provide a list of groups, you may not have configured the mail server information correctly. In the Pan window select **Tools**, **News Servers**. Use this dialog box to edit or add the correct information for your news server.

2 Select Group

Scroll through the list of groups (there are a lot of them) and then select the group you want to open and view posts that the group contains. The Download Headers for Group dialog box opens.

> **TIP**
>
> To filter the list of groups by a keyword, type the keyword in the **Find** box and then press **Enter**. This shows you a subset of the group list based on the keyword.

3 Download Headers

In the **Download Headers for Group** dialog box new headers will be downloaded (meaning the titles of recent posts to the group). If you want to download a greater (or fewer) number of posts, select the **Download Recent Headers** option button and use the number drop-down list to specify a number. Then select **Execute**.

4 View Message and Message Threads

To view a post, select the post in the upper pane of the post list. To view threads (responses) to the post, double-click the expand button to the left of the post. The contents of the currently selected post appear in the bottom pane of the Pan window.

5 Post Message

To post a message as a follow-up to the currently selected post, select the **Followup to Newsgroup** icon on the Pan toolbar (the second button from the left). Or if you want to post a new message (not related to the current post), select the **Post to Newsgroup** button (the first button on the toolbar). In either case a new post window opens.

Enter the text for your post in the message area of the Post window. If you are creating a new post (not related to a current post) enter a subject for the post. After entering the post information, select the **Send Now** button, and the post will be sent. It may take some time (depending on the news server) for your post to appear in the group.

After you have finished browsing groups and posts and finished posting your own messages, select the **Close Window** button to close the Pan window.

> **TIP**
>
> As you browse through the various groups, you will find groups that you want to access often. Right-click on the group in the group list and select **Subscribe**. The group is marked with a subscribe icon. You can quickly find your subscribed groups in the group list. Select the **All Groups** drop-down list and select **Subscribed**. Only your subscribed groups appear in the group list.

88 About Other NLD Internet Communication Tools

NLD offers other Internet communication tools that you can use. These tools include an Internet Relay Chat client, a videoconferencing client, and an FTP client.

Internet Relay Chat (IRC) is the grandfather (or grandmother if you prefer) of Internet chat platforms. Users log on to IRC channels, which are discussion groups that allow real-time conversations between the participants in that channel.

IRC provides channels for many subject areas. It is actually a good place to gather information about computers, gardening, or just about anything else. However, like Usenet, some channels will definitely make you blush, and you may want to avoid the channels that offend your sensibilities (which you have to decide).

To use IRC (select **Internet** and then **IRC Client**), you connect to a network (there are many IRC networks, such as Dalnet). After you are connected to a network, you can select a channel and participate in a chat on that channel.

The X-Chat IRC client allows you to participate in IRC channel chats.

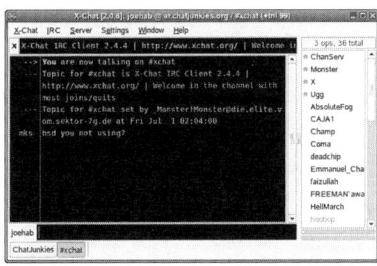

NOTE

IRC channels are moderated by owner of that channel (the person who originated the channel). They have the ability to knock users out of the channel for inappropriate behavior. So, behave.

Another Internet tool provided by NLD is the GnomeMeeting voice and videoconferencing software. This software allows you to do voice and videoconferencing over the Internet using a microphone and an optional USB webcam (or other camera configuration).

GnomeMeeting provides the ability to communicate via text, voice, or video over the Internet. In terms of voice communication, connect a microphone to

215

CHAPTER 9: Using Other Internet Tools

your system and then run the GnomeMeeting Configuration Druid, which runs the first time you start GnomeMeeting or can be started from the Edit menu.

In terms of configuring GnomeMeeting for videoconferencing, USB webcams can be a problem because many manufacturers of these small USB cameras don't provide support for the Linux platform. You can attempt to use the Configuration Druid to get your video camera running. If it does not work, you need to do some research on the Web, and you may be able to get GnomeMeeting up and running with your webcam or other video camera. Start you research at wwww.gnomemeeting.org.

Another tool that you may need in certain circumstances is the gFTP client. FTP or File Transfer Protocol is the protocol used to download and upload files on the Internet. Web browsers such as Firefox have FTP capabilities built in, so most of the time you don't necessarily need an FTP client. However, if you need to access an FTP server that requires a username and a password to download or upload files, you need an FTP client such as gFTP.

The gFTP client allows you to access FTP sites that require a username and password.

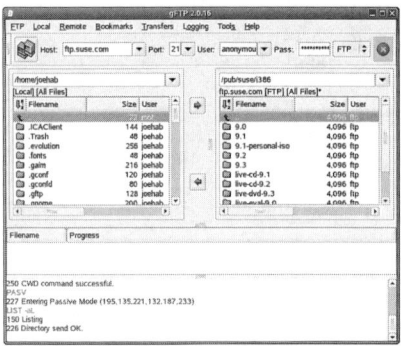

To use gFTP (select **Programs**, **Internet**, **More**, and then **FTP Client**), you need to know the URL for the FTP site (typically ftp://sitename.com) and your username and password. All three of these items are entered in the gFTP window. You can then connect to the site and view the folders and files available on the site. The gFTP site provides a number of bookmarked FTP sites that you can explore using gFTP (select a site from the **Bookmarks** menu).

PART III

Using Productivity and Collaboration Software

10 Working with OpenOffice.org Applications 219

11 Creating Documents with OpenOffice.org Writer 237

12 Creating Spreadsheets with OpenOffice.org Calc 273

13 Creating Presentations with OpenOffice.org Impress 301

14 Managing Email and Contacts with Novell Evolution 331

15 Staying Organized with Novell Evolution 367

16 Using Novell iFolder 391

CHAPTER 10

Working with OpenOffice.org Applications

IN THIS CHAPTER:

- 89 About OpenOffice.org
- 90 Start OpenOffice.org Applications
- 91 Configure OpenOffice.org Global Options
- 92 About Sharing Documents with Microsoft Office Users
- 93 Start a New File
- 94 Save a Document
- 95 Open an Existing Document
- 96 Get Help in OpenOffice.org

CHAPTER 10: Working with OpenOffice.org Applications

Most of us end-users spend our time on the computer working with a variety of software tools that allow us to create documents, spreadsheets, and presentations. An easy-to-use and powerful set of productivity applications is really a must. NLD provides OpenOffice.org, an integrated and complete software suite of productivity applications.

This chapter takes an introductory look at OpenOffice.org. Our discussion includes global configuration options and issues related to sharing files with Microsoft Office users.

89 About OpenOffice.org

OpenOffice.org is an open source, cross-platform suite of productivity applications. OpenOffice.org includes applications that allow you to create documents, spreadsheets, presentations, and drawings. The NLD OpenOffice.org installation, which has been adapted for NLD by Novell, includes the following applications:

- Writer—A powerful document processor that allows you to create every possible type of document from simple letters to brochures to complex reports that contain data from the other OpenOffice.org applications. Writer also makes it easy to create tables of contents and indexes and provides autocomplete and autoformat options that make it easy to create any document quickly.

- Calc—A spreadsheet application that provides all the tools that you need to create invoices, balance sheets, and budgets and chart the data in a variety of chart formats. Calc also provides advanced tools for "What If" analysis of data and provides a number of wizards to help you work with more advanced analysis features.

- Impress—An application that allows you to create simple slideshows and advanced multimedia presentations that include pictures, sound, and other multimedia content such as video. Impress also provides drawing and diagramming tools that allow you to create an impressive array of highly informative slides for your presentations.

- Draw—A drawing tool that allows you to create simple and complex drawings to include in your OpenOffice.org documents, spreadsheets, and presentations. Draw is particularly useful for creating flowcharts and other complex diagrams.

90 Start OpenOffice.org Applications

NOTE

At the time of the writing of this book, OpenOffice.org version 1.1.4 was the most recent "stable version" of this application suite. A version 2 is in the works and will include a database application. Because Novell has "fine-tuned" the version of OpenOffice.org that accompanies NLD, it is unclear when version 2 will be available for NLD and which applications will be included in newer versions of the suite.

The OpenOffice.org applications use an XML (eXtensible Markup Language) file format as the default format when you save a document or other file in one of the Open.Office.org applications. OpenOffice.org embraces XML as the default file format because XML files can readily be opened by a variety of applications. Because OpenOffice.org is open source, the developers of the application suite chose a default file format that is also open and nonproprietary.

KEY TERM

XML—XML or eXtensible Markup Language was developed by the World Wide Web Consortium and is a markup language that allows for the creation of extended tags (a tag language like HTML). It provides a universal file format that can be embraced by many different types of applications.

Because the OpenOffice.org applications share a number of tools and a common interface, you will find that the learning curve for taking advantage of more advanced features in the applications is fairly flat; meaning that you will be up and running in all the applications in no time. Let's take a look at how you start the various applications and then we can look at configuring OpenOffice.org options.

90 Start OpenOffice.org Applications

The OpenOffice.org applications (Write, Calc, Impress, and Draw) can be opened from the Programs menu. You can also launch one of the applications from the window of any of the other applications by selecting a new file that requires that application. For example, if you are in Write, you can select **File**, **New** from the menu and start a new spreadsheet, which opens Calc.

✔ **BEFORE YOU BEGIN**

89 About OpenOffice.org

CHAPTER 10: Working with OpenOffice.org Applications

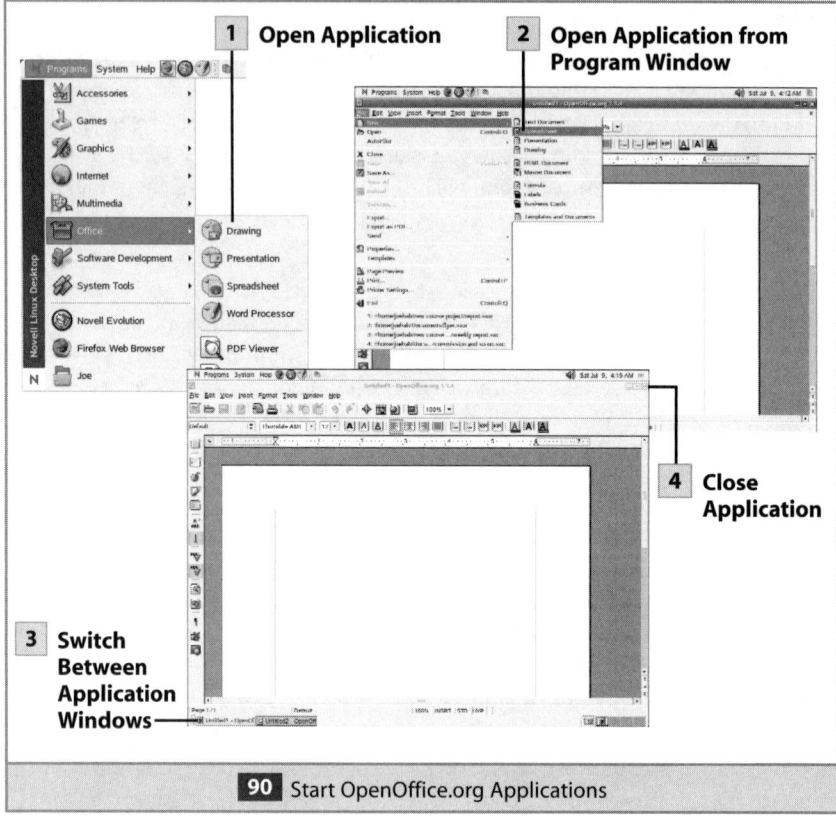

90 Start OpenOffice.org Applications

1 Open Application

From the NLD desktop, select **Programs**, **Office** from the menu. Select one of the application icons to start the appropriate application: **Drawing**, **Presentation**, **Spreadsheet**, or **Word Processor**. A new application window opens.

TIP

You can quickly start Writer using the **Word Processor** icon provided in the top panel of the NLD desktop.

2 Open Application from Program Window

You can also open a new drawing, presentation, spreadsheet, or document window from any of the OpenOffice.org applications. From within one of the application windows, select **File**, **New**, and then select **Text Document**, **Spreadsheet**, **Presentation**, or **Drawing**. A new application window opens for the OpenOffice.org application that creates the document type that you chose on the New submenu.

3 Switch Between Application Windows

You can quickly switch between application windows open on the NLD desktop. Select the icon for the application window you want to switch to on the desktop's lower panel.

TIP

If you have multiple application windows open on the NLD desktop and want to keep all the applications open but clear up your workspace, right-click on the bottom panel icon for any open application window. On the shortcut menu select **Move to Another Workspace** and then select one of the workspaces listed. This keeps the application window open but moves it to another of the virtual workspaces provided by NLD. To switch between workspaces, use the icons on the far right of the bottom panel.

4 Close Application

After you have completed working with an application, select the **Close** button for that window (or select **File**, **Exit**). Make sure that you save any changes to the current document if alerted when closing the application.

91 Configure OpenOffice.org Global Options

You can configure a number of global options that affect all the OpenOffice.org applications. These global options include user data (such as your name and other information), the view settings for the applications, the folder paths for graphics and your saved files, and appearance settings such as colors and boundaries.

✔ **BEFORE YOU BEGIN**

89 About OpenOffice.org

→ **SEE ALSO**

96 Get Help in OpenOffice.org

CHAPTER 10: Working with OpenOffice.org Applications

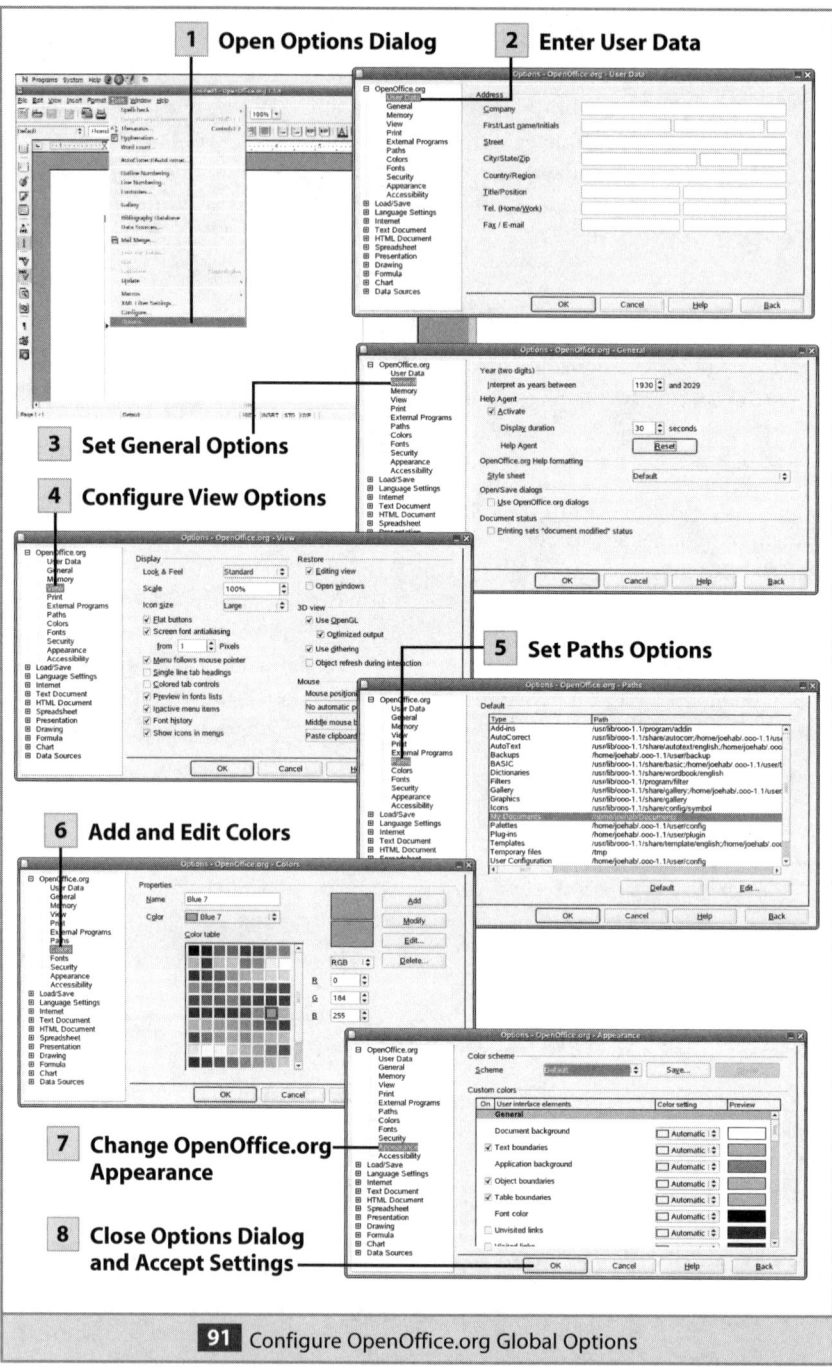

91 Configure OpenOffice.org Global Options

91 Configure OpenOffice.org Global Options

1 Open Options Dialog

From any of the OpenOffice.org application windows, select **Tools**, **Options**. The Options dialog box opens. To view all the global options, expand the OpenOffice.org category (double-click on **OpenOffice.org**) in the left pane of the dialog box.

NOTE

Other global options include security, printing, and external program options. You may want to leave these settings at the default as you begin your explorations of the various applications. The Options dialog box also provides access to settings for languages, text documents, spreadsheets, and presentations. These settings allow you to fine-tune the look and the features of the individual applications such as Writer and Calc. I would suggest that you begin using the applications with specific settings at the default (feel free to edit the global settings excluding security, print, and external programs). You can then fine-tune settings specific to an application or document type as you become more familiar with the OpenOffice.org applications.

2 Enter User Data

Select the **User Data** option. Enter the information including name, address, and so on. This information is used by the OpenOffice.org applications when you use a template to create a letter or send a fax or email directly from one of the applications.

3 Set General Options

Select the **General** options. These settings relate to the date, the Help Agent, and the document status. The date information is best left at the default. The Help Agent is also enabled by default (the Help Agent provides context-sensitive help as you perform certain tasks in OpenOffice.org). If you do not want to use the Help Agent, clear the Help Agent **Activate** check box. If you want documents to require that you save changes after printing, select the **Printing Sets "Document Modified" Status** check box.

4 Configure View Options

Select the **View** options. To change the look and feel of OpenOffice.org, select the **Look and Feel** drop-down list and select Macintosh, X Window, or OS/2 (the standard uses the default NLD view settings). Set other view options by selecting or clearing the appropriate check box (such as the heading or font options). If you want to set mouse positioning settings (where the mouse pointer automatically appears in a dialog box), select the **Mouse Positioning** drop-down list and select **Default Button** or **Dialog Center** (no automatic positioning is the default).

TIP

If you need help setting a particular option, select the **Help** button in the Options dialog box.

5 Set Paths Options

Select the **Paths** options. All the path options are determined when OpenOffice.org is installed on your computer (when NLD is installed). Use caution when changing the paths for any of the items other than Graphics or My Documents. OpenOffice.org may not operate properly if you do. To change the default location for saving and opening files, select **My Documents** and then **Edit**. The Select Path dialog box opens. Browse for the new path and then click **OK**. The new path appears in the Options dialog box.

6 Add and Edit Colors

Select the **Colors** option. You can add colors to the color palette or edit existing colors (for use in your applications as fill colors, frame colors, or font colors). To add a new color, type a name in the Name box and then click **Add** (you then need to modify the color). To modify the new color or an existing color, select the **Modify** button and then specify the Red (R), Green (G), and Blue (B) mix for the color using the color spinner boxes. If you want to delete a color, select the color in the Color drop-down list, and then select **Delete**. Click **Yes** to delete the color.

TIP

You can switch from RGB colors to CMYK colors. Select the **RGB** drop-down list and select **CMYK**. You can now "mix" colors using the Cyan, Magenta, Yellow, and Black spinner boxes.

7 Change OpenOffice.org Appearance

Select the **Appearance** option. General settings and more specific settings (such as settings for text documents and spreadsheets) are available in this option dialog box. Use the check boxes to enable or disable an appearance setting such as Text Boundaries or Table Boundaries. To change the color and appearance setting for one of the enabled options (such as Text Boundaries), select the drop-down list to the right of the option and make a selection from the list (Automatic is the default setting for all options).

8 Close Options Dialog and Accept Settings

After you have made your selections for the various global options provided in the Options dialog box, click **OK** to close the dialog box and accept the new settings.

92 About Sharing Documents with Microsoft Office Users

OpenOffice.org makes it easy for you to share documents, spreadsheets, and presentations with users of Microsoft Office (Word, Excel, and PowerPoint). You can save your OpenOffice.org files in a format that can be opened by a Microsoft Office application. For example, you can save your Writer documents in a Word document format.

OpenOffice.org can save files in Microsoft Office file formats.

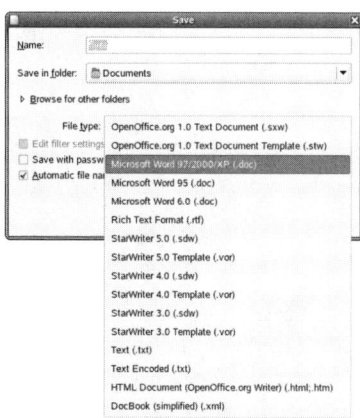

CHAPTER 10: Working with OpenOffice.org Applications

You can also email documents, spreadsheets, and presentations directly from one of the OpenOffice.org applications (select **File**, **Send** from an OpenOffice.org application window). An option is provided that attaches the document in a Word or Excel format. This means that the recipient of the email can immediately open the sent file in the Microsoft Office application required.

In cases where you must open a file created in Microsoft Office, you can open the file in the appropriate OpenOffice.org application immediately. Just select **Open** from the OpenOffice.org application's Function bar and then browse to locate the file and then open it. OpenOffice.org opens the document, spreadsheet, or presentation without a hitch. You can then save changes that you make to the file in the original Microsoft Office format or use Save As to save the document in the native OpenOffice.org XML file format.

93 Start a New File

You can start a new blank document, spreadsheet, or presentation from the OpenOffice.org File menu or from the **New** button on the Function bar. You can also start new documents or presentations based on a template. For example, you can quickly create business cards or mailing labels by choosing one of these options from the New submenu. You can also select from two presentation templates in the Templates and Documents dialog box (opened from the New submenu).

> ✔ **BEFORE YOU BEGIN**
>
> 90 Start OpenOffice.org Applications

1 Open New Blank Document

From any of the OpenOffice.org application windows, select the **New** button on the Function bar. The new document opens.

2 Open New File from New Menu

You can also open a new document, spreadsheet, presentation, or drawing from any of the OpenOffice.org applications. Select **File**, **New** from the menu. On the New submenu, select the type of file that you want to create (such as Text Document, Spreadsheet, and so on). If the new file is not the type of file created in the current application, a new application window opens (with the appropriate application) for the new document.

93 Start a New File

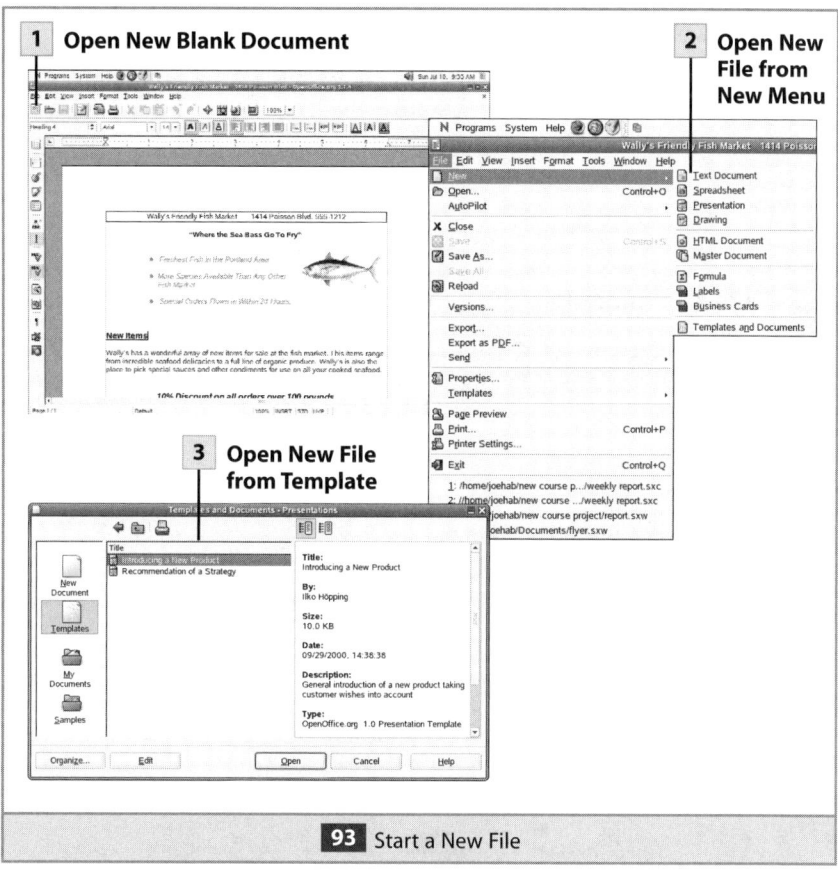

93 Start a New File

NOTE

The OpenOffice.org applications share a common interface. The top toolbar in the application window is the Function bar. It provides quick access to commands that allow you to open and save documents. The toolbar below the Function bar is the Object bar. It allows you to add formatting attributes to text and other items such as bold and italics. It also provides alignment commands such as Center. The vertical toolbar on the left of the application window is the Main toolbar. It provides quick access to tools such as Spell Check and allows you to insert objects into a file such as charts, Math objects (using OpenOffice.org Math), and floating frames.

3 Open New File from Template

From the New submenu (select **File**, **New**), select **Templates and Documents**. This opens the Templates and Documents dialog box. To create a new Impress presentation from one of the templates provided (such as Introducing a New Product), select the template and then click **Open**.

94 Save a Document

After you have started a new document and entered some information, you will want to save your work. The first time you select the Save command the Save As dialog box opens.

> ✔ **BEFORE YOU BEGIN**
>
> 90 Start OpenOffice.org Applications
> 93 Start a New File

1 Open Save As Dialog

From any of the OpenOffice.org application windows, select **File**, **Save**. The Save dialog box opens.

TIP

You can quickly save a new document by using the **Save Document** button on the Function bar.

2 Enter Filename

Enter a new name for the file in the **Name** box.

3 Select Path

The default path for saving your files is the Documents folder (in your Home folder). To choose a different folder, select the **Browse for Other Folders** link. You can then select a folder as the path.

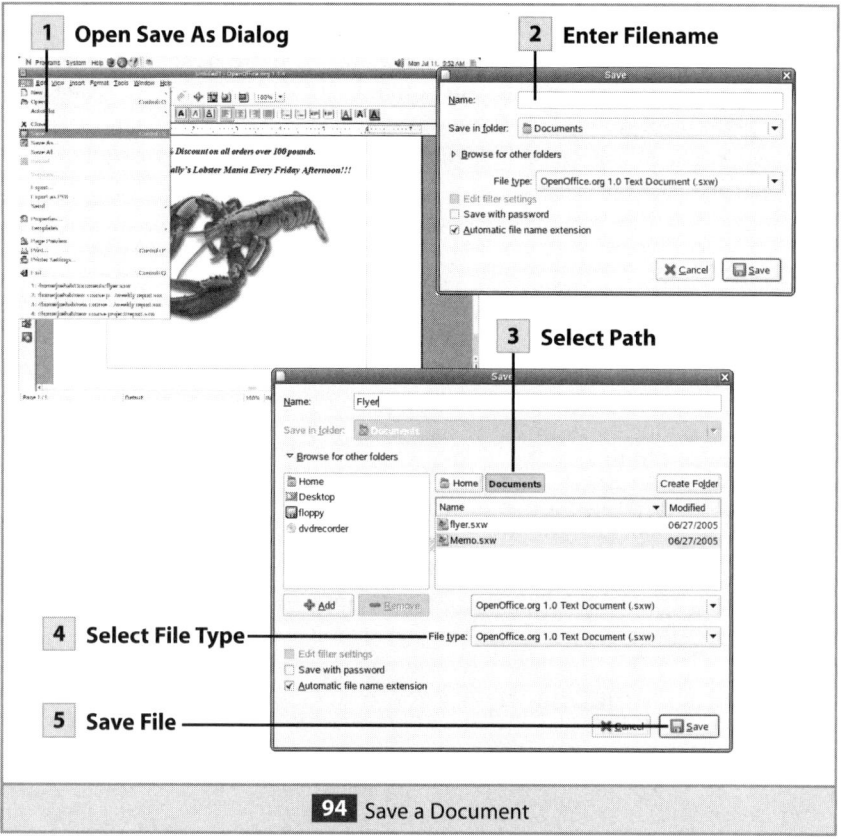

4 Select File Type

OpenOffice.org saves your new files in the default OpenOffice.org file formats. If you want to change the file format for this saved file, select the **File Type** drop-down list and select a new format.

5 Save File

After you have entered a name and made other selections related to the file, click the **Save** button to save the file.

> **TIP**
>
> After you have saved the document, you can quickly save changes that you make as you work; select the **Save Document** button on the Function bar. If you want to change the name, location, or file type of a previously saved document, select **File, Save As**. Enter the new filename and other information in the Save As dialog box and then click **Save**.

95 Open an Existing Document

To read or edit an existing document you must first open it from the appropriate applications.

> ✔ **BEFORE YOU BEGIN**
>
> 90 Start OpenOffice.org Applications
> 93 Start a New File
> 94 Save a Document

1 Access Open Dialog

From any of the OpenOffice.org application windows, select **File, Open**. The Open dialog box appears.

> **TIP**
>
> You can quickly open a file using the **Open File** button on the Function bar.

2 Select File

Use the folder icons provided (double-click to open a folder or location in the left pane) to locate the file that you want to open and then select the file in the file list.

> **TIP**
>
> The Open dialog box browses for all document types. If you want to browse for only one file type, such as text documents or spreadsheets, select the **File Type** drop-down list and select one of the file types provided. This filters the file list by that file type.

96 Get Help in OpenOffice.org

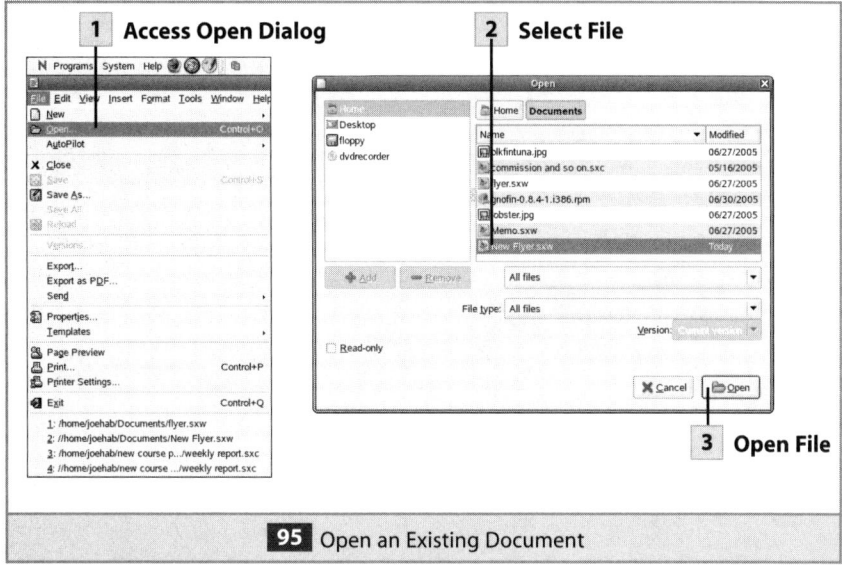

95 Open an Existing Document

3 Open File

To open the file, select the **Open** button.

TIP

You can also open your OpenOffice.org files (and any files for that matter) using Nautilus. Open Nautilus (select **Programs**, **Accessories**, **File Manager**) and browse for the file. After you have located the file, double-click it to open the file in the appropriate OpenOffice.org application.

96 Get Help in OpenOffice.org

There will be times when you need to get help as you work in the OpenOffice.org applications. OpenOffice.org supplies three different features that help you get your work done.

First, the Help system allows you to browse the Help contents and search for help on specific topics. Second, the Help Agent, provides context-sensitive help on a particular task or feature. Third, OpenOffice.org provides tips for all the buttons on the various toolbars. You can expand these tips for increased information by selecting **Help**, **Extended Tips** from the menu.

CHAPTER 10: Working with OpenOffice.org Applications

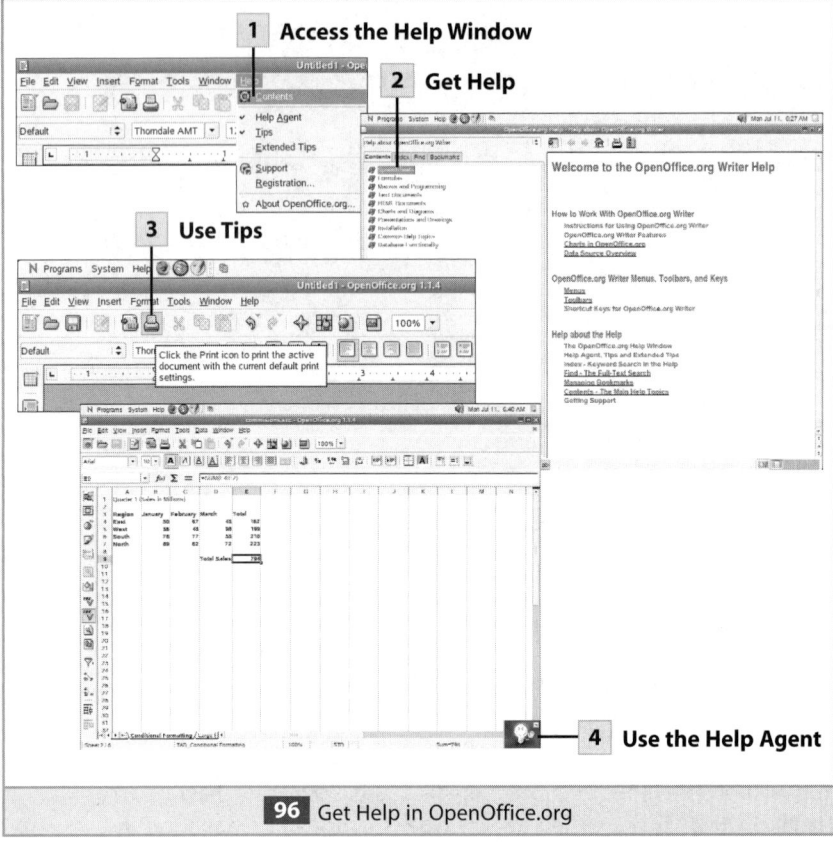

96 Get Help in OpenOffice.org

1 Access the Help Window

To open the Help window, select **Help, Contents** from the menu.

2 Get Help

To browse the topics in the Help window double-click on a "book" in the left pane of the Help window. To open a particular topic, double-click that topic. The topic appears in the right pane of the Help window.

To search the index by keywords, select the **Index** tab on the left pane of the Help window. Type keywords to search the index. To open a topic in the Index list (which appears in the left pane based on your keywords), double-click that topic.

To search the Help contents by search terms, select the **Find** tab. Type keywords in the Search term box and then select **Find**. To view a found topic, double-click any of the topics that appear as a result of your search.

TIP

To bookmark a help topic, right-click on the topic and then select **Add to Bookmarks**. You can then access this topic at any time by selecting the **Bookmarks** tab in the Help window.

3 Use Tips

Place the mouse pointer on any of the toolbar icons to view a tip for that tool. If you have enabled Extended Tips on the Help menu, you will receive an extended tip for your tools.

4 Use the Help Agent

The Help Agent provides context-sensitive help as you perform certain tasks. As you work in an application, the Help Agent appears in the lower right of the application window. Click the Help Agent and the Help window opens, displaying help on the feature that you are currently using.

CHAPTER 11

Creating Documents with OpenOffice.org Writer

IN THIS CHAPTER:

- 97 About OpenOffice.org Writer
- 98 Use the AutoPilot to Create a Document
- 99 Format Characters
- 100 Format Paragraphs
- 101 About Writer Styles
- 102 Use the Stylist
- 103 Create a Paragraph Style
- 104 Insert Headers, Footers, and Page Numbers
- 105 Use Format Page Options
- 106 Move Text
- 107 Insert a Table
- 108 Insert a Text Frame
- 109 Place Graphics in a Document
- 110 Do a Mail Merge
- 111 About Printing in Writer
- 112 Print a Document

CHAPTER 11: Creating Documents with OpenOffice.org Writer

The most frequently used application on any system would have to be the word processor. In this chapter we take a closer look at OpenOffice.org Writer. Writer is a complete document processor and desktop publishing application that makes it easy to create a variety of document types.

97 About OpenOffice.org Writer

Writer provides all the features and tools that you would expect from a word processing application. You can add headers/footers to documents, insert tables, insert frames that hold a variety of objects, and merge addresses with form letters and labels.

You can start Writer from the Programs menu (select **Programs**, **Office**, **Word Processor**). You can also start Writer from the **Word Processor** icon on the top panel.

Writer's command set is easily accessed from the menu system in the Writer application window. Writer also provides both default and optional toolbars that allow you to quickly access a particular feature. The default toolbars are

- Function bar—This toolbar resides below the menu system and provides access to commands such as New, Open File, and Print File Directly. It also provides access to specialized tools such as the Navigator (which allows you to quickly move to a specific place in a document such as a table or text frame) and the Stylist (which provides easy access to the styles in the current document).

- Object bar—This toolbar resides below the Function bar and by default provides access to commands related to formatting such as font, font size, alignment, and numbered and bulleted lists. When you select a button on the Main toolbar such as Show Draw Functions, the formatting tools on the Object bar are replaced with a set of drawing tools.

- Main toolbar—This toolbar is the vertical toolbar on the left of the Writer window. It provides quick access to a number of features including the Insert Table and Insert Object commands and the Spell Check feature.

You can customize any of the toolbars. Right-click to the right of the Function bar or Object bar and select **Customize** from the shortcut menu. The Customize dialog box allows you to add or remove buttons from a selected toolbar.

97 About OpenOffice.org Writer

The Writer toolbars provide quick access to a number of commands and Writer features.

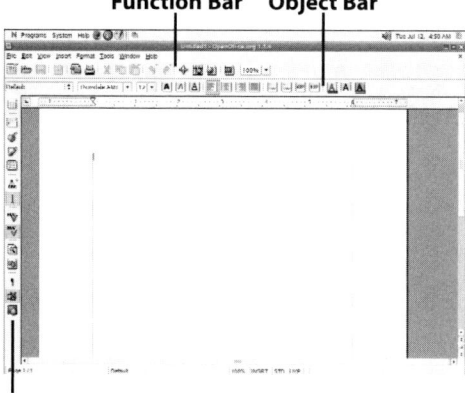

Function Bar **Object Bar**

Main Toolbar

You can customize the Writer toolbars.

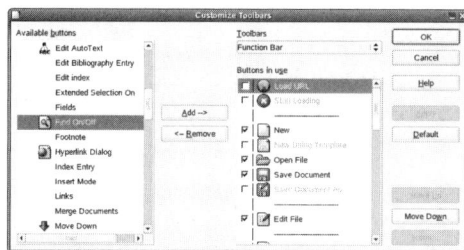

The best way to navigate a multipage document is with the Navigator. It allows you to quickly jump to a particular object in a document such as a heading, frame, table, or graphic. It also provides a page spinner box that allows you to move quickly to any page in the document. The Navigator is opened using the **Navigator** button on the Function bar.

TIP

You can also open the Navigator by selecting the **Navigator** button on the vertical scrollbar, which also provides Next Page and Previous Page buttons.

CHAPTER 11: Creating Documents with OpenOffice.org Writer

Use the Navigator to move to a particular page or object in your document.

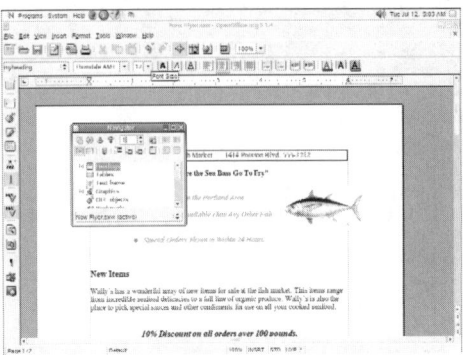

NOTE

Because the OpenOffice.org applications share a common interface, you can also apply the things that you learn as you use Writer, such as customizing toolbars, to the other application windows.

98 Use the AutoPilot to Create a Document

One of the easiest ways to create a new document and have Writer walk you through the various steps of creating that document is to use the AutoPilot. The AutoPilot allows you to create "specialty" documents such as agendas, memos, and reports. The AutoPilot walks you through each step as you create the document.

✔ **BEFORE YOU BEGIN**

97 About OpenOffice.org Writer

1 Start AutoPilot for New Document

From the Writer window (select **Programs**, **Office**, **Word Processor**), select **File**, **AutoPilot**. Select one of the AutoPilot documents such as **Memo**.

98 Use the AutoPilot to Create a Document

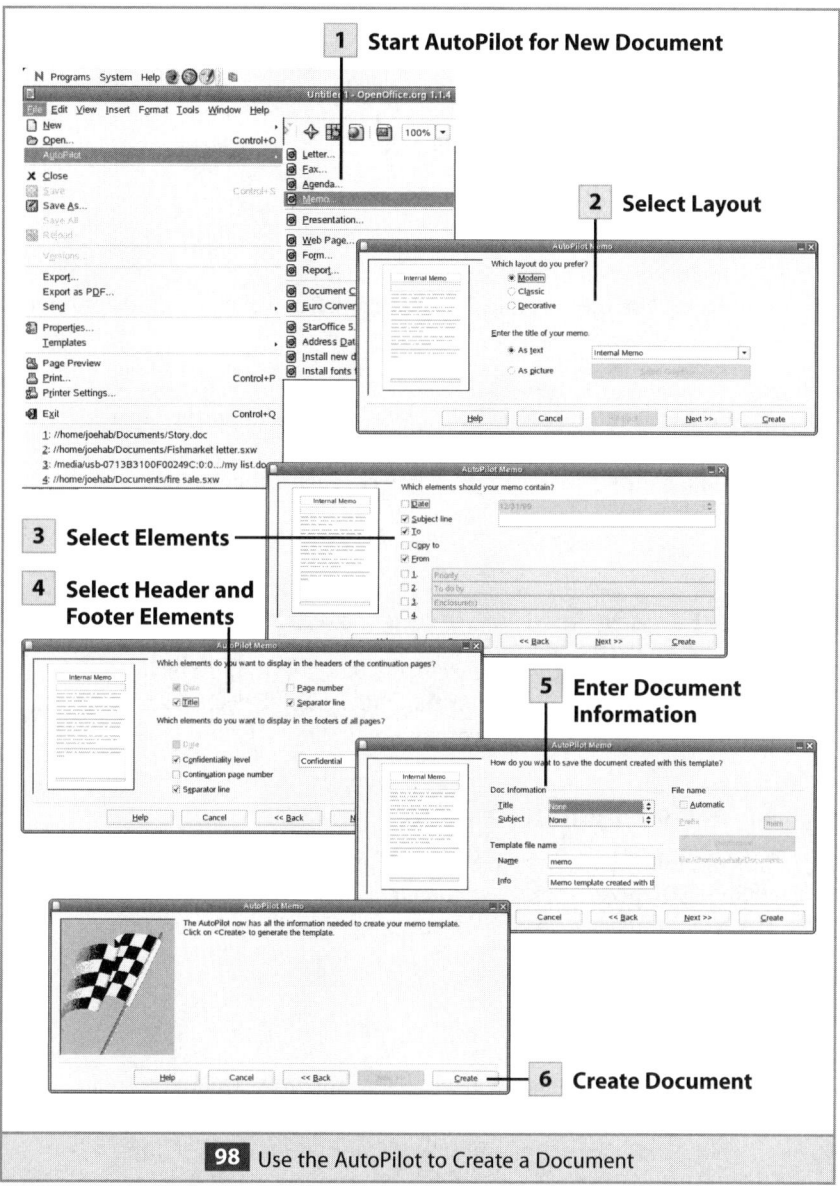

NOTE

The steps provided by the AutoPilot vary for the different document types (such as fax, agenda, memo, and so on). The steps provided here show how to create an AutoPilot memo.

2 Select Layout

On the first AutoPilot screen select a layout for the new document (in this case a memo). Use the drop-down list to select a title for your memo (you can also use a graphic as the title). Then select **Next** to continue.

3 Select Elements

On the next screen select the elements that you want to include in the document. Use the check boxes as needed. Then click **Next** to continue.

> **TIP**
>
> The AutoPilot documents take advantage of the personal information that you entered in the OpenOffice.org global settings. To enter your name and other information, go to the Options dialog box (select **Tools, Options**). Enter your information under User Data.

4 Select Header and Footer Elements

On the next screen select the elements that you want to include in the header and footer of the document (the memo). Select check boxes as needed. Then click **Next** to continue.

5 Enter Document Information

Enter the document information such as title and subject. Check the **Automatic** check box to save the file using the title information. You can choose a destination for the file using the **Destination** button. Click **Next** to continue.

6 Create Document

The last screen provided by the AutoPilot appears. Click **Create** to create the document. The document appears in the Writer window including the various elements that you selected during the AutoPilot process. Additional text to be entered will be marked by placeholder text. Select the placeholder text and type the required text (such as the body of the memo) to complete the document.

TIP

Remember to save your document by selecting the **Save Document** button on the Function bar.

99 Format Characters

Formatting text characters can be done on-the-fly as you type or edit using the font formatting commands on the Object bar. You can also change character formatting attributes in the Character dialog box.

✔ **BEFORE YOU BEGIN**

97 About OpenOffice.org Writer

1 Select Text

Select the text that you want to format in the document. Click and drag to select text, double-click to select words, or triple-click to select lines.

TIP

You can toggle the various font attributes buttons on the Object bar on and off as needed as you type, if you want. Typically, it is almost faster to format the text after the fact, after you have typed your rough draft.

2 Select Font Attributes from Object Bar

After the text is selected, select a character formatting attribute from the Object bar such as **Font**, **Bold**, **Italics**, and so on. You can also use the **Font Color** button to change the font color.

TIP

Place the mouse on any button on the Object bar for a tip related to that button. If you want to see more information, select **Help, Extended Tips**. This provides more detailed tips for the various toolbar buttons.

CHAPTER 11: Creating Documents with OpenOffice.org Writer

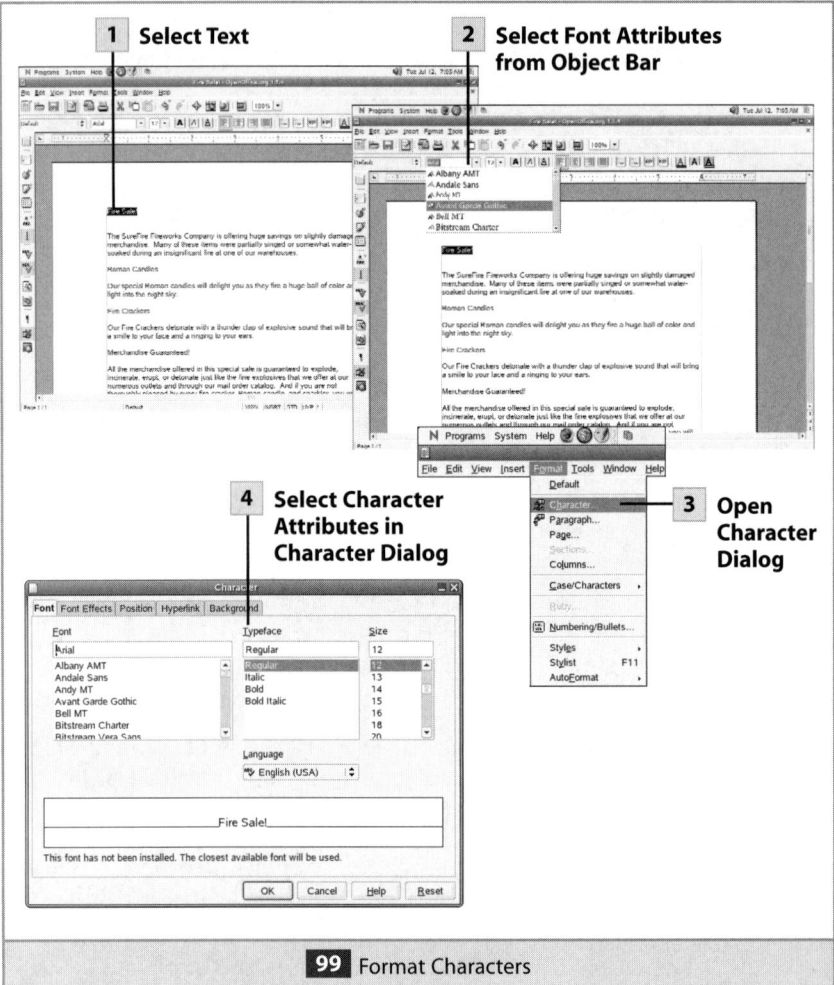

99 Format Characters

3 Open Character Dialog

To have access to all the font attribute and alignment possibilities for selected text you can use the Character dialog box; select **Format**, **Character**. The Character dialog box opens.

4 Select Character Attributes in Character Dialog

In the Character dialog box, set character attributes such as font, font size, and typeface on the **Font** tab.

100 Format Paragraphs

To change font color and add attributes such as underlining, select the **Font Effects** tab. This tab also provides character effects such as all capitals and embossing.

To make the selected text superscript or subscript, select the **Position** tab and select the appropriate options. On this tab, you can also change the spacing for the selected text and rotate text.

To add a background to the selected text, select the **Background** tab. Select a color for the background. When you have finished working in the Character dialog box, click **OK**.

100 Format Paragraphs

You can change paragraph formatting attributes using buttons on the Object bar, such as the alignment buttons—Align Left, Centered, and Align Right. You can also increase and decrease the indent for the paragraph. To control paragraph attributes such as line spacing, numbering attributes, and border formats, you need to access the Paragraph dialog box.

> ✔ **BEFORE YOU BEGIN**
>
> **97** About OpenOffice.org Writer

1 Select Paragraph

Select the paragraphs that you want to format in the document (if you are formatting only one paragraph, place the cursor in that paragraph). If you want to format all the paragraphs in the document, select **Edit**, **Select All**.

2 Select Paragraph Formatting

To change the paragraph formatting for the selection, select a button on the Object bar such as the **Increase Indent** button (or an attribute such as a numbered or bulleted list).

NOTE

We normally think of paragraphs as several sentences, but every line followed by a line break (the Enter key) is really a paragraph in terms of formatting attributes particularly when you use the numbered or bulleted list formats.

CHAPTER 11: Creating Documents with OpenOffice.org Writer

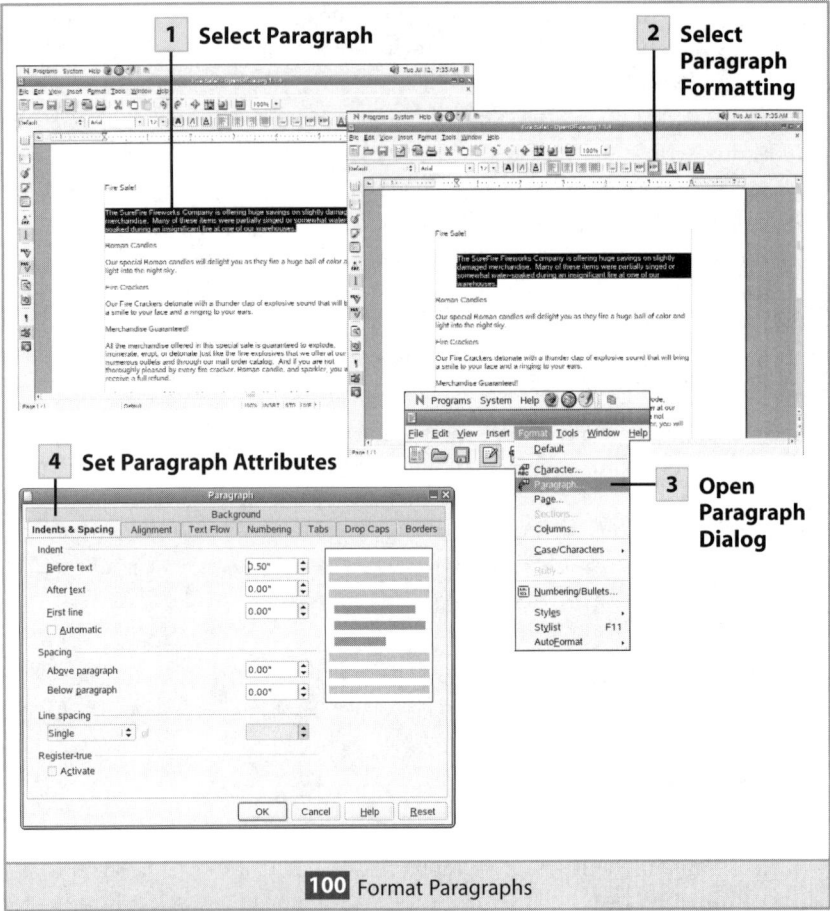

100 Format Paragraphs

3 Open Paragraph Dialog

To access additional paragraph formatting attributes, you need to open the Paragraph dialog box. Select **Format**, **Paragraph**. The Paragraph dialog box opens.

4 Set Paragraph Attributes

On the Indents & Spacing tab set the indent, spacing before and after, and the line spacing for the paragraph as needed.

Select the **Alignment** tab. Set the alignment for the selected paragraph (or paragraphs) by selecting the **Left**, **Right**, **Center**, or **Justified** option buttons.

101 About Writer Styles

TIP

The Numbering tab allows you to control the numbering in your numbered lists. You can choose to start at a certain number or restart a numbered list with the current paragraph.

To set border options for the paragraph or paragraphs, select the **Borders** tab. Select one of the line arrangements to enable borders or use the user-defined grid to specify your own line arrangement (click in the grid to place a line). Use the Style list to select a style for the border. To set a color for the border lines use the Color drop-down list. When you have finished selecting your paragraph formatting settings, click **OK**.

TIP

You can set tabs for the selected paragraph or paragraphs on the Tabs tab of the Paragraph dialog box. However, it is easier to create tabs directly on the Writer ruler. With a paragraph or paragraphs selected, select the tab type on the far left of the ruler (the default tab type is Left) and then click on the ruler at the position where you want to place the tab. Every paragraph (meaning every line followed by a line break) can have its own unique tab settings.

101 About Writer Styles

When you are working with a document that requires that you use the same set of character or paragraph formatting attributes on text throughout the document, you will want to take advantage of styles. A style is a grouping of formatting attributes identified by a style name.

KEY TERM

Style—A collection of formatting attributes that have been saved under a style name.

For example, you may be formatting a number of headings that use the same font size, color, and alignment (perhaps all the headings are centered). You can create a style (a paragraph style) that contains these formatting elements and then assign it to your various headings as needed.

Writer styles are cataloged and assigned using the Stylist. The Stylist allows you to quickly switch between style types and add new styles as needed. So, you can take advantage of a number of premade styles, and you can create your own styles.

Two of the most commonly used styles are character and paragraph styles. A character style is used to assign formatting attributes to a word. For example, you might want to bold and italicize terms that show up in a document. All you have to do is click on the word and then assign the character style from the Stylist.

> **KEY TERM**
>
> ***Character style***—A collection of saved character formatting attributes used to format words in a document.

> **KEY TERM**
>
> ***Paragraph style***—A collection of both character and paragraph formatting attributes that have been saved under a style name.

Paragraph styles allow you to combine paragraph attributes, such as alignment, and character formatting attributes. You can then assign the style to an entire paragraph of text by clicking inside the paragraph and selecting the style from the Stylist.

The great thing about styles is that you can assign them as needed. And then if you decide that you don't like the way a particular style looks in the document, you can edit the style and change the formatting attributes it assigns to text. All the text that was previously assigned the style will be updated to the edited version of the style. Bottom line: Styles save you a lot of time when you are creating documents that use a lot of formatting.

> **NOTE**
>
> Writer also provides additional style types other than character and paragraph styles. There are frame styles (used for different types of frames depending on the object inside a frame), page styles (a first page style can be used to format a first page without headers and footers in the rest of the document), and numbering styles (can be used to format numbered lists with different looks).

102 Use the Stylist

The Stylist provides a number of predefined styles including character and paragraph styles. The Stylist can be opened by selecting the **Stylist** button on the Function bar.

✔ BEFORE YOU BEGIN

101 About Writer Styles

1 Open Stylist

Select the **Stylist** button on the Function bar to open the Stylist.

TIP

You can dock the Stylist. Hold down the **Ctrl** key and drag the Stylist to the left side of the Writer window. The Stylist will be docked to the left of the Main toolbar. To undock the Stylist hold down the **Ctrl** key and drag the Stylist (by the top of the Stylist pane) back onto the Writer application window.

2 Select Word or Paragraph

Place the cursor (click the I-beam) in the word or paragraph that you will assign the style to. To assign a style to multiple words or paragraphs select the words or paragraph.

3 Assign Style

Double-click a style in the Stylist to assign it to the text or paragraph.

TIP

Use the buttons on the top left of the Stylist to switch between the different types of styles available such as character and paragraph.

CHAPTER 11: Creating Documents with OpenOffice.org Writer

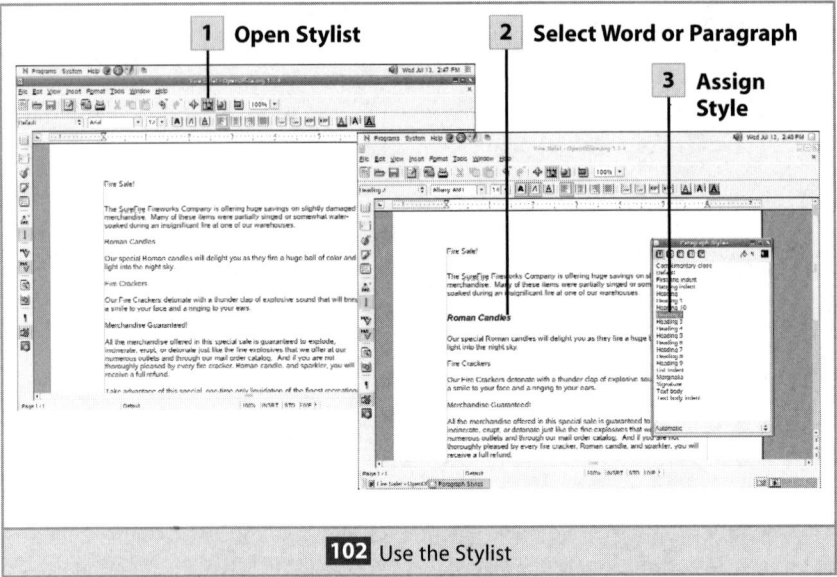

102 Use the Stylist

103 Create a Paragraph Style

You can create your own styles, which are then added to the Stylist for easy access. Styles can quickly be created by formatting text or paragraphs and then creating a new style based on the current formatting of selected text or paragraphs.

Paragraph styles, which are often the most useful style to create, can contain both font attributes and paragraph attributes such as alignment. So, you can create your own heading styles or special paragraph styles and then apply them as needed.

✔ **BEFORE YOU BEGIN**

101 About Writer Styles
102 Use the Stylist

1 Format Paragraph

Format a paragraph with character and paragraph formatting attributes as needed.

103 Create a Paragraph Style

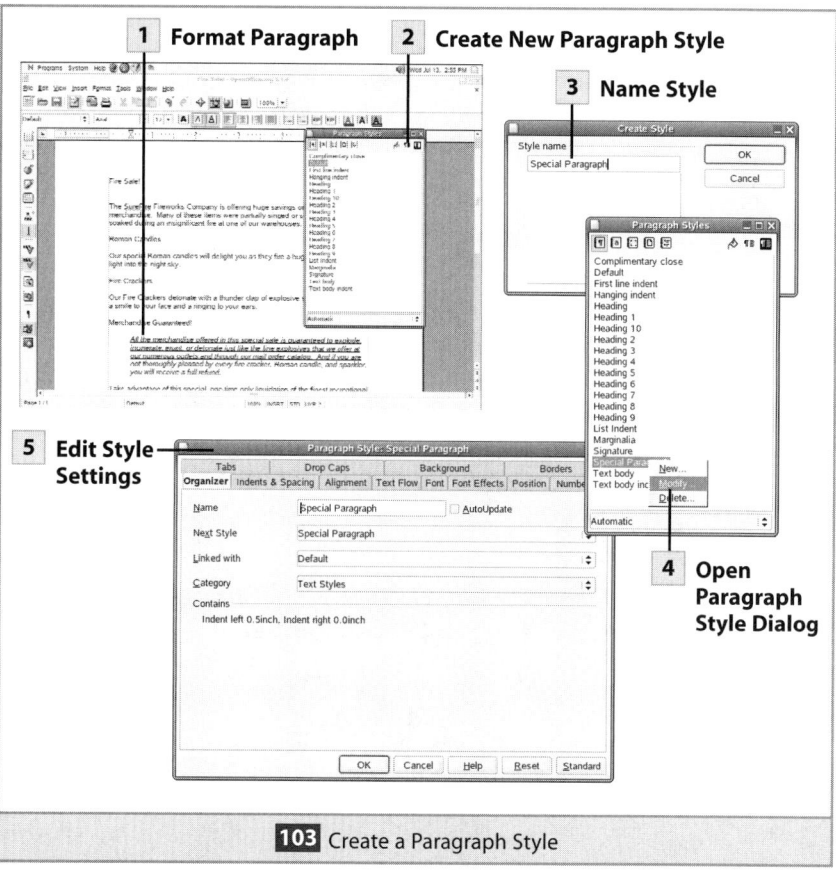

103 Create a Paragraph Style

2 Create New Paragraph Style

In the Stylist window (select the **Stylist** button on the Function bar if the Stylist is not open), select the **New Style from Selection** button. The Create Style dialog box opens.

3 Name Style

Type a name for the style in the Create Style dialog box; then click **OK**. The new style appears in the Stylist's style list. You can now assign the style to other paragraphs as needed.

251

CHAPTER 11: Creating Documents with OpenOffice.org Writer

4 Open Paragraph Style Dialog

You can edit the various formatting options for a style that you have created. Right-click on the style in the Stylist's style list and select **Modify**. The Paragraph Style dialog box opens.

5 Edit Style Settings

Use the various tabs in the Paragraph Style dialog box to change the formatting options for the style. After you have completed your changes, click **OK**. You can now assign the edited style to text in the document.

TIP

You can also update a style by changing the formatting on a paragraph that has been assigned the style. Then in the Stylist, select the **Update Style** button in the upper right of the Stylist window.

104 Insert Headers, Footers, and Page Numbers

Information that you want to repeat at the top (header) or bottom (footer) of the pages in the document can be inserted using the Page Style dialog box (select **Format, Page**). Typically, you do not place headers and footers on the first page of a document. However, Writer provides the option of having a different header/footer on the first page of the document (as opposed to the header/footer on the rest of the document pages).

Headers and footers are useful when you want to place a draft number on the pages of a document or place your name and the date on all the pages in the document. More importantly, you can automatically number the pages of the document by entering a page number field in a header or footer.

1 Open Page Style Dialog

Because headers and footers are typically not placed on the first page, go to the second page of your document and place the cursor on that page. Select **Format, Page** from the menu. The Page Style dialog box opens.

2 Enable Header/Footer

In Page Style dialog box, select the **Header** (or Footer) tab. To enable the header (or footer) select the **Header On** (or Footer On) check box.

104 Insert Headers, Footers, and Page Numbers

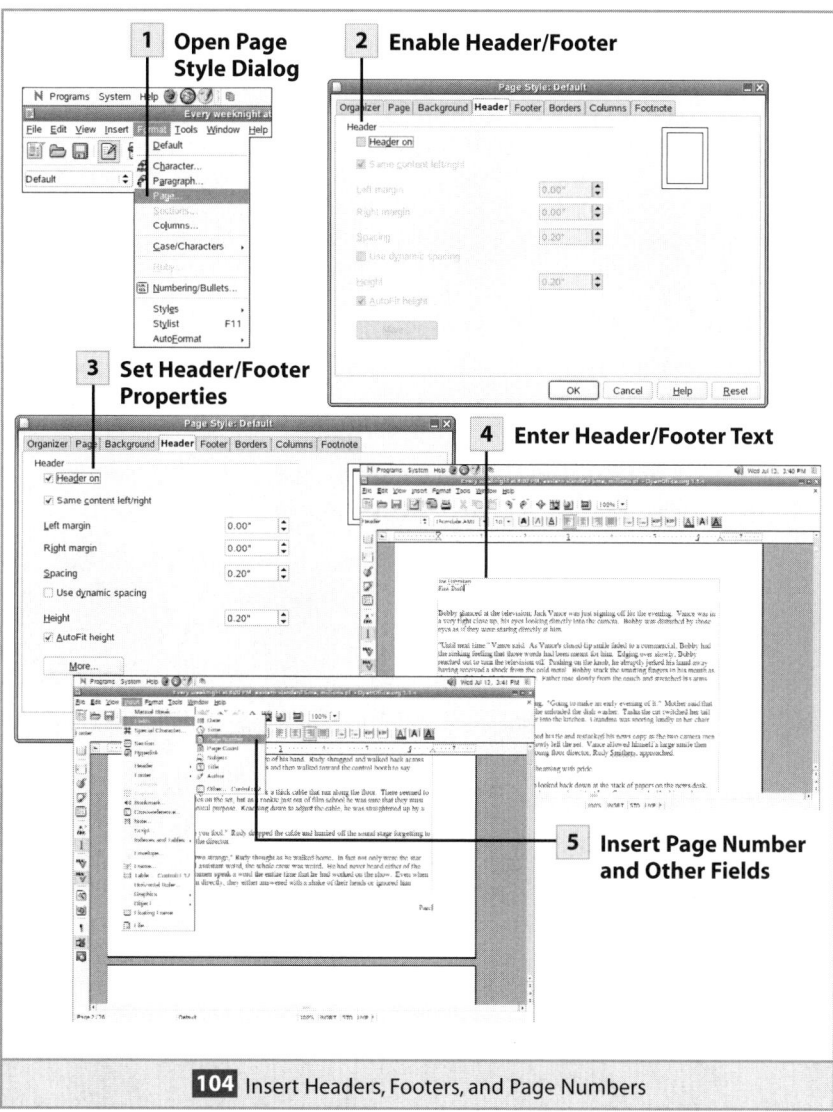

TIP

Obviously, you can have both headers and footers on your document's pages. Enable both headers and footers in the Page Style dialog box, if you want to use both in your document.

3 Set Header/Footer Properties

After you enable the header or footer feature on the Header or Footer tab, you can set the distance from the header to the margins (Left Margin and Right Margin settings) and the height of the header or footer. The default Autofit Height setting allows the header or footer to accommodate all the text that you place in the header or footer. After you have completed setting the options for the header or footer (or both), click **OK**.

4 Enter Header/Footer Text

Click in the header or footer. Enter the header or footer text as needed. You can format the text in the header or footer as you would format text in the document itself.

5 Insert Page Number and Other Fields

Headers and footers typically contain information such as the date or page numbers. You can enter these items into the header or footer as fields. To enter a field in a header or footer (such as the page number field), place the cursor in the header or footer where you want to place the field. Select **Insert**, **Fields**, and then select a field (such as **Page Number**) from the list of available fields. This places the field in the header or footer.

TIP
You can have a different header and footer on the first page of your document, if you want. To place a header or footer on the first page, select **Insert**, **Header**, **First Page** (or Footer and then First Page). Then enter the first page header or footer information including any fields that you want to use.

---

105 Use Format Page Options

Headers and footers settings are set using the Page Style dialog box. This dialog box also allows you to control other page settings such as the margins for the document, the page orientation for pages (portrait or landscape), and the borders and footnotes for the document.

✔ BEFORE YOU BEGIN

104 Insert Headers, Footers, and Page Numbers

105 Use Format Page Options

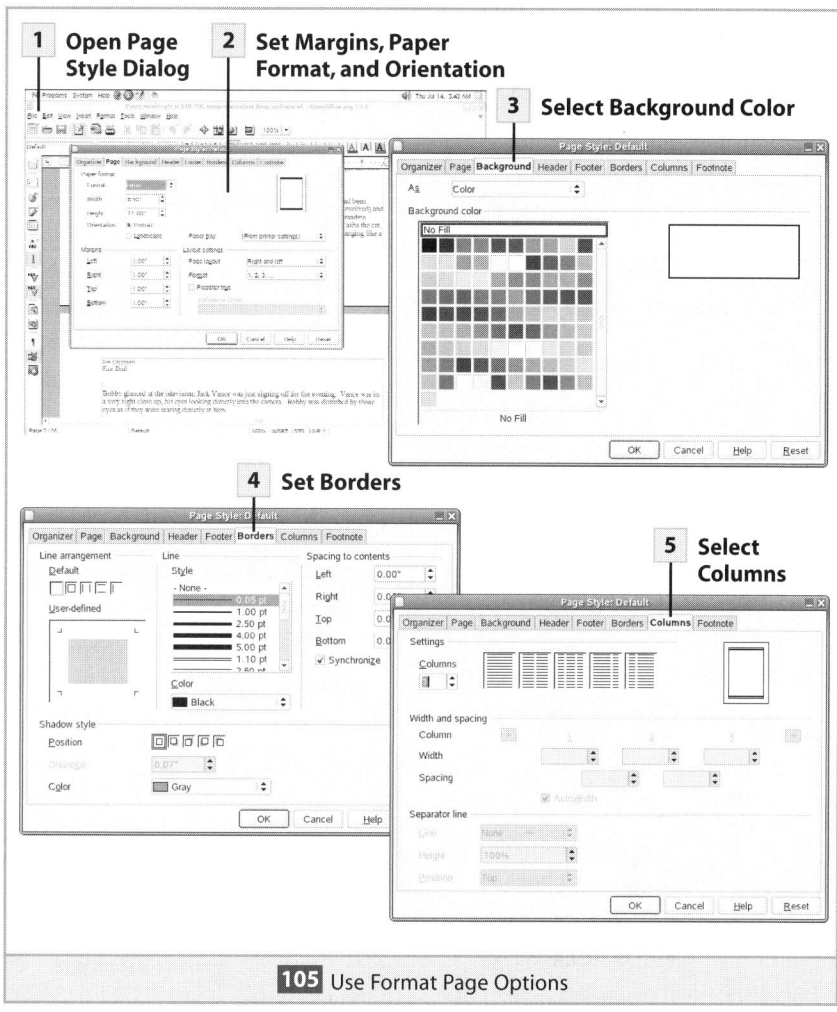

105 Use Format Page Options

1 Open Page Style Dialog

Select **Format**, **Page** from the menu. The Page Style dialog box opens.

NOTE

The Organizer tab of the Page Style dialog box can be used to change the current page style. This allows you to quickly format your document pages for endnotes or footnotes using a page style from the Next Style drop-down list.

2 Set Margins, Paper Format, and Orientation

In the Page Style dialog box, select the **Page** tab. To change the paper format (Letter, Legal, and so on), select the **Format** drop-down list and make a selection. Use the margin spinner boxes to set the top, bottom, left, and right margins for the document.

TIP

The settings in the Page Style dialog box are designed to affect all the pages in the document. You can also create documents that have pages with different margins, orientation, and other attributes such as borders or backgrounds. This can be done by adding a section to the document. You can insert sections at any point in the document (you enter a name for each section that you create). This allows you to create a single document with multiple sections, meaning different page layouts throughout the document. The easiest way to create a new section in an existing document is to select the text that you want to apply the style to. Then select **Insert**, **Sections**. The Sections dialog box allows you to name the section and select settings for the new section such as columns, backgrounds, and footnotes. Sections can also be edited as needed.

3 Select Background Color

Select the **Background** tab. Use the color palette to select a color for the background.

4 Set Borders

Select the **Borders** tab. Select one of the default border styles or use the user-defined pane to create your own custom borders. Use the **Line Style** and **Color** drop-down lists to set the options for the borders. If you want to have a shadow on the borders, select the shadow position and then select the color for the shadow.

5 Select Columns

You can format all the pages in the document with columns (very useful when you are creating a newsletter). The column settings take effect on the pages starting at the current cursor position. So, if you want columns on all the pages, press **Ctrl+Home** to go to the top of the document (otherwise, place the cursor where you want the columns to start). Select the **Columns** tab and select one of the column presets. If you want to set your own columns, select the number of columns in the **Columns** spinner box. You can then set the spacing between the columns.

After you have finished selecting your page style settings, click **OK** to accept the new settings for the document. The Page Style dialog box closes.

106 Move Text

The document editing process usually entails moving text from one place to another within the document. Writer makes it easy for you to move text with the Cut and Paste commands. You can also drag and drop selected text anywhere in the document or drag text from one document to another.

1 Drag Text to New Location

Select the text that you want to move. Drag the selected text to a new location in the document. The mouse pointer becomes a drag-and-drop pointer as you drag the text.

2 Cut Selected Text

If you don't like dragging text, you can use Cut and Paste. Select the text that you want to move and then select **Edit**, **Cut**. The text is removed from the document.

TIP

You can cut and paste text faster using the **Cut** and **Paste** buttons on the Function bar.

3 Paste Selected Text

Place the cursor in the document at the position where you want to paste the text that was cut. Select **Edit**, **Paste** to paste the text into the document.

TIP

The Paste Special command on the Edit menu allows you to paste text without the formatting that has been assigned to it.

CHAPTER 11: Creating Documents with OpenOffice.org Writer

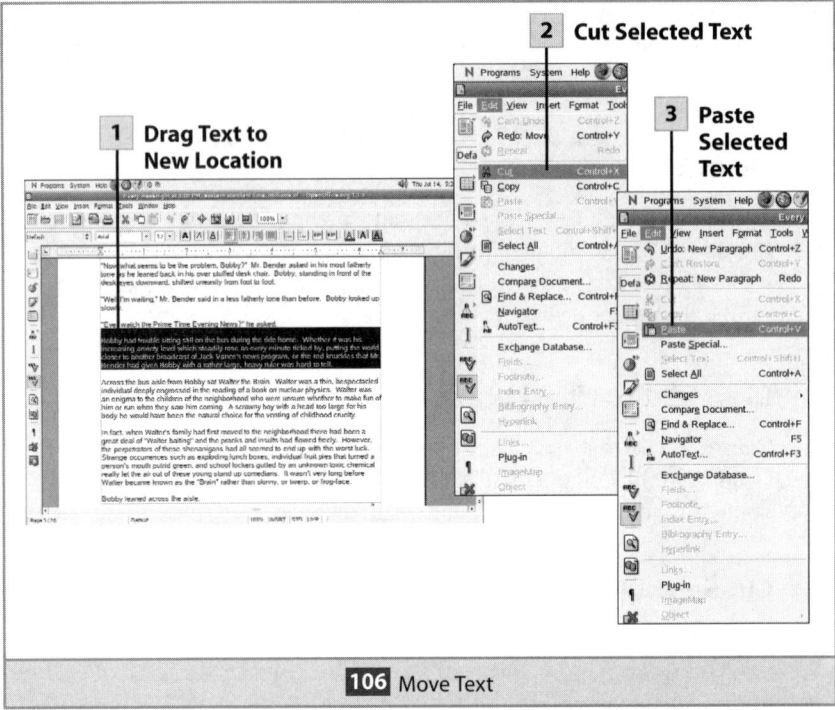

106 Move Text

107 Insert a Table

Writer tables are made up of columns and rows, allowing you to arrange text in a tabular format. The intersection of a column and a row is referred to as a cell.

There are two ways to add a table. You can add a table from the Main toolbar's Insert button. This option allows you to choose the number of rows and columns in the table with the mouse. You can also select **Insert**, **Table** to open the Insert Table dialog box. This dialog box allows you to specify the number of rows and columns and also autoformat the new table.

1 Insert Table from Main Toolbar

Select the arrow at the top of the Insert button on the Main toolbar. In the toolbox that appears, point at the table button and drag to select the number of rows and columns for the table. When you release the mouse, the table is inserted into the document.

107 Insert a Table

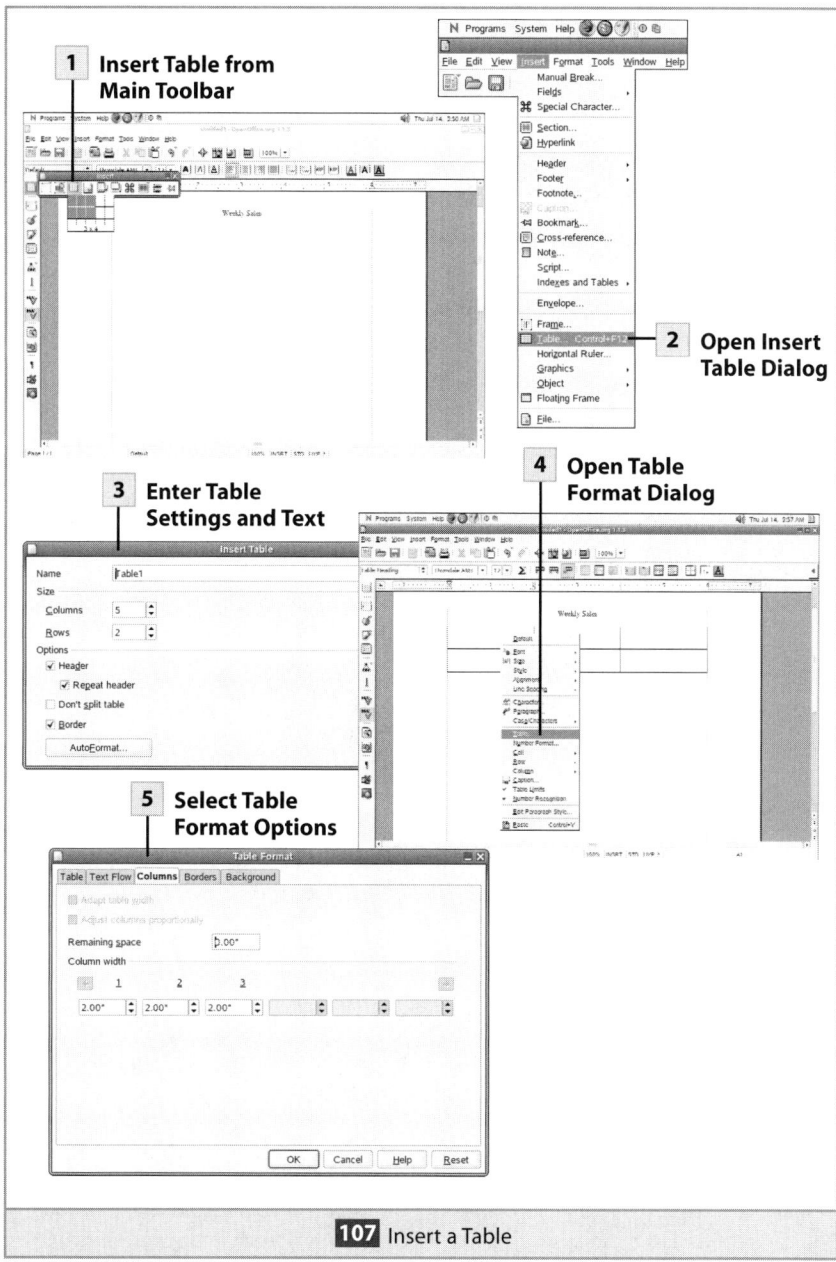

2 Open Insert Table Dialog

If you don't want to insert the table from the Insert button, you can use the Insert menu. Select **Insert, Table**. The Insert Table dialog box opens.

3 Enter Table Settings and Text

In the Insert Table dialog box enter the number of columns and rows for the table and then click **OK**. You can now enter text into the table. Click in any of the cells and enter the data. You can quickly move forward through the cells in the table by pressing the **Tab** key (go backward with **Shift+Tab**).

TIP

You can quickly assign an autoformat to your table in the Insert Table dialog box by clicking the **AutoFormat** button.

4 Open Table Format Dialog

You can format your table. The formatting options include column width, borders, and backgrounds. Right-click on the table and select **Table** on the shortcut menu. The Table Format dialog box opens.

5 Select Table Format Options

On the **Columns** tab set the width for each of the table's columns. To add a border or a background select the **Borders** or **Background** tab, respectively, and make your selections for these settings. After you have completed setting the table format options, click **OK**.

TIP

You can change the width of the columns in the table by dragging a column border.

TIP

You can autoformat a table, which provides a number of ready-made formats that include different combinations of cell backgrounds and table grid formats. Select **Format, Autoformat** (when you are in the table). Select an autoformat from the list and then click **OK**.

108 Insert a Text Frame

Text frames allow you to add text boxes to your documents. These frames can be placed anywhere on the page, and options can be set for how the regular document text flows around the frame. You can insert a new frame from the Insert menu (select **Insert, Frame**). However, the easiest way to insert the frame is to use the **Insert** button on the Main toolbar. This allows you to create the frame and size it on-the-fly.

1 Insert Text Frame from Main Toolbar

Select the arrow at the top of the Insert button on the Main toolbar. In the toolbox that appears, select the **Insert Frame Manually** button. When you move the mouse pointer onto the document, it will appear as a large plus (+) symbol. Hold down the left mouse button and drag the pointer to create the frame (drag over and then down to create the size of rectangle that you want to create for the frame). When you release the mouse the frame is inserted in the document.

TIP

You can move or resize the frame as needed. Place the mouse pointer on one of the frame borders until the sizing handle appears. Drag to change the size and shape of the frame. To move the frame, drag the frame to a new location or drag the anchor for the frame that appears to the left of the frame near the left margin.

2 Enter Text in Frame

Click the I-beam inside the frame and type the text that you want to place in the frame. You can format the text and change the text alignment (left, center, right, and so on) after typing the text. Click outside the frame when you have finished typing.

TIP

You can format the text in a frame as you would any other text in the document. You can change fonts, size, color, and layout such as columns.

CHAPTER 11: Creating Documents with OpenOffice.org Writer

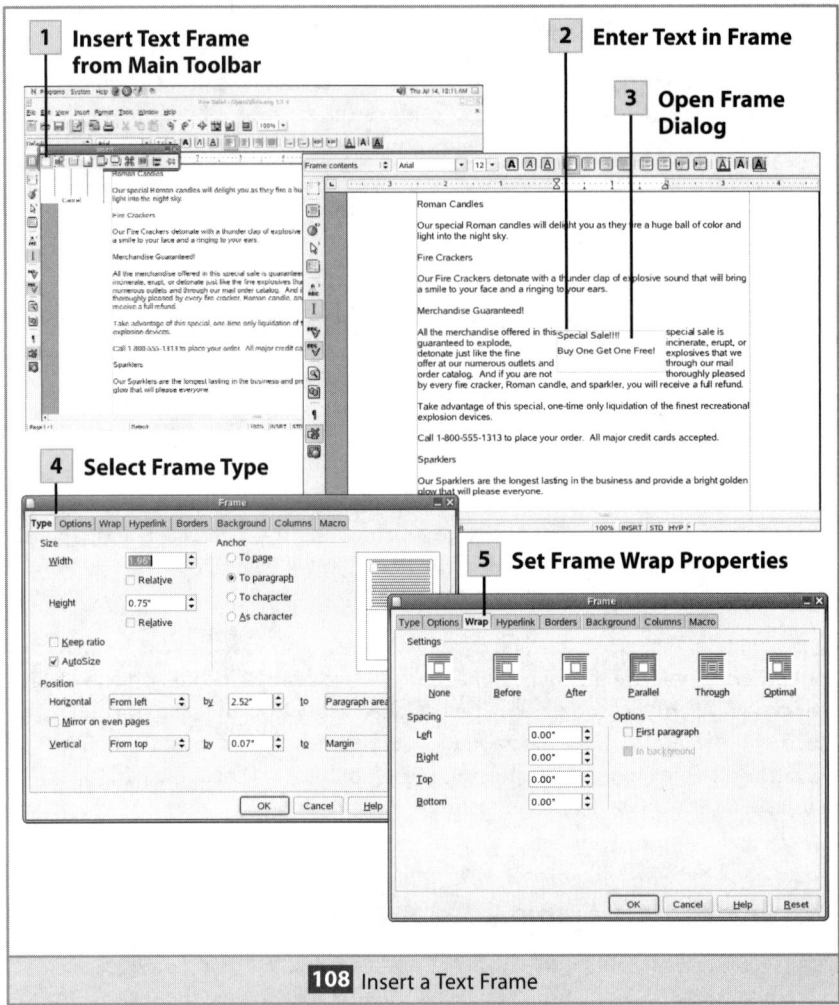

108 Insert a Text Frame

3 Open Frame Dialog

You can control the settings for the text frame in the Frame dialog box. Click once on the frame border to select it and then double-click on the frame (or right-click on the frame and select **Frame**); the Frame dialog box opens.

4 Select Frame Type

On the **Type** tab select the anchor type for the frame (**To Page**, **To Paragraph**, **To Character**, and so on). You can also change the vertical and horizontal position of the frame on the Type tab.

TIP

You can also format the frame for borders, backgrounds, and columns in the Frame dialog box. Select a tab (such as **Background**) and then select the properties you want to apply to the frame.

5 Set Frame Wrap Properties

To change how the document text wraps in relation to the frame, select the **Wrap** tab. Select one of the wrap settings: **None**, **Before**, **After**, **Parallel**, **Through**, or **Optimal**. You can also control the spacing around the frame using the **Spacing** spinner boxes. After you have finished working in the Frame dialog box, click **OK** to return to the document.

TIP

You can also insert floating frames into a document; select **Insert**, **Floating Frame**. A floating frame can contain any type of object: a picture, another document; it is up to you. Floating frames can be dragged to any position on the page.

109 Place Graphics in a Document

Images that you place in your documents can be informational (such as a picture of a house that you are writing about) or can be used as desktop publishing elements that just add interest to the document. You can add graphics to your documents from files (meaning image files on your computer) or directly from a scanner attached to your computer.

1 Open Insert Graphics Dialog

Select **Insert**, **Graphics**, **From File** from the menu. The Insert Graphic dialog box opens.

CHAPTER 11: Creating Documents with OpenOffice.org Writer

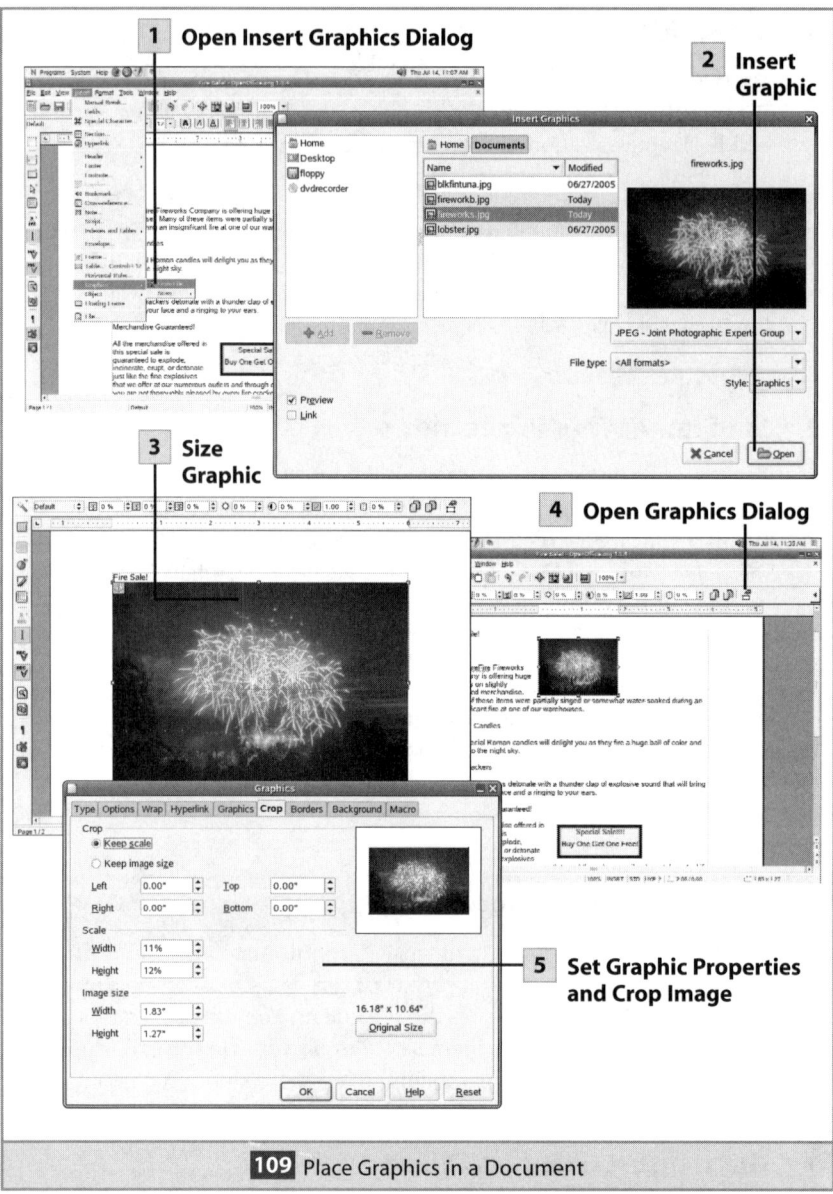

109 Place Graphics in a Document

TIP

You can also draw your own images for your documents within the Writer application window. Select the **Show Draw Functions** button on the Main toolbar, and the Object bar shows the various drawing tools available (replacing the formatting buttons normally shown on the Object bar). Use the tools as needed.

2 Insert Graphic

In the Insert Graphic dialog box browse to find the image that you want to place in the document. Select the file and then select **Open**.

3 Size Graphic

Place the mouse pointer at one of the corners of the inserted graphic (to maintain the height/width ratio) and when the sizing tool appears drag diagonally to size the picture.

4 Open Graphics Dialog

When the graphic is selected, the Object bar provides a set of tools for editing the image; for example, you can use the **Red**, **Green**, and **Blue** buttons to adjust the RGB ratios for the picture. To open the Graphics dialog box for the picture (and adjust settings) select the **Graphics Properties** button on the Object bar (the first button on the right of the toolbar).

5 Set Graphic Properties and Crop Image

In the Graphics dialog box you can adjust the type, wrap, borders, and backgrounds for the image (select the appropriate tab and configure options as needed). You can also crop the image in the Graphics dialog box. Select the **Crop** tab on the Graphics dialog box. Use the **Left**, **Right**, **Top**, and **Bottom** spinner boxes to crop the image as needed. As you adjust the cropping settings, crop marks appear on the preview image on the Crop tab. After you have completed configuring the settings for the image, click **OK**.

TIP

You can set the transparency for the image on the Object bar (when the image is selected); use the transparency spinner box on the Object bar. This allows you to add special effects such as watermarks to a document because you can then choose to have the text in the document to wrap through (on the Wrap tab of the Graphics dialog box, select **Through**) the image, which in effect uses the graphic as a background for the text.

CHAPTER 11: Creating Documents with OpenOffice.org Writer

110 Do a Mail Merge

No matter what your business, it is useful to be able to create a form letter and then create individual letters for a list of people. Writer walks you through the process of creating a form letter and merging the letter with a data source that provides the names and addresses of the individuals you want to receive the letter. You can also do mail merges to other document types such as envelopes. The easiest data source to prepare for your mail merges is the Contact list in Evolution (the NLD personal information manager and email client).

✔ BEFORE YOU BEGIN

154 About the Evolution Address Book
155 Create a New Contact

1 Type Letter

The best first step in preparing for the mail merge is to start a new document and create your form letter. You can type the body text and add fields to the document such as the date field (select **Insert**, **Fields**, **Date**).

2 Begin Mail Merge Process

To begin the mail merge process, select **Tools**, **Mail Merge**. The Mail Merge dialog box opens.

3 Select Current Document

Select **From This Document** in the Mail Merge dialog box and then click **OK**.

4 Select Data Source

A warning box opens telling you that a data source has not been set up for the merge. Click **OK** to close the box. The Address Data Source AutoPilot opens. Select **Evolution** as the data source. Then click **Next**.

TIP

You need to set up your data source, meaning enter your contacts in Evolution before performing the mail merge. You can then specify the contacts that should be included in the merge.

110 Do a Mail Merge

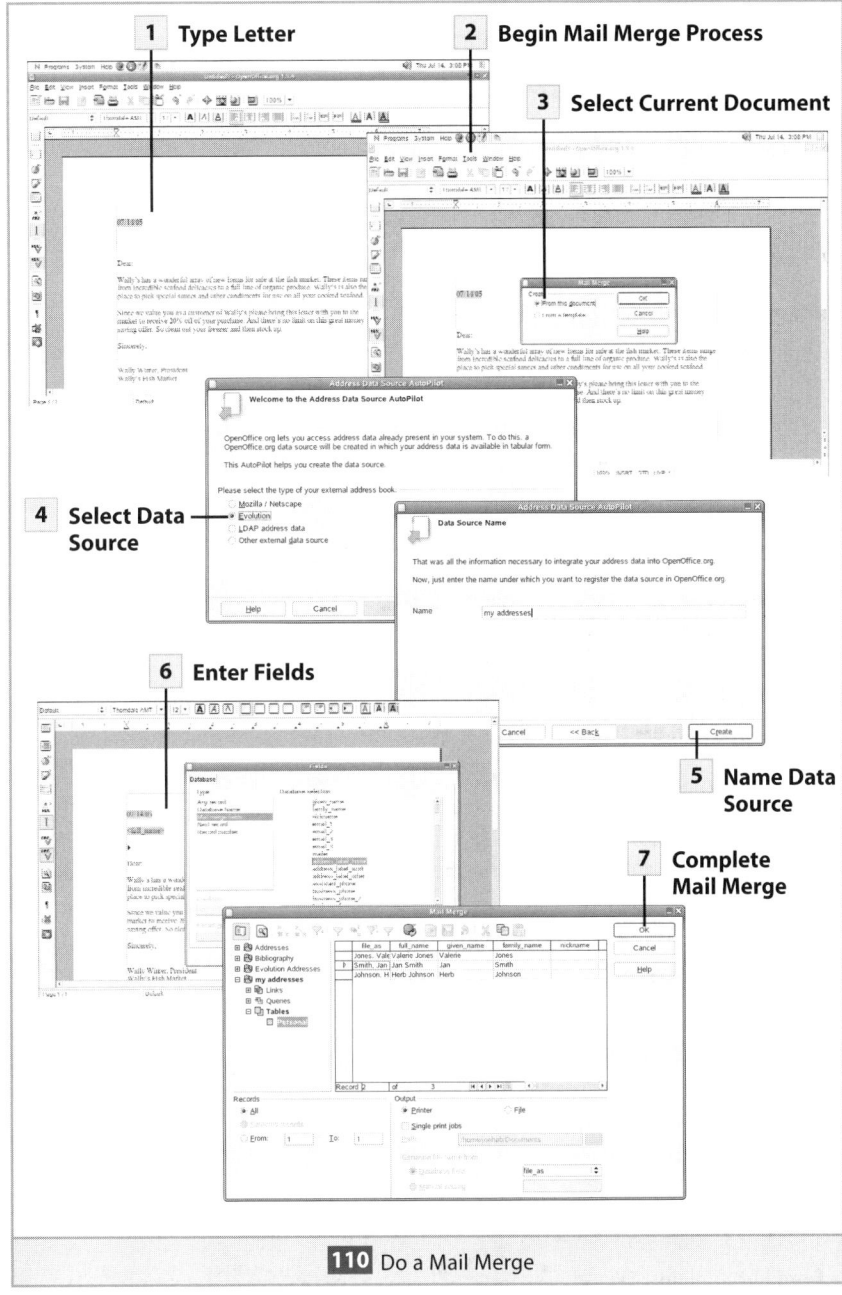

> **NOTE**
>
> You can use other databases as your data source. This depends on the access that you have to internal databases (on your computer) or external database sources on the network. For example, programs such as Novell GroupWise, which can hold contact information, can be accessed as the data source.

5 Name Data Source

On the next AutoPilot screen you are asked to enter a name for the data source. This is a "friendly" name, so type the name you want to use and then click **Create**. A message box opens letting you know that the data source is now available to the OpenOffice.org application. You can access the data source anytime from OpenOffice.org by pressing **F4**. Click **OK** to close the message box. The Fields dialog box opens.

6 Enter Fields

You must enter merge fields into the form letter. The fields are placeholders for items such as name, address, and so on. The Fields dialog box allows you to access the fields in your data source and then insert them into the appropriate places in the form letter (or other merge document).

Expand the data source to view the available fields. (It will be named with the name you provided in step 5.) Click in the letter to place the cursor where you want to place a field. Then click in the Fields dialog box, select the field, and then select **Insert**. The field placeholder is placed in the letter. After you have finished inserting the fields, click **Close**.

7 Complete Mail Merge

The Mail Merge window opens. Select the Output for the merge: **Printer** or **File**. If you select File, you can specify a filename; select the **Manual Setting** option and then enter a filename. A number is placed after the filename you provide for each letter that you save as a file, meaning each letter exists as a separate file.

All the records in the data source are used by default. If you want to use only some of the records, select the records. Click a record with the mouse and then hold down the **Ctrl** key to select other records. Or you can specify a range of records using the **From** option.

111 About Printing in Writer

When you are ready to complete the merge, click **OK**. The merged letters are printed or saved as individual files, depending on the output option you chose.

111 About Printing in Writer

Despite the web, email, and all other forms of electronically dealing with documents today, there are still times when you may find it necessary to print out a hard copy of a document.

> ✔ **BEFORE YOU BEGIN**
>
> 35 About Printing and NLD
> 36 Add and Configure a Printer
> 37 Print to a Printer

Writer can print to any printer that has been installed on your system. This includes local and network printers that have been installed through CUPS. You can quickly print a document by selecting the **Print File Directly** button on the Function toolbar. This sends the print job to the default printer using the default print settings.

If you want to be able to choose from the different printers that you have access to, you will want to print via the Print dialog box (select **File**, **Print**). The Print dialog box allows you to select the printer, the page range to print, and other options related to the print job.

You can preview your print jobs using the Page Preview feature (select **File**, **Page Preview**). The Preview window allows you to zoom in and out on a page and view multiple pages as they would print.

> **NOTE**
>
> You can also print a document to a file. This file can then be printed on any computer regardless of whether you have OpenOffice.org. You can also export Writer documents as PDF (Adobe Acrobat files). This is useful because the standard document type for most websites is now the PDF file format. The PDF format also preserves all your formatting, graphics, and so on. To export a document as a PDF, select **File**, **Export as PDF**. Provide a filename and then save the newly created PDF file.

112 Print a Document

Printing a document in most applications follows a few very similar steps. This task will show you specifcally how to print a document in Writer.

✔ BEFORE YOU BEGIN

111 About Printing in Writer

1 Open Print Dialog

With the document you want to print open in the Writer window, select **File**, **Print**. The Print dialog box opens.

2 Set Print Options

In the Print dialog box use the printer **Name** drop-down box to select the printer you will use for the print job. Specify the print range for the document if you are not printing the entire document. If you want to print multiple copies of the document, use the **Number of Copies** spinner box to specify the number of copies.

TIP

You can set other options for your print job. Select the **Options** button in the Print dialog box. The Printer Options dialog box opens. You can select the objects you want to print in the document (such as graphics and tables) and change the order of the print job. When you close the Printer Options dialog box you are returned to the Print dialog box.

3 Print Document

After you have specified the options related to the print job, click **OK**. The document will be sent to your printer.

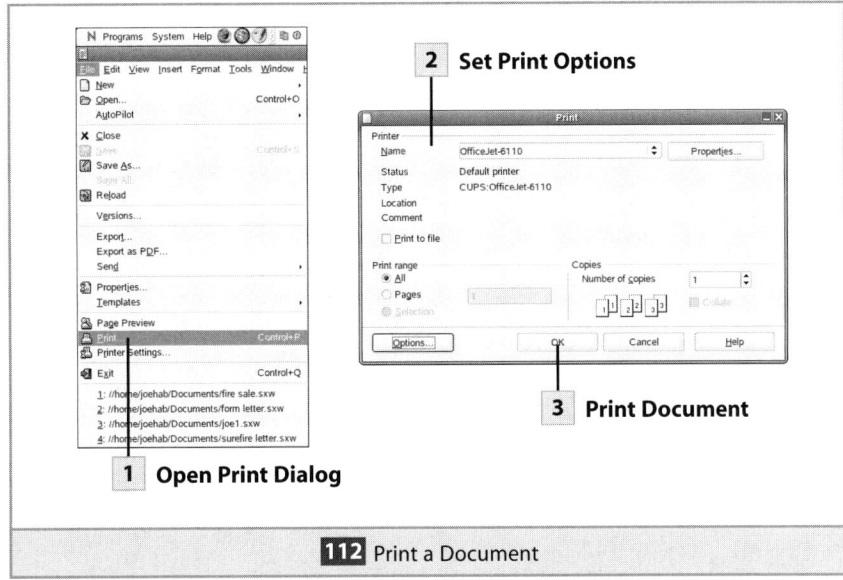

CHAPTER 12

Creating Spreadsheets with OpenOffice.org Calc

IN THIS CHAPTER:

- **113** About OpenOffice.org Calc
- **114** Enter Text and Data
- **115** Enter Dates
- **116** About Creating Formulas
- **117** Create a Formula
- **118** About Calc Functions
- **119** Use the Function AutoPilot
- **120** Select and Format Spreadsheet Cells
- **121** Insert and Delete Columns
- **122** Insert and Delete Rows
- **123** Insert, Name, and Delete Sheets
- **124** Sort and Filter Data
- **125** About Calc Charts
- **126** Insert and Format a Chart
- **127** Print a Spreadsheet

CHAPTER 12: Creating Spreadsheets with OpenOffice.org Calc

Everyone on occasion has to do some number crunching in the form of invoices, balance sheets, or budgets. OpenOffice.org provides Calc, a full-featured and easy-to-use spreadsheet program. In this chapter, we look at how to create basic spreadsheets and take advantage of Calc's many features including functions, chart creation, and the printing of spreadsheets.

113 About OpenOffice.org Calc

Calc provides all the capabilities and features that you would expect from a spreadsheet program. It provides you with the ability to create both simple and complex spreadsheets. And because it shares a common interface with the other OpenOffice.org applications, such as Writer, the working environment where you create your spreadsheets will be immediately familiar no matter which of the other OpenOffice.org applications you use most often.

The Calc application window provides the same toolbars as the other OpenOffice.org applications. There is the Function bar, Object bar, and Main toolbar. These toolbars provide many of the same button and functions as you will find in the other applications. However, the Calc Object bar and Main toolbar provide access to tools that are specific to working in a spreadsheet, such as tools for sorting data and formatting tools that make it easy to format numerical data as currency or percentages.

The Calc application window is also different from the other OpenOffice.org applications in that it is designed to create spreadsheets. The Calc window contains an additional toolbar called the Formula bar, which provides access to Calc built-in formulas (called functions) and provides a box that shows you the contents of the currently selected cell.

So, if Calc is designed to create a spreadsheet, what do spreadsheets look like? *Spreadsheet* is really a generic term that refers to the file type that is created. When you work in Calc you are actually working on a particular sheet. Each sheet consists of columns and rows. The intersection of a column and a row is referred to as a *cell*. You can place data in each cell. Each spreadsheet file, which is the file that you save when you save your work in Calc, can consist of multiple sheets.

Each sheet contains 256 columns, and each column is designated by a letter such as A, B, C, and so on. After Z the letters repeat AA, AB, and so on until you get to IV the last column in the sheet.

Each sheet has 32,000 rows available. Each row is designated by a number (1, 2, 3, to 32000).

So, with 256 columns and 32,000 rows, you have 8,192,000 cells in a sheet. Each cell has an address based on the column and row that intersect to create the cell; for example, a cell in column A and row 1 would be Cell A1.

TIP

Don't be intimidated by the fact that there are so many columns, rows, and cells in each sheet. Even large spreadsheets use only a fraction of the cells provided. The fact that each spreadsheet can contain multiple sheets means that you can break your spreadsheets down into smaller endeavors by using multiple sheets. For example, each quarter of the year could be placed on a separate sheet instead of placing the entire year on one sheet. Sure, there is certainly room for a lot of data on one sheet, but in terms of viewing and printing data, using multiple sheets is easier on the eyes and makes it easier to print your work.

When you build a spreadsheet (meaning a sheet, really), you enter text and numbers into the various cells. The true power of Calc is its capability to perform a wide variety of mathematical calculations on the numerical data that you enter on the sheets. It also provides you with the ability to create a chart based on the data, which provides a pictorial view of the data and the results of formulas in the sheet.

114 Enter Text and Data

To create your spreadsheets you will enter text, which serves as descriptive data such as column or row headings; numbers, which have numerical significance (meaning they can be acted on by formulas); and formulas and functions (formulas you create; functions are built into Calc). Entering text and numerical data is straightforward. You click on a cell with the mouse and then you enter the information that you want in the cell. When you press Enter the cell selector moves down to the next cell in the column.

✔ **BEFORE YOU BEGIN**

97 About OpenOffice.org Writer

1 Start Calc

From the NLD desktop, Select **Programs**, **Office**, **Spreadsheet**. The Calc window opens.

CHAPTER 12: Creating Spreadsheets with OpenOffice.org Calc

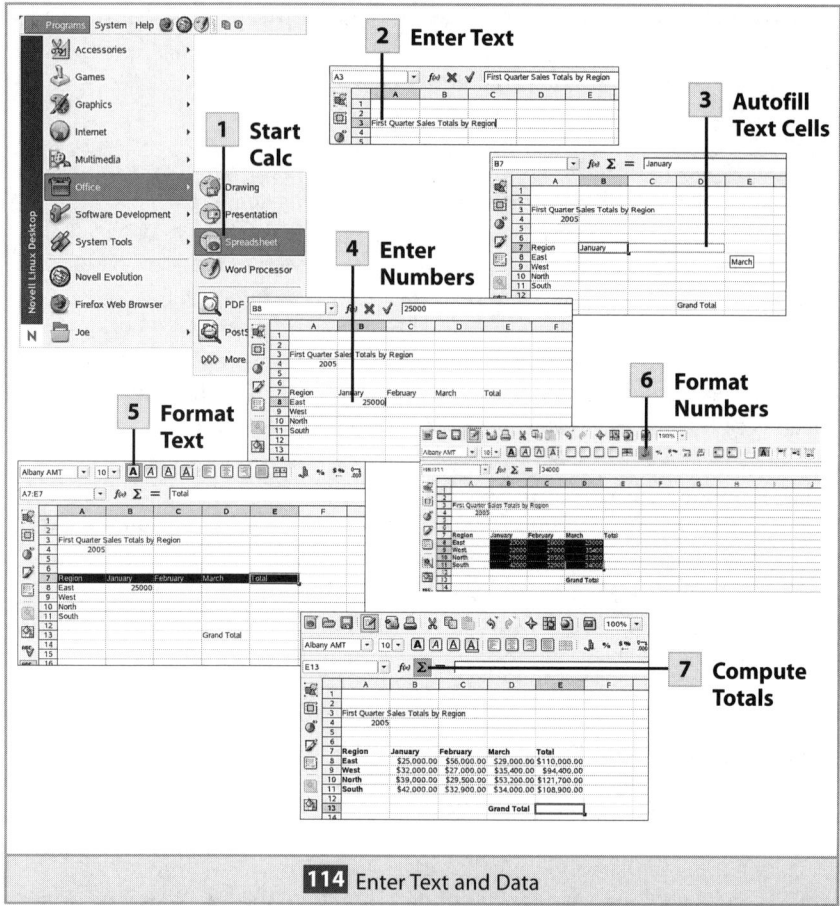

114 Enter Text and Data

2 Enter Text

Click in a cell that will contain text. Then type the text. After you have completed entering the text, press **Enter**. The text is placed in the cell, and the cell selector moves to the next cell down. Enter other text as needed. Notice that text is aligned left in the cells.

TIP

You can also enter typed text in a cell by pressing an arrow key. This moves you to another cell in the direction of the arrow key selected.

3 Autofill Text Cells

You can save some typing of text labels by using the autofill feature. This fills adjacent to the current cell based on the contents of the currently selected cell. For example, if the current cell contains January, you can autofill the cells to the right of the cell with February, March and so on.

Click on the first cell in the series you want to create (such as a cell containing January). Place the mouse pointer on the lower-right corner of the selected cell. The mouse becomes a plus symbol. Drag the fill handle (the small black box on the cell) to create the series and autofill the adjacent cells (you can drag up, down, or right as needed).

NOTE

Autofill is pretty slick; it can pick up on series that you need to create. For example, typing Region 1 and then using autofill produces Region 2, Region 3, and so on. Autofill can also be used for days of the week (Monday, Tuesday, and so on), and it can fill in a series of numbers. For example, you place 2 in a cell and then 4 in an adjacent cell (below or to the right). When you drag to use autofill, a series of 2, 4, 6, 8, and so on is created.

4 Enter Numbers

Select a cell that will contain a numerical value. Type the number and then press **Enter** (or use one of the arrow keys).

TIP

If you need to change an entry (text or number) click in the cell and type the new data. If you want to edit an entry, select the cell and then use the **Input** line (on the Formula bar) to enter the entry. Press **Enter** when finished.

TIP

If you exceed the column width with an entry (text or number), the entry will be truncated when you enter data in the cell to the right of the "long" entry. You can quickly correct this by dragging the column border (the border in the column heading area) for the column to accommodate the entry. You can also double-click the column boundary for a "best fit," which accommodates the longest entry in the column automatically.

5 Format Text

After you have entered your text labels, you can format them. Select the cell or cells that you want to format. Then select a formatting option such as **Bold** on the Object bar. You can also add borders and background colors for selected cells using the Object bar. After formatting the cells, click in any other cell to deselect the formatted cells.

6 Format Numbers

Numerical values can appear as standard numbers, currency, and percentages (and have a varying number of decimal places). To format numbers for a particular number type such as currency, select the cells to be formatted and then select a format option on the Object bar such as **Currency**.

> **TIP**
>
> You can access more formatting options for selected cells in the Format Cells dialog box. Select **Format, Cells**. This provides access to numerical formatting and formatting for font attributes and borders and background colors.

7 Compute Totals

You can quickly derive a total for a row or column of numbers using the Sum function. This function (a built-in formula) automatically selects the cells to be used to compute the total by selecting adjacent cells containing numerical values (a group of adjacent cells is referred to as a range).

> **KEY TERM**
>
> *Range*—A group of adjacent and contiguous cells. Ranges are used in formulas and functions to compute the results. You can also select a range of cells for formatting.

Click in the cell where you want to place the Sum function and then click the **Sum** function button on the Formula bar. The cell range to be acted on by the function will be highlighted in a blue box. If you need to adjust the cell selection, click and drag to select the appropriate cells. Then press **Enter** to enter the Sum function in the cell.

TIP

You can also drag to copy a formula or function. For example, if you have several like ranges of numerical values in rows, you can use Sum to compute the first total and then drag the Sum function to the other total cells to compute their totals. The Sum function is actually copied using the autofill handle, and it adjusts to the new row values, giving you the correct total for each range of numbers.

115 Enter Dates

Although dates appear as dates (August 11, 2005, for example) in your Calc sheets, these dates actually have numerical significance. For example, you might need to calculate the number of days between two different dates. You can actually subtract the earlier date from the later date and be provided the number of days that they differ.

The date is actually seen by Calc as a numerical value; so when you enter 11/22/2005, you see it as a date, but Calc sees it as a number—the number of days that have elapsed since January 1, 1900. So, Calc sees 11/22/2005 as 38,678.

1 Enter Date

In Calc, click on a cell that will hold a date. Type the date; you can enter the date as November 22, 2005 or as 11/22/2005. Press **Enter**.

2 Open Format Cells Dialog

You can change the format (appearance of the date). Select a cell or cells containing dates and then select **Format**, **Cells**. The Format Cells dialog box opens.

3 Format Date

The Numbers tab of the dialog box will be selected. Select a format for the date in the **Format** list. After you have completed your selection, click **OK**.

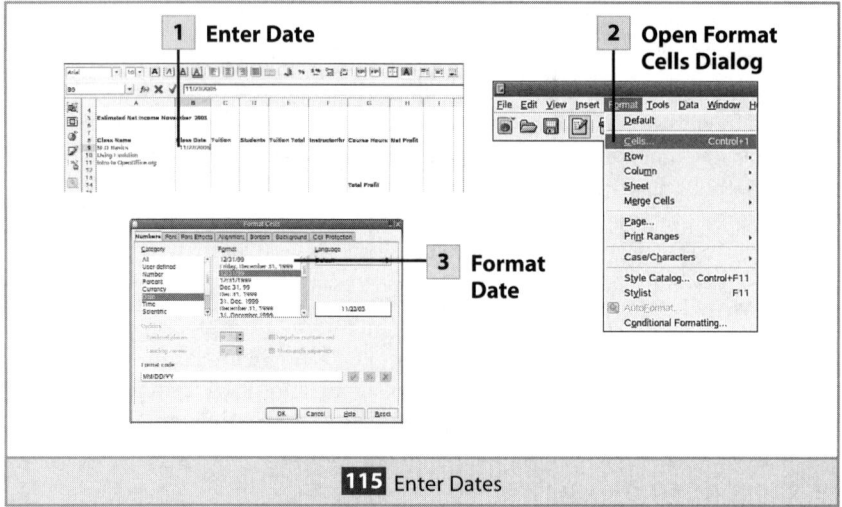

115 Enter Dates

116 About Creating Formulas

Calc is designed to do calculations. Although many built-in formulas and functions are provided by Calc, in some situations you will need to build your own formulas. These formulas typically involve simple math operations such as subtraction, multiplication, and division.

All formulas that you create must begin with the equal sign (=). This tells Calc that the information that follows the equal sign is a formula. To designate what type of calculation you want Calc to perform you use a mathematical operator (see Table 12.1).

TABLE 12.1
Mathematical Operators

OPERATOR	PERFORMS	EXAMPLE
+	Addition	=A1+B1
−	Subtraction	=A1-B1
*	Multiplication	=A1*B1
/	Division	=A1/B1
^	Exponentiation	=A1^2

You enter the cell addresses for the cells that will be acted on by the formula. For example, B5*C5 multiplies the contents of B5 times the contents of C5.

When you design your own formulas, keep the natural order of math operator precedence in mind: Exponents are computed first, then multiplication and division, followed by addition and subtraction. To force the precedence you can place portions of your formula in parentheses. This part of the formula is computed first.

117 Create a Formula

Calc makes it easy to add simple formulas in your spreadsheet.

✔ BEFORE YOU BEGIN

116 About Creating Formulas

1 Start Formula

Select the cell that will contain the formula. Type an equal sign (=) or select the **Function** button (the big equal sign on the Formula bar).

2 Select Cell

Select the first cell that will be included in the formula (selecting the cell is better than typing the cell address because it avoids typos). The cell address appears in the cell where you are creating the formula.

3 Enter Operator and Select Second Cell

Type the operator for the formula. For example, type an asterisk (*) for multiplication. Then select the second cell that will be acted on by the formula. Press **Enter** to complete the formula. The results of the formula appear in the cell where you built the formula. To view the formula itself, select the cell and view the formula on the Formula bar's Input line.

TIP

After you create the formula, you can use the autofill feature to copy the formula to other cells or use **Copy** and **Paste** to copy the formula to other cells.

CHAPTER 12: Creating Spreadsheets with OpenOffice.org Calc

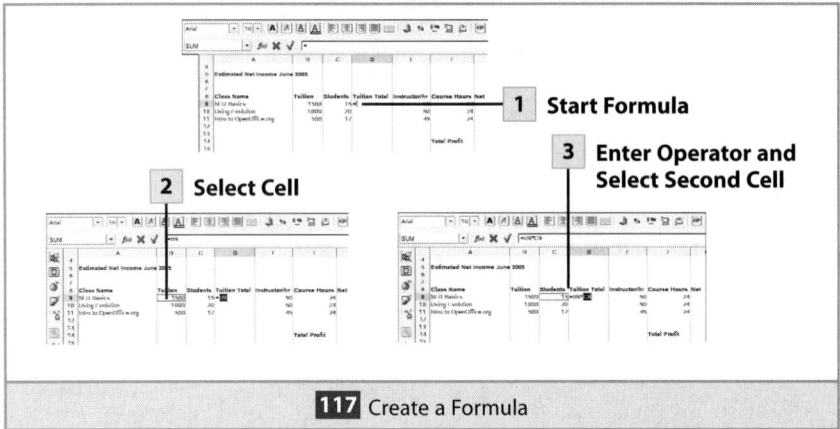

117 Create a Formula

118 About Calc Functions

Functions are built-in formulas that can do everything from add a range of values to provide an average for a range of cells to figure out the payment amount for a loan at a particular interest rate. Functions consist of two parts: the function name (such as =Average) and the range of cells that the function should act on. Calc provides many functions broken down into different categories (see Table 12.2). A statistical category includes functions such as average, maximum, and minimum. A financial category provides functions that allow you to calculate returns on investment and loan payment amounts among other finance-related calculations.

TABLE 12.2
Some of the Calc Function Categories

CATEGORY	EXAMPLE	PURPOSE
Date and Time	TODAY	Enters the current date
Financial	PMT	Calculates loan payments
Logical	IF	Returns a true or false answer to a conditional statement
Mathematical	COS	Calculates the cosine of an angle
Statistical	AVERAGE	Calculates the average for a range of cells

The easiest way to enter a function is through the Function AutoPilot. The AutoPilot allows you to select a particular function from the function list and then specify the cells that the function should act on. The AutoPilot also provides information about a selected function and makes it easy for you to get help as you work with a particular function.

282

119 Use the Function AutoPilot

Calc's AutoPilot simplifies the task of creating complex formulas and functions with your spreadsheet data.

> ✔ **BEFORE YOU BEGIN**
>
> 118 About Calc Functions

1 Select Cell and Start AutoPilot

Select the cell that will contain the function. Then select the **AutoPilot: Functions** button on the Formula bar. The AutoPilot: Functions dialog box opens.

2 Select Function

In the AutoPilot dialog box use the **Category** drop-down list to select the function category you want to view. To select a function, use the **Function** scroll box. After you have selected your function, click **Next**.

3 Shrink AutoPilot

On the next AutoPilot screen you must provide the range of cells that you want the function to act on. The easiest way to specify the range is to shrink the AutoPilot. Select the **Shrink** button in the Number 1 range box on the right of the AutoPilot. The AutoPilot dialog box shrinks or rolls up, allowing you to view the data on the sheet.

4 Select Cell Range

Select the range of cells to be used in the function. Then press **Enter**. The AutoPilot dialog box reappears (unshrinks).

5 Enter Function

To enter the function in the cell, click **OK**. The function is placed in the cell, showing the results.

CHAPTER 12: Creating Spreadsheets with OpenOffice.org Calc

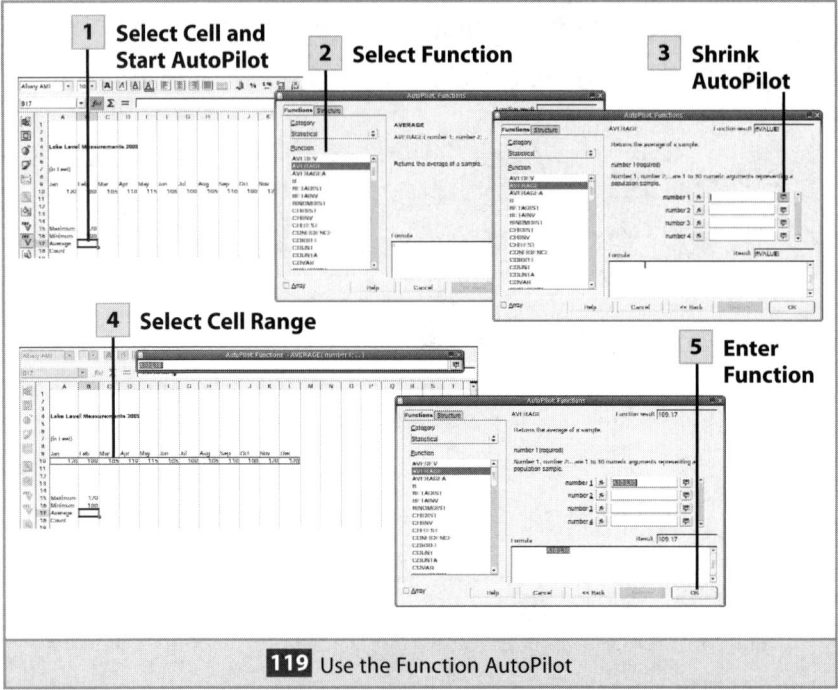

119 Use the Function AutoPilot

TIP

When you use some functions such as the AVERAGE function, you may want to decrease the number of decimal places shown in the functions results so that only "whole" numbers are represented. Use the **Number Format: Delete Decimal Place** button on the Object bar to reduce the number of decimal places shown in the function's results.

TIP

If the results of your function show as ####, this means that the column width can't accommodate the results of the function. Widen the column as needed to view the function results.

120 Select and Format Spreadsheet Cells

It makes sense to build your sheets by entering text, numerical values, and your formulas and functions before formatting the data on the sheet. You can then select ranges of cells and format them with different font attributes and numerical formats, and add borders or backgrounds to highlight certain cells or ranges of cells on the sheet.

You can use the various formatting options on the Object bar (Bold, Italics, Currency, Percentage, and so on). More options are available in the Format Cells dialog box. You can also format the entire spreadsheet using the AutoFormat feature.

1 Select Cell Range

Select the cell range that you want to format.

2 Open Format Cells Dialog

Select **Format**, **Cells** from the menu. The Format Cells dialog box opens.

3 Select Format Options

Use the tabs on the Format Cells dialog box to select formatting options for the selected cell range. The **Numbers** tab allows you to select a number format for a cell range containing numerical values. The **Font** tab provides access to font attributes. The **Alignment** tab allows you to change the alignment of the data in the selected cells. The **Borders** tab allows you to select a border for the selected cells or create a custom border. Use the **Background** tab to select a background color for the selected cells. After you have selected your options, click **OK**.

4 Open AutoFormat

You can also select a range of cells that includes the entire spreadsheet. You can then apply an AutoFormat to the cell range.

Select the range of cells and then select **Format**, **AutoFormat**. The AutoFormat dialog box opens.

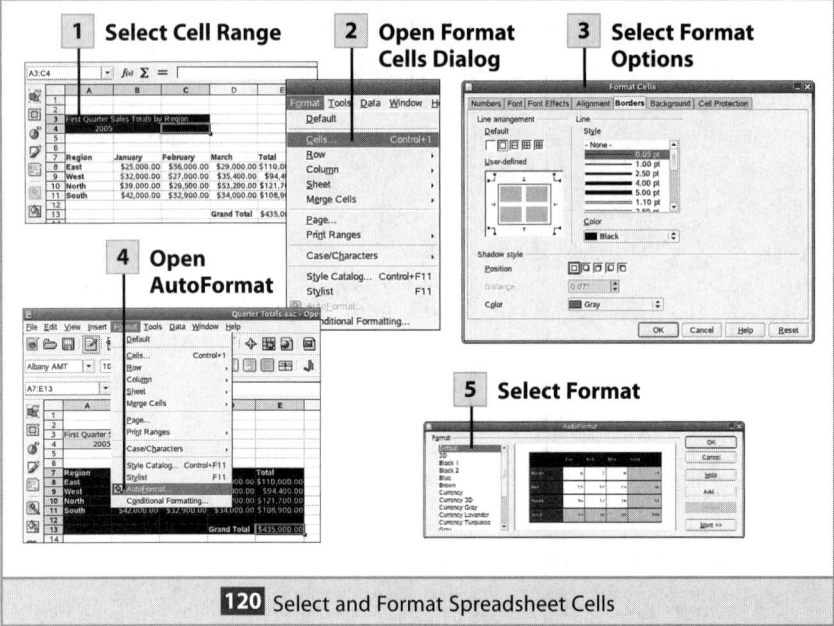

120 Select and Format Spreadsheet Cells

5 Select Format

Select a format in the **Format** list and then click **OK** to close the AutoFormat dialog box and return to the sheet. The selected cell range will be formatted with your AutoFormat selection.

TIP

If you select the **More** button in the AutoFormat dialog box, you can specify which items are formatted by AutoFormat. You can toggle options on or off such as Number format, Borders, and Alignment.

121 Insert and Delete Columns

You will find that even well-planned spreadsheets sometimes require that you add or delete columns from the sheet. You can insert one or multiple columns and delete columns as needed.

121 Insert and Delete Columns

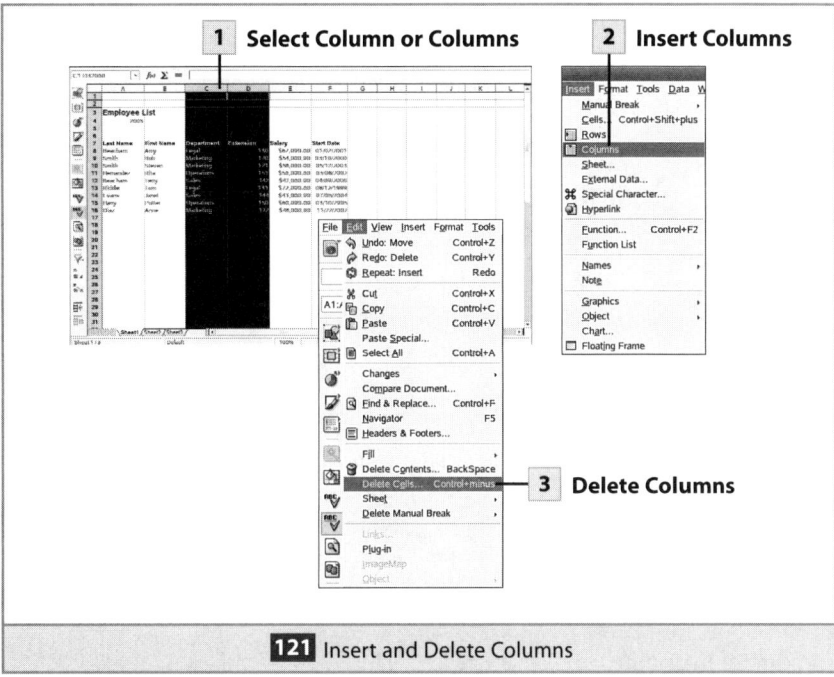

121 Insert and Delete Columns

1 Select Column or Columns

Select the column or columns where you want to insert new columns. Click the column heading to select a column or drag to select multiple columns. The number of columns that you select dictates how many new columns are inserted.

2 Insert Columns

Select **Insert**, **Columns**. The new column or columns are inserted into the sheet. The selected column or columns are pushed to the right.

287

TIP

After you insert a new column you can click and drag data in other cells into the empty column if you are rearranging information in a sheet.

3 Delete Columns

To delete columns select the column or columns that you want to delete (as in step 1). Select **Edit, Delete Cells**. The column or columns are removed from the sheet. Remember that when you delete a column you also delete its contents.

TIP

If you want to delete the contents of a column and not the column itself, select a column or columns. Then select **Edit, Delete Contents**.

122 Insert and Delete Rows

You can insert and delete rows in a sheet. This allows you to add or remove information as needed.

1 Select Row or Rows

Select the row or rows where you want to insert new rows. Click the row indicator (the row number) to select the rows. Drag across multiple row indicators to select multiple rows.

2 Insert Rows

Select **Insert, Rows** from the menu. The new rows or rows are inserted into the sheet. The rows or rows that were selected are pushed down by the newly inserted row or rows.

3 Delete Rows

Select a row or rows as shown in step 1. Select **Edit, Delete Cells** to delete the selection.

123 Insert, Name, and Delete Sheets

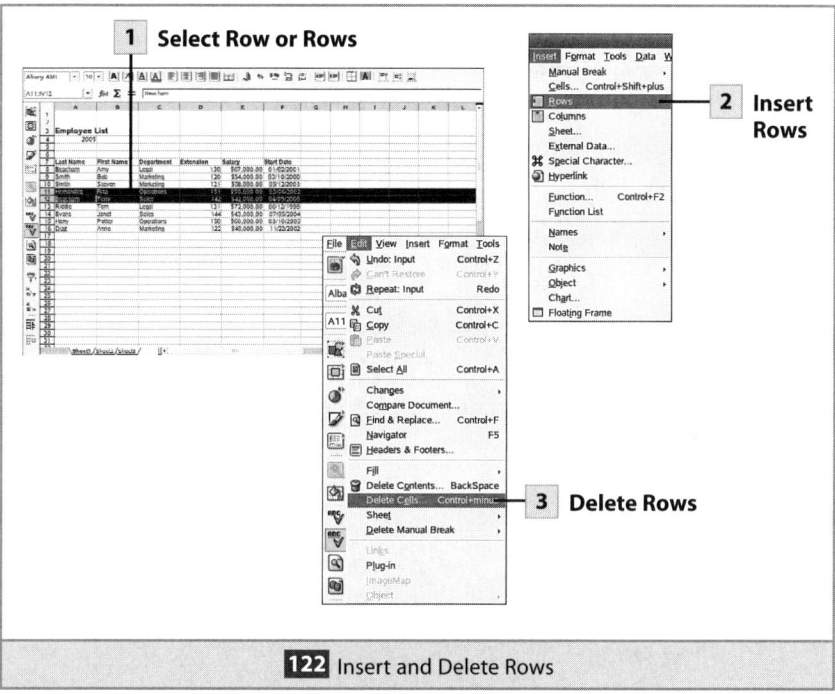

122 Insert and Delete Rows

123 Insert, Name, and Delete Sheets

You can add or delete sheets from a Calc spreadsheet as needed. You can also name each sheet, making it easier to locate a particular sheet in the spreadsheet.

1 Open Insert Sheet Dialog

Click on a **Sheet** tab to select that sheet. The new sheet can be placed to the left or right of the currently selected sheet. Select **Insert**, **Sheet** from the menu. The Insert Sheet dialog box opens.

2 Insert Sheet

Select a Position option for the new sheet (**Before Current Sheet** or **After Current Sheet**). Use the **No. of Sheets** spinner box to specify the number of sheets that you want to insert. You can type a name for the newly inserted sheet (or sheets) in the **Name** box. After you have completed the information for the new sheet, click **OK**. The sheet is inserted into the spreadsheet.

CHAPTER 12: Creating Spreadsheets with OpenOffice.org Calc

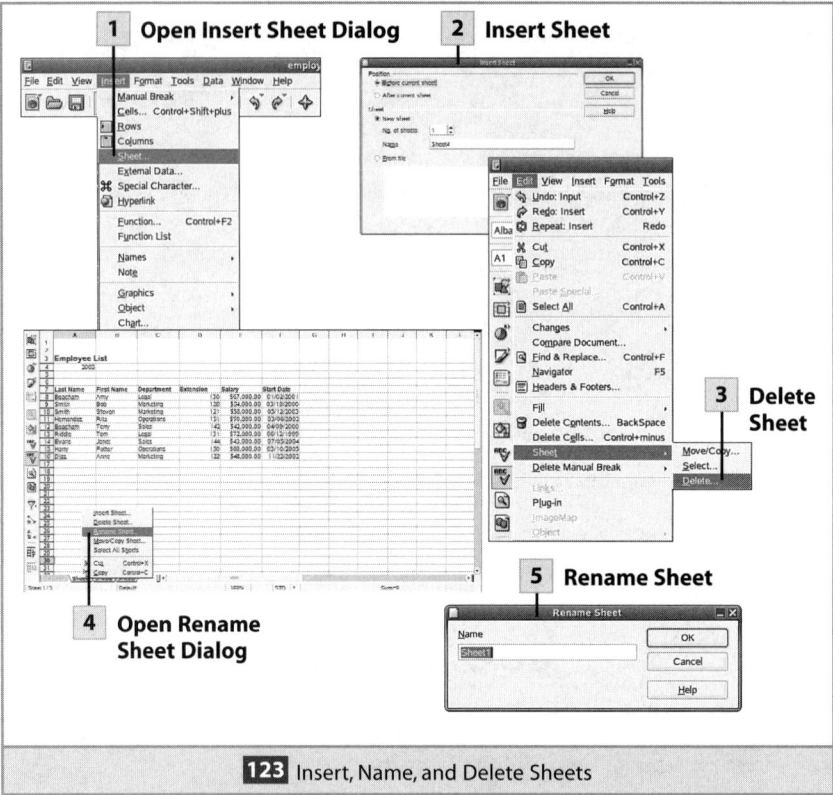

123 Insert, Name, and Delete Sheets

TIP

You can also insert a spreadsheet file into your current spreadsheet using the Insert Sheet dialog box. Select the **From File** option button. Then use the **Browse** button to locate the Calc file that you want to insert into the current spreadsheet.

3 Delete Sheet

With the sheet that you want to delete open in the Calc window, select **Edit**, **Sheet**, **Delete**. You are asked whether you want to permanently delete the sheet; select **Yes**. The sheet is removed.

TIP

You can also select multiple sheets (if you want to delete more than one sheet). Select **Edit**, **Sheet**, **Select**. The Select Sheets dialog box opens. Select the sheets in the dialog box and then click **OK**. You can now delete all the selected sheets, Using the **Edit**, **Sheet**, **Delete** commands.

4 Open Rename Sheet Dialog

You can rename your sheets to give them more descriptive names. Right-click on any sheet's name tab (at the bottom of the sheet) and select **Rename Sheet** from the shortcut menu.

5 Rename Sheet

In the Rename Sheet dialog box type a new name for the sheet and then click **OK**.

TIP

You can rearrange your sheets as needed. Grab a sheet by its name tab and drag it to a new location in relation to the other sheets in the spreadsheet.

124 Sort and Filter Data

When you work with large sheets containing data such as employees, products, or lists, it is useful to be able to sort and filter the data. Calc provides you with the ability to sort spreadsheet data and also to filter data; in effect, these features (and other database features provided by Calc) allow you to use Calc for database management.

1 Open Define Range Dialog

The first thing you need to do is identify the database for Calc. Select all the data in your database list including your column headings (these are actually used to identify the column that will be used when sorting the items in the list). Select **Data**, **Define Range**. The Define Database Range dialog box opens.

CHAPTER 12: Creating Spreadsheets with OpenOffice.org Calc

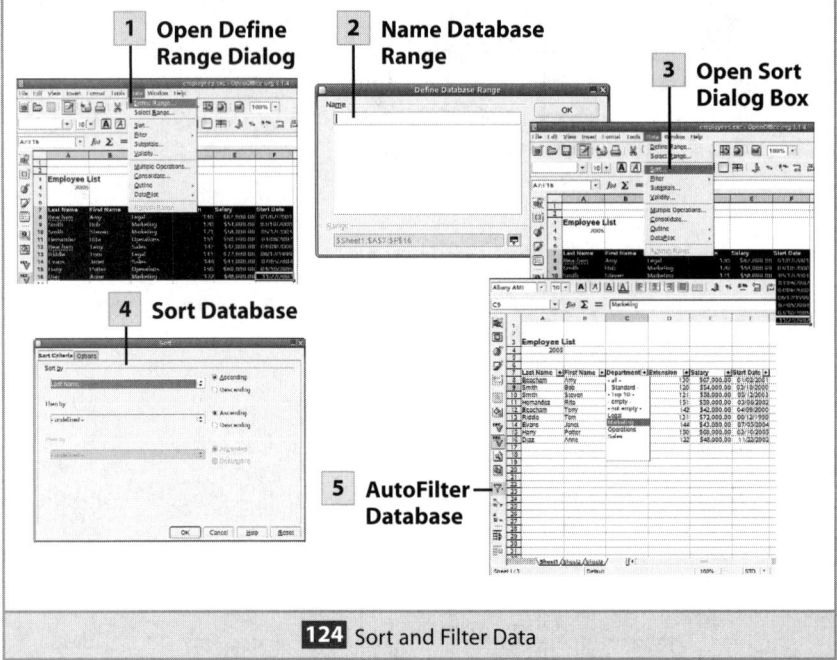

124 Sort and Filter Data

2 Name Database Range

Type a name for your database in the **Name** box of the Define Database Range dialog box. You can enter any descriptive name; this is not a filename. The name is used to identify the database (the selected list) only. Click **OK**.

3 Open Sort Dialog Box

Now you can sort the database by a particular field (column heading). Click in any cell that is part of the database list that you named in step 2. Select **Data**, **Sort**. The Sort dialog box opens.

4 Sort Database

Select the first field drop-down box to select the field (column heading) that you want to use to sort the list. If you want to select a secondary sort criterion (or even a third), use the additional criteria drop-down lists provided.

Click **OK**. The database list is sorted based on the criteria that you set.

TIP

You can also quickly sort a database or a selected list using the **Sort Ascending** or **Sort Descending** buttons on the Main toolbar. Only select the items in the list to use these buttons. Do not select your column headings (the field names that you used to describe the columns such as Name, Address, and so on); they will end up being sorted with the other data.

5 AutoFilter Database

You can also quickly filter your data; meaning view a subset of the data based on a particular field and its contents. For example, you could view all your clients in Indiana by doing an autofilter of a State field where the criterion is "Indiana".

Select the **AutoFilter** button on the Main toolbar. A set of drop-down lists appears to the right of each of your column headings. Select a list and choose a field parameter (the drop-down list shows each of the entries that you have entered in that particular field). As soon as you select an entry in the field drop-down box, the database list will be filtered based on the selection.

You can further filter the database by selected parameters for any of the other fields using that field's drop-down list. After you have finished filtering the database list, select the **AutoFilter** button. The Database list appears in its entirety, and the autofilter drop-down lists for each column heading disappear.

TIP

You can also create more complex filters that allow you to filter using conditional statements. To open the Standard Filter dialog box, select **Data**, **Filter**, **Standard Filter**. Select the field or fields that you want to filter the list by and include conditional statements as needed.

125 About Calc Charts

Charts provide pictorial representations of the data in your spreadsheet. Charts can be used to emphasize trends shown by the data, and charts often make it easier for someone looking at the data to understand what the data really means.

Calc provides a number of different chart types that can be used to depict your numerical data. Some of the most useful chart types are

293

- Line charts—Line charts are used to show change over time. They emphasize the highs and the lows in the data. Line charts can show business growth over time or the sinking of a particular stock fund over time.
- Column/bar charts—These types of charts are useful for comparing how different groups of data points compare. For example, you can see how different sales regions compare in terms of quarterly or yearly sales. Column charts can also contain multiple data points so that you could chart data related to all four quarters of the year, with each quarter represented as a separate column for each of your sales regions.
- Area charts—These charts are useful for showing trends over long periods of time because they emphasize the general direction of the data points (whether values are going up or going down). Rather than the severe peaks and valleys that you see in line charts, area charts emphasize the area under the graph line, showing a gradual rise or drop over time rather than the short-term fluctuations shown by line charts.
- Pie charts—Pie charts show how the parts relate to the whole. For example, if you want to view pictorially how your budget money is spent by category (such as supplies, salaries, and so on), a pie chart could be used to view each spending category and its percent in relation to the whole budget.

NOTE

Calc also provides scatter charts and net charts. Scatter charts are used to identify data clusters, which show a correlation between data points. Net charts show how uniform a set of data points are that have been plotted.

When you create a chart in Calc, you are walked through the steps of selecting the chart type and adding labels or other information to the chart. A new chart can be created as an object on an existing sheet in your spreadsheet (such as the same sheet that contains the data), or you can choose to place the chart on a new sheet.

126 Insert and Format a Chart

Often you may want to add a chart to your spreadsheet either to present the information to others or to help yourself visualize the data. The following steps will help you do that.

✔ **BEFORE YOU BEGIN**

125 About Calc Charts

126 Insert and Format a Chart

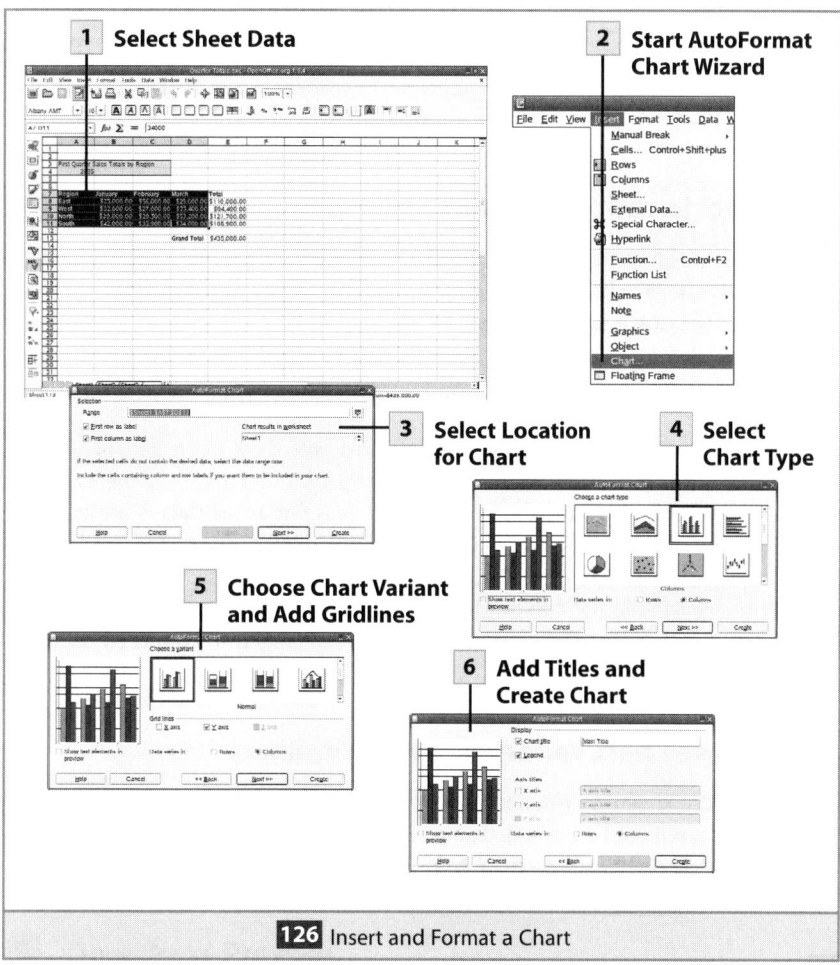

126 Insert and Format a Chart

1 Select Sheet Data

Select the data that you want to chart. Include row or column headings so that the data points can be labeled and a legend can be created for the chart.

2 Start AutoFormat Chart Wizard

Select **Insert**, **Chart** from the menu. The AutoFormat Chart Wizard opens.

295

CHAPTER 12: Creating Spreadsheets with OpenOffice.org Calc

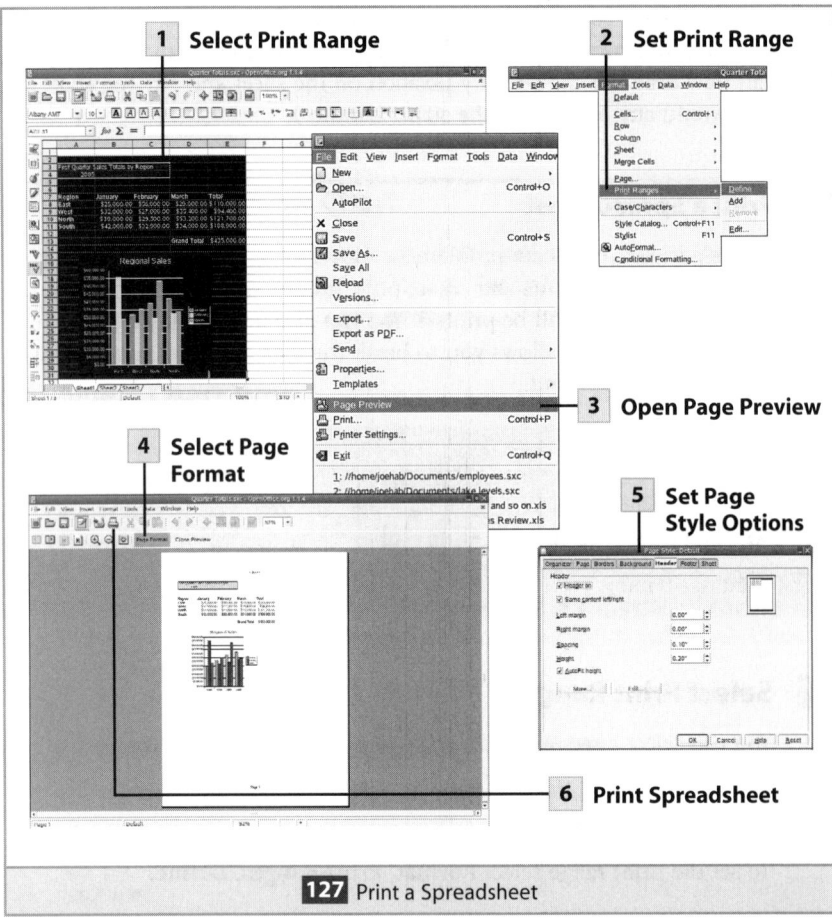

127 Print a Spreadsheet

4 Select Page Format

You may want to add information in the header or footer of the pages of your sheet printout. This allows you to add page numbers, the date, and other repeating information on each page. You can also add borders and backgrounds to the pages of your printout.

Select the **Page Format** button on the Page Preview window's Object bar. The Page Style dialog box opens.

5 Set Page Style Options

In the Page Style dialog box you can set page, border, and background settings using the appropriate tab. To set header or footer settings, select the **Header** or **Footer** tab. Set the header or footer spacing and margins using the appropriate spinner box.

To place information in the header or footer, select the **Edit** button on the Header or Footer tab. The Header or Footer dialog box opens.

Enter the information that you want to appear in the header or footer using the Left Area, Center Area, and Right Area panes. To enter information such as page number or date in a header or footer use the buttons provided below the header or footer area panes. After you have completed inserting the information for the header or footer, click **OK**. This returns you to the Page Style Dialog box. Click **OK** to close the dialog box.

6 Print Spreadsheet

When you are ready to send your previewed print job to the default printer, select the **Print File Directly** button on the Page Preview window's Function bar. The printout is sent to the printer.

TIP

You can also print the spreadsheet via the Print dialog box. This allows you to select the printer that you want to use for the print job and also allows you to set print options. Select **File**, **Print** to open the Print dialog box.

CHAPTER 13

Creating Presentations with OpenOffice.org Impress

IN THIS CHAPTER:

- 128 About OpenOffice.org Impress
- 129 Create a New Presentation
- 130 Insert a New Slide
- 131 Add Text to a Slide
- 132 Modify Slide Layout
- 133 Change Slide Design
- 134 Use the Object Bar
- 135 Insert Graphics and Other Objects
- 136 Select a Slide Transition
- 137 Add Slide Animation Effects
- 138 Change the Workspace View
- 139 Rehearse Slide Show Timings
- 140 Change Slide Show Settings
- 141 Run the Slide Show
- 142 Print Slides, Notes, and Handouts

CHAPTER 13: Creating Presentations with OpenOffice.org Impress

Planning and then actually getting up in front of a group of people to give a presentation can be nerve wracking for even the most seasoned presenter. OpenOffice.org provides Impress, a presentation application that makes it easy for you to create a presentation that provides both insight and impact in relation to any subject matter.

In this chapter we take a look at how to create a presentation using Impress. We begin with a look at the options for creating a new presentation and then concentrate on the various aspects of creating presentation slides including the insertion of text and graphics.

128 About OpenOffice.org Impress

OpenOffice.org Impress provides all the tools that you need to create both simple and complex presentations. You can create simple text slides and then add animation effects and slide transitions. You can even add multimedia content such as sound and other media objects to your slides to create full-blown multimedia presentations.

The Impress application window provides the same overall layout as the other OpenOffice.org applications such as Writer and Calc. You have the Function bar, Object bar, and Main toolbar, which give you access to most of the tools that you need to create your presentations. Impress also provides additional toolbars such as the Presentation toolbar, which makes it easy for you to quickly insert a new slide or change the slide design or layout.

The Impress application window provides the workspace and toolbars embraced by the other OpenOffice.org applications.

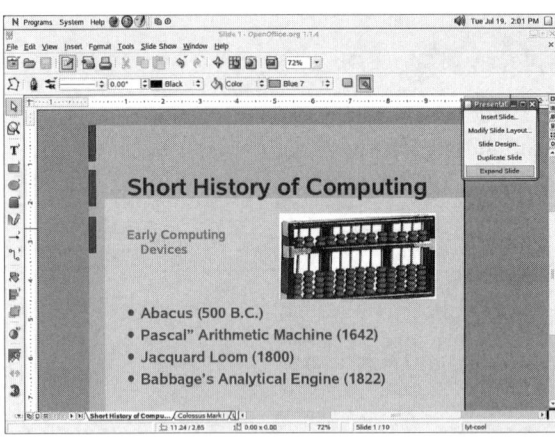

Impress also provides different options for the output of your presentations. Although most of us think of these types of presentations being shown primarily on a computer (or video projection system), Impress also makes it easy for you to design your presentations for other types of outputs such as overheads, papers, and actual 35mm slides.

Impress provides a fairly slide-centric approach to creating your presentation; in the default Drawing view you are able to concentrate on each slide as you add text and other objects to the slide. Then slide transitions and animation effects can be added on a slide-by-slide basis. However, you can also use different workspace views, such as the Outline view and the Slides view, which allow you to easily move content from slide to slide or rearrange the slides in the presentation, respectively.

129 Create a New Presentation

Impress provides the AutoPilot Presentation Wizard, which walks you through the process of creating a new presentation. The wizard allows you to select a background for the slides in the presentation and quickly add a standard slide transition for the slides in the presentation.

✔ BEFORE YOU BEGIN

128 About OpenOffice.org Impress

1 Start Impress

Select the **Programs**, **Office**, **Presentation**. The AutoPilot Presentation Wizard opens.

TIP

If you don't want the AutoPilot Presentation Wizard to appear each time you start Impress, select the **Do Not Show This Dialog Again** check box on the first wizard screen. When you open Impress in the future, you are taken directly to the Impress workspace and a new blank slide opens. You can then open existing presentations as needed. If you do want to use the AutoPilot to create a new presentation, select **File**, **AutoPilot**, **Presentation**.

CHAPTER 13: Creating Presentations with OpenOffice.org Impress

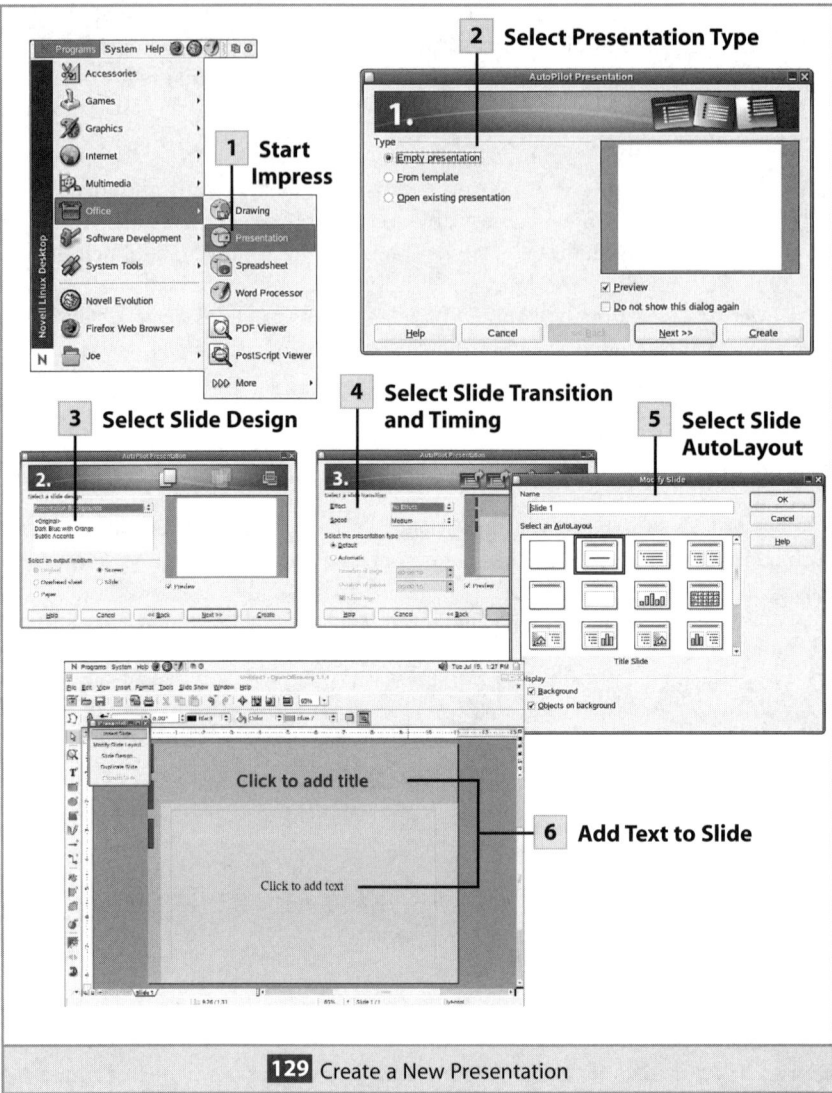

129 Create a New Presentation

2 Select Presentation Type

On the first wizard screen select a new presentation type such as **Empty Presentation** or **From Template**. If you select **From Template** a list of templates appears. Select a template from the drop-down list. To continue, click **Next**.

> **TIP**
>
> If you want to open an existing presentation from the AutoPilot Wizard, select the **Open Existing Presentation** option.

3 Select Slide Design

On the next screen select a slide design from the **Presentation Backgrounds** drop-down list. To select an output medium (other than the default: Screen), select the appropriate option button such as **Overhead Sheet** or **Paper**. After making your selections, click **Next** to continue.

4 Select Slide Transition and Timing

On the next wizard screen you are provided the option of selecting a slide transition for the slides in the presentation. Select a transition type from the **Effect** drop-down list (such as Fly in from Left or Dissolve). To set the speed of the transition select the **Speed** drop-down list and select a speed (Medium is the default).

If you want to create a self-running automatic presentation, select the **Automatic** option button. You can then set the page and pause duration timings using the appropriate spinner box. After you have configured the settings on this wizard screen, select **Create** to continue.

> **NOTE**
>
> You do not have to select a transition type for your slides in the AutoPilot Presentation Wizard window. You can add transitions to your slides using the **Slide Show** menu (and then **Slide Transition**) as you create each of the slides.

5 Select Slide AutoLayout

The Modify Slide dialog box opens. This allows you to set the AutoLayout for the first slide in the presentation. This layout is typically Title Slide layout. You can also enter a name for the slide. This is a descriptive name, which is saved with the slide's properties. After selecting the slide layout and entering the optional slide name, click **OK**. The new slide appears in the Impress window in the Drawing view, which is used to add text and other objects to the slide (only one slide is shown in the Drawing view at a time).

6 Add Text to Slide

Placeholder text is provided on the new slide. Select any of the placeholder text and enter your slide text as needed.

TIP

To save your new presentation, select the **Save Document** button on the Function bar. In the Save As dialog box provide a name and a location for the new file; then select **Save**.

130 Insert a New Slide

As you create your slide presentation, you will need to enter new slides. The quickest way to insert a new slide is using the Presentation toolbar. You can also insert a new slide using the Insert menu.

✔ BEFORE YOU BEGIN

128 About OpenOffice.org Impress
129 Create a New Presentation

1 Activate Presentation Toolbar

If the Presentation toolbar is not open in the Impress workspace, select the **View**, **Toolbars**, **Presentation**. The Presentation toolbar appears.

TIP

You can dock the Presentation toolbar in the Impress workspace. For example, if you want to dock the Presentation toolbar on the right side of the workspace, hold down the **Ctrl** key and then drag the Presentation toolbar to the right border of the Impress window. When you dock the Presentation toolbar you are provided access to a series of buttons at the bottom of the toolbar that allow you to quickly switch the current view in the workspace.

2 Insert New Slide

On the Presentation toolbar, select **Insert Slide**. The Insert Slide dialog box appears.

131 Add Text to a Slide

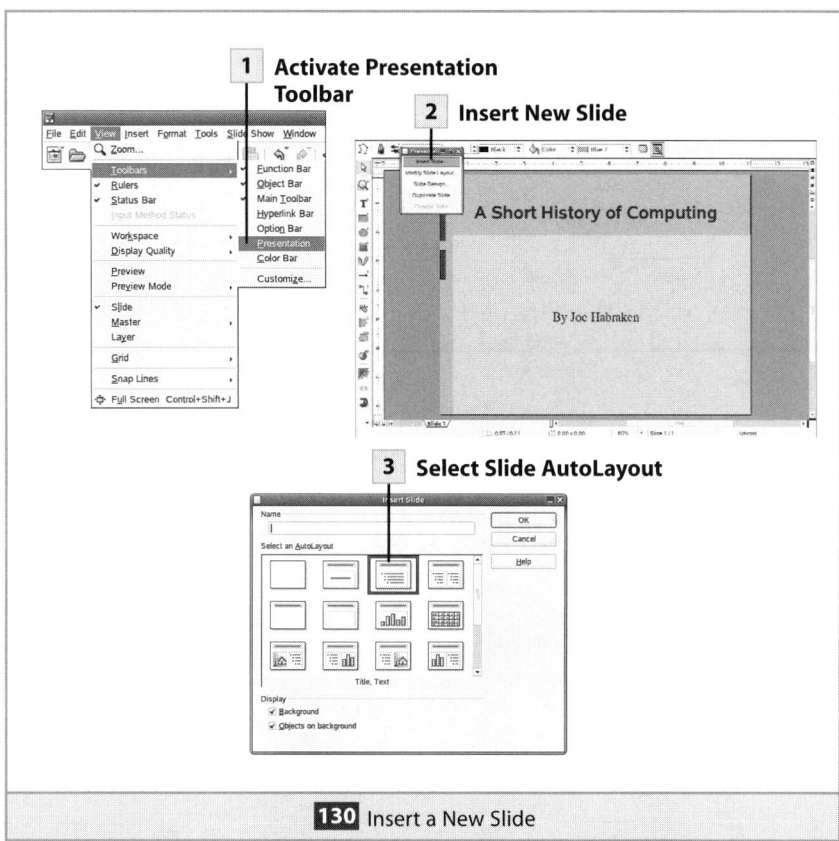

130 Insert a New Slide

3 Select Slide AutoLayout

In the Insert Slide dialog box type an optional name for the slide. Select a layout for the new slide from the AutoLayouts provided (the Title, Text layout is selected by default after you have created a title slide for the presentation). After making your selection, click **OK**. The new slide appears in the Impress workspace.

131 Add Text to a Slide

After you've created a slide, you can add text to it by selecting any of the placeholder text on the slide and then typing your text as needed. In some situations you may want to add text to a slide in a new text box. You can add text boxes, text boxes where the text fits the frame (making the font size dependant on the frame size), and you can also add callouts that allow you to provide information related to a certain part of an image, chart, or other inserted object.

307

CHAPTER 13: Creating Presentations with OpenOffice.org Impress

✔ **BEFORE YOU BEGIN**

130 Insert a New Slide

1 Select Text Tool

Insert a new slide or use a current slide in a presentation. On the Main toolbar, select the **Text** button's arrow and select one of the text tools such as **Text** or **Fit Text to Frame** (this changes the font to mimic the size of the drawn frame).

TIP

You can move from slide to slide in your presentation using the navigation buttons at the bottom of the workspace. To select a particular slide, click on the tab for that slide. The slide tabs show the name that you entered when you created the slide.

2 Draw Text Box

Use the mouse to "draw" a text box on the current slide. When you release the mouse a cursor appears in the text box.

3 Enter Text

Type the text that you want to place in the text box.

TIP

You can drag the text box by its border to any location on the slide. If you want to change the size or shape of the text box after you have entered text, use the sizing handles on the text box. After text is in the text box, you can select the text using the I-beam and then format the text using the font formatting and alignment tools on the Object bar.

4 Add Callout to Slide

Callouts allow you to draw attention to a particular place on a diagram or picture. Select the **Text** button's arrow (as in step 1) and then select the Callouts tool. Drag the mouse from the item that you want to "point out" with the callout to a position where you want the callout's text box to appear. Then release the mouse.

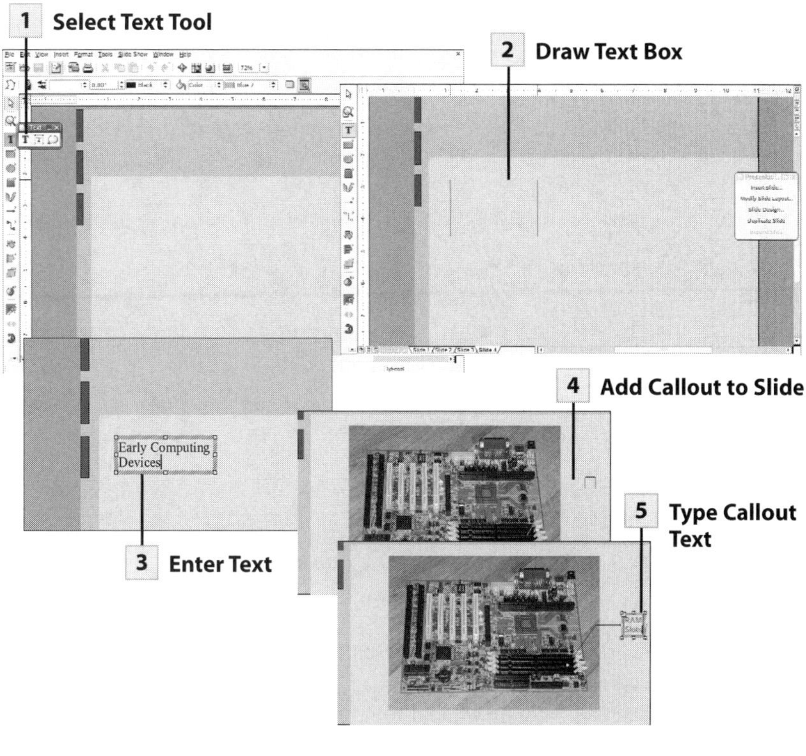

132 Modify Slide Layout

⁵ Type Callout Text

Type and format the text in the callout's text box as needed. You can drag the callout to position it more precisely on the slide.

132 Modify Slide Layout

You can modify the layout for the current slide in the Drawing view. Because layout changes can affect text and objects already on the slide, you may want to finalize the layout for a slide before adding items to the slide.

✔ **BEFORE YOU BEGIN**

130 Insert a New Slide

309

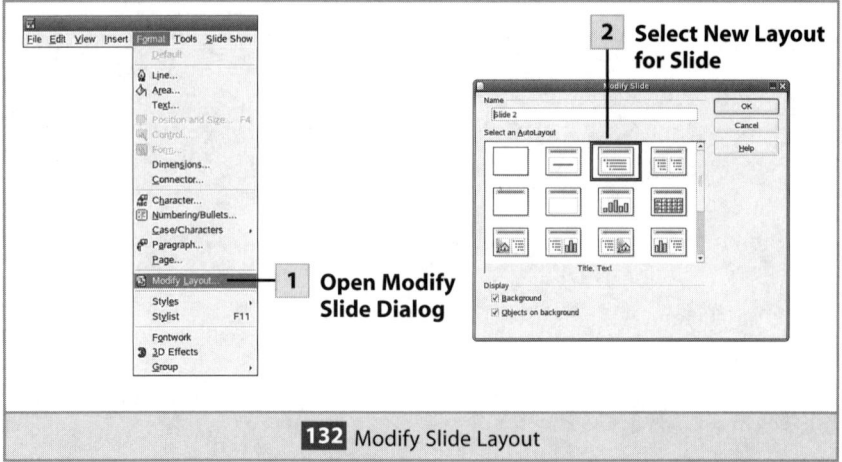

132 Modify Slide Layout

1 Open Modify Slide Dialog

Open the slide in the Drawing view. Select **Format**, **Modify Layout**. The Modify Slide dialog box opens.

TIP

You can also use the Presentation toolbar to duplicate the current slide. This allows you to change the layout for the slide and see how the change affects the text and objects already on the slide.

2 Select New Layout for Slide

Select a new layout for the slide in the Modify Slide dialog box. Then click **OK** to accept the selection.

TIP

Changing the slide layout negates you from "undoing" any changes made to the slide before you change the layout. Although changing the layout preserves current objects on the slide, it may make them look a little strange when the new layout places additional new objects on the slide.

133 Change Slide Design

You can change the slide design for a slide or slides in your presentation. This changes the background color and the design elements provided by the previous design. As with slide layouts, it makes sense to select the slide design before you enter a lot of text or other objects on the slides. This allows you to arrange objects on a slide so that they complement the design elements provided by the selected design. When you select a different design, you are actually selecting a template that is applied to the slides.

1 Open Slide Design Dialog

Open the slide in the Drawing view that you want to edit. Select **Format**, **Styles**, **Slide Design**. The Slide Design dialog box opens.

TIP

You can also open the Slide Design dialog box from the Presentation toolbar. Select **Slide Design**.

2 Load Slide Designs

Recently used designs are listed in the Slide Design dialog box. To load other available designs, select the **Load** button. The Load Slide Design dialog box opens.

3 Choose Design for Loading

Select **Presentation Backgrounds** in the Categories box of the Load Slide Design dialog box. This lists the slide designs available. Select a design and then click **OK**. You are returned to the Slide Design dialog box.

TIP

You can download additional templates and slide designs from the OpenOffice.org website. The template page URL is http://documentation.openoffice.org/Samples_Templates/User/template/index.htm The template page provides links for downloading the templates and also provides information on the folder that you should place the templates in so that Impress can load them when you want to access them. This template page also provides templates for other OpenOffice.org applications such as Writer and Calc.

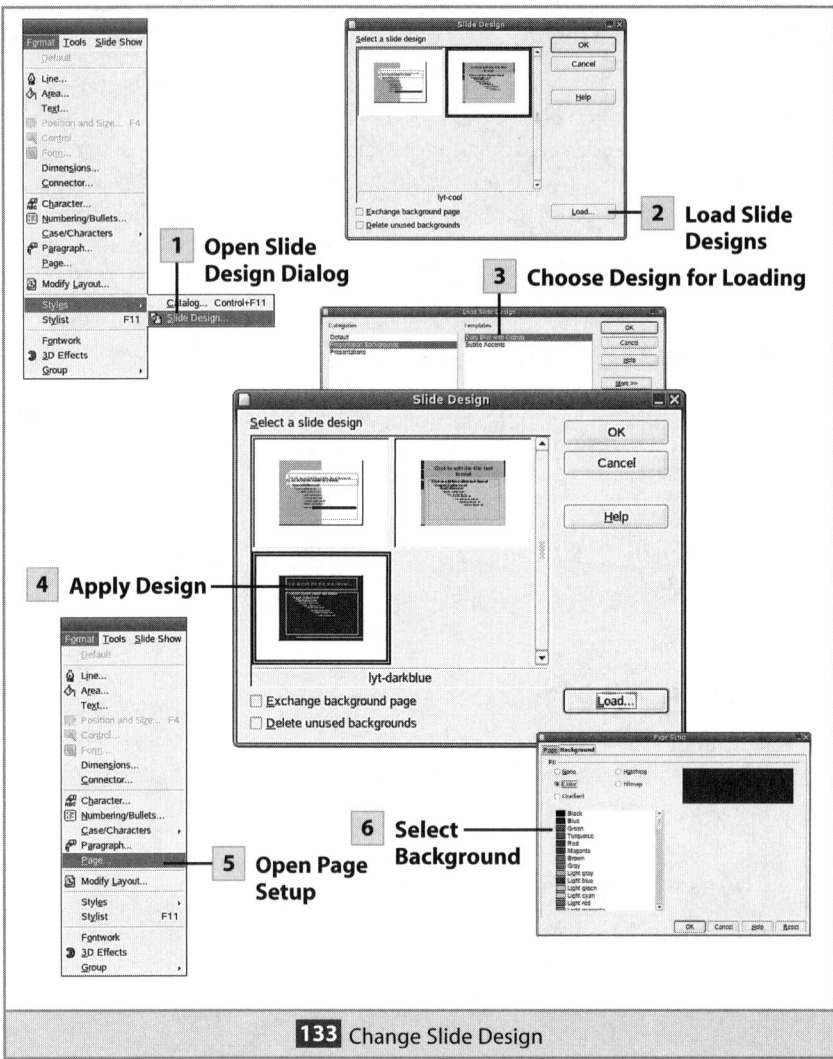

133 Change Slide Design

4 Apply Design

Select the newly loaded design in the Slide Design dialog box. Then click **OK** to apply the design to the current slide.

5 Open Page Setup

You can change the background for the current slide; select **Format**, **Page**. The Page Setup dialog box opens. Select the **Background** tab if necessary.

134 Use the Object Bar

6 Select Background

Use the option buttons on the Background tab to select the type of background to apply to the slide: **Color**, **Gradient**, **Hatching**, or **Bitmap**. Then select the background for the slide from the currently selected background type. When you are ready to apply the new background, click **OK**.

TIP

You can change the background color and design elements for all the slides in a presentation. This allows you to add objects to all your slides such as a company logo or other repeating elements. You change the overall design of the slides in the presentation by editing the master slide. Select **View**, **Master**, **Drawing** from the menu. Be careful not to change the text box format provided on the master. You can, however, add or replace the design elements on the master. You can also change the background. Select **Format**, **Page**. Use the Page Setup dialog box to change the background for the master. You can then return to the slide view; select **Format**, **Slide**.

134 Use the Object Bar

The Object bar provides tools specific to the currently selected object on your slide. For example, when you work with a text object (a text box) the Object bar provides font formatting and alignment tools. When you work on a drawn object (such as an ellipse drawn using the Mail toolbar Ellipse tool), the Object bar provides tools that can be used to format the line style, color, and background color for the drawn object.

1 Use Text Formatting Tools

Select the text in a text box. The Object bar changes to the text formatting tools. Use the font formatting tools such as the **Font** box to select a new font and the **Size** box to select a new font size. You can also enable other formatting attributes such as **Bold** and **Italic**. To change the alignment for the selected text, select one of the alignment buttons such as **Centered**.

313

CHAPTER 13: Creating Presentations with OpenOffice.org Impress

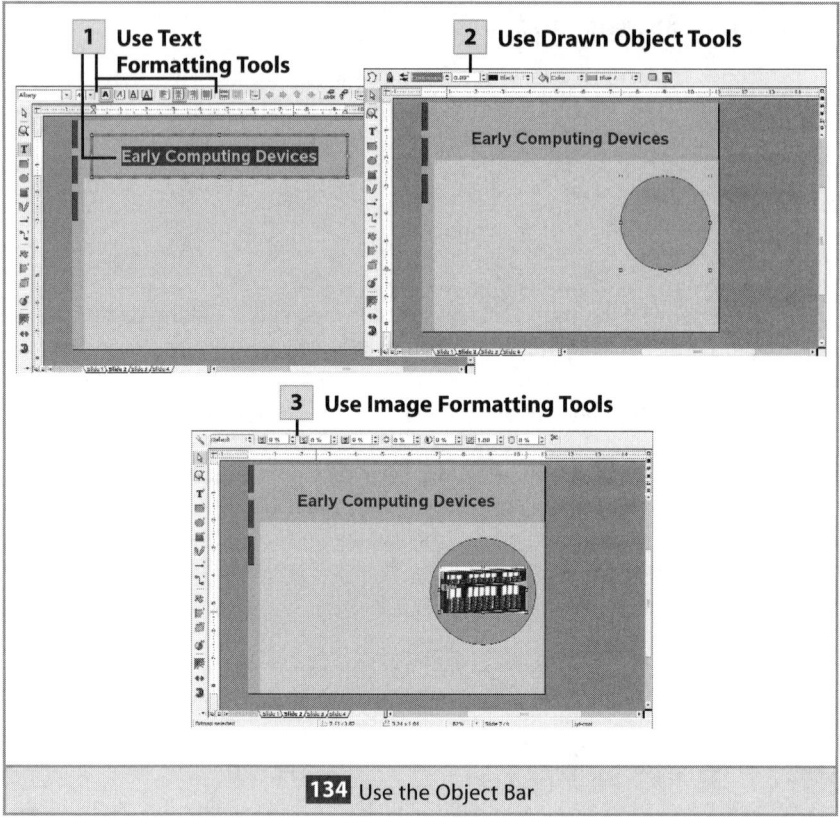

134 Use the Object Bar

2 Use Drawn Object Tools

Draw an object such as an ellipse using the Ellipse tool on the Main toolbar. With the drawn object selected use the Object bar tools such as the **Line Style**, **Line Width**, or **Line Color** tools to format the object. To change the fill color for the object, select the **Area Style/Filling** drop-down list and select a new color.

3 Use Image Formatting Tools

Insert a graphic on a slide (select **Insert**, **Graphics**). When the graphic is selected, the Object bar provides tools for formatting the graphic. Use the Red, Blue, Green spinner boxes to change the basic color mix for the graphic. Use the Brightness and Contrast spinner boxes to lighten or darken the image as needed.

135 Insert Graphics and Other Objects

You can insert graphics and other objects to enhance the slides in your presentation. Graphics can be informative, such as a picture that provides information related to the slide content, or used just to add interest to your slides, such as a design element. You can also insert other objects (just about anything really), such as video and sound or application objects such as Calc spreadsheets and charts. Any application that you run on your system can actually be the host for an object placed on a slide.

1 Open Insert Graphics Dialog

Select **Insert**, **Graphics** from the menu. This opens the Insert Graphics dialog box.

TIP

You can search for open source and free clipart and images on the Web. A good place to start is www.openclipart.org. You can browse for specific clipart on this site or download the entire library.

2 Insert Graphic

In the Insert Graphics dialog box browse your folders as needed to locate the graphic. Then select the graphic file and then select **Open**. The graphic is placed on the slide. You can drag the graphic to a new location or size it as needed. Tools for modifying the graphic are available on the Object bar.

TIP

OpenOffice.org allows you to use graphics in a number of different graphic file formats including .bmp, .eps, .gif, .jpg, and .png.

3 Open Gallery

You can find a number of 3-D graphics, textures, and other graphic objects to add to your slides in the Gallery. Select the **Gallery** button on the Function bar. The Gallery opens at the top of the workspace.

CHAPTER 13: Creating Presentations with OpenOffice.org Impress

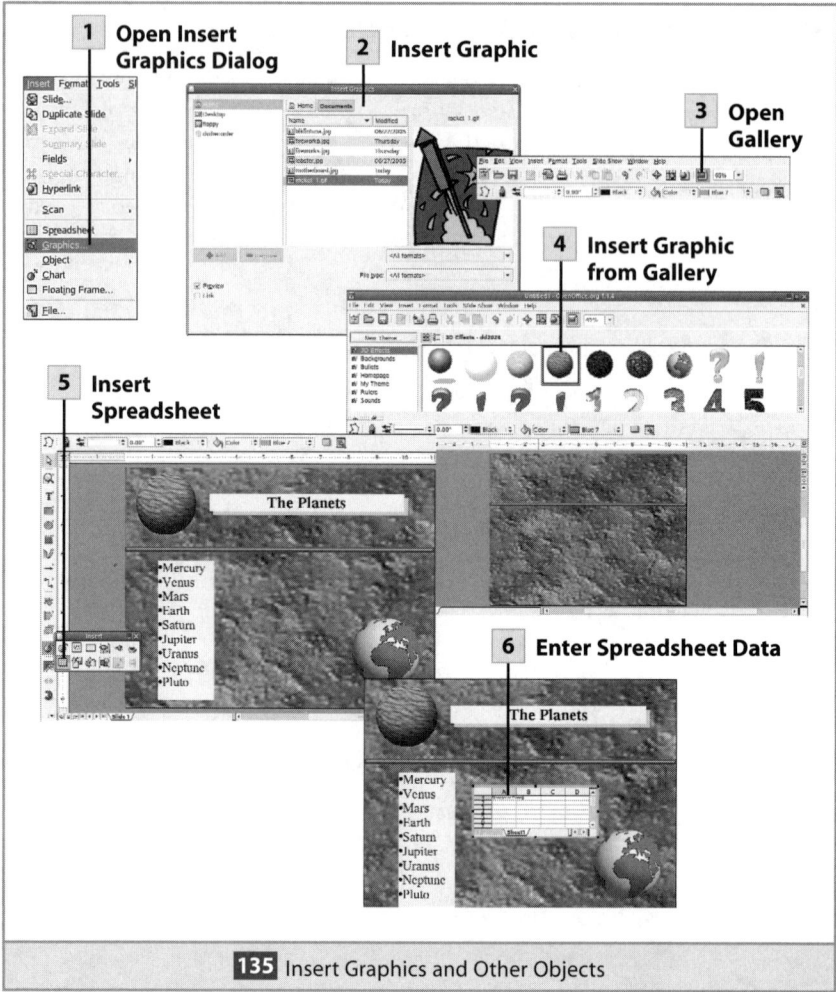

135 Insert Graphics and Other Objects

4 Drag Graphic from Gallery

Select one of the Gallery categories such as **3D Effects**, **Bullets**, or **Rulers**. Drag an object from the Gallery to the current slide. After the object is on the slide, you can move and size it as needed.

TIP

You can also drag sounds from the Gallery to your current slide. To see a more descriptive listing of the sounds in the Gallery's Sound category, select the **Detailed View** button at the top of the Gallery pane.

TIP

To place repeating graphics or other objects such as a text box containing the date, slide show title, or your name, open the master slide (select **View**, **Master**, **Drawing**) and then place items on the master. You can insert fields such as the Date and Author (select **Insert**, **Fields**) at the top or bottom of the master slide and add a company logo or other graphic to the master. Remember that objects that you place on the master appear on all the slides in the presentation. Take advantage of the different design objects in the Gallery to build eye-catching master slides.

5 Insert Spreadsheet

You can place other objects on your slides including charts and spreadsheets. To insert a new spreadsheet on a slide, select the **Insert** button's arrow on the Main toolbar and then select **Spreadsheet** from the object list. A new blank spreadsheet is placed as an object on the slide.

6 Enter Spreadsheet Data

When the spreadsheet object is selected the toolbars provide the tools that you would normally have access to in Calc. Enter data in the spreadsheet as needed. When you click outside the spreadsheet object, the toolbars provide the Impress tools normally available in the Impress workspace.

TIP

You can drag text boxes, images, and other objects off a slide and park these objects in the gray area of the workspace. This allows you to "accumulate" objects for a particular slide and then arrange them as needed or actually move them to a different slide.

136 Select a Slide Transition

Slide transitions allow you to add some interest and glitz to your slide presentations. A transition uses a special effect (such as dissolve), and each slide in a presentation can be assigned a different transition type. You see the transitions as you advance from the current slide to the next slide during your slide show.

CHAPTER 13: Creating Presentations with OpenOffice.org Impress

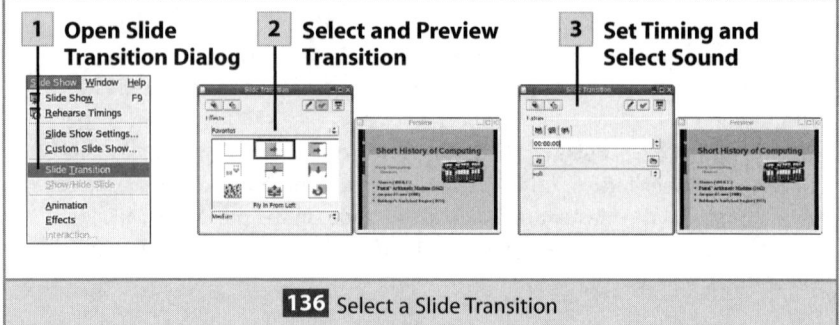

136 Select a Slide Transition

1 Open Slide Transition Dialog

To add a transition to the current slide, select the **Slide Show**, **Slide Transition** from the menu. The Slide Transition dialog box opens.

2 Select and Preview Transition

Select the **Preview** button on the top right of the Slide Transition dialog box (this allows you to preview the transition). Then select a transition from the transition list. Select the **Assign** button (the check mark button); a preview of the transition appears in the Preview window when you assign the transition to the slide (using the Assign button).

3 Set Timing and Select Sound

Select the **Extras** button on the top left of the Slide Transition dialog box. This screen allows you to add automatic timings for the transition and add a sound effect to the transition.

Select the **Automatic Transition** button and then use the time spinner box to set the timing for the transition. To add a sound effect to the transition, select the **Sound** button and then select a sound from the list. When you select the **Assign** button, the timing and the sound are assigned to the transition and you receive a preview in the Preview window. After you have completed your transition settings, you can close the Slide Transition dialog box and the Preview box.

137 Add Slide Animation Effects

Another way to add special effects to your presentation slides is to take advantage of animation effects. These effects can be assigned to a particular object on a slide such as a text box or graphic.

There are "regular" effects that are used to control the entry of an object (or objects) onto the slide (such as a dissolve), and there are also text effects. A text effect can be used to animate the text in a text box such as a bulleted list. For example, assigning the **Fly in from Left** text effect to a text box causes each item in the list to fly in from the left (separately) when you click the mouse (a mouse click is required for each item in the list).

> ✔ **BEFORE YOU BEGIN**
>
> 135 Insert Graphics and Other Objects

1 Select Object

Select an object on the current slide (or select multiple objects by using the mouse to drag a selection frame around those objects).

2 Open Animation Effects Dialog

Select **Slide Show**, **Effects** from the menu. The Animation Effects dialog box opens. Select the **Preview** button in the Animation Effects dialog box so that you can view a preview of any effects you apply to the selected object or objects.

3 Select Object Effect

If you want to apply an animation effect to an object (any object), select the effect category in the **Effects** drop-down list (such as Favorites, Cross-fading, and so on). Then select an effect in the effect box.

To change the speed of the effect, select the **Speed** drop-down list and select **Slow**, **Medium**, or **Fast**. To apply the effect and view a preview (in the Preview window), select the **Assign** button (check mark).

CHAPTER 13: Creating Presentations with OpenOffice.org Impress

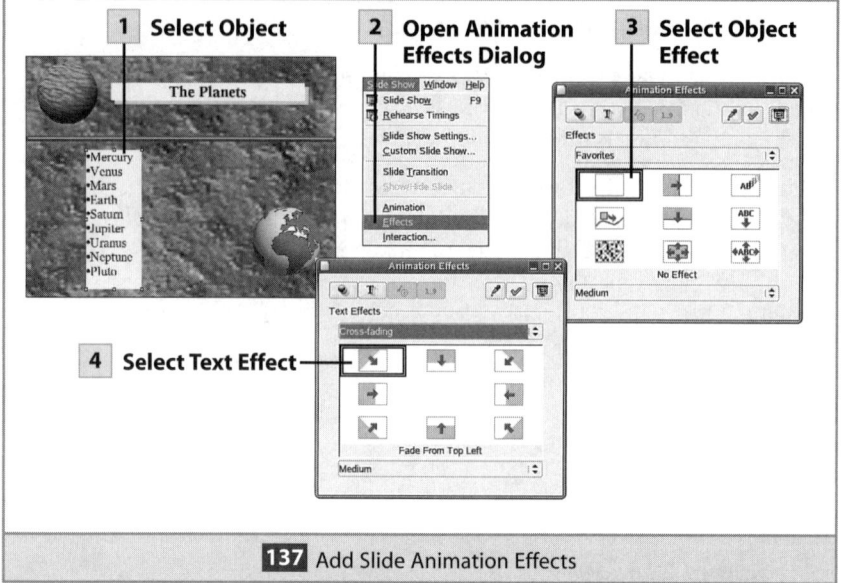

137 Add Slide Animation Effects

TIP

You can also select a sound to accompany your animation effects. After selecting an effect, select the **Extras** button. On the Extras screen select the Sound button and select a sound to accompany the effect. You can also select **Fade Object to Color** on the Extras screen and select a color to be used for the fade.

TIP

You can configure the order that objects appear on the slide when you have set effects for multiple objects. In the Animation Effects dialog box, select the **Order** button. The Order list appears for the slide, listing all the objects on the slide. Drag objects in the list to select the order entry for the various items. Remember to select **Assign** after making any changes to the animation effect settings.

4 Select Text Effect

If you want to apply a text effect rather than an object effect (as discussed in step 3), select the **Text Effects** button in the Animation Effects dialog box. Select the Text Effects drop-down list and select an effect from the list (such as Cross-fading, Fly In, and so on). Then select one of the effects shown in the Effect box.

After selecting the effect, select the **Assign** button to apply the effect to the text box. A preview of the effect will appear in the Preview window.

After you have finished applying your object or text effects, close the Animation Effects dialog box and then the Preview window.

138 Change the Workspace View

After you create slides in the Draw view, you might want to take a "bigger picture" look at your presentation. Impress provides different workspace views including the Outline, Slides, and Notes views.

The Outline view allows you to see your presentation as an outline and makes it easy to move text (particularly bulleted lists) from one slide to another. You can use the Slides view to quickly view all the slides and change the slide order as needed. The Notes view allows you to view a notes area for each slide, which provides space for you to type notes related to each slide, allowing you to build your presentation script (what you will say) as you create the slides.

1 Select Workspace View

To select a workspace view, select **View**, **Workspace**, and then select one of the views provided on the Workspace submenu such as **Outline View**.

2 View Presentation as Outline

Open the Outline view (select **View**, **Workspace**, **Outline View**). Use the Main toolbar outline buttons, such as **First Level** or **All Levels**, to shrink or expand the slide text shown, respectively. When you select **First Level** to shrink the slide content to the slide titles only, you can easily drag slides to a new location in the outline.

TIP

You can quickly view the presentation slide show from the current slide in the Outline view. Select the **Slide Show** button on the Main toolbar.

3 Rearrange Slides in the Slides View

Open the Slides view (select **View**, **Workspace**, **Slides View**). This view shows all the slides in the presentation as thumbnails. You can rearrange your slides in this view. Drag a slide to a new location as needed.

CHAPTER 13: Creating Presentations with OpenOffice.org Impress

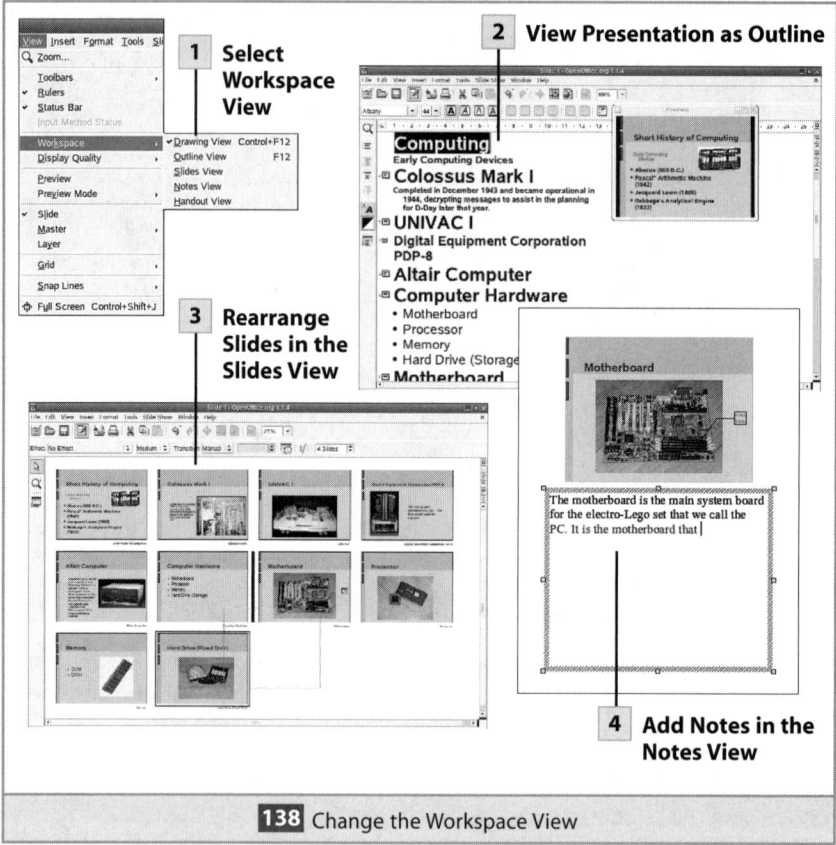

138 Change the Workspace View

TIP

You can quickly assign a transition effect to a slide in the Slides view. Select the slide (or slides by dragging a selection frame around the slides) and then select the transition effect using the **Effect** drop-down list on the Object bar. If you want to see a preview of the effect, open the Preview window; select **View**, **Preview**.

TIP

When you are in the Slides view, you can quickly open any of the slides in the Drawing view by double-clicking on the slide.

4 Add Notes in the Notes View

Open the Notes view (select **View**, **Workspace**, **Notes View**). The current slide is represented by a thumbnail, and a text box appears below the slide. Enter text as needed to the notes text box. This can be notes you will use when you give your presentation or reminders related to the presentation.

TIP

When you print a presentation from the Print dialog box, you can select to print the notes that you have typed on the various slides.

139 Rehearse Slide Show Timings

The Rehearse Slide Show Timings feature allows you to set up the timings for an automated presentation. You actually run the slide show, and a timer appears in the bottom-left corner of the screen. You can then deliver your "speech" and talk about the content of each slide as you would when giving the presentation. When you want to "set" the onscreen duration for a particular slide and move onto the next slide, you click on the timer on the slide show window.

These timing settings are saved with your presentation. The next time you run the automated presentation, the slides change based on the timings that you set during your "dry run" of the presentation. Because setting transition effects is another aspect of readying a slide show, the best place to select transitions and set and review the automatic slide timings is the Slides view.

1 Open Slides View

The fastest way to choose transitions for your slides and then run the Rehearse Timings feature is the Slides view; select **View**, **Workspace**, **Slides View** from the menu.

2 Set Transitions to Automatic

Select all the slides in the presentation and then set the **Transition** drop-down list to **Automatic**.

CHAPTER 13: Creating Presentations with OpenOffice.org Impress

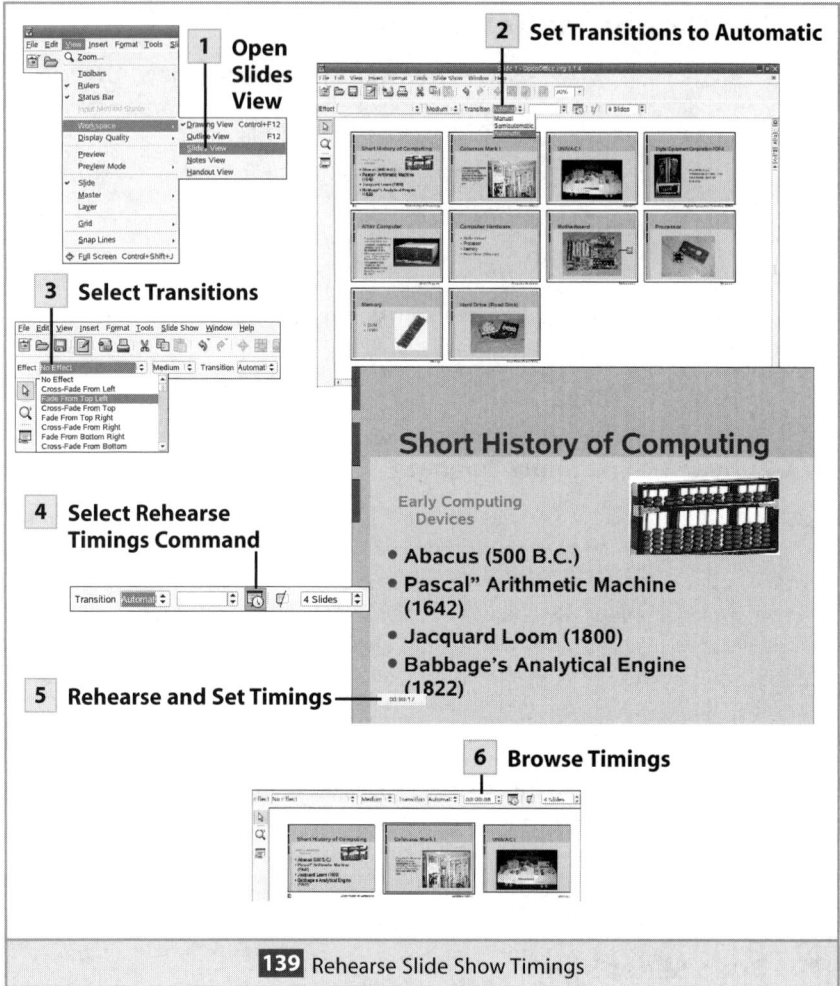

139 Rehearse Slide Show Timings

TIP

If you want all the animation effects that you have added to your slides to play automatically but don't want to have the slides advance until you click the mouse or press the spacebar, select **Semiautomatic** in the Transition drop-down list.

3 Select Transitions

Select a slide or slides and then select a transition from the **Effect** drop-down list. Repeat as needed to set a transition for each slide. You can also set the speed for the transition using the Speed drop-down list to select **Slow**, **Medium**, or **Fast**.

4 Select Rehearse Timings Command

After you have selected your transitions and set the transition mode to automatic, you can set the timing for each slide during the rehearsal. Select the **Rehearse Timings** button on the Object bar.

5 Rehearse and Set Timings

The slide show begins, and the timer appears in the bottom left of the presentation screen. Rehearse your presentation; when you are ready to set the timing for the current slide and advance to the next slide, click on the **Timer**. Repeat as necessary to set all the timings for the presentation slides.

6 Browse Timings

After you complete your presentation, you are returned to the Slides view. Click on a slide to view the timer setting for that slide (it will correspond to the time you set during the rehearsal). You can edit the times (for your slides) by using the Time spinner box as needed.

140 Change Slide Show Settings

You can configure a number of settings related to the slide show using the Slide Show dialog box. You can select where the slide show should begin (select the slide) and configure other settings such as the pause time for restarting an automatic presentation and settings related to the mouse pointer.

1 Open Slide Show Dialog

From any of the workspace views (Drawing view, Slides view, and so on), select **Slide Show**, **Slide Show Settings** from the menu. The Slide Show dialog box opens.

2 Configure Slide Show Settings

To set a new start point for the slide show (other than slide 1), select the **From** option button. Then select the slide from the **Slide** drop-down list. To set the slide show to run in the application window rather than the entire computer screen, select the **Window** option button.

CHAPTER 13: Creating Presentations with OpenOffice.org Impress

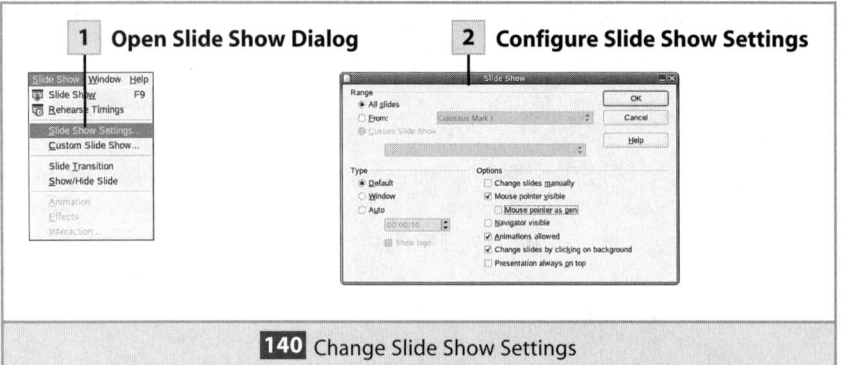

140 Change Slide Show Settings

TIP

You can also select a custom slide show in the Slide Show Settings dialog box. A custom slide show is a slide show that you have configured using the current presentation slides. A custom slide show can present the slides in any order you want. To create a custom slide show (or shows) based on the slides in the current presentation, select **Slide Show, Custom Slide Show**, In the Custom Slide Show dialog box, select **New** to create a custom slide show. (You can select the slides and the order of the slides for the custom slide show.) You can create as many custom shows as you want based on the slides in the presentation.

If you want to set a pause duration (really the intermission time before restarting the presentation) for an automatically running presentation, select the **Auto** button and use the spinner box to set the pause duration (a Pause slide appears at the end of the slide show and stays on the screen until the slide show restarts).

TIP

If you want to run manually a slide show that has been configured as an automatic slide show, select the **Change Slides Manually** check box.

To use the mouse as a pen during the presentation (this allows you to draw on the screen), select the **Mouse Pointer as Pen** check box. After you have completed making your selections in the dialog box, click **OK**.

141 Run the Slide Show

After you have created your slides, configured your transitions and timings, and added animation effects to the objects on your slides, you are ready to run the slide show. You can run the slide show from any of the workspace views. If you have configured the mouse pointer as a pen, you can highlight information on your slides as needed. You can also jump to a particular slide during the slide show using the Navigator.

TIP

If you want the Navigator to be visible during the entire slide show, select the **Navigator Visible** check box in the Slide Show dialog box. Otherwise, you can open the Navigator with the **F5** function key.

1 Run Slide Show

Select **Slide Show**, **Slide Show** from the menu. The slide show begins to run on the computer.

TIP

You can also start the slide show by pressing **F9** or by clicking the **Slide Show** button on the Main toolbar. The slide show starts from the currently displayed slide, so make sure that you are at the beginning of the presentation before starting the slide show.

2 Highlight Content with Mouse

If you configure the mouse as a pen (in the Slide Show dialog box), you can draw on the screen highlighting information for your audience. Hold down the left mouse button and draw as needed.

3 Use Navigator

Click the left mouse button to go forward one slide. Click the right mouse button to go back one slide. If you need to move to a particular slide because of a question from the audience, you can use the Navigator. Press the **F5** function key. The Navigator appears. Use the Navigator to jump to a particular slide. After you have finished showing the slide show, you are returned to the Impress window.

CHAPTER 13: Creating Presentations with OpenOffice.org Impress

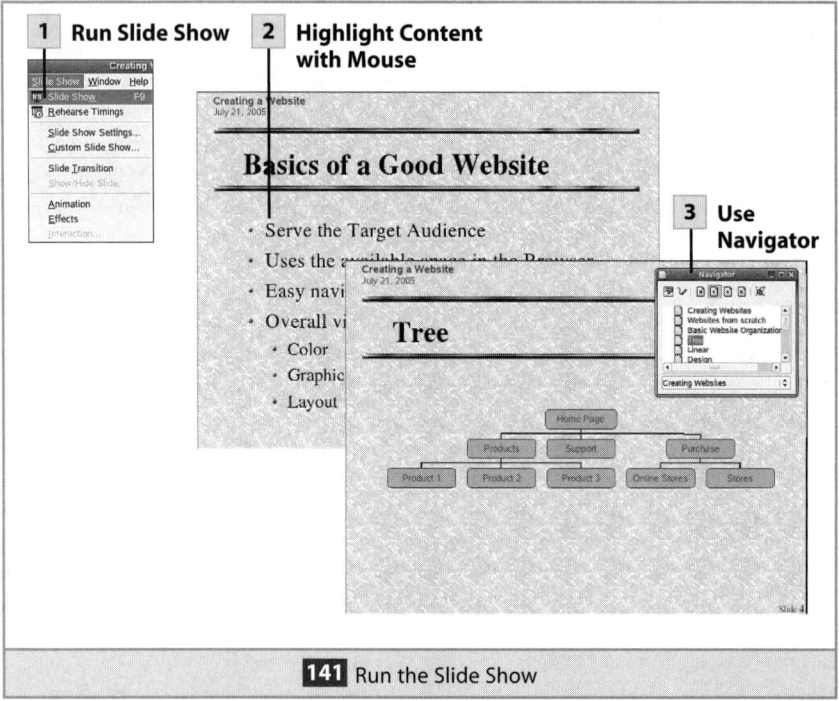

141 Run the Slide Show

TIP

You can stop the slide show at any point by pressing **Escape**.

142 Print Slides, Notes, and Handouts

You can print your slides for reference and also print your notes and create handouts for your audience. The various print settings for a presentation are available in the Print dialog box.

✔ **BEFORE YOU BEGIN**

35 About Printing and NLD
36 Add and Configure a Printer
37 Print to a Printer

142 Print Slides, Notes, and Handouts

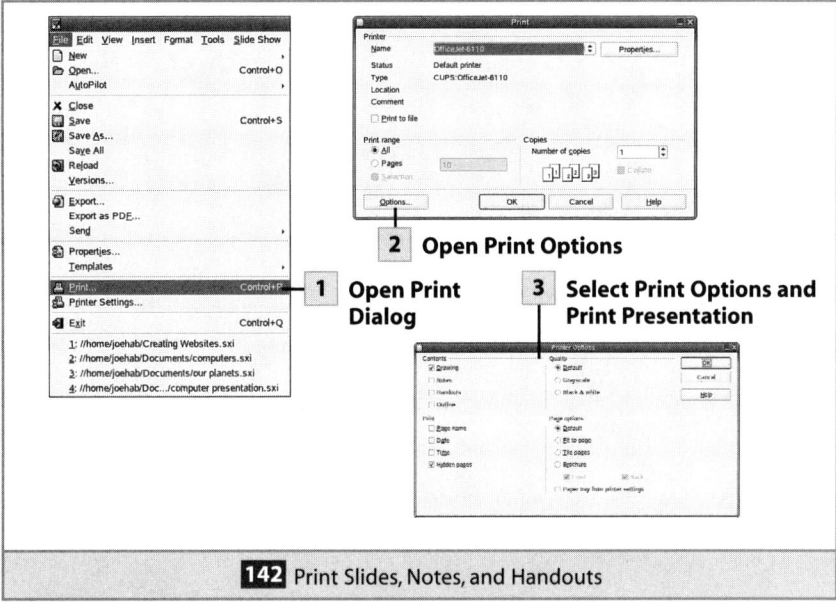

142 Print Slides, Notes, and Handouts

1 Open Print Dialog

Select **File**, **Print**. The Print dialog box opens. You can select the print range and the number of copies on this screen.

2 Open Print Options

To print handouts or notes, you need to access the print options. Select the **Options** button. The Printer Options dialog box opens.

3 Select Print Options and Print Presentation

Use the **Contents** check boxes to determine the type of printout that you want to create such as **Notes**, **Handouts**, or **Outline**. You can also select the output for the printout such as **Grayscale** or **Black & White** (select the appropriate option button). After you have completed your selection of print options, click **OK**. You are returned to the Print dialog box. Click **OK** again to send the print job to the currently selected printer.

329

CHAPTER 14

Managing Email and Contacts with Novell Evolution

IN THIS CHAPTER:

- 143 About Novell Evolution
- 144 Add an Email Account to Evolution
- 145 About Email and Evolution
- 146 Compose and Send Email
- 147 Send an Email with an Attachment
- 148 Receive and Reply to Email
- 149 Work with Received Email Attachments
- 150 Read, Sort, and Search Your Email
- 151 Organize Your Email
- 152 Use the Junk Mail Filter
- 153 Create Virtual Folders
- 154 About the Evolution Address Book
- 155 Create a New Contact
- 156 Edit an Existing Contact
- 157 Create Contact Lists
- 158 Search for Contacts
- 159 Use Categories to Group Contacts
- 160 Import Contacts

CHAPTER 14: Managing Email and Contacts with Novell Evolution

Keeping your various communications channels open and organized is essential no matter what your job. You need to keep your email organized, have quick access to contacts, make and keep appointments, and complete tasks on time.

Evolution is a groupware product designed for collaboration and communication between users and a personal information manager (PIM) that can serve as your email client, contact manager, and appointment calendar. Evolution provides an easy-to-use interface that makes it easy for you to take advantage of all its powerful features.

143 About Novell Evolution

Novell Evolution is a perfect example of a groupware client. It is designed to allow groups of users to communicate and collaborate. Groupware products such as Novell Evolution provide email, help enable group scheduling, and give access to local and global contacts.

Evolution can serve as the email client and calendar and contact manager on a number of different network communication platforms such as SUSE Linux communication servers, Novell GroupWise servers, and Microsoft Exchange communication servers. The type of server environment isn't really all that important to Evolution users because the email features and other features such as the calendar and contacts work seamlessly no matter the network platform.

NOTE

Evolution can be synchronized with Palm handheld devices allowing you to take your Evolution contacts and calendar on the road.

The real concerns of the end-user are related to how Evolution allows you to juggle emails, contacts, and appointments and still stay organized. Evolution is installed during the NLD installation process. When you open Evolution, you are provided with an environment that makes it easy for you to access mail, contacts, and a number of other tools.

NOTE

The first time that you start Evolution you are walked through the process of adding an email account to the Evolution configuration (if an email account has not been preconfigured for you by your system administrator).

The Evolution window is divided into three main areas. At the top of the window are the Menu bar and the toolbar. The toolbar actually provides tools

143 About Novell Evolution

specific to the folder that you are currently using; so the buttons available on the toolbar when you are working with mail are different from those provided when you work with your contacts.

NOTE
A Search bar is provided below the toolbar, making it easy to quickly search for items in the currently selected folder.

On the left side of the Evolution window is the Folder list. The Folder list allows you to quickly access the various Evolution folders. There is a Shortcut bar at the bottom of the Folder list. The shortcuts provided on the bar make it easy for you to access specific Evolution features such as mail, contacts, and the calendar.

On the right side of the Evolution window is a list pane that shows a list of your emails, contacts, or appointments (depending on whether you have Mail, Contacts, or Calendars selected). A preview pane is also provided that allows you to preview the email currently selected in the list.

Evolution provides an easy-to-navigate interface for managing emails, contacts, and your calendar.

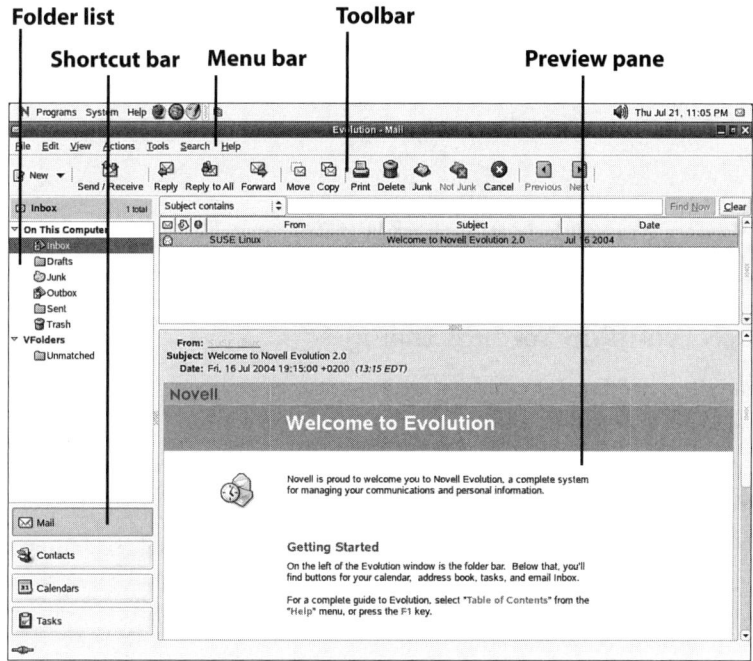

CHAPTER 14: Managing Email and Contacts with Novell Evolution

If you used a previous email, contacts, and calendar manager, you will find that Evolution provides tools that you can use to import information saved in other groupware applications and email clients. So, you can hit the ground running in terms of responding to email and managing your contacts and calendar.

144 Add an Email Account to Evolution

✔ **BEFORE YOU BEGIN**

81 Configure an Email Client

The first time you start Evolution you are walked through the process of configuring the settings for your email account. Evolution can serve as the email client for both corporate email accounts and Internet-only email accounts and can be the client for multiple email accounts.

Because your first email account is configured during the initial setup of Evolution (the first time you start the software), this task looks at adding additional email accounts (no matter the type of account). You can easily add a new email account at any time on an as-needed basis.

1 Start Evolution

Select **Programs**, **Novell Evolution** from the menu. The Evolution window opens on the desktop.

TIP

You can also start Evolution by selecting the **Evolution** icon on the desktop's top panel.

2 Open Evolution Settings Dialog

To add an email account to the Evolution configuration, select **Tools**, **Settings**. The Evolution Settings dialog box opens.

3 Open Evolution Account Assistant

In the Evolution Settings dialog box, make sure that the **Mail Accounts** icon is selected and then select **Add**. The Evolution Account Assistant opens. Select **Forward** to bypass the introductory screen.

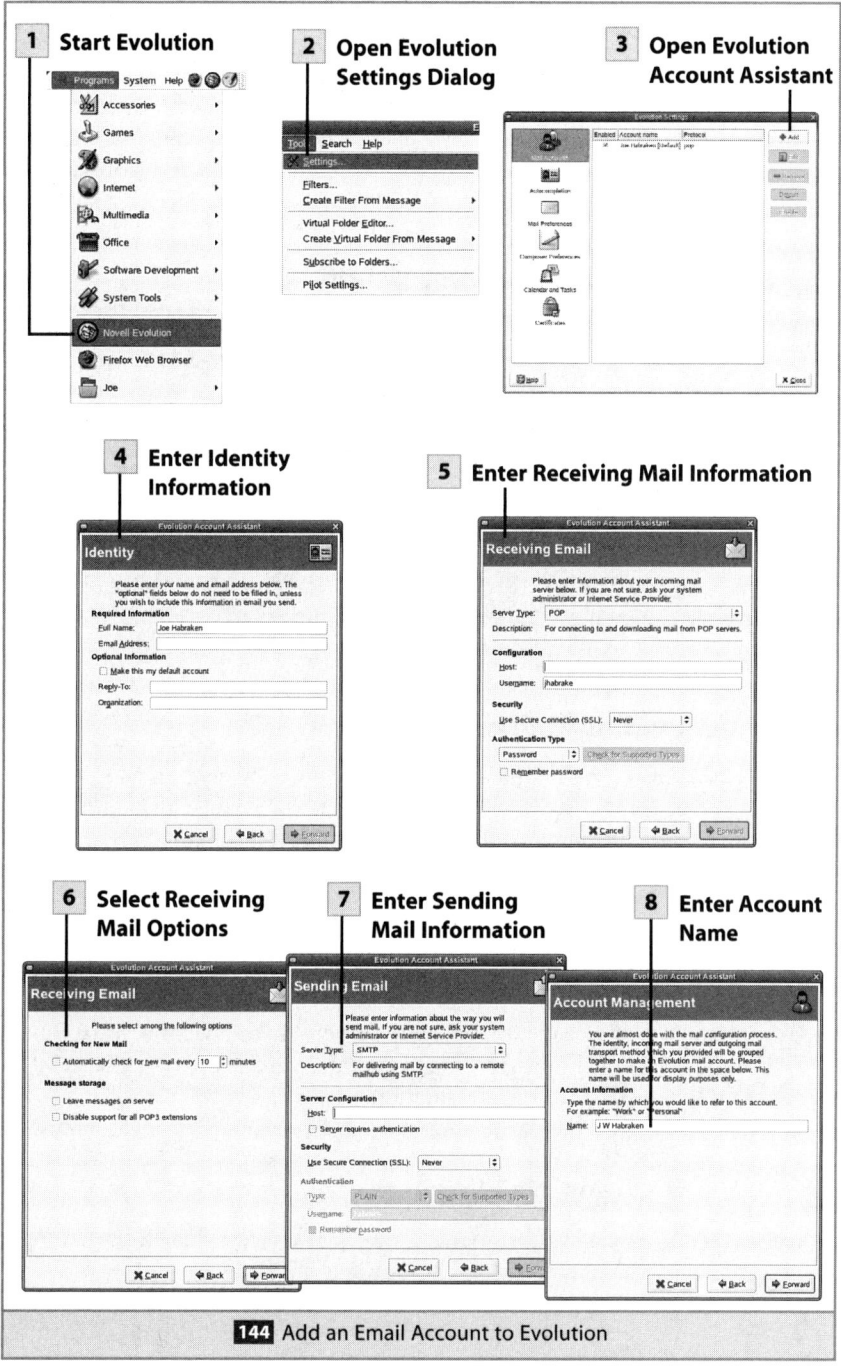

4 Enter Identity Information

Enter your name and email account on the Identity screen. If the account will be the default account, select the **Make This My Default Account** check box. You can also enter optional text such as reply to and organizational information (which appears on all sent emails). Select **Forward** to continue.

5 Enter Receiving Mail Information

Select the **Server Type** drop-down box and select the type of server that you use to receive email. You also need to enter the hostname for the server (such as pop-server.mail.company.com or variation for a pop mail server) in the **Host** box. Type your username in the **Username** box.

6 Select Receiving Mail Options

On the next screen select the **Automatically Check for New Mail** check box if you want to have Evolution periodically check for new mail. Set the time frame for the automatic checks and then select **Forward** to continue.

7 Enter Sending Mail Information

On the next screen you enter information related to sending mail. Select the **Server Type** drop-down list to select the server type for sending mail. In the **Host** box type the name of the server. After entering the information, select **Forward** to continue.

8 Enter Account Name

On the next screen enter the name that you want to use to refer to this account. Type the name in the **Name** box and then select **Forward** to continue. The final Assistant screen appears; select **Apply**. The account is added to your Evolution configuration.

---

145 About Email and Evolution

When you configure an email account for Evolution, a set of email-related folders is created for you automatically. These folders are

145 About Email and Evolution

- Inbox—Messages received via your email account (or accounts) are placed by default in the Inbox.
- Drafts—When you are working on a message and want to save it before completion, the draft of the message is saved to the Drafts folder. The incomplete message can be reopened and completed as needed.
- Junk—Mail that is tagged as "junk" by the Evolution Junk Email filter is placed in the Junk folder.
- Outbox—Mail that has been completed but not sent is held in the Outbox. When you select **Send/Receive**, all email in the Outbox is sent.
- Sent—A copy of each of your sent emails is saved in the Sent folder.
- Trash—When you delete an email (or other items such as contacts), the item is placed in the Trash folder. You can undelete items from the Trash folder if needed. You can also configure Evolution to automatically empty the Trash folder when you exit Evolution.

Obviously, these folders are designed to help you manage your email messages, particularly those sent and received. You can also create your own subfolders for any of the default email folders as needed (right-click on a folder and then select **New Folder**). You can also keep your email organized and easily accessible by creating rules and filters that allow messages to be viewed in special folders called vFolders.

NOTE

A *vFolder* or *virtual folder* is really a view of email messages that meet certain rule criteria. For example, you can set up a vFolder that lists all the emails from a certain person or that contain certain keywords in the message subject. A vFolder isn't really a place because the message still resides in an actual folder such as the Inbox. vFolders are created by setting up a rule (or rules) for the vFolder. When you open a vFolder, it lists all the messages that meet the criteria that have been configured for that vFolder.

CHAPTER 14: Managing Email and Contacts with Novell Evolution

146 Compose and Send Email

Composing and sending email is one of the most essential communication tasks today. Evolution does this as well as any email application.

✓ BEFORE YOU BEGIN

145 About Email and Evolution

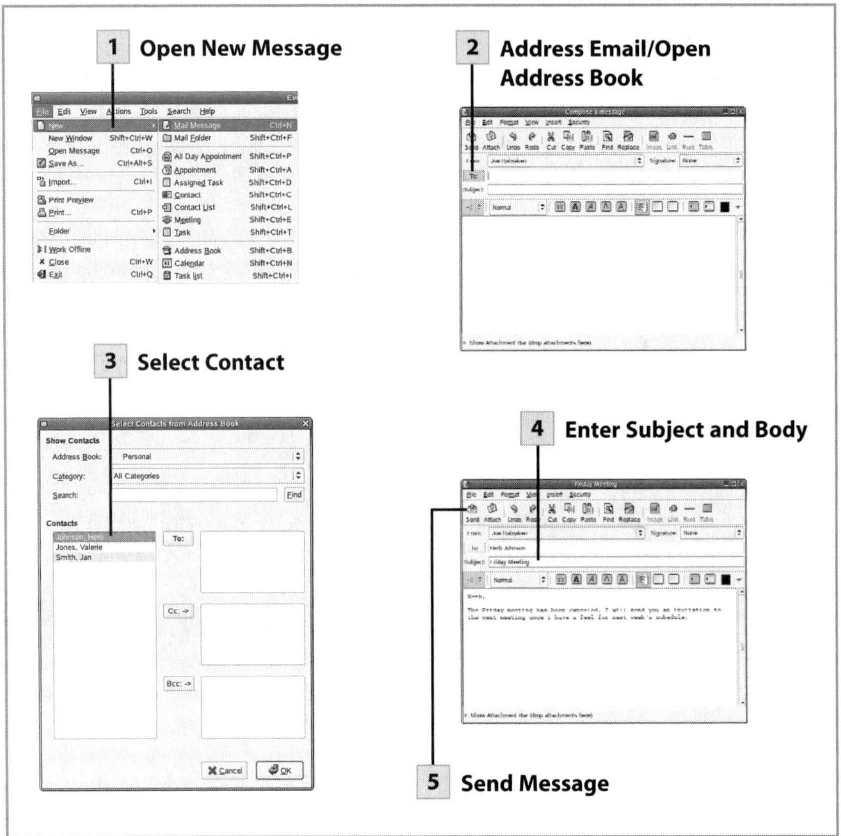

146 Compose and Send Email

146 Compose and Send Email

1 Open New Message

From the Evolution application window (select **Programs**, **Evolution**), select **File**, **New**, **Mail Message**.

TIP

When you have the Inbox selected (or any of the mail folders), you can quickly start a new email by selecting the **New** button on the toolbar.

2 Address Email/Open Address Book

To address the email, type a valid email address in the **To** box. If you want to select the email address from the address book, select the **To** button. The Address Book opens.

3 Select Contact

Select a contact or contacts and then select **To:**, **Cc:** (copy), or **Bcc:** (blind copy; main addressee does not see these email addresses) as needed. (You can add contacts in this way only if contacts have been added to your contact list.) After you have finished addressing the email, click **OK**.

4 Enter Subject and Body

Type a subject and a body for the message.

5 Send Message

Select the **Send** button on the message. The message goes to your Outbox temporarily and then is sent to the recipient or recipients.

NOTE

A copy of the sent message is saved in your Sent folder.

CHAPTER 14: Managing Email and Contacts with Novell Evolution

147 Send an Email with an Attachment

You can send files as email attachments. This makes it easy to send a document or spreadsheet to a coworker. It also makes it easy to send pictures of your weekend trip to your friends. You can attach multiple attachments to an email.

✓ BEFORE YOU BEGIN

146 Compose and Send Email

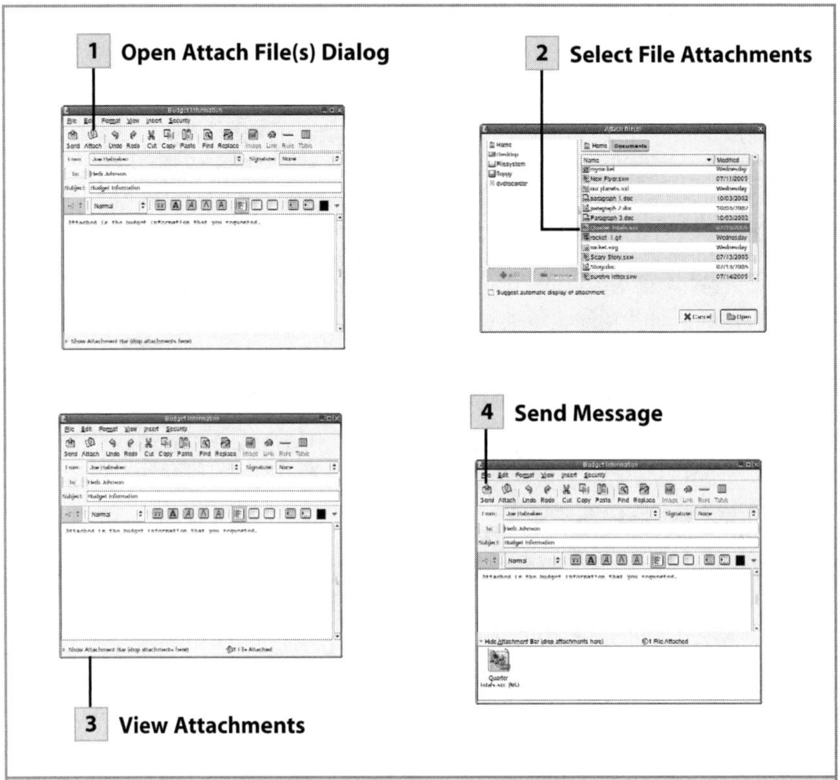

1 Open Attach File(s) Dialog

2 Select File Attachments

3 View Attachments

4 Send Message

147 Send an Email with an Attachment

1. Open Attach File(s) Dialog

On a new mail message (select **New** on the toolbar), select the **Attach** button on the message toolbar.

TIP

You can also open Nautilus and drag files onto a message when you want to send them as an attachment. Select the **Show Attachment Bar** link at the bottom of the message window and then drag files onto the bar as needed.

2. Select File Attachments

In the Attach File(s) dialog box, select the file or files that you want to attach to the message. Then select **Open**. You are returned to the message window.

3. View Attachments

Select the **Show Attachment Bar** link at the bottom of the message. This allows you to view the icons for the files attached to the message.

TIP

To remove an attachment, select the attachment in the attachment pane at the bottom of the message and press **Delete**.

4. Send Message

When you are ready to send the message, select the **Send** button on the message toolbar.

148 Receive and Reply to Email

Newly received messages are placed in your Inbox (unless you have set up a rule that sends that particular message to the Junk or other folder). You can quickly reply to any received message or forward that message to another recipient if necessary.

CHAPTER 14: Managing Email and Contacts with Novell Evolution

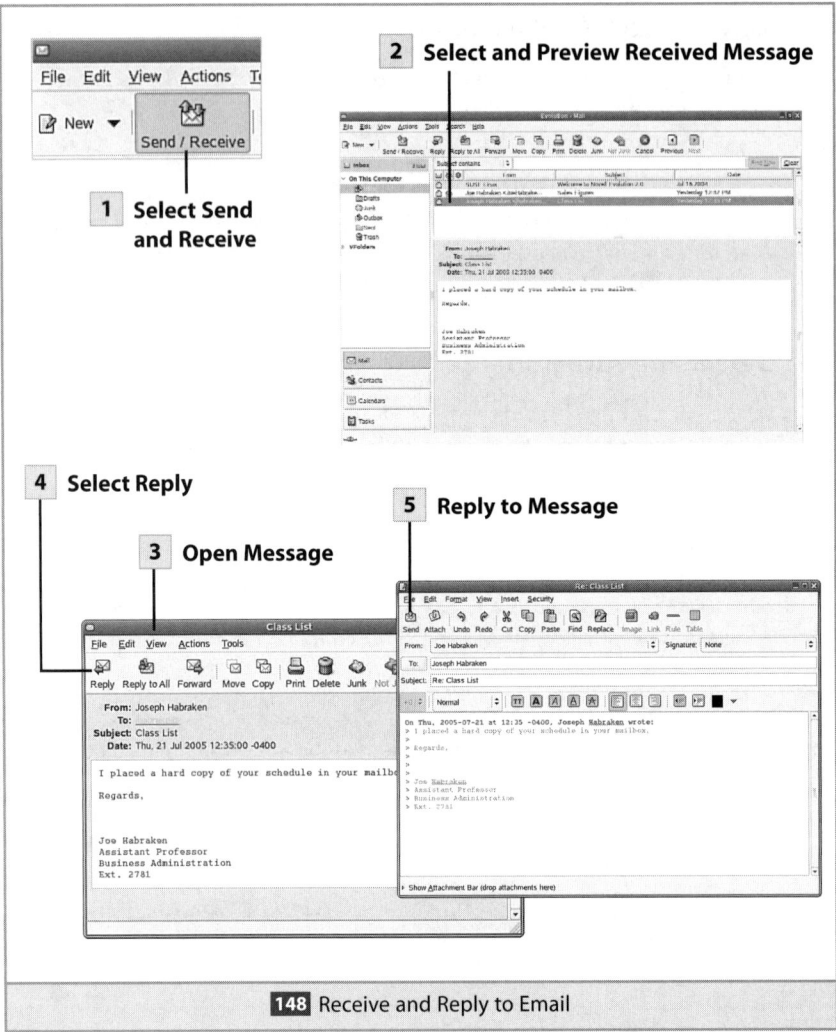

148 Receive and Reply to Email

1 Select Send and Receive

To check your mail server for new mail, select **Send/Receive** on the Evolution toolbar. New email messages are placed in your Inbox (and any unsent messages are sent from your Outbox).

342

149 Work with Received Email Attachments

2 **Select and Preview Received Message**

Select a newly received message to view it in the Preview pane.

3 **Open Message**

If you want to open a message in a separate window, double-click the message.

4 **Select Reply**

To reply to the message select **Reply** on the message toolbar (or on the Evolution toolbar if you are previewing the message). A new message window opens for your reply.

TIP

To send the reply message that you create to all the recipients of the original message, select **Reply All**. This sends the reply to the original sender and all the original recipients.

5 **Reply to Message**

Add text and other information as needed to your reply message (including attachments if applicable). Then select **Send**.

TIP

You can also forward a selected or open message. Select the **Forward** button on the toolbar. Then address the forwarded message and add additional body text as needed.

149 Work with Received Email Attachments

Some of the messages that you receive will certainly contain attachments. You can open attachments directly from the received email, or you can choose to save the attachments before opening.

✔ **BEFORE YOU BEGIN**

148 Receive and Reply to Email

343

CHAPTER 14: Managing Email and Contacts with Novell Evolution

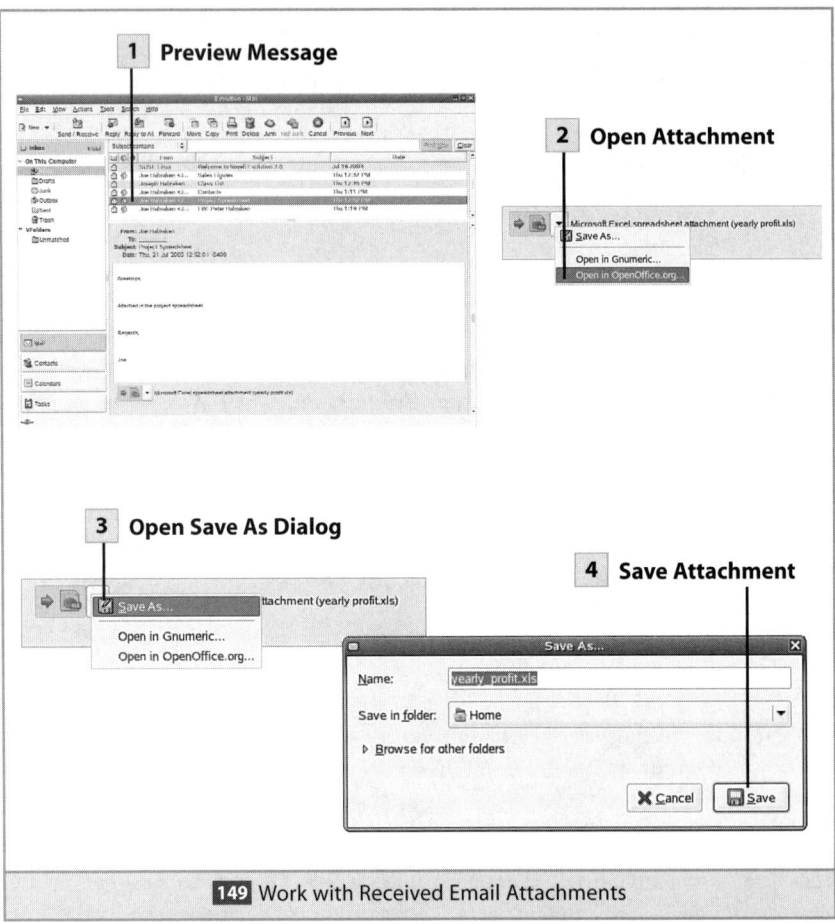

149 Work with Received Email Attachments

1 Preview Message

In the Inbox, select a message that has a file attachment.

2 Open Attachment

To open the attachment in an NLD application such as OpenOffice.org, select the drop-down arrow to the right of the attachment icon (at the bottom of the Preview pane). Select the application that you want to open the attachment in. The file opens in the application in a new window.

3 Open Save As Dialog

If you would rather save the file for later consideration (instead of opening it immediately), select the drop-down arrow to the right of the attachment icon. Then select **Save As**.

4 Save Attachment

In the Save As dialog box browse for a folder to save the file in. You can change the filename if needed. Then select **Save**. The file is saved to the selected folder.

TIP

To browse for other folders in the Save As dialog box, select the **Browse for Other Folders** link.

150 Read, Sort, and Search Your Email

To read a message all you have to do is select that message and then view it in the Preview pane. Sometimes, however, you may find it difficult to find a particular message. Evolution makes it easy for you to sort your messages by date, subject, or any of the informational columns shown above the message list (in any mail folder such as the Inbox). You can also quickly search for a message using the Search toolbar.

1 Read Message

Select a message in the **Inbox** or any folder to view that message in the Preview pane.

2 Sort Email

Email is sorted by date (this is the default). To sort the mail in the current folder (such as the Inbox) by one of the other mail columns, select the heading of that column such as **Subject**. The mail is sorted alphabetically in ascending order by subject. If you want to sort descending (or unsort the messages) by a particular column, right-click on that column and select **Sort Descending**.

CHAPTER 14: Managing Email and Contacts with Novell Evolution

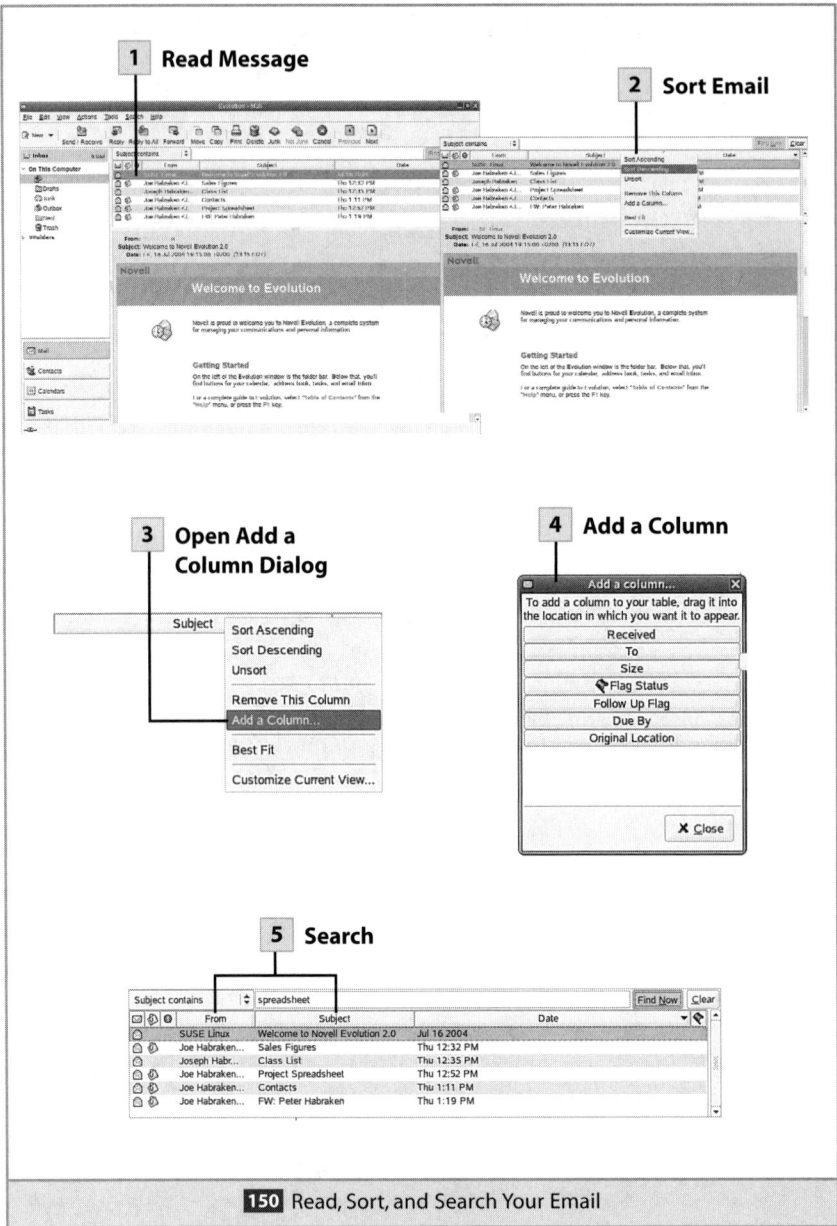

150 Read, Sort, and Search Your Email

TIP

To change the width of a column in the message list so that you can see the longest entry in that column (such as the email subjects), right-click on that column heading and select **Best Fit**.

3   Open Add a Column Dialog

You can add additional columns to the message pane. Right-click on one of the current columns and select **Add a Column**.

4   Add a Column

Drag a column listed in the Add a Column dialog box to the column area of the message list. The column is added. You can then use the column to sort the messages in the currently selected folder.

TIP

If you want to remove a column from the message list, right-click the column heading and select **Remove This Column**.

5   Search

You can quickly search for email messages in the Inbox (or any mail folder). Select the **Rule** drop-down list and select a search criterion such as Subject Contains, Subject Does Not Contain, Sender Contains, and so on. After selecting the criterion, enter the search parameter (keywords) in the Search box. When you are ready to search, select the **Find Now** button. The message list is filtered by your search parameters, and only the messages meeting the search parameters are listed in the message list.

TIP

If you need to do a search with multiple search criteria (say you want to search by Subject Contains and Sender Contains, using more than one rule at a time), select **Advanced Search** in the **Rule** drop-down list and then add criteria to the Advanced Search dialog box to conduct your complex search as needed.

TIP

To reset the search feature and show all messages in the message list, select the **Clear** button.

151 Organize Your Email

When you receive large numbers of email, it is certainly worth your while to keep these messages organized. You can add flags to emails to "tag" for future reference. For example, you can add the Call follow-up flag, which reminds you to call the sender of a particular message.

You can also keep your email organized by moving incoming mail to folders that you create. For example, you may create a folder related to a certain project and then move all the email related to that project to the folder. You can move email easily by dragging email from one folder to another folder. Another way to get email into a specific folder is to use a filter. A filter uses criteria that you set to locate a message. The filter also includes instructions related to what the filter should do with the message such as move the message to a folder that you have specified.

1 Open Create Folder Dialog

If you are going to use filters to move mail to specific folders, create the folders as needed. Right-click on a folder such as **Inbox** and then select **New Folder** on the shortcut menu.

2 Create Folder

In the Create Folder dialog box, specify a name for the new folder and then select **Create**. The folder is added to the Folder list. Create other folders as needed.

3 Open Filters Dialog

Now you can create a filter (or filters as needed). Select **Tools, Filters**.

4 Open Add Rule Dialog

In the Filters dialog box, select **Add** to create a new filter rule. The Add Rule dialog box opens.

151 Organize Your Email

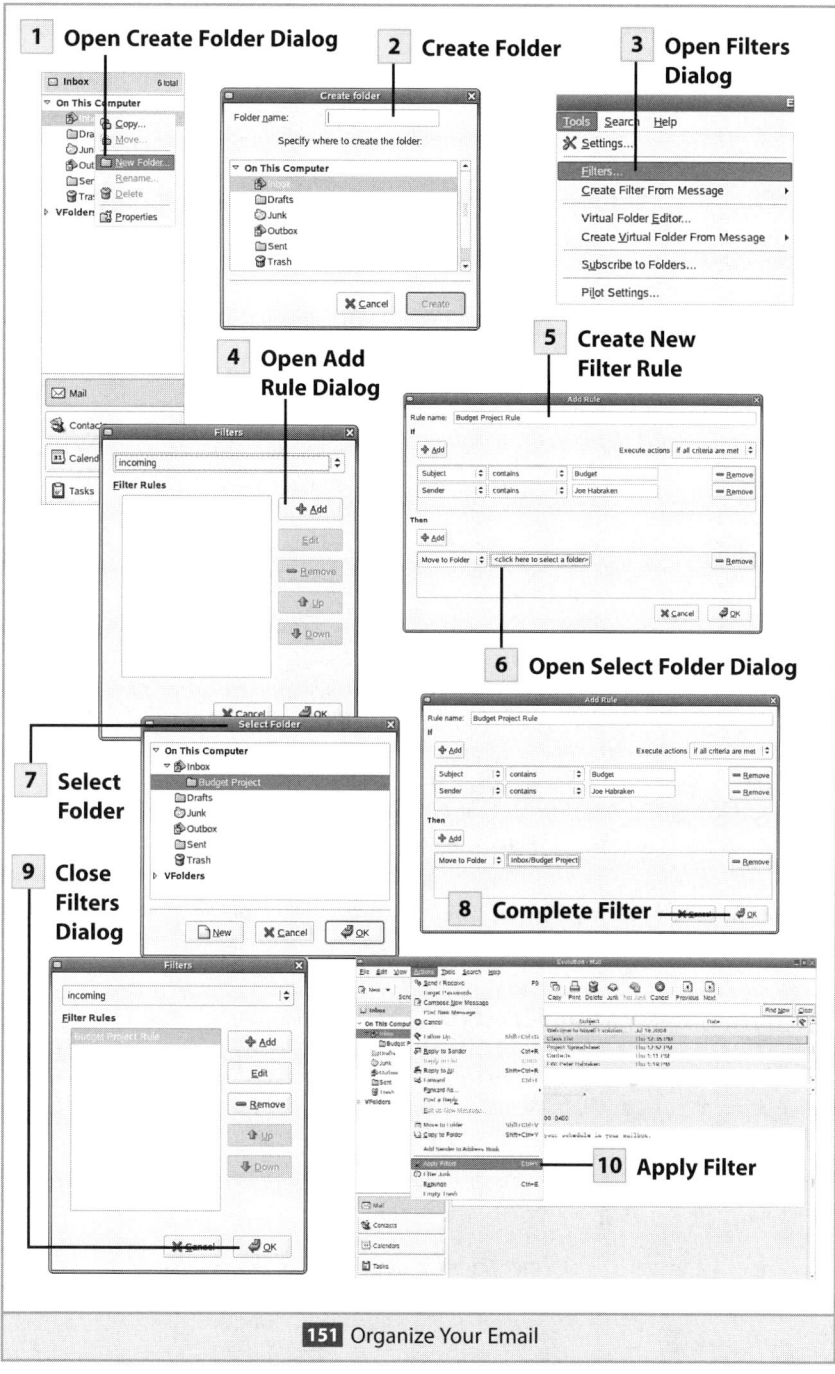

151 Organize Your Email

5 Create New Filter Rule

In the Add Rule dialog box, type a name for the new rule. In the **If** area of the dialog box, specify your criteria. Select the first criteria drop-down box and select the part of the message that will be used by the filter such as Sender, Recipient, Subject, and so on. Then type the criteria that will be used by the filter. For example, if you want to filter all the emails from Mary Smith, select **Sender** in the drop-down list and then type **Mary Smith** as the criteria.

Add other criteria for the rule using the If **Add** button. If you use multiple criteria, select the **Execute Actions** drop-down list and select either **If All Criteria Are Met** or **If Any Criteria Are Met** (depending on how you want the criteria used).

In the **Then** area of the Add Rule dialog box, select the drop-down list and select the action that you want to take place when the filter rule criteria is met by a message, such as **Move** to **Folder**, **Copy** to **Folder**, **Delete**, and so on. You can add multiple actions using the **Add** button if necessary.

TIP

You can create filters based on the currently selected message. Select a message in the message list and then select **Tools, Create Filter From Message**, and then select the part of the message that you will base the filter on from the submenu such as **Filter on Subject, Filter on Sender**, and so on. The Add Filter Rule dialog box opens. The criteria for the filter rule will be set based on information in the email. For example, if you selected **Filter on Sender** on the submenu, the rule is set to filter mail based on the selected email's sender. You can add criteria as needed and specify what you want done to messages that meet this rule's criteria (such as move to a particular folder).

6 Open Select Folder Dialog

To specify a folder to be used when the rule criteria is met (when you are using actions such as Move to Folder or Copy to Folder), select the **Click Here to Select a Folder** box. This opens the Select Folder dialog box.

7 Select Folder

Select a folder in the Select Folder dialog box and then click **OK**. You are returned to the Add Rule dialog box.

TIP

Your filters don't necessarily have to move, copy, or delete the messages that they act on. Filters can also be used to color code messages, and you can automatically assign follow-up flags to messages using filter rules.

8 Complete Filter

After specifying the criteria and the actions for the filter rule, click **OK**. You are returned to the Filters dialog box.

9 Close Filters Dialog

Your new rule will appear in the Filters dialog box. Click **OK** to close the Filters dialog box.

10 Apply Filter

Select a message or messages in the Inbox or any folder. Select **Actions**, **Apply Filters**. Selected messages that match the rule criteria are acted on by the filter (such as being moved to a different folder). All new mail automatically is acted on by the filter.

152 Use the Junk Mail Filter

We are all inundated with junk email: spam! Evolution provides a junk mail filter that detects suspected junk email and removes it to the Junk folder. You can actually train the junk mail filter by letting the feature know when you have received junk email. You select the email and then mark the email as junk using the Junk button on the Evolution toolbar.

1 Open Evolution Settings Dialog

Select **Tools**, **Settings** from the menu. In the Evolution Settings dialog box, select the **Mail Preferences** icon.

NOTE

The Evolution Settings dialog box is where you configure the various settings for your mail accounts, mail preferences, and settings for your calendar and tasks. Select one of the setting icons such as Calendar and Tasks to configure settings such as the time zone, the start of the work week, and when reminders should be provided for your scheduled appointments.

CHAPTER 14: Managing Email and Contacts with Novell Evolution

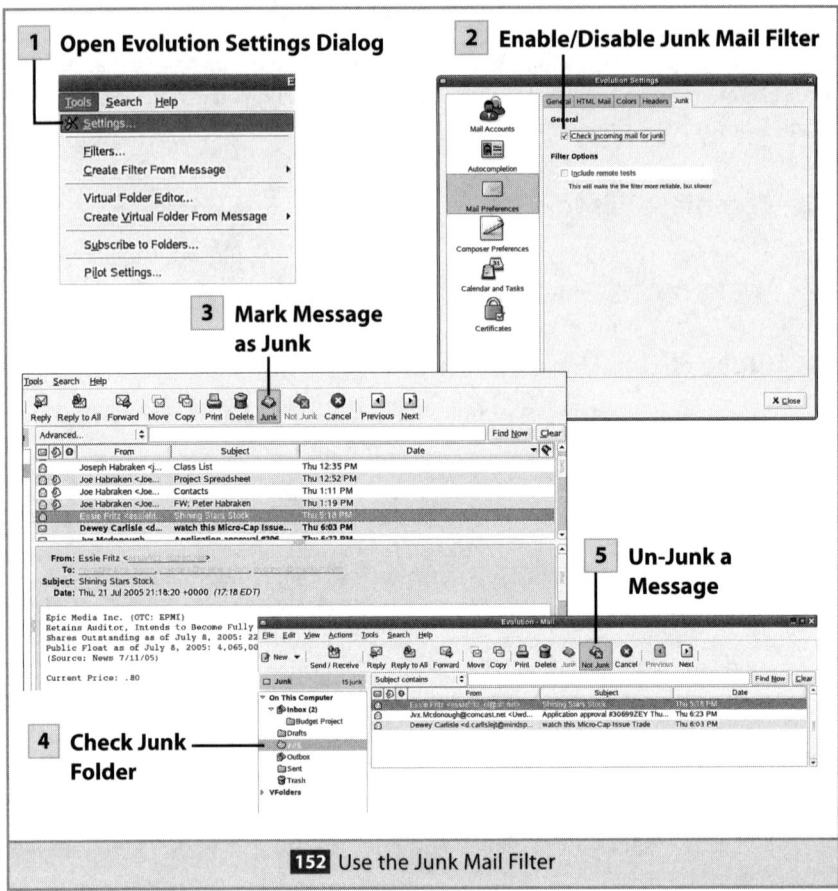

152 Use the Junk Mail Filter

2 Enable/Disable Junk Mail Filter

Select the **Junk** tab. The Junk filter is enabled by default. If you want to disable the filter, deselect the **Check Incoming Mail for Junk** check box. After you have finished viewing the Junk settings, close the Evolution Settings dialog box.

NOTE

If your network provides a server that performs remote tests to block spam and junk mail, you can enable the remote test feature. Select the **Include Remote Tests** check box on the Junk tab.

3 Mark Message as Junk

In your Inbox (or other mail folder) select a message that is junk (you can select multiple messages). Select the **Junk** button on the toolbar to send the message to the Junk folder. This also teaches Evolution that the message (taking into consideration sender and content) should be treated as junk in the future.

4 Check Junk Folder

To open the Junk folder select the **Junk** icon in the Folder list. Any junk messages are listed in the folder.

5 Un-Junk a Message

If a message has been sent to the Junk folder that is not junk, select the message. Then select the **Not Junk** button on the toolbar.

TIP

After viewing junk mail in the Junk folder (and un-junking messages that are not junk), you can select the messages in the Junk folder and delete them.

153 Create Virtual Folders

Virtual folders or vFolders are not actually folders but views of messages that meet the criteria of a particular rule. So, a vFolder is a combination of a search and a filter (or filters) and allows you to quickly access messages that meet certain criteria.

✔ BEFORE YOU BEGIN

151 Organize Your Email

1 Open Virtual Folder Editor

In the Evolution window select **Tools**, **Virtual Folder Editor**. The vFolders dialog box opens.

CHAPTER 14: Managing Email and Contacts with Novell Evolution

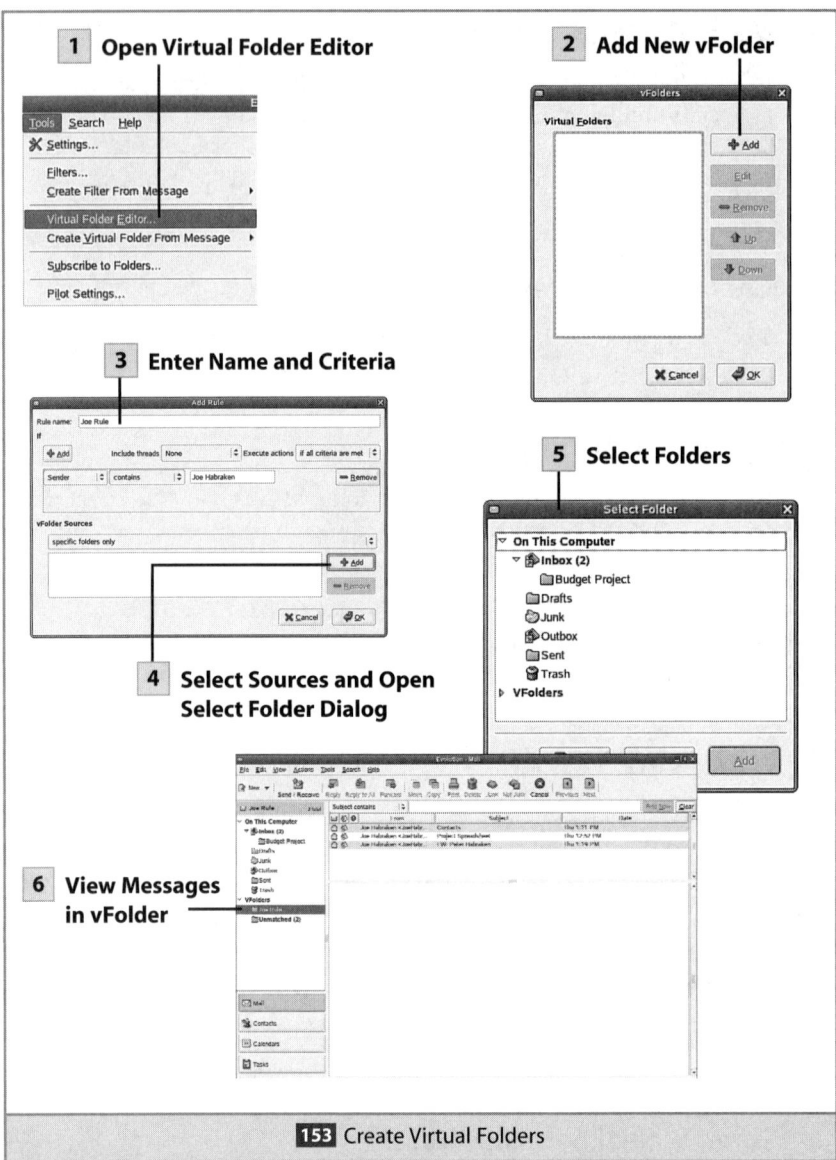

153 Create Virtual Folders

TIP

You can also quickly create a vFolder based on a selected message. Select **Tools**, **Create Virtual Folder From Message**, and then select one of the choices on the submenu such as **VFolder on Subject**. This opens a new Virtual Folder dialog box (the Add Rule dialog). You then set the criteria and folders to be filtered as needed to create the vFolder.

2 Add New vFolder

In the vFolders dialog box click the **Add** button to open the Add Rule dialog box.

3 Enter Name and Criteria

Type a name for the new vFolder rule (this will also be the name of the vFolder). In the **If** area of the dialog box, specify your criteria. Select the first criteria drop-down box and select the part of the message that will be used by the filter such as **Sender**, **Recipient**, **Subject**, and so on. Then type the criteria that will be used by the filter.

Add other criteria for the rule using the If **Add** button. If you use multiple criteria, select the **Execute Actions** drop-down list and select either **If All Criteria Are Met** or **If Any Criteria Are Met** (depending on how you want the criteria used).

NOTE

Creating vFolders is similar to creating filters. You set the criteria for the virtual folder (there can be a number of conditions that must be met for the vFolder) and then the filter dictates what appears in the vFolder when you access it from the Folder list.

4 Select Sources and Open Select Folder Dialog

You also need to specify the folders that the vFolder rule searches when compiling the message list that appears in the vFolder. If you want to provide the vFolder with a look at all your local or network folders, select the **vFolder Sources** drop-down list and make a selection such as **With All Local Folders**.

If you want to specify a folder or folders, select the **Add** button.

5 Select Folders

In the Select Folder dialog box, select the folder or folders you want to use as the source for the vFolder. Then select **Add**.

After setting the criteria and the source folders, click **OK** to close the Add Rule dialog. Click **OK** again to close the vFolders dialog box.

6 View Messages in vFolder

Now you can view the messages that meet the criteria of the vFolder rule by looking in the vFolder. In the Folder list, expand the **vFolders** list and then select the vFolder that you created. The messages listed in the vFolder are all messages that meet the criteria of the rule that you created for the vFolder.

NOTE

The Unmatched vFolder, which is created automatically, shows you all the messages that don't appear in the vFolders that you have created in Evolution.

154 About the Evolution Address Book

The Evolution address book or contact list provides you with the ability to enter contacts including information on each contact such as name, email address, phone number, and both home and business addresses. Each contact that you enter is shown as an address card in the contacts list when the Address Book is selected in the Evolution window (when the Contacts shortcut is selected below the Folder list).

You can quickly change the view of the contact list by selecting **View**, **Current View**, and then selecting one of the views on the submenu such as **Phone List** or **By Company**. You can also use the Search box to quickly find a contact or contacts.

NOTE

You can share contact information easily with nearly any co-worker user no matter what email or groupware program he uses. Select a contact in the address book and then select **File, Save as VCard**. Saving the address information as a vcard allows you to email the vcard file as an attachment. Most contact management and groupware products can then "read" the vcard so that the information can be added to that groupware product's contact list.

The information that you record for each contact depends on what you need to know about that particular contact. For example, in the case of personal contacts or co-workers you may only need to enter their names and email addresses. In the case of clients you may want to enter all the information that you have regarding them, such as work address, home address, multiple telephone numbers, and email addresses.

Contacts are shown as address cards by default.

The Contact Editor is used to create and edit contacts. The Contact Editor provides three tabs in its window:

- Contact—This tab is used to record the contact's name and other basic information such as email address, phone number, and instant messaging account names (if applicable).
- Personal—This tab allows you to enter information such as home page address and the contact's job information (such as company and title).
- Mailing Address—This tab provides space for you to enter both the home and work addresses of the individual (and includes space for additional optional addresses).

After you create a new contact, you can edit his information at any time. You can also delete contacts that you no longer need.

155 Create a New Contact

Contacts can be added as needed to the Evolution address book. You can enter all the information for a particular contact when you first create the entry in the address book. Or you can add information for the contact over time as you accumulate it.

CHAPTER 14: Managing Email and Contacts with Novell Evolution

✔ **BEFORE YOU BEGIN**

154 About the Evolution Address Book

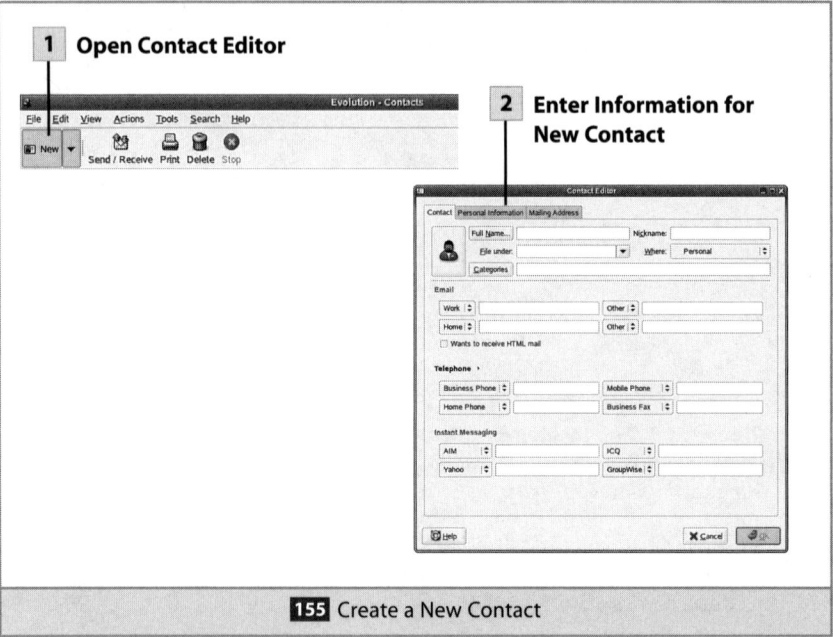

155 Create a New Contact

1 **Open Contact Editor**

With the Address Book selected in the Evolution window (select the **Contacts** shortcut), select the **New** button on the Evolution toolbar. The Contact Editor opens.

TIP

You can also quickly open the Contact Editor to create a new contact by double-clicking on any of the white space in the Address Book (not on an existing card).

2 **Enter Information for New Contact**

Enter the contact's information on each of the tabs (Contact, Personal Information, Mailing Address) provided in the Contact Editor window. After you have completed entering the information, click **OK**. The contact is added to the Address Book.

156 Edit an Existing Contact

You can quickly edit any of your existing contacts. This allows you to update contact information as needed.

✔ **BEFORE YOU BEGIN**

155 Create a New Contact

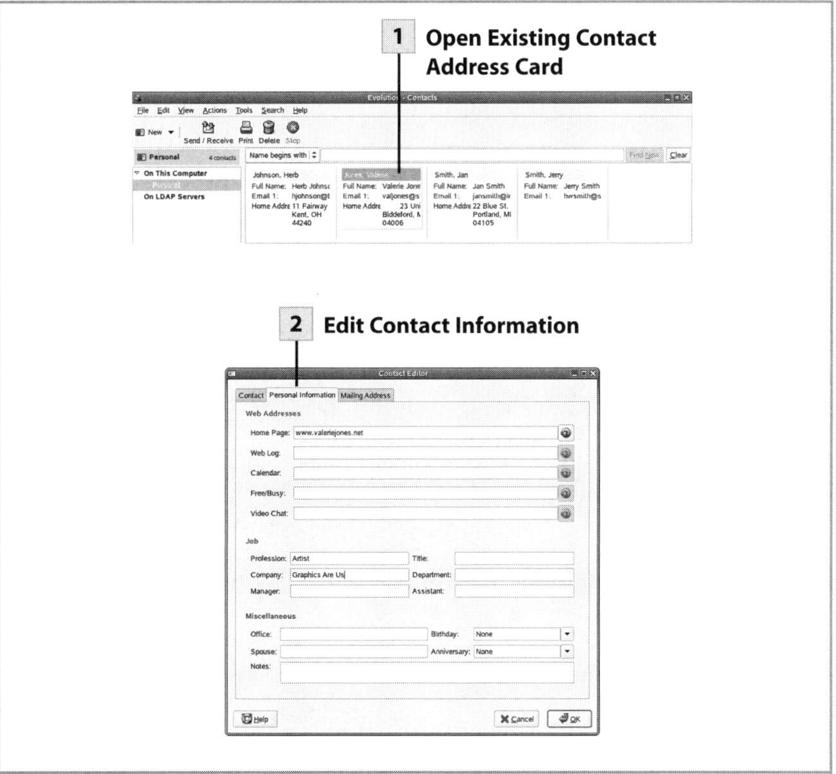

1 Open Existing Contact Address Card

2 Edit Contact Information

156 Edit an Existing Contact

1 Open Existing Contact Address Card

With the Address Book selected in the Evolution window (select the **Contacts** shortcut), double-click on the contact's address card that you want to edit. The Contact Editor opens with the contact's current information.

2 Edit Contact Information

Edit the contact's information as needed on the tabs provided by the Contact Editor. After you have completed editing the information, click OK.

157 Create Contact Lists

You can quickly create a contact list that serves as an alias or nickname for several contacts in the address book. For example, you may be working with a group of people who all need to receive email updates from you. You can create the contact list (which is saved as a separate card in the address book) and then add the contacts to it. Sending an email to the contact list sends the email to all the contacts that you included in the contact list.

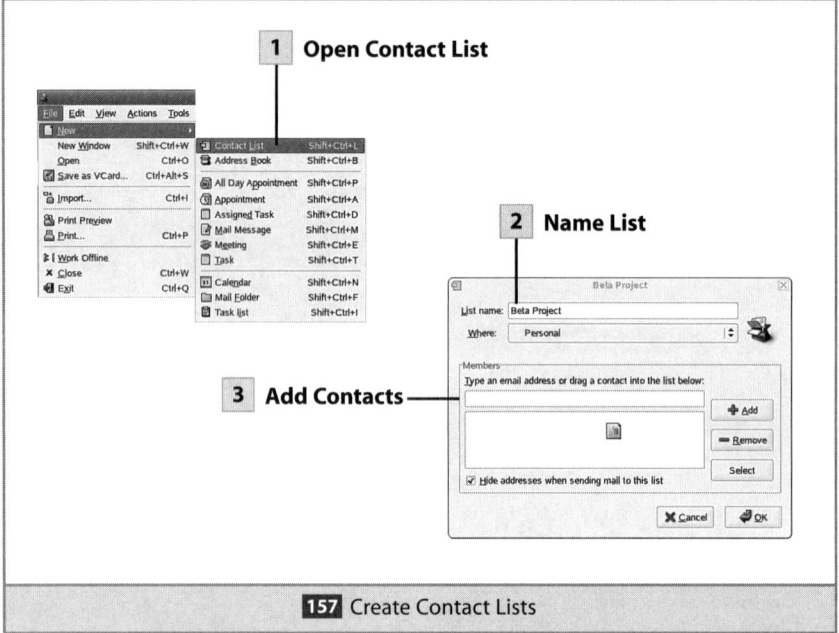

157 Create Contact Lists

1 Open Contact List

In Evolution with the address book open, select **File**, **New**, and then **Contact List**. The Contact List dialog box opens.

2 Name List

Type a name for the new list in the **List Name** box.

3 Add Contacts

To add contacts drag the contact from the address book list to the **Members** box in the Contact List dialog box. After adding contacts to the list (as needed), click **OK**. The Contact List is added to the address book as an address card.

TIP

You can also type an email address in the Members box and then click add to add an email address to the contact list that is not currently entered in the address book.

158 Search for Contacts

You can quickly search for contacts that meet a set of criteria using the Search bar. Searches can be conducted using any of the fields in an address book entry.

1 Select Search Type

Select the **Search** drop-down arrow and select the search type such as **Name Begins With** or **Category Is**.

2 Enter Search Text and Run Search

Enter the search criteria (in most cases a text string) for the search and then select **Find Now**. The results of the search appear in the Address Book pane.

3 Clear Search

To clear the search and view all entries in the Address Book, select the **Clear** button on the far right of the Search bar.

CHAPTER 14: Managing Email and Contacts with Novell Evolution

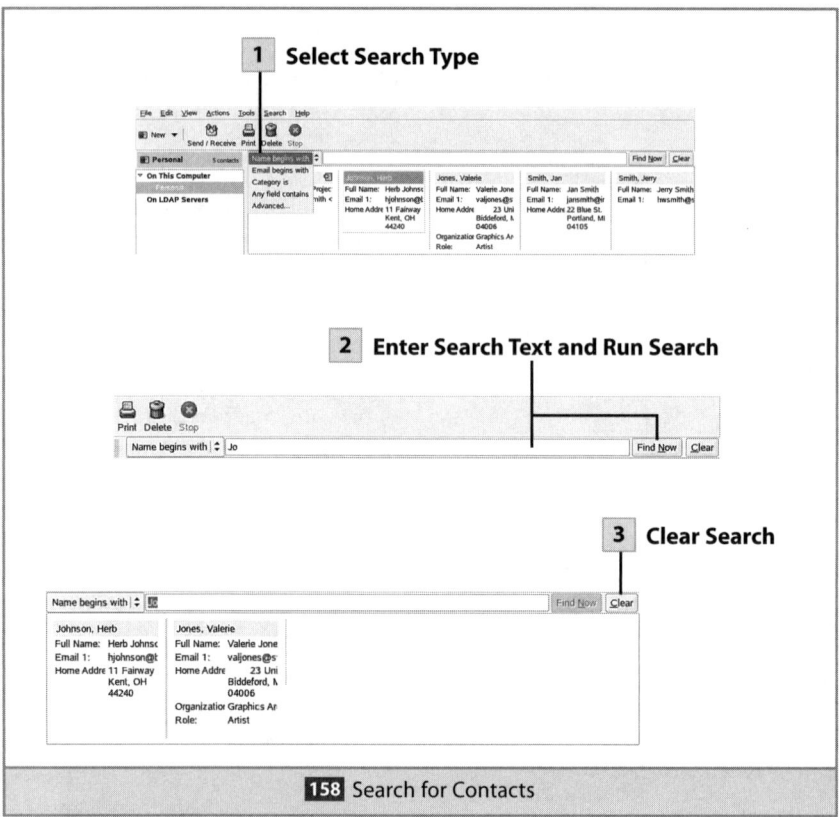

158 Search for Contacts

159 Use Categories to Group Contacts

You can assign a category or categories to the contacts in the Address Book. Assigning a category, such as Key Customer, to specific contacts allows you to group those contacts. You can then use this "grouping" as a way to quickly search for all "key customers."

1 Open Edit Categories Dialog

In the Contact Editor window for a new or existing contact (double-click an existing contact to open the Contact Editor), select the **Categories** button.

TIP

An address card can be assigned multiple categories.

160 Import Contacts

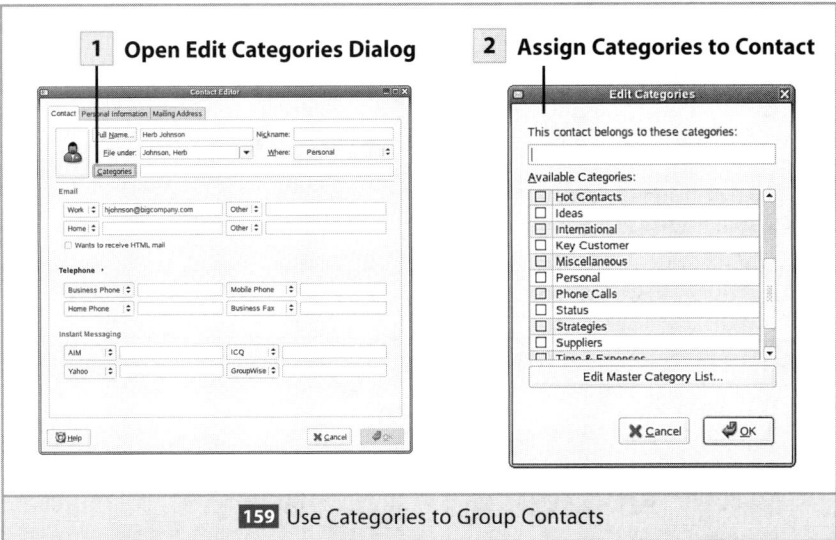

1 Open Edit Categories Dialog **2** Assign Categories to Contact

159 Use Categories to Group Contacts

2 Assign Categories to Contact

In the Edit Categories dialog box, select the check box for a category or categories. After you have finished selecting the categories for the contact, click **OK**. This returns you to the Contact Editor. After you have finished editing the information for the contact, click **OK**.

TIP

A number of existing categories are provided by Evolution by default. You can also create your own categories. In the Edit Categories dialog box select the **Edit Master Category List** button. The Edit Global Category List dialog opens. Select the **Click Here to Add Category** box and then add a new category. Repeat as needed to build a list of custom categories.

160 Import Contacts

You can import contacts from existing address books or email software (installed on your NLD system), or you can import files from other contact management software. You must export and save the data using the other contact management software before you can attempt to import it into Evolution (meaning the data must exist as a file). Because Evolution serves as the default email and address book manager for NLD (meaning, you probably have not been running other address book or email software on your NLD installation), most situations will involve an import of data from another groupware product.

363

CHAPTER 14: Managing Email and Contacts with Novell Evolution

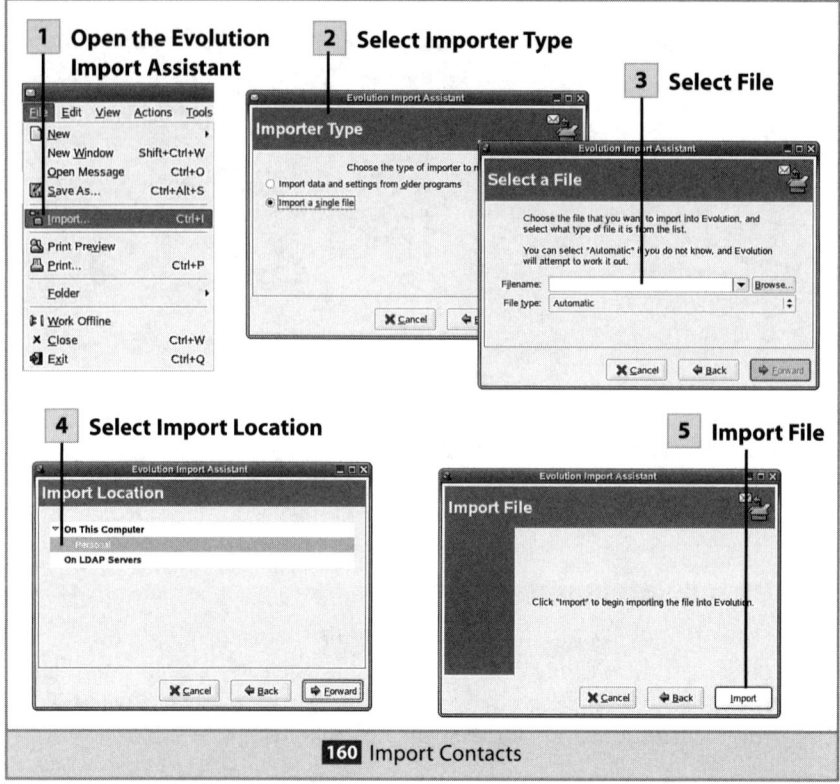

160 Import Contacts

1. Open the Evolution Import Assistant

In the Evolution window select **File**, **Import**. To begin the import process, select **Forward** on the initial Import Assistant screen.

2. Select Importer Type

On the next screen select the type of import that you want to perform: **Import Data and Settings from Older Program** or **Import a Single File**.

If you select Import Data and Settings from Older Program, select **Forward**, and Evolution scans your system for address book, email, and calendar files created in other Linux software applications. When the files are ready to import, you can select the **Import** button (and skip steps 4 and 5).

If you select Import a Single File, select **Forward** to continue the process.

3 Select File

On the next screen enter the file that you want to import. You can use the **Browse** button to locate the file. After specifying the file, select **Forward** to continue.

4 Select Import Location

On the next screen specify the location for the import. Because you are importing "personal" information, you will, in almost all cases, select **Personal** (On This Computer). Select **Forward** to continue.

5 Import File

Select the **Import** button. The information (contacts, email messages, appointments—depending on the contents of the import file) is added to the appropriate folder in Evolution.

TIP

If you have been using Microsoft Outlook as your groupware software, you need to download an open source tool called Outport to help you save your contact, email, or calendar information for import into Evolution. The Outport open source software is available for download to a Microsoft Windows system using the URL http://www.outport.sourceforge.net. The website provides all the information that you need to download Outport and then prepare your Outlook information for import into Evolution.

TIP

You can also quickly start a new contact based on a mail or calendar entry. This isn't really an import, but it does allow you to start a new contact based on information that you have received. Just right-click on an email address or email message in the **Inbox** or other mail folder and then select **Add Sender to Contacts** on the shortcut menu. This creates a new address card that can then be edited as needed.

CHAPTER 15

Staying Organized with Novell Evolution

IN THIS CHAPTER:

- 161 About the Evolution Calendar
- 162 Create Appointments
- 163 Send a Meeting Invitation
- 164 Manage Appointments and Meetings
- 165 Create Tasks
- 166 Create Assigned Tasks
- 167 Create Task Lists
- 168 Use Calendar Views
- 169 Set Evolution Preferences
- 170 About Synchronizing a Handheld Device with Evolution
- 171 Delete Evolution Items

CHAPTER 15: Staying Organized with Novell Evolution

Everyone needs to keep a calendar. Tracking appointments and job tasks (as well as personal tasks) can be a headache if a system isn't available that provides appointment reminders and allows you to view tasks in progress and completed tasks.

The Evolution calendar makes it easy for you to manage both your appointments and your tasks. Evolution also provides you with the ability to pull a meeting together quickly by sending electronic invitations to the participants and tracking their responses to the invitation.

161 About the Evolution Calendar

The Evolution calendar serves as an easy-to-use time-management tool that allows you to enter appointments (including recurring appointments), events, and tasks. The default view for the calendar shows the current day and any appointments scheduled for that day. The current month and the following month are also shown. A task list is also provided in the Evolution window, making it easy to monitor entered tasks and quickly add new tasks as needed.

The Evolution default calendar view allows you to quickly view your appointments for the day and monitor your task list.

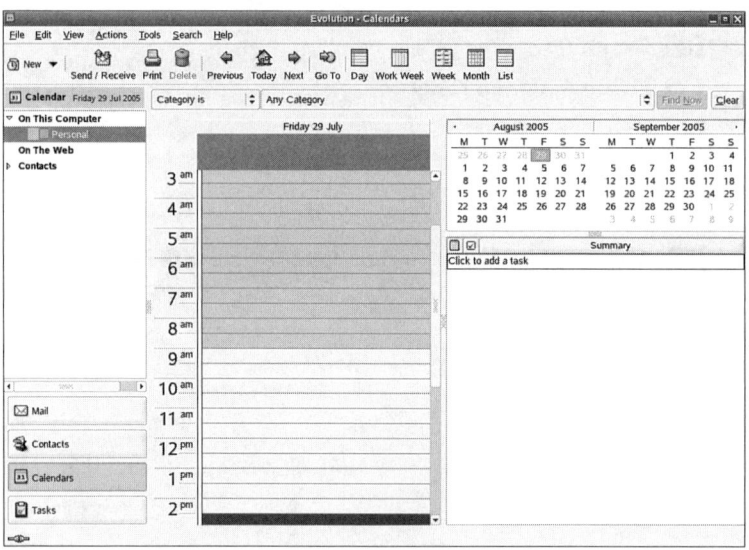

162 Create Appointments

You may note that the shortcut icon for the calendar is actually called Calendars, and there is a good reason for the plural. You can quickly create a new calendar (the default is Personal) by right-clicking an existing calendar and then selecting **New Calendar** from the shortcut menu. Name the new calendar, and you are ready to add appointments to the calendar.

When you use multiple calendars, the different calendars actually overlay each other in the Evolution window. Each calendar that you create is assigned a color code. Any appointments that have been entered in a particular calendar are color coded using the calendar color assigned when you created the new calendar.

So, you can have a personal calendar (the default), a work calendar, a special project calendar—as many calendars as you need. The color coding allows you to differentiate an appointment on your personal calendar from your work calendar.

Different views are also provided for the calendar pane, with the default being the current day. You can also quickly switch to a work week or month view of your calendars using the View menu.

162 Create Appointments

You can create a new appointment for the current day or a future date (by selecting the date on the months shown). Appointment information that you enter includes an appointment summary, location, and starting time, and you can also set a reminder for the appointment. Appointments that you specify as All Day appear in the gray header area of the current day (or the day that you placed the appointment on).

1 Open New Appointment

In the Evolution calendar window (select **Calendars** shortcut), select the **New** drop-down button on the toolbar and select **Appointment**. The Appointment dialog box opens.

TIP

You can quickly start a new appointment by double-clicking on a blank space on your daily calendar.

CHAPTER 15: Staying Organized with Novell Evolution

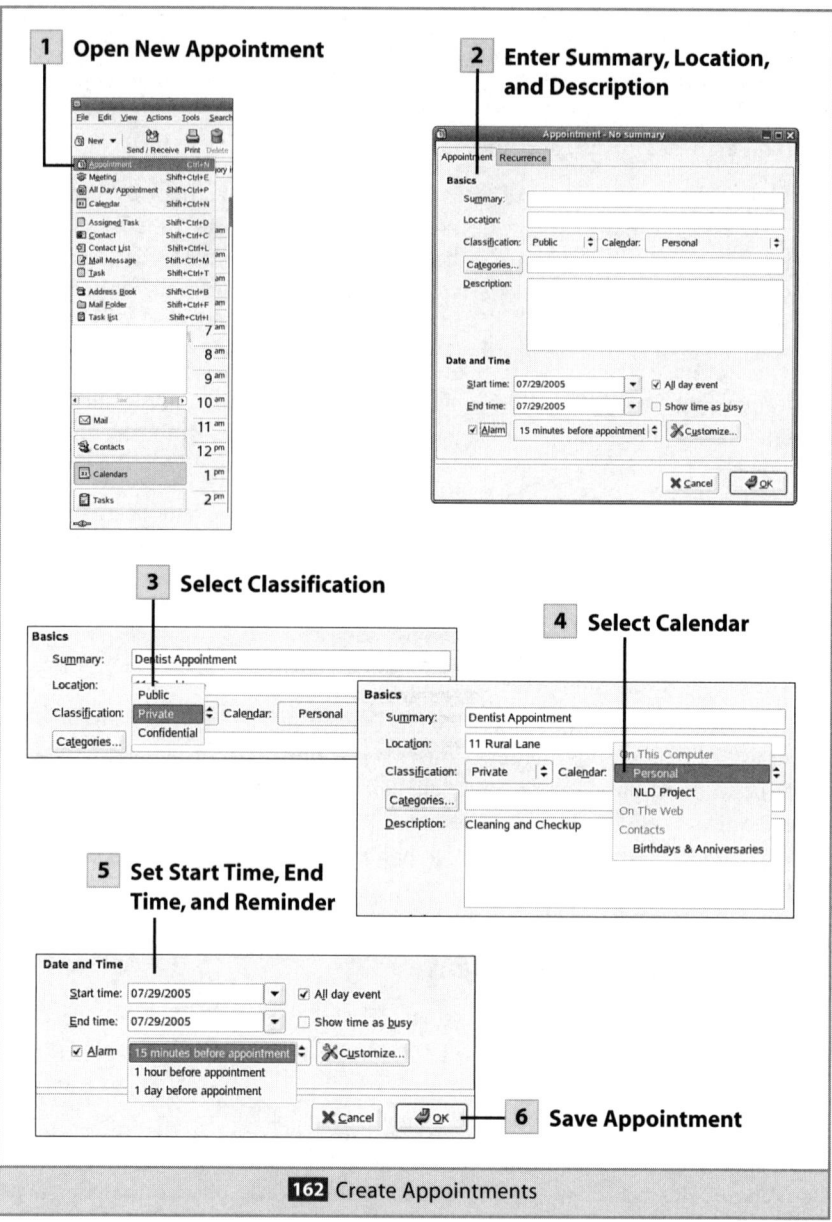

162 Create Appointments

162 Create Appointments

TIP

Make sure that the calendars you want to view in the calendar pane are selected in the Calendar list on the left side the Evolution window (select the check box for each calendar you want to view).

2 Enter Summary, Location, and Description

Enter a summary for the appointment. You can also type an optional location and description for the appointment.

3 Select Classification

To classify the appointment as Public, Private, or Confidential select the **Classification** drop-down list and make a selection.

NOTE

Marking an appointment as private or confidential is really only necessary when you are using group calendars on a network. In this type of groupware environment, public appointments would be available to other users; private appointments would not.

4 Select Calendar

Select the **Calendar** drop-down box and select the calendar for the appointment. The calendar you select determines the color-coding for the appointment.

5 Set Start Time, End Time, and Reminder

Use the **Start Time** and **End Time** drop-down lists to set the start and end times for the appointment, respectively. To set a reminder for the appointment, select the **Alarm** drop-down list and make a selection on the list (such as **1 Hour Before Appointment**).

TIP

If the appointment is an all-day event, select the **All Day Event** check box to mark the entire day as "busy."

371

TIP

If you want to customize the alarm for the appointment, select the **Customize** button. You can then customize your alarm by selecting the **Add** button in the Add Alarm dialog box. Custom alarms can start a particular program or play a particular sound when the alarm is triggered.

6 Save Appointment

After you have finished entering the information and the time frame for the appointment, click **OK**. The appointment is added to your calendar.

TIP

For a recurring appointment, select the **Recurrence** tab on the appointment's dialog box. Select the **This Appointment Recurs** check box and then use the spinner boxes to set the time period for the appointment's recurrence.

163 Send a Meeting Invitation

Evolution makes it easy for you to schedule a meeting and notify the participants. Invitations can quickly be sent to your contacts and others via email. When you create a new meeting you are also creating a new appointment on your calendar.

1 Open New Meeting

To start a new meeting select the **New** drop-down arrow on the toolbar and then select **Meeting**. A new Appointment dialog opens with Scheduling and Invitations tabs included.

NOTE

Because you are the organizer of the meeting, Evolution automatically includes you as a participant.

2 Open Select Contacts from Address Book Dialog

To type a new participant into the meeting list, select **Add** and then type the name or email address of the participant. You can also quickly add participants for the meeting from your address book. Select **Contacts** on the Invitations tab.

163 Send a Meeting Invitation

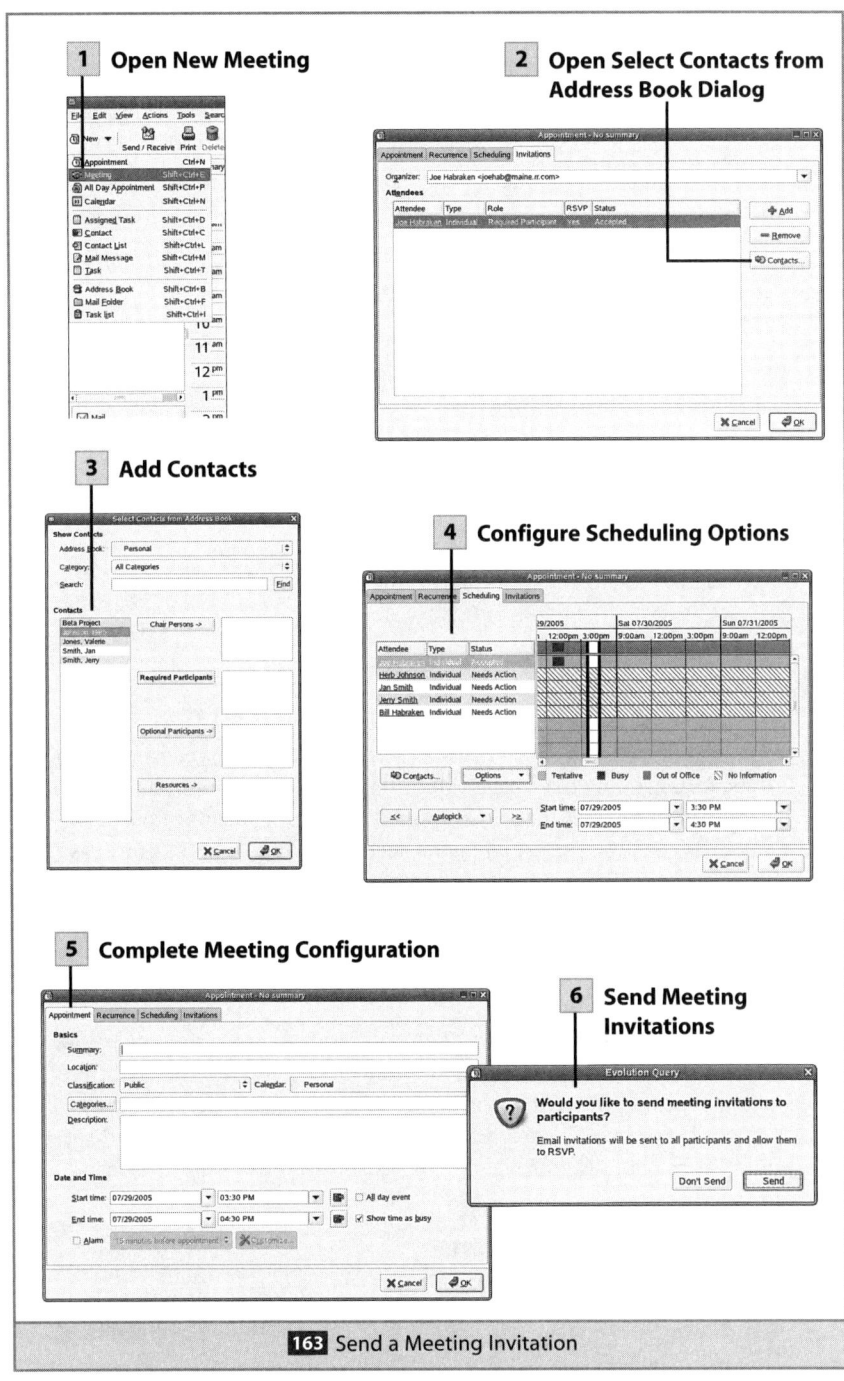

3 Add Contacts

In the Select Contacts from Address Book dialog box, select a contact from the list and then add them to the meeting by clicking the appropriate button: **Chair Persons**, **Required Participants**, and so on. After you have finished adding contacts, click **OK** to return to the Appointment dialog box.

4 Configure Scheduling Options

Select the **Scheduling** tab. Use the drop-down lists to set the date and the start and end times for the meeting. Or you can drag the bracketed time block on the Time/Date pane to set the time and date. You can also quickly add additional contacts by selecting the **Contacts** button.

TIP
You can add an attendee to the Attendee list by typing in the person's email address. This allows you to add participants who you do not have in your address book.

TIP
On a corporate network that allows users to share calendar data, you can quickly select a time for a meeting that will avoid all conflicts. After entering all the participants for the meeting, select (on the Scheduling tab) the **AutoPick** button's drop-down arrow and then select an option such as **All People and Resources** or **Required People**.

5 Complete Meeting Configuration

Select the **Appointment** tab of the new meeting. Enter a summary, location, and a description (as needed). You can also set an alarm (for you) for the meeting; select the **Alarm** check box and then set the time for the reminder. After you have entered the information (and checked the date and time for the meeting), click **OK**. An Evolution Query box opens.

6 Send Meeting Invitations

Evolution asks whether you want to send the meeting invitations to the participants. Click **OK** to close the query box and send the invitations. The invitations require a response from all invitees.

164 Manage Appointments and Meetings

> **NOTE**
>
> The invitation email that is received by your invitees makes it easy for a potential attendee to respond. The email provides a series of buttons at the top of the message such as Accept, Decline, and Propose New Time. Responses to your invitation appear in your Evolution Inbox. The response email that you receive has a "slick" Update Respondent Status button that allows you to quickly change the status of that respondent on the actual meeting dialog box (on the Scheduling tab); all you do is click the **Update Respondent Status** button in the email message.

164 Manage Appointments and Meetings

The Evolution calendar makes it easy for you to manage your appointments and meetings. Days that hold appointments appear in bold on the month calendars shown in the Calendar pane. You can easily move an appointment or meeting to a new time and date. Appointments can also be edited as needed. You can also respond to meeting requests that will place a new meeting appointment on your calendar when you accept a meeting invitation.

1 Select Calendars to View

In the Calendar view, select or deselect calendars in the Calendar list as needed (select or deselect the appropriate check boxes). Appointments and meetings only show on the current day for the calendars currently selected.

2 Open Existing Appointment

Double-click an existing appointment on the currently selected day. The appointment's dialog box opens.

3 Edit Appointment

Edit the appointment as needed (including date and time) and then click **OK** to close the appointment.

> **TIP**
>
> You can move appointments from one of your calendars to any of your other calendars. Right-click an appointment and select **Move to Calendar**. The Select Destination dialog box opens. Select the calendar that will serve as the destination for the appointment and then click **OK**. Moving an appointment to a different calendar does not change the time or date of the appointment. It does change the color coding of the appointment based on the calendar that served as the destination.

CHAPTER 15: Staying Organized with Novell Evolution

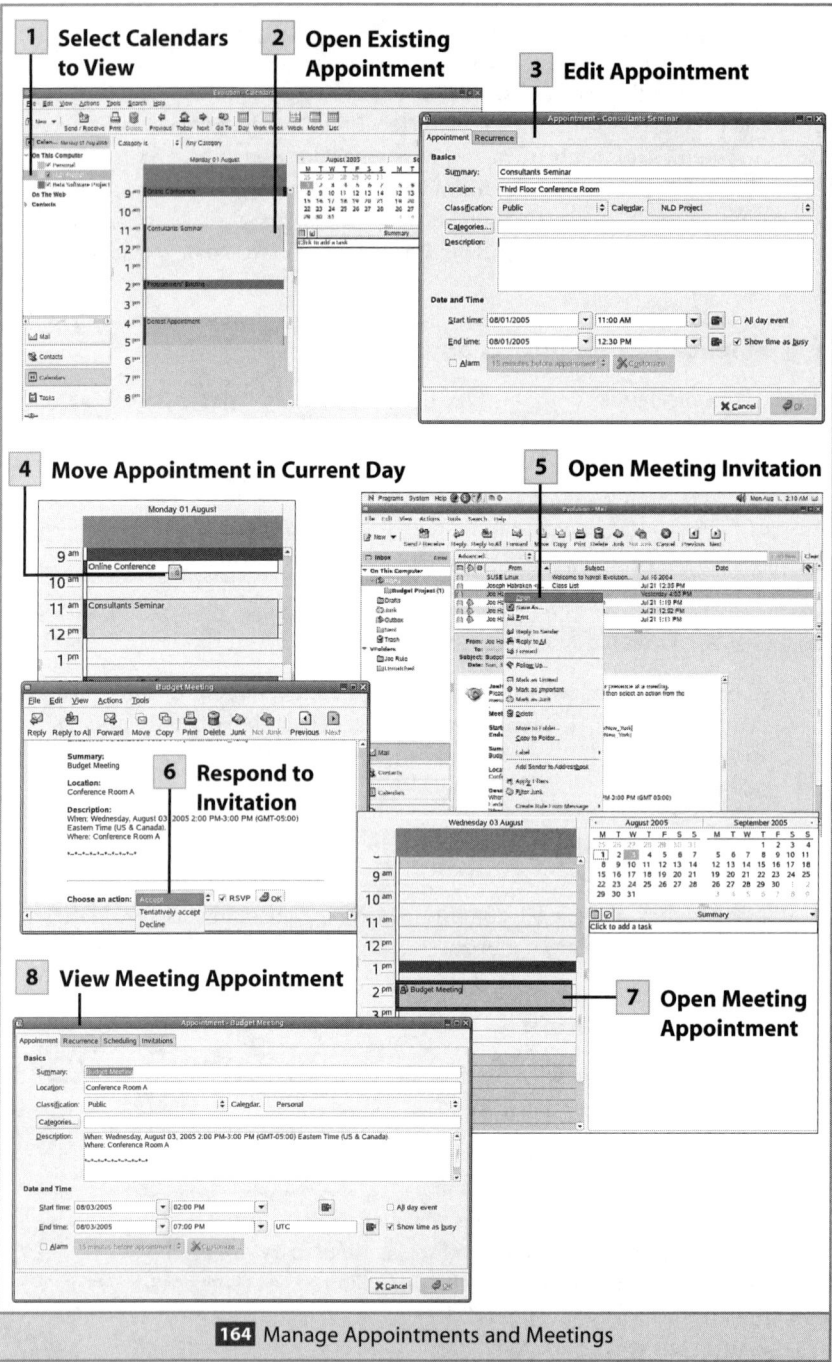

164 Manage Appointments and Meetings

4 Move Appointment in Current Day

To move an appointment on the current day drag the appointment to a new time.

5 Open Meeting Invitation

You must accept or reject meeting invitations that you receive. In your Inbox open a meeting invitation; right-click on the invitation message and select **Open** or double-click on the message.

6 Respond to Invitation

Scroll to the bottom of the invitation message. Select the **Choose an Action** drop-down list and then select **Accept**, **Tentatively Accept**, or **Decline**. A response message is sent to the originator of the meeting invitation.

7 Open Meeting Appointment

When you accept an invitation to a meeting, a new appointment is placed on your calendar for the meeting. To open a meeting appointment, double-click the appointment.

8 View Meeting Appointment

The meeting appointment opens. View the appointment for location and other information related to the meeting. After you have finished reading the information, close the appointment dialog.

---

165 Create Tasks

You can view tasks in the Calendar view in the Task pane or you can switch to the Task view (select the **Task** shortcut icon). You can create tasks for your own to-do list or assign tasks to others. You can also create multiple task lists (the same as creating multiple calendars) that allow you to color-code tasks (dependant on the task list the task is held in).

1 Select Task View

To switch to the Task view, select the **Task** shortcut.

CHAPTER 15: Staying Organized with Novell Evolution

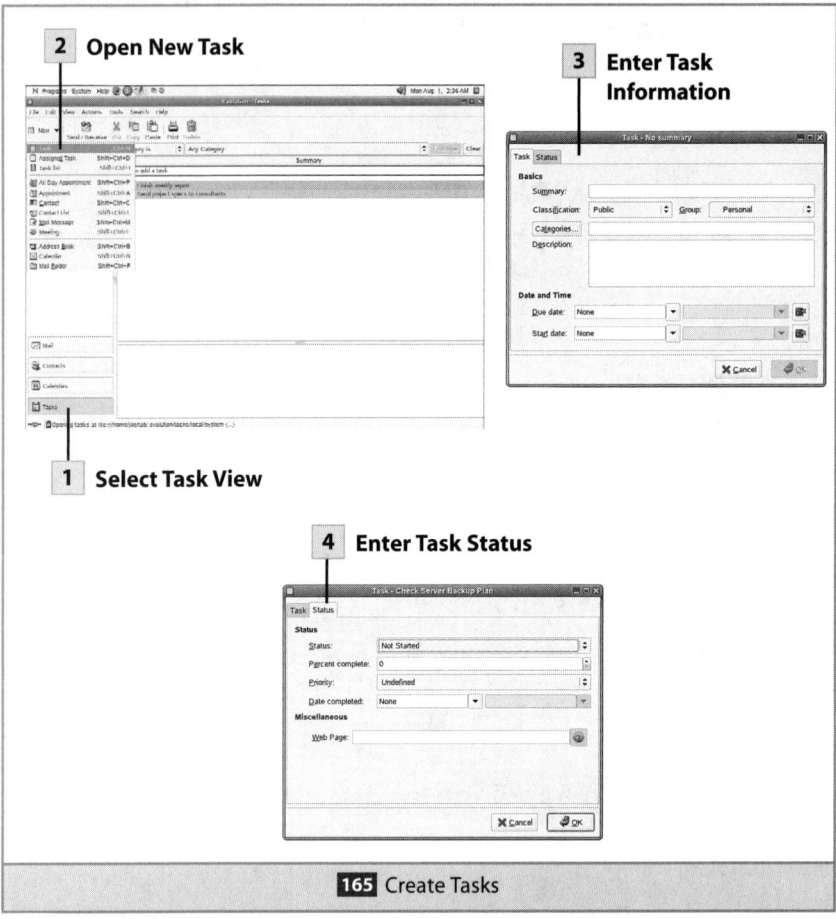

165 Create Tasks

2 Open New Task

To create a new task, select the **New** drop-down arrow on the toolbar and then select **Task**. A new task dialog box opens.

3 Enter Task Information

On the Task tab of the new task dialog box enter the summary and description for the task. In the Date and Time area of the Task tab use the drop-down lists to set the **Due Date** and **Start Date** for the task as needed.

TIP

To quickly start a new task click in the **Click to Add a Task** box in the Task pane. Type the name of the new task. To edit the task, including setting the task status, double-click the task in the Task list.

④ Enter Task Status

Select the **Status** tab of the task's dialog box. Set the status of the task; select the **Status** drop-down list and then select **In Progress**. To set the priority, select the **Priority** drop-down list and then select **High**, **Normal**, or **Low**. To close the dialog box and add the task to the Task list, click **OK**.

TIP

After you have completed a task, you can select the task's check box in the Task list. Or you can open the task (double-click the task), select the **Status** tab, and then select **Completed** on the **Status** drop-down list.

166 Create Assigned Tasks

You can assign tasks to co-workers or subordinates. When you assign a task, the assignee has the option of accepting or rejecting the task.

① Open Assigned Task

Select the **New** drop-down arrow on the toolbar and then select **Assigned Task**. A new task dialog box opens.

② Open Select Contacts from Address Book Dialog

Task participants are entered on the task's Assignment tab. You are added as a participant automatically (you can remove yourself using the **Remove** button if you want). To add additional participants from your address book select the **Contacts** button. The Select Contacts from Address Book dialog box opens.

379

CHAPTER 15: Staying Organized with Novell Evolution

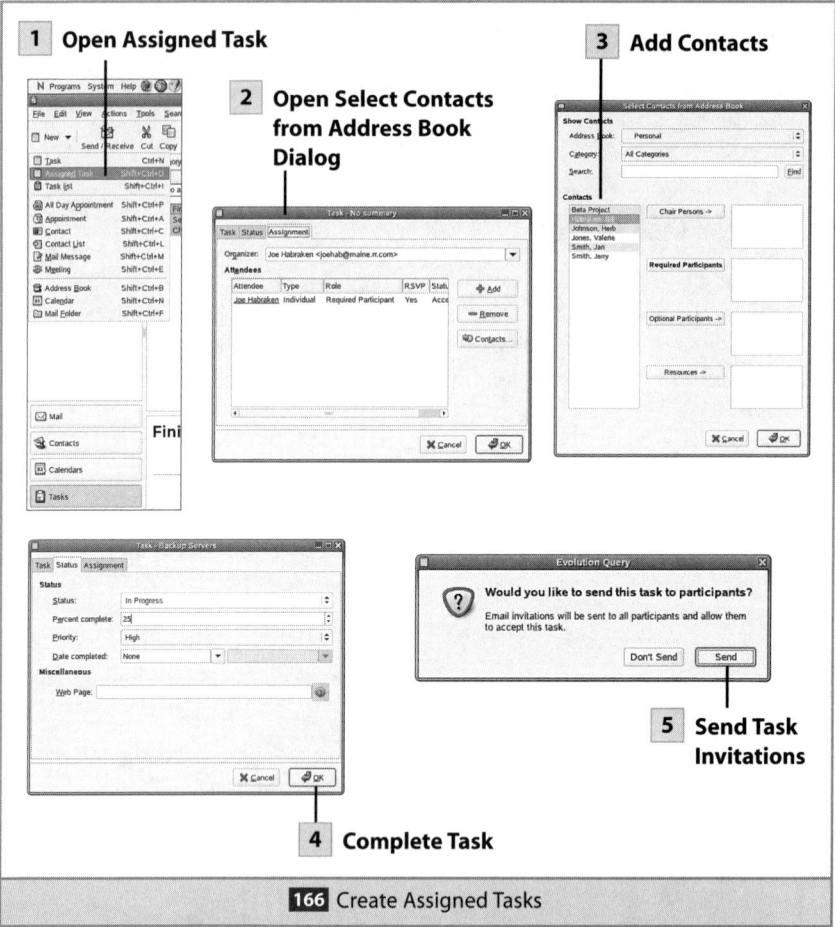

166 Create Assigned Tasks

3 Add Contacts

Select contacts and then select **Required Participants** to add them to the task participant list. After you have finished adding participants, click OK.

4 Complete Task

Enter information on the task's Task and Status tabs as needed. After you have completed entering information related to the assigned task, click OK.

5 Send Task Invitations

An Evolution Query dialog box opens asking you whether you want to send the task participants an email invitation. Click **Send**.

NOTE

When you send task invitations, invitees have the option of accepting or declining the task. Email responses from the invitees appear in your Inbox when the various invitees respond.

167 Create Task Lists

You can create multiple task lists. Each task list appears in the left pane of the Task view. Each task list has its own color coding, so you can have task lists for various projects that you are working on. All tasks appear in the Task view when all lists are selected. To view the tasks in a particular list, make sure that it is the only list selected in the left pane of the List view.

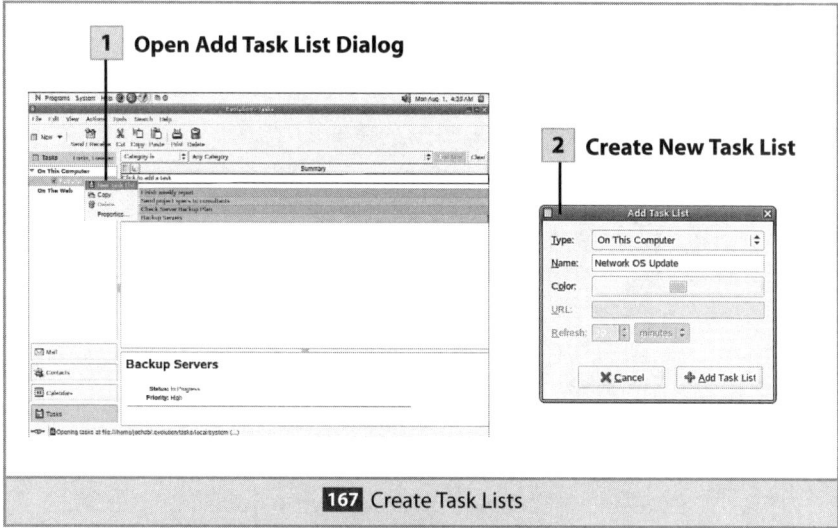

167 Create Task Lists

1 Open Add Task List Dialog

Right-click on an existing task list in the left pane of the Task view (such as the Personal task list). On the shortcut menu select **New Task List**.

2 Create New Task List

Enter a name for the task list and select a color for the list (which is used to color code tasks in that list). To create the new list select **Add Task List**.

When you create a new task, you can assign it to a particular task list on the task's Task tab using the **Group** drop-down list.

168 Use Calendar Views

Viewing tasks and your calendar simultaneously is easily accomplished in the Calendar view. You can also change the current view of the calendar to better view your daily appointments (in a list) or view.

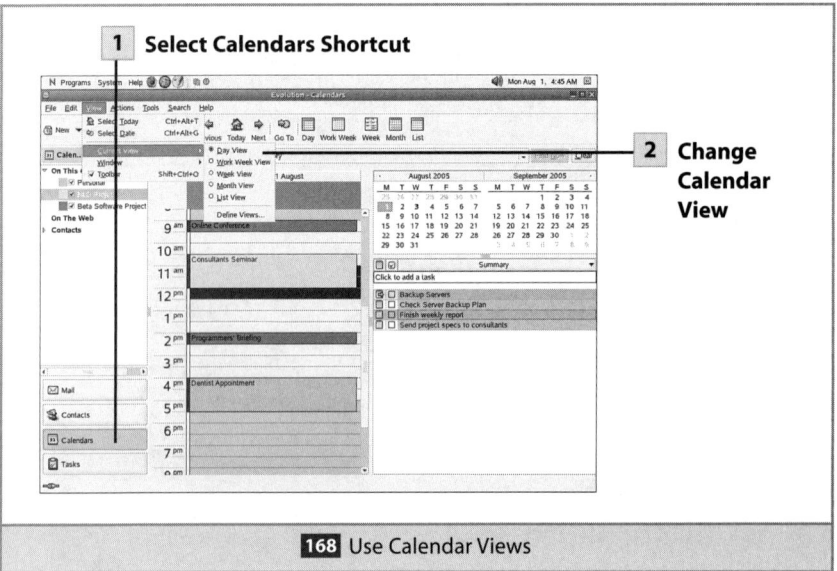

168 Use Calendar Views

1 Select Calendars Shortcut

Select the **Calendars** shortcut to view your calendars and the task list.

2 Change Calendar View

Select **View**, **Current View**. Select one of the following views from the submenu:

- Day View—The default view shows the current day and appointments.

169 Set Evolution Preferences

- Workweek View—Shows the current workweek in a grid, with appointments shown for each workweek day.
- Week View—Shows the current seven-day week and appointments scheduled on each day.
- Month View—Shows the current month and appointments scheduled on each day of the month.
- List View—Lists the current day's appointments in a list.

169 Set Evolution Preferences

You can set the various preferences for Evolution, including mail, calendar, and task preferences, in the Evolution Settings dialog box.

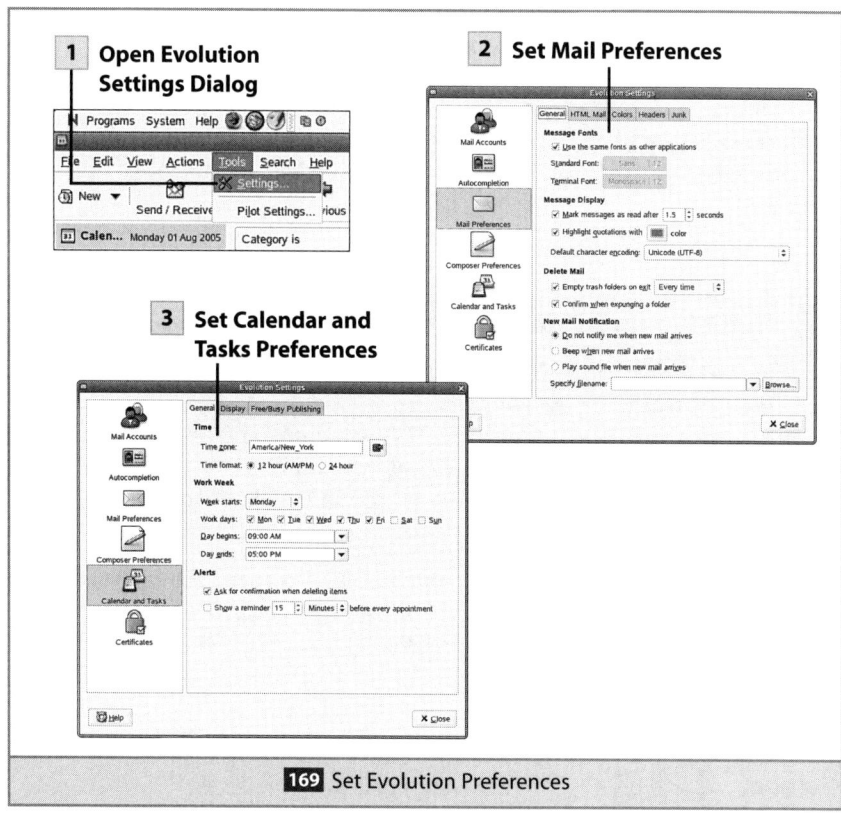

CHAPTER 15: Staying Organized with Novell Evolution

1   Open Evolution Settings Dialog

To open the Settings dialog box, select **Tools, Settings**.

2   Set Mail Preferences

Select the **Mail Preferences** icon. You can then set mail preferences including message fonts, message notification settings, and the headers shown for each email message (such as To:, From:, CC:, and so on).

3   Set Calendar and Tasks Preferences

Select the **Calendar and Tasks** icon. Set preferences as needed including time zone, work week parameters, and alert settings. After you have completed setting your preferences, select **Close** to close the Settings dialog box.

TIP

To set preferences related to composed messages select the **Composer Preferences** icon in the Settings dialog box. You can set preferences such as having all messages sent as HTML and automatically including a smiley face on every message.

---

170   About Synchronizing a Handheld Device with Evolution

You can synchronize handheld devices that run the Palm operating system with Evolution. The first thing that you must do is set up communication between the NLD system and your Palm device. The second phase of the setup is selecting the conduits that allow you to move information from your various Evolution folders, such as the calendar and the address book to the Palm device (and vice versa).

The easiest way to set up the initial communication between the Palm device and Evolution is to run the Gnome-Pilot Wizard. The wizard walks you through the steps of linking your Palm handheld organizer with Evolution. You start the Gnome-Pilot Wizard from inside Evolution; select **Tools, Pilot Settings** from the Evolution menu.

After the Gnome-Pilot Wizard has started, the first screen provided by the wizard can be quickly bypassed by selecting **Forward**. The second screen requires you to enter important information for creating the link between the handheld

170 About Synchronizing a Handheld Device with Evolution

device and Evolution. You must specify the port type (Serial, USB, for example) and the actual port that will be used for the Palm to Evolution communication. The default is /dev/pilot, but other ports such as ttyUSB0 or ttyUSB1 can be used.

NOTE

You need read and write access to connect to a port such as a USB or serial port. So, connecting a handheld device to an NLD system when you are not running as root, poses some of the same problems that burning CDs or DVDs do (meaning root privileges are required to access devices). You can use commands such as chown and chmod at the command line, when logged in as root using the su (superuser) command, to gain access to ports. For example, you can run the command chmod 777 /dev/ttyUSB0 to access the first USB port on a system. Successfully connecting to a Palm device may require help from your system administrator or require some additional research on your part to get the Palm device and your system talking when you are not logged in to the system as root.

Specify the port and port type for the communication between the Palm device and Evolution.

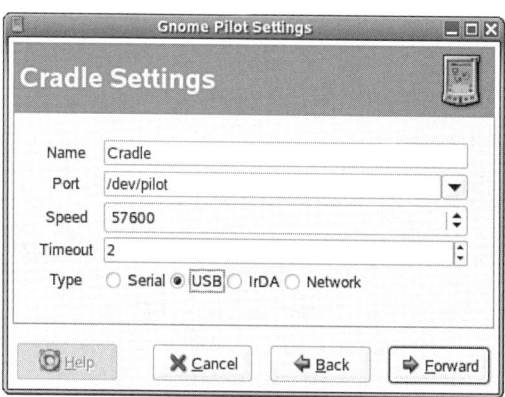

After the port and port type are specified, the wizard walks you through the steps of synchronizing with the Palm device for the first time. You can specify whether you have synced the device with other groupware software in the past or are synchronizing the device with a groupware product (such as Evolution) for the first time. In either case, a username and unique ID are negotiated between the handheld device and your system.

385

CHAPTER 15: Staying Organized with Novell Evolution

After your system and the handheld device have been synchronized for the first time, you can configure the conduits that allow you to synchronize email, appointments, or tasks between Evolution and the Palm device. You can access the Pilot Settings (including the conduit settings) by selecting **Tools**, **Pilot Settings** from the menu after you have run the initial synchronization.

The Pilot Settings dialog box provides three tabs: Pilots, Devices, and Conduits. The Pilots tab lists the device that was identified during the initial synchronization. The Devices tab shows the cradle and communication port (such as a USB port) that was configured by the Gnome-Pilot Wizard.

The Pilot Settings dialog box shows the settings that were configured when you ran the Gnome-Pilot Wizard.

The Conduits tab is used to configure how Evolution and the handheld device share information. You will have different conduits listed on the Conduit tab such as Eaddress, which is for synchronizing the address book, and Ecalendar, which is used for synchronizing your appointments. You select a conduit and then enable it by selecting the **Enable** button. To configure the conduit, you select the conduit (such as EAddress) and then select **Settings**. Selecting **Settings** opens a Conduit Settings dialog box for the selected conduit.

You then must determine how you want Evolution and the handheld device to handle the information shared during subsequent synchronizations. In the Conduit Settings dialog box you select the **Action** drop-down list. You can then select from the following:

- Synchronize—New data is shared between Evolution and the device (no matter where the new information resides), and information deleted in Evolution or the Palm device is removed from Evolution and the handheld device.

- Copy from Pilot—New information is copied from the Palm device to Evolution.

- Copy to Pilot—New information is copied from Evolution to the Palm device.

- Merge from Pilot—New data is copied to Evolution, and any data deleted on the handheld device is also deleted from Evolution.

- Merge to Pilot—New data is copied to the handheld device from Evolution, and any information that has been deleted from Evolution is also deleted from the handheld device.

Conduits are configured to determine how information is dealt with during the synchronizing of Evolution and the handheld device.

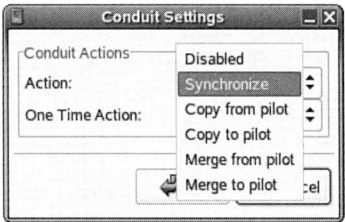

Configure all the conduits that you want to synchronize. You can then synchronize Evolution and your Palm device as needed. After you have configured your conduits, you can synchronize Evolution and your handheld device as needed by pressing the sync button on your handheld device's cradle.

171 Delete Evolution Items

The end result of deleting items in Evolution really depends on the item you are deleting. Deleted messages are placed in the Trash folder. This allows you to recover the message if it has been deleted inadvertently. When you delete contacts, appointments, and tasks, you aren't really given a second chance in terms of recovering the deleted item. They are removed from Evolution completely.

387

CHAPTER 15: Staying Organized with Novell Evolution

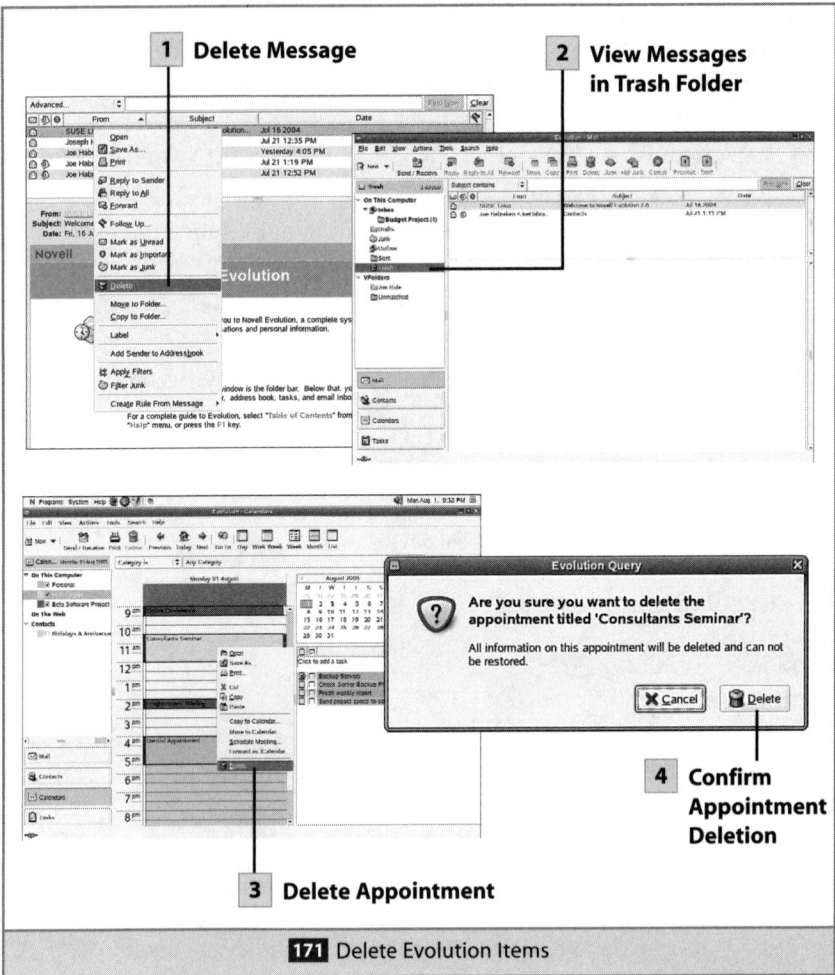

171 Delete Evolution Items

1 Delete Message

With the **Inbox** selected, right-click on any message and select **Delete** from the shortcut menu. The message is deleted from the Inbox.

TIP

You can select multiple messages and then delete them by pressing the **Delete** key.

2 View Messages in Trash Folder

Select the **Trash** folder in the Folder list. Deleted messages are held in the Trash folder until you empty the trash or exit Evolution (and have configured Evolution to automatically empty the Trash folder on exiting).

TIP
To configure Evolution to automatically empty the Trash folder on exiting, go to the **Mail Preferences** in the Evolution Settings dialog. Select the **Empty Trash Folders on Exit** check box on the General tab of the Mail Preferences.

TIP
You can undelete a message in the Trash folder (which returns it to the folder that held it before the deletion). Right-click on the message and select **Undelete**.

3 Delete Appointment

When you delete items such as appointments or tasks, you don't have the luxury of recovering them from a Trash folder (as you do with messages). With the **Calendars** shortcut selected, right-click on an appointment on the daily calendar. Select **Delete** from the shortcut menu.

4 Confirm Appointment Deletion

An Evolution Query dialog box opens that lets you know that the item will be permanently deleted from Evolution; select **Delete** to remove the item.

CHAPTER 16

Using Novell iFolder

IN THIS CHAPTER:

- 172 About Novell iFolder
- 173 Start the iFolder Client
- 174 Access iFolder from the Desktop
- 175 Access Your iFolder from a Web Browser
- 176 About Synchronizing Files
- 177 Manually Synchronize Files
- 178 View Files in the iFolder Conflict Bin
- 179 Set iFolder Preferences

CHAPTER 16: Using Novell iFolder

Having the ability to access important files from any computer, even a computer that is not running NLD, provides a number of possibilities for working on the road and collaborating with other users. Novell iFolder is a network service that allows you to access a dedicated folder either from any workstation running NLD or from any computer's web browser. This chapter provides a basic overview of the client side of iFolder.

172 About Novell iFolder

Novell iFolder is a network and Net service that allows you to access a personal folder on a server (the iFolder server can be a NetWare, SUSE, or Microsoft Windows server configured with the iFolder service). The items in the local folder are synchronized with your iFolder on the server. This provides seamless access to the files that you need as if they exist locally, and it also backs up these files in the iFolder on the server.

You can access your folder on the iFolder server from any computer that provides access to an iFolder client. NLD provides an iFolder client that is installed during the NLD installation process.

In cases where you have access to a computer but not to an iFolder client, you can access your iFolder from any computer that has a web browser. As files are moved over the network and/or the Internet, they are encrypted, protecting your data.

173 Start the iFolder Client

The iFolder client is the easiest way to access your online iFolder. The client software is installed by default during the NLD installation.

1 Start iFolder Client

From the NLD desktop, select **Programs**, **Accessories**, **Novell iFolder**. The Login dialog box opens.

2 Enter Logon Information

Enter your user ID, password, and the name of the iFolder server. After you have completed entering the information, select **Login**. The first time you log in, the Novell iFolder Location dialog opens.

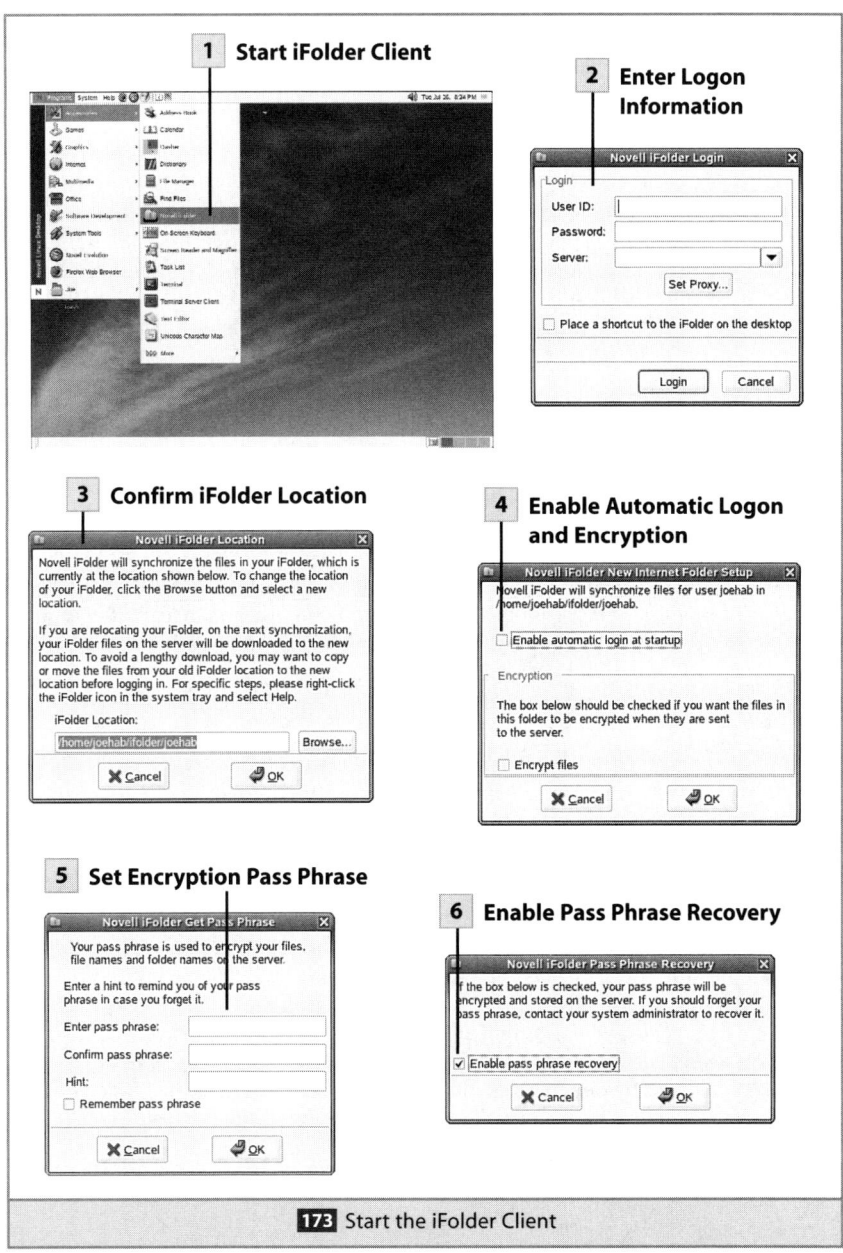

> **NOTE**
>
> The server name can be entered as a DNS friendly name, or the IP address of the server can be entered.

3 Confirm iFolder Location

The Novell iFolder Location dialog box shows the default location for your new iFolder. You can edit the path if you want, even using a directory in which you already have files. To accept the default (or your modified path), click **OK**. The Novell iFolder New Internet Folder Setup dialog box opens.

4 Enable Automatic Logon and Encryption

The next step in the process of configuring your new iFolder provides you with the option of having automatic logon to the iFolder server at the startup of your NLD system and also gives you the option of encrypting your files. Select the **Enable Automatic Login at Startup** check box to log on to the iFolder server at NLD startup.

If you are going to access your iFolder via an Internet connection (rather than an internal network), you may want to enable the file encryption feature; select the **Encrypt Files** check box. Click **OK**. If you choose to encrypt files, the Novell iFolder Get Pass Phrase dialog box opens.

5 Set Encryption Pass Phrase

Enter a pass phrase and then reenter the pass phrase to confirm it. Enter a hint that helps you remember your pass phrase (if necessary). Click **OK** to continue the iFolder initialization process.

> **NOTE**
>
> The pass phrase can be one word or multiple words. Spaces are legal characters. Keep the pass phrase simple enough so that you can remember it easily but complex enough that it will not be easy to guess.

6 Enable Pass Phrase Recovery

Select the **Enable Pass Phrase Recovery** check box. This makes it possible for your network administrator to provide you with your pass phrase if you cannot remember it. Click **OK**.

This ends the initialization process. An iFolder icon appears on the NLD desktop for your new iFolder.

NOTE

You only have to go through all the initialization steps the first time you use the iFolder client to log on to the iFolder server. In the future providing the username and password will log you immediately on to the server.

174 Access iFolder from the Desktop

After you have logged on successfully to the iFolder server, an icon is placed on the desktop for your local iFolder. You can use this icon to quickly open your iFolder as needed. To keep the files up-to-date in the local iFolder, it is periodically synchronized with your iFolder on the server.

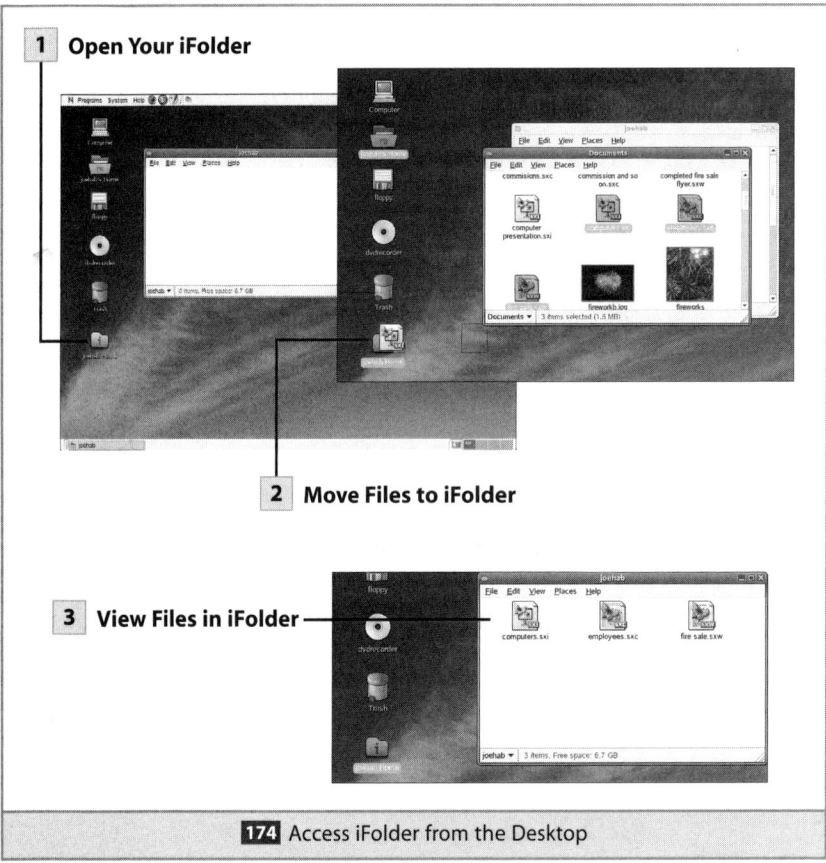

1. Open Your iFolder
2. Move Files to iFolder
3. View Files in iFolder

174 Access iFolder from the Desktop

1. Open Your iFolder

Double-click the **iFolder** icon on the NLD desktop. The iFolder opens. The iFolder is empty the first time you open it, unless you specified a directory that already contains files.

2. Move Files to iFolder

Open a Folder on your hard drive using Nautilus. To move files from a local folder (on your computer) to the iFolder, drag the files as needed onto the iFolder icon on the desktop.

3. View Files in iFolder

To view or access the files in your iFolder double-click the desktop **iFolder** icon. A Nautilus window opens showing the iFolder contents.

NOTE

You can treat the iFolder as you do any other folder on your system. Copy or move files to the iFolder, delete files in the iFolder, and double-click a file to open the application that the file was created in. You can also specify the iFolder as the destination to save a file as you work in an application such as OpenOffice.org Writer or Calc. Bottom line: It is the same as other folders that you access locally on your computer, except that it gets synchronized in the background to your iFolder on the server.

175 Access Your iFolder from a Web Browser

You can also access your iFolder from any computer that has Internet access and a web browser installed (if your iFolder server is reachable via the Web).

1. Access iFolder Server via the Web

Open a web browser on any computer with an Internet connection. Enter the DNS name or the IP address of your iFolder server in the address box and then click **Go** (or press **Enter**). You are taken to the main page of the iFolder server.

Because most web browsers support Java, the easiest way to log on and access the iFolder is to use the Java client that runs inside your browser window. Select the **Login** link on the left side of the browser window. The Java Login client opens.

175 Access Your iFolder from a Web Browser

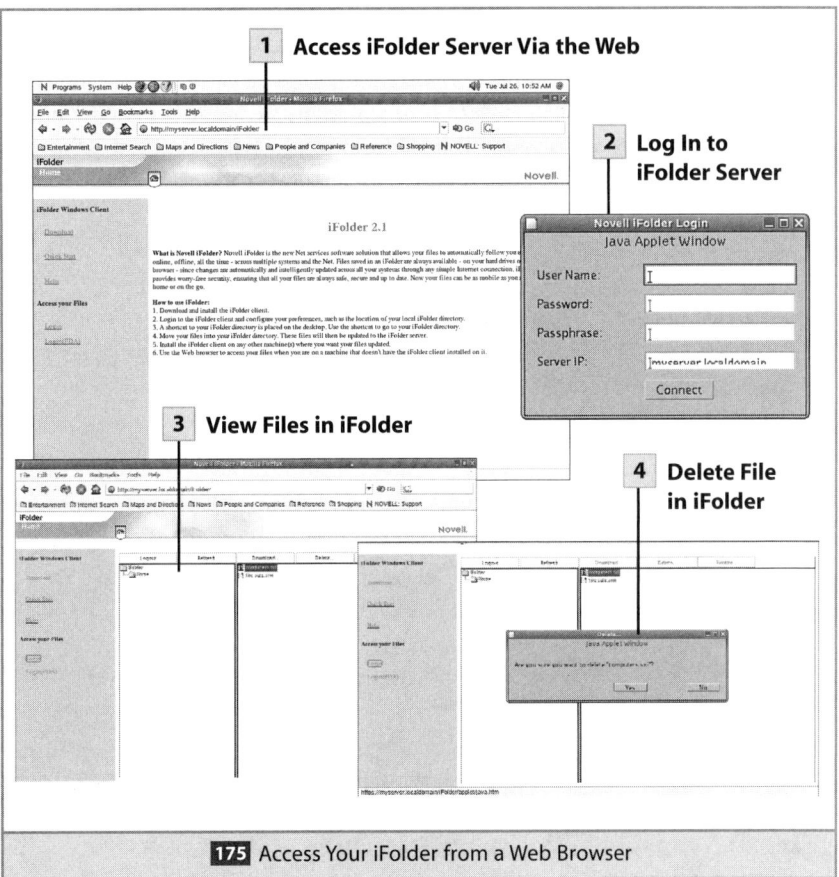

175 Access Your iFolder from a Web Browser

TIP

For web browsers that do not support Java or for access to the iFolder using a handheld device with web access, use the **Login (PDA)** link in the browser window to log on. You will be able to download the files but not upload them to your iFolder nor delete any files from the server.

2 Log In to iFolder Server

In the Java client Login window provide your username, password, and pass phrase. Then click **Connect**.

[3] View Files in iFolder

The iFolder appears in the browser window. To view the files in your folder, double-click the folder in the Folder list. Files appear in the File list. If you want to use one of the files on the current computer, select the file and then click **Download**. This downloads the file to the computer you are currently working on.

TIP

You can also upload files to your iFolder using the web client. Select your iFolder (don't open it) in the browser window and then select **Upload**. An Upload dialog box opens. Specify the file that you want to upload and then upload the file (or files). The file is added to your iFolder.

[4] Delete File in iFolder

You can delete files from the iFolder using the web client. Select a file and then select **Delete**. In the Delete dialog box that opens, select **Yes** to delete the file.

176 About Synchronizing Files

Because you can access your iFolder from multiple workstations, even over the Web, it is necessary for the iFolder on the server to be synchronized with the iFolder on your NLD system (the system you use most often). Synchronization makes sure that the same files are available in the iFolder no matter where you are when you log on to the server.

Files are automatically synchronized between the server and your computer when you use the iFolder client to log on to the server (on your NLD system). You can also activate synchronization manually from the iFolder applet that resides in the top panel.

When there is a conflict during synchronization, affected files are held in a conflict bin. For example, let's say that you are working on a file on your NLD desktop that resides in your iFolder. Then you go to a remote system and download the file using the web client. You then complete working on the file. And let's say that you don't need the file any longer, so you delete it from the iFolder using the web client.

The next time that you log on to the iFolder server on your NLD system (using the iFolder client) synchronization takes place. However, there will be a conflict because the file that you deleted using the web client is not on the server; it is in your local iFolder. Instead of just deleting the file, the file in question is placed in your conflict bin. This allows you to review the file and decide whether it should also be deleted from the local iFolder on your NLD system.

177 Manually Synchronize Files

Occasionally you may find the need to manually synchronize you iFolder with your NLD system.

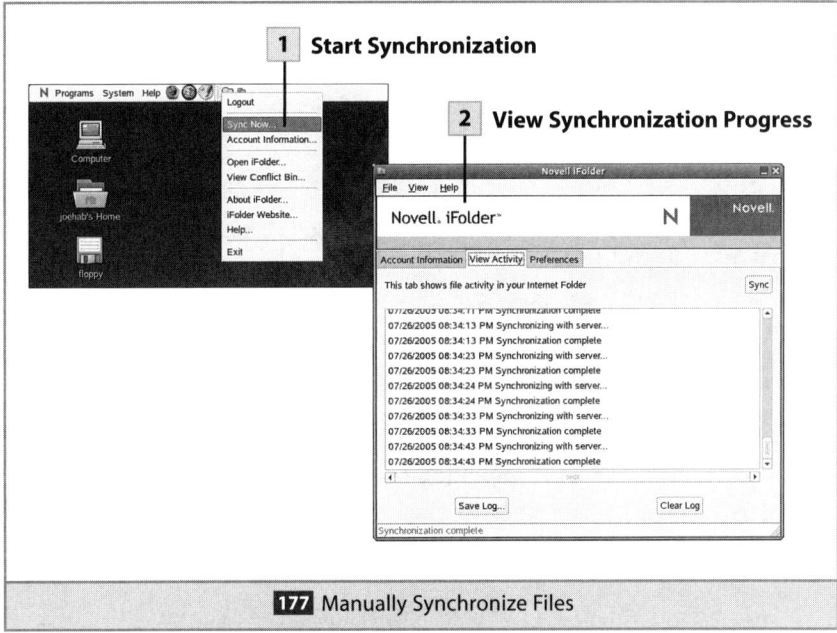

177 Manually Synchronize Files

1 Start Synchronization

Select the **iFolder** icon in the top panel. On the menu that appears select **Sync Now**. The Novell iFolder dialog box opens.

2 View Synchronization Progress

The manual synchronization is posted on the View Activity tab of the Novell iFolder dialog box. You can scroll through the log information to view all the recent activity related to synchronization between your local iFolder and the iFolder server. After you have completed viewing the log, you can close the Novell iFolder dialog box.

178 View Files in the iFolder Conflict Bin

After you synchronize with the iFolder server (at logon or manually), files may be placed in the conflict bin. You can access the conflict bin and determine what to do with the files found there.

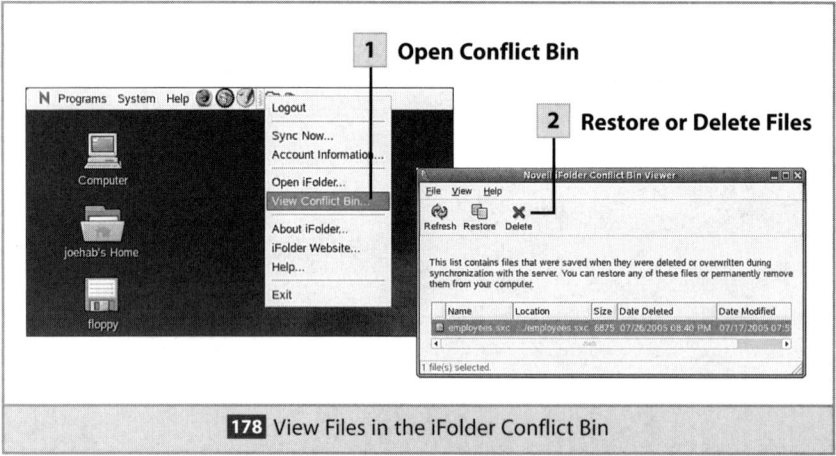

178 View Files in the iFolder Conflict Bin

1 Open Conflict Bin

Select the **iFolder** icon in the top panel and then select **View Conflict Bin**. The conflict bin opens.

2 Restore or Delete Files

Files listed are a result of conflicts found during synchronization. To place a file back in your local iFolder that was removed during synchronization, select the file and then select **Restore**.

If files listed in the conflict folder are no longer needed and were not the result of a "true" conflict, you can select the files and then click **Delete** to delete them as needed. After you have finished working in the conflict bin, close the dialog box.

179 Set iFolder Preferences

You can review your iFolder account settings and set preferences related to synchronization between your local iFolder and the iFolder server. Settings and preferences are accessed via the Novell iFolder dialog box.

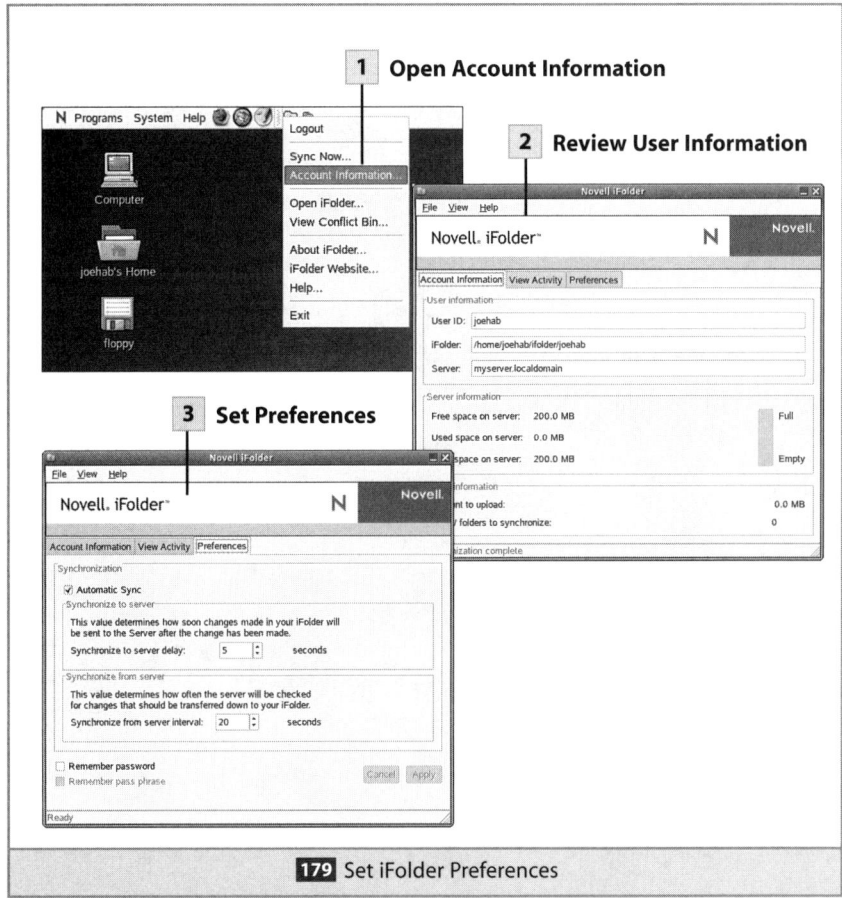

179 Set iFolder Preferences

1 Open Account Information

Select the **iFolder** icon in the top pane of the NLD desktop. Then select **Account Information**. This opens the Account Information tab of the Novell iFolder dialog box.

2. Review User Information

The Account Information tab provides all the information related to your user ID, iFolder, and the iFolder server that you use. The amount of space available on the server and the amount of space that you have used are also provided on this tab.

3. Set Preferences

Select the **Preferences** tab. The **Automatic Sync** check box is enabled by default. If you want to turn off Automatic Sync, clear the check box (only do this if advised to do so by your network administrator). You can also change the default timing for the synchronization delay (the delay between changes to the local iFolder and synchronizing with the server) and the syncing interval, which is the time between sync operations from the server. You can change these timings as needed using the spinner boxes provided. If you want the iFolder client to remember your password, select the **Remember Password** check box.

Any changes that you make to the settings should be applied by selecting **Apply**. After you have finished working with the dialog box, you can close it.

Index

A

acceleration options for mouse, configuring, 95

Accessibility and Assistive Technology Support (GNOME), 66
    Assistive Technology Support, 69-70
    keyboard mouse, 69
    keyboard shortcuts, 70
    sticky keys, 68

accessing
    files from USB memory sticks (Nautilus File Manager), 138-140
    iFolder
        desktop icon, 395-396
        from web browsers, 396-398
    recent files in Nautilus File Manager, 137-138

Accessories submenu tools
    calculator, 11
    dictionary, 11
    file manager, 11

accounts (email)
    adding (Evolution), 202-205, 334-336
    configuring, 200
        addresses, 201
        client tool, 202

accounts

for corporate environments, 201
for home/small office use, 201
IMAP servers, 202
passwords, 201
POP3 servers, 201
SMTP servers, 201
identity information (Evolution), 336
receive mail options (Evolution), 336
send mail options (Evolution), 336

Acrobat Reader, PDF files, 104
Actions option (Logon Manager), graphical greeters, 23
Add Bookmark dialog box, 187-188
adding
    applications
        Red Carpet, 154-156
        YaST, 154
    items to menus, 63-65
    user accounts, 17
        user versus administrator rights, 20

Address Book (Evolution), 356-357
    contact lists, creating, 360-361
    contacts
        creating, 357-358
        editing, 359-360
        grouping, 362-363
        importing, 363-365
        searching, 361

addresses (email), 201
administrators, printers, deletion of, 106-107
adware, Mozilla Firefox browser protections, 5
alarms for appointments, setting (Evolution), 372
ALSA (Advanced Linux Sound Architecture), 107-108

animation effects, presentations, setting (Impress), 319-321
anti-virus packages, 5
AOL Instant Messenger (AIM), 206
Appearance settings (GNOME desktop), 66
applets
    desktop icons, creating, 59-61
    Resolution Switcher, 5
    Volume Control, 5

applications
    adding
        Red Carpet, 154-156
        YaST, 154
    desktop icons, creating, 59-61
    Help Center, opening, 42-44
    installing
        Red Carpet, 164
        from tar archives, 168-170
        YaST, 165-168
    nonsession managed, 112
    Novell Evolution groupware features, 10
    OpenOffice.org
        Calc program, 8
        closing, 223
        Database User Tools program, 8
        Draw program, 8
        Impress program, 8
        opening, 221-222
        Writer program, 8
    quickstart icons, 37
        adding to desktop panels, 62-63
    removing (YaST), 167-168
    RPM files, installing, 160-162
    running from Run Application dialog box, 45

searching on subscribed channels (Red Carpet), 162-163
session managed, 112
updating
   Red Carpet, 154-160
   YaST, 154
virtual desktop, opening, 39

appointments
calendar (Evolution)
   alarms, 372
   classifications, 371
   creating, 369-372
   deleting, 387-389
   editing, 375
   moving, 377
   recurring, 372
   reminder options, 371
   viewing, 375
   views, 382-383

archiving files (File Roller), 144-147
area charts in spreadsheets (Calc), 294
.arj file format (archives), 144
ARPAnet, email roots, 200
arranging desktop icons, 61
assigning tasks (Evolution), 379-381
Assistive Technology Support
dasher package, 69
deactivating, 70
enabling, 69
gnome-mag package, 69
gnopernicus package, 69
gok package, 69

AT&T Bell Labs, UNIX development, 4
attachments (email)
opening (Evolution), 343-344
reading (Evolution), 345
saving (Evolution), 345
sending (Evolution), 340-341
sorting (Evolution), 345

audio on slides, adding (Impress), 316
autofill feature (Calc), 277
autoformatting tables in documents (Writer), 260
autologon options for iFolder client, 394
automatic synchronization of iFolder files, 398-399
AutoPilot (Writer) documents, creating, 240-243
autoYaST tool
automated NLD installations, 12-13
partitions, creating during installations, 13-14

B

back ups
archiving (File Roller), 149-151
creating (System Backup), 148-149
restoring from (Restore System utility), 148-149
restoring from archival status (File Roller), 151-152

background colors
documents
   setting (Writer), 254-257

backgrounds
color options, changing, 70-73
slide presentations, applying (Impress), 313
wallpaper images
   changing, 70-73
   screen placement, 72

bar charts in spreadsheets (Calc), 294
bookmarks for websites
creating (Mozilla Firefox), 187
deleting (Mozilla Firefox), 191

bookmarks for websites

editing (Mozilla Firefox), 189-191
importing/exporting (Mozilla Firefox), 189
moving (Mozilla Firefox), 189-191
naming (Mozilla Firefox), 188
sorting (Mozilla Firefox), 191-192
viewing list of (Mozilla Firefox), 188

boot loader, execution of, 20-21

booting process, 20

message displays, 21-22

borders in documents, setting (Writer), 254-257

bottom panel as GNOME desktop element, 33

Browse Icons dialog box, 59

browsing

files (Nautilus File Manager), 129-131
web pages
History list (Mozilla Firefox), 185-186
Mozilla Firefox, 176-180

buddy lists for IM sessions (Gaim Instant Messenger), 209

Build Search Index dialog box (Help Center), 44

built-in functions for formulas

date and time category (Calc), 282
financial category (Calc), 282
logical category (Calc), 282
math category (Calc), 282
statistical category (Calc), 282

burning

CDs, 11
files to CDs/DVDs (K3b software), 140-144

buttons on mouse, configuring, 95

C

Calc (OpenOffice.org), 220, 274

Formula bar, 274
Function bar, 274
Object bar, 274
spreadsheets
area charts, 294
bar charts, 294
cell formatting, 285-286
cell selection, 285-286
cells, 275
chart formatting, 294-297
chart insertion, 294-297
column insertion/deletion, 286-288
columns, 274
data entry, 275-278
data formatting, 278
data, filtering, 291-293
data, sorting, 291-293
date entry, 279
formulas, built-in functions, 282
formulas, copying, 279
formulas, creating, 280-281
formulas, Function AutoPilot, 283-284
functionality of, 275
line charts, 294
pie charts, 294
printing, 297-299
row insertion/deletion, 288
rows, 274
scatter charts, 294
sheet insertion/deletion, 289-291
size of, 274
text entry, 275-278
text formatting, 278

commands

calculator tool (Accessories submenu), 11
calendar (Evolution)
    appointments
        alarms, 372
        classifications, 371
        creating, 369-372
        deleting, 387-389
        editing, 375
        moving, 377
        recurring, 372
        reminder options, 371
        viewing, 375
        views, 382-383
    color coding, 369
    default view of, 368-369
    meeting invitations
        responding to, 377
        RSVPs, 375
        sending, 372-375
    multiple, 369
    preferences, setting, 383-384
categories, contacts, assigning to (Evolution), 362-363
cd command (change directory), 50-51
CDs
    burning, 11
    burning (K3b software), 140-144
cells in spreadsheets
    autofill feature (Calc), 277
    Calc (OpenOffice.org), 275
    compute totals (Calc), 278
    formatting (Calc), 285-286
    ranges (Calc), 278
    selecting (Calc), 285-286
channels, Internet Relay Chat (IRC), 215
character styles, applying (Writer), 247-248

charts in spreadsheets
    area type (Calc), 294
    bar type (Calc), 294
    formatting (Calc), 294-297
    inserting (Calc), 294-297
    line type (Calc), 294
    pie type (Calc), 294
    scatter type (Calc), 294
click speeds for mouse, configuring, 95
client (iFolder)
    autologon options, 394
    encryption pass phrases, 394-395
    folder location, 394
    launching, 392-395
    logon information, 392
clients (email), configuring, 202
clipart, OpenClipart.org website, 315
Clock applet, date and time settings, 39, 41
clock setting, Universal Coordinated Time (UTC), 42
closing OpenOffice.org applications, 223
colors of GNOME desktop, changing, 70-73
columns
    documents, setting (Writer), 254-257
    message list, adding (Evolution), 347
    spreadsheets
        Calc (OpenOffice.org), 274
        inserting/deleting (Calc), 286-288
command line
    accessing, 47-49
    exiting, 53
commands
    case-sensitivity of, 51
    file management
        cd (change directory), 50-51
        copy (copy file), 50

commands

ls (list), 50-51
mkdir (make directory), 50-52
rm (delete file), 50
rmdir (remove directory), 50-52
help information, viewing, 49
Linux Forum website, complete listing of, 51
recently used, viewing, 51
shell commands, 47
system, 53-54
    date (time settings), 53
    df (free disk space), 53-54
    du (total disk space), 53-54
    free (memory stats), 53-54
    kill (terminate), 53
    ps (current processes), 53-55
    su (root account), 56
compute totals, spreadsheet cells (Calc), 278
configuring
    global options for OpenOffice.org, 223-227
    hardware settings, Settings dialog box, 88-90
    keyboard settings
        Keyboard Preferences dialog box, 91-93
        Mouse Preferences dialog box, 94-96
    printer settings, 96-102
    system settings, Settings dialog box, 88-90
Conflict Bin (iFolder), files, viewing after synchronization, 400
Contact Editor (Evolution), tab options, 357
contacts, Address Book (Evolution)
    creating, 357-361
    editing, 359-360

    grouping, 362-363
    importing, 363, 365
    searching, 361
Controls subtheme, GNOME desktop, 79-80
cookies
    accepting, 194-195
    deleting, 196
    function of, 192
    handling, 193
    rejecting, 194-195
copy command (copy file), 50
copying files in Nautilus File Manager, 136-137
Create Launcher dialog box
    icons
        creation, 59-61
        URL pointers, 61
    quickstart icon creation, 63
CUPS (Common UNIX Print System), 96-97
cursors, mouse, configuring, 95

D

dasher package (Assistive Technology Support), 69
data in spreadsheets
    entry of (Calc), 275-278
    filtering (Calc), 291-293
    formatting (Calc), 278
    sorting (Calc), 291-293
Database User Tools program (OpenOffice.org), 8
date and time settings, changing, 39-41
date command (time settings), 53
dates in spreadsheets, entry of (Calc), 279
Day View calendar (Evolution), 382

downloading

deleting
- columns in spreadsheets (Calc), 286-288
- desktop icons, 61
- files (Nautilus File Manager), 134-136
- iFolder files, 398
- printers, 106-107
- rows in spreadsheets (Calc), 288
- sheets from spreadsheets (Calc), 289-291

dependencies in software, Red Carpet issues, 155-156

desktop
- background colors, changing, 70-73
- iFolder icon, accessing, 395-396
- wallpaper images
  - changing, 70-73
  - screen placement, 72

Desktop Background Preferences dialog box, Add Wallpaper button, 73

desktop icons
- arranging, 61
- as GNOME desktop element, 33
- removing, 61

desktop panels, quickstart icons
- adding to, 62-63
- removing, 63

df command (free disk space), 53-54

dictionary tool (Accessories submenu), 11

disabilities, accessibility settings
- Assistive Technology Support, 69-70
- keyboard mouse, 69
- keyboard shortcuts, 70
- sticky keys, 68

distributions
- free versus purchased versions, 6
- lack of end-user capabilities, 5
- Linux flavors, 4
- Mandrake Linux, 4
- RedHat Linux, 4
- SUSE Linux, 4
- viruses, lack of threat, 5

documents
- existing, opening (OpenOffice.org), 232-233
- exporting in PDF format (Writer), 269
- form letters, mail merging (Writer), 266-269
- icons, creating, 61
- multipage, navigating (OpenOffice.org), 239-240
- new, starting (OpenOffice.org), 228, 230
- OpenOffice.org, sharing with Microsoft Office users, 227-228
- PDF files, 104
- printing, 102-104, 269-270
- saving (OpenOffice.org), 230-231
- Writer, creating via AutoPilot (OpenOffice.org), 240-243

downloading
- files via Mozilla Firefox, 178
- newsgroups to Pan News Reader, 212-213
- pictures to Mozilla Firefox, 178
- slide designs to Impress application, 311
- templates to Impress application, 311

Drafts folder (Evolution), 337
Draw (OpenOffice.org), 8, 220
drivers for printers, selecting, 101
du command (total disk space), 53-54
dual-boot systems, partition creation considerations, 14
DVDs
- burning (K3b software), 140-144
- playing, 11

E

editing user accounts, 17
email
- account configuration, 200
  - addresses, 201
  - client tool, 202
  - corporate environments, 201
  - homes/small offices, 201
  - IMAP servers, 202
  - passwords, 201
  - POP3 servers, 201
  - SMTP servers, 201
- Evolution, 332
  - accounts, adding, 202-205, 334-336
  - accounts, identity information, 336
  - accounts, receive mail options, 336
  - accounts, send mail options, 336
  - Address Book, 356-357
  - Address Book, contact creation, 357-358
  - Address Book, contact groups, 362-363
  - Address Book, contact imports, 363-365
  - Address Book, contact list creation, 360-361
  - Address Book, contact modifications, 359-360
  - Address Book, contact searches, 361
  - composing, 338-339
  - Contact Editor, 357
  - Drafts folder, 337
  - filter rules, creating, 348-351
  - Folder list, 333
  - folder organization, 348-351
  - forwarding, 343
  - Inbox, 337
  - interface appearance, 333
  - Junk folder, 337
  - junk mail filter, 351-353
  - Menu bar, 332
  - messages, deleting, 387-389
  - opening attachments, 343-344
  - Outbox, 337
  - platforms support, 332
  - preferences, setting, 383-384
  - Preview pane, 333
  - reading, 341-345
  - replying to, 343
  - saving attachments, 345
  - searching, 347
  - sending, 339
  - sending with attachments, 340-341
  - Sent folder, 337
  - Shortcut bar, 333
  - sorting, 345, 347
  - synchronizing with Palm devices, 332
  - toolbar, 332

Trash folder, 337
vFolders, 337
vFolders, creating, 353-356
vFolders, viewing messages, 356
historical roots, 200

emblems (Nautilus File Manager)
file/folder icons, 124
folders, adding to, 128

emoticons in IM sessions, inserting (Gaim Instant Messenger), 210

encryption, pass phrases (iFolder client), 394-395

end-users, NLS development, 5

events, sounds, associating, 108

Evolution (email tool), 202, 332
accounts
adding, 202-205, 334-336
identity information, 336
receive mail options, 336
send mail options, 336
setup configuration, 202-205
Address Book, 356-357
contact lists, creating, 360-361
contacts, creating, 357-358
contacts, editing, 359-360
contacts, grouping, 362-363
contacts, importing, 363-365
contacts, searching, 361
appointments, deleting, 387-389
calendar
appointments, alarms, 372
appointments, classification of, 371
appointments, creating, 369-372
appointments, editing, 375
appointments, moving, 377
appointments, recurring, 372
appointments, reminder options, 371
appointments, viewing, 375, 382-383
color coding, 369
default view of, 368-369
meeting invitations, 372-377
multiple, 369
Contact Editor, tab options, 357
Drafts folder, 337
email, deleting, 387-389
Folder list, 333
Inbox, 337
interface appearance, 333
Junk folder, 337
Menu bar, 332
messages
column width, 347
composing, 338-339
filter rules, creating, 348-351
folder organization, 348-351
forwarding, 343
junk mail filter, 351-353
opening attachments, 343-344
reading, 341-345
replying to, 343
saving attachments, 345
searching, 347
sending, 339
sending with attachments, 340-341
sorting, 345
Outbox, 337
Outlook information, importing to (Outport tool), 365
Palm devices, synchronization, 332, 384-387

411

platforms support, 332
preferences, setting, 383-384
Preview pane, 333
Sent folder, 337
Shortcut bar, 333
tasks
    assigning, 379-381
    creating, 377-379
    marking as completed, 379
    multiple lists, 381-382
    status of, 379
toolbar, 332
Trash folder, 337
vFolders, 337
    creating, 353-356
    messages, viewing, 356

existing documents, opening (OpenOffice.org), 232-233

exiting command line, 53

extracting archival files (File Roller), 144-147

F

Failsafe GNOME, GUI troubleshooter, 23

Failsafe Terminal, GUI Troubleshooter, 23

file associations
    automatic configuration of, 115
    system settings, configuring, 90, 114-117

file manager tool (Accessories submenu), 11

File Roller
    backup files
        archiving, 149-151
        restoring from archival status, 151-152

files
    archiving, 144-147
    extracting from archives, 144-147

files
archiving (File Roller), 144-147
back ups
    archive creation (File Roller), 149-151
    creating (System Backup), 148-149
    restoring from archival status (File Roller), 151-152
burning to CDs/DVDs (K3b software), 140-144
desktop icons, creating, 59-61
directories, 120-122
downloading (Mozilla Firefox), 178
extracting from archives (File Roller), 144-147
hierarchical structure overview, 120-122
iFolder
    deleting, 398
    viewing on Conflict Bin, 400
management commands
    cd (change directory), 50-51
    copy (copy file), 50
    ls (list), 50-51
    mkdir (make directory), 50-52
    rm (delete file), 50
    rmdir (remove directory), 50-52
managing (Nautilus File Manager), 50
Nautilus File Manager
    accessing from USB memory sticks, 138-140
    browsing, 129-131

formatting

copying, 136-137

deleting, 134-136

moving, 136-137

opening, 129-131

preferences, behavior options, 125

preferences, configuring, 122-126

preferences, icon caption options, 125

preferences, list columns options, 125

preferences, preview options, 126

preferences, view options, 124

recent, accessing, 137-138

saving to USB memory sticks, 138-140

searching, 131-134

permissions, 128

restoring from back ups (Restore System utility), 148-149

servers, accessing remotely (iFolder), 392

standard folders, 120-122

synchronizing between web server and NLD system (iFolder), 398-400

trash, emptying options, 125

viewing (iFolder), 396

filtering data in spreadsheets (Calc), 291-293

filters

junk mail (Evolution), 351-353

messages, rules creation (Evolution), 348-351

floating frames, documents, inserting (Writer), 263

Folder list (Evolution), 333

folders

desktop icons, creating, 59-61

iFolder client, default location of, 394

messages, organization of (Evolution), 348-351

Nautilus File Manager

adding emblems to, 128

adding notes to, 128

copying, 127

creating, 126

deleting, 128

moving, 127

preferences, behavior options, 125

preferences, configuring, 122-126

preferences, icon caption options, 125

preferences, list columns options, 125

preferences, preview options, 126

preferences, view options, 124

permissions, 128

Font Preferences dialog box, 74-76

fonts

GNOME desktop

family selection, 75

preference settings, 74-76

rendering options, 75

Pick a Font dialog box, 74-76

footers in documents, inserting (Writer), 252-254

form letters, mail merges, creating (Writer), 266-269

formatting

cells (Calc), 285-286

charts in spreadsheets (Calc), 294-297

413

formatting

paragraphs, Writer (OpenOffice.org), 245-247
tables in documents (Writer), 260
text characters, Writer (OpenOffice.org), 243-245

Formula bar, Calc (OpenOffice.org), 274
formulas
   built-in functions
      date and time category (Calc), 282
      financial category (Calc), 282
      logical category (Calc), 282
      math category (Calc), 282
   built-in functions (Calc), 282
   mathematical operators (Calc), 280-281
   spreadsheets
      built-in functions (Calc), 282
      copying (Calc), 279
      creating (Calc), 280-281
      Function AutoPilot(Calc), 283-284

forwarding messages (Evolution), 343
free command (memory stats), 53-54
Free Software Foundation (FSF), GNU Project, 6
FTP sites, gFTP client, 216
Function AutoPilot (Calc), 283-284
Function bar
   Calc (OpenOffice.org), 274
   Impress (OpenOffice.org), 302
   Writer (OpenOffice.org), 229, 238
functions
   formulas
      date and time category (Calc), 282
      financial category (Calc), 282
      logical category (Calc), 282
      math category (Calc), 282
   FunctionAutoPilot (Calc), 283-284

G

Gaim Instant Messenger, 206
   buddy lists, 209
   configuring, 207
   logon sessions, 208
   message exchanges, 209
   messages, emoticon use, 210
gFTP client, FTP site access, 216
global options for OpenOffice.org, configuring, 223-227
GNOME Add a Printer utility, 96-102
GNOME (GNU Network Object Model Environment) desktop, 7
   appearance of, 7-8
   Appearance settings category, 66
   background colors, changing, 70-73
   bottom panel, 33
   command line, accessing, 47-49
   creation of, 32
   date and time settings, changing, 39-41
   desktop icons, 33
   elements of, 33
   fonts
      family selection, 75
      preference settings, 74-76
      rendering options, 75
GNOME.org, 32
gnome-session documentation tool, 113
GNU licensing, 6
hardware settings, 58
Hardware settings category, 66

Help Center, opening, 42, 44
Home folder
   closing, 35
   maximizing, 35
   opening, 35
icons
   creating, 59-61
   rearranging, 35
items, adding to menus, 63-65
menu system
   Programs, 36-37
   System, 36-37
modification options, 58
navigating, 34-35
Personal settings category, 65-70
personalizing, 58
programs, running from the Run Application dialog box, 45-46
quickstart icons, 33
   adding to desktop panels, 62-63
screensavers
   display modes, 76
      energy saving settings (Display Power Management compliance), 78
   locking options, 78-79
   previewing, 77
   selecting, 76-78
   timing settings, 78
System settings category, 66
themes, 58
   adding, 82-85
   Controls subtheme, 79-80
   custom creation, 82-85
   downloading, 80
   file extension, 84

Icons subtheme, 79-80
   selecting, 80-82
   Window Border subtheme, 79-80
top panel, 33
virtual desktop, 33
   applications, opening, 39
   management of, 37-39
   returning to original state, 39
   switching between, 38-39
wallpaper images
   changing, 70-73
   screen placement, 72
windows
   minimizing, 36
   preference settings, 85-86
   rolling up, 86
Workspace Switcher, 33
X Window System, 32-33

GNOME Terminal
command line, accessing, 47-49
entries, clearing, 49
file management commands
   cd (change directory), 50-51
   copy (copy file), 50
   ls (list), 50-51
   mkdir (make directory), 50-52
   rm (delete file), 50
   rmdir (remove directory), 50-52
system commands, 53-54
   date (time settings), 53
   df (free disk space), 53-54
   du (total disk space), 53-54
   free (memory stats), 53-54
   kill (terminate), 53
   ps (current processes), 53-55
   su (root account), 56

gnome-mag package (Assistive Technology Support), 69
gnome-session tool, 113
GNOME.org, 7, 32, 80
GnomeMeeting videoconferencing tool, 215-216
gnopernicus package (Assistive Technology Support), 69
GNU (GNU's not Unix) Project
    Free Software Foundation (FSF), 6
    Linux development, 6
    software, 6
        free versus purchased versions, 6
        GNOME desktop, 6
        licensing strategy, 6
        Mozilla Firefox browser, 6
        OpenOffice.org, 6
        other platforms, 6
GNU.org, distribution licensing, 6
gok package (Assistive Technology Support), 69
Google, searching (Mozilla Firefox), 176
graphics
    documents, inserting (Writer), 263-265
    OpenClipart.org website, 315
    slides, adding (Impress), 315-317
grouping contacts in Address Book (Evolution), 362-363
groupware, 10
GUIs (graphical user interfaces)
    as replacement for command-line environments, 6
    GNOME desktop, 7
        adding items to menus, 63-65
        appearance of, 7-8
        Appearance settings category, 66

bottom panel, 33
closing Home folder, 35
color options, 70-73
command line, accessing, 47-49
creation of, 32
date and time settings, 39-41
desktop icons, 33
elements of, 33
font options, 74-76
font options, family selection, 75
font rendering options, 75
GNOME.org, 32
hardware settings, 58
Hardware settings category, 66
Help Center, 42-44
icons, creating, 59-61
icons, rearranging, 35
maximizing Home folder, 35
menu system, 36-37
minimizing windows, 36
modification options, 58
navigating, 34-35
opening Home folder, 35
Personal settings category, 65-67
Personal settings category, accessibility options, 68-70
personalizing, 58
quickstart icons, 33, 62-63
running programs from Run Application dialog box, 45-46
screensaver lock options, 78-79
screensaver options, 76-78
System settings category, 66
themes, 58, 80
themes, adding, 82-85
themes, custom creation, 82-85

themes, downloading, 80
themes, file extension, 84
themes, selecting, 79-82
top panel, 33
virtual desktop, managing, 37-39
virtual desktop, opening applications, 39
virtual desktop, returning to original state, 39
virtual desktop, switching between, 38-39
wallpaper options, 70-73
windows, preference settings, 85-86
windows, rolling up, 86
X Window System, 32-33
KDE, 7
selecting at logons, 23

H

handouts for slide show presentations, printing (Impress), 328-329
Happy GNOME greeter, 23
hard drives
    minimum space requirements, 13
    partitions
        Linux versus Windows assignments, 13
        root, 13-14
        swap, 13-14
hardware
    clock settings, 42
    NLD requirements
        hard drive space, 13
        memory, 13
        processors, 13
        video display, 13

settings
    configuring, 88-90
    keyboard options, 89-93
    mouse options, 89, 94-96
    printer options, 89, 96-102
    screen resolution options, 89
    sound options, 89
Hardware settings (GNOME desktop), 66
headers in documents, inserting (Writer), 252-254
Help Center
    advanced searches, 44
    Build Search Index dialog box, 44
    content topics
        generating search indexes, 44
        printing, 42
        searching, 42-44
    Glossary tab, 44
    navigation area, 42
    opening (GNOME desktop), 42-44
    Search tab, 44
    view window, font sizes, 42
Help system (OpenOffice.org)
    accessing, 233-235
    topics
        bookmarking, 235
        browsing, 234
History list for web pages, accessing (Mozilla Firefox), 185-186
Home folder
    closing, 35
    maximizing, 35
    opening, 35
HP DirectJet technology, 97

I

icons
- Browse Icons dialog box, 59
- Create Launcher dialog box, URL pointers, 61
- documents, creating, 61
- GNOME desktop
  - arranging, 61
  - creating, 59-61
  - removing, 61
- menus, dragging from, 59
- rearranging, 35

Icons subtheme (GNOME desktop), 79-80

ICQ IM, 206

iFolder
- account settings, 401-402
- automatic file synchronization process, 398-399
- client
  - autologon options, 394
  - encryption pass phrases, 394-395
  - folder location, 394
  - launching, 392-395
  - logon information, 392
- desktop icon, accessing from, 395-396
- files
  - deleting, 398
  - remote access, 392
  - synchronizing between web server and NLD system, 398-400
  - viewing, 396
  - viewing in Conflict Bin, 400
- function of, 392
- local files, moving to, 396
- manual file synchronization process, 399-400
- preferences, setting, 401-402
- user information, 402
- web browsers, accessing from, 396-398

IMAP servers (Internet Message Access Protocol), 202

importing
- contacts from Address Book (Evolution), 363-365
- Outlook information to Evolution (Outport tool), 365

Impress (OpenOffice.org), 220, 302
- Function bar, 302
- Object bar, 302, 313
  - drawn object tools, 314
  - image formatting tools, 314
  - text formatting tools, 313
- Presentation bar, 302
- presentations
  - animation effects, 319-321
  - audio additions, 316
  - creating, 303-305
  - graphics additions, 315-317
  - handouts, printing, 328-329
  - master slides, 317
  - Notes view, 321-323
  - Outline view, 321-323
  - saving, 306
  - slide backgrounds, 313
  - slide design changes, 311-313
  - slide insertion, 306-307, 310
  - slide layout, modifying, 309
  - slide show execution, 327
  - slide show modifications, 325-326
  - slide show timings, 323-325
  - slide text, 306-308

Slides view, 321-323
spreadsheet additions, 317
transition effects, 305, 317-318
type templates, 304
Inbox (Evolution), 337
indexes in Help Center, generating, 44
inserting
    charts in spreadsheets (Calc), 294-297
    columns in spreadsheets (Calc), 286-288
    floating frames in documents (Writer), 263
    graphics
        in documents (Writer), 263, 265
        to slide presentations (Impress), 315-317
    rows in spreadsheets (Calc), 288
    sheets in spreadsheets (Calc), 289-291
    tables in documents (Writer), 258-260
    text frames in documents (Writer), 261-263
Install and Remove Software tool (YaST), 154
installing
    applications
        from tar archives, 168-170
        Red Carpet, 164
        YaST, 165-168
    desktop themes, 84
    NLD, 15
        partitions creation, 13-14
        root account creation, 15-16

        user account creation, 15-16
        YaST (Yet Another Setup Tool), 12-13
    package updates for applications (Red Carpet), 156-158
    printers to networks, 96
    RPM files, 160-162
instant messaging
    AOL Instant Messenger (AIM), 206
    commercial options, 206
    Gaim Instant Messenger, 206
        buddy lists, 209
        configuring, 207
        emoticons, 210
        logon sessions, 208
        message exchanges, 209
    ICQ IM, 206
    Internet Relay Chat (IRC), 206
    Jabber IM, 206
    MSN IM, 206
    Yahoo! IM, 206
interface (Evolution), 333
Internet Relay Chat (IRC), 206, 215
invitations to meetings
    responding to (Evolution), 377
    RSVPs (Evolution), 375
    sending (Evolution), 372-375

J - K

Jabber IM, 206
java file format (archives), 144
Junk folder (Evolution), 337

K3b software, CDs/DVDs, burning files to, 140-144
KDE (K Desktop Environment), 7

Keyboard Preferences dialog box, 91-93
keyboards
  cursor blink speeds, 92
  layouts, configuring, 93
  mouse, accessibility settings, 69
  repeat key times, 92
  settings, configuring, 89-93
  shortcut actions, enabling, 70
  sticky keys, enabling, 68
  typing breaks, enabling, 92
kill command (terminate), 53

L

Language option (Logon Manager), 22
launching
  applications via quickstart icons, 37
  iFolder client, 392-395
layouts of keyboards, configuring, 93
lha file format (archives), 144
line charts in spreadsheets (Calc), 294
Linux
  as alternative to Windows OS, 4
  distributions, 4
  open source, 4
  Torvalds, Linus, 4
  UNIX as basis for, 4
  viruses, lack of threat, 5
Linux Forum website, commands listing, 51
Linux.org, software searches, 161
List View calendar (Evolution), 383
local files, moving to iFolder, 396
Lock Screen tool (screensavers), 78-79
log offs
  process, 25-29
  System menu options
    Logout, 25-27
    Restart, 25
    Shutdown, 25-29

log ons
  iFolder client, 392
  requirements
    passwords, 20
    valid usernames, 20
    usernames/password entries, 22, 25
Logoff dialog box, GNOME desktop settings, 25
Logon Manager
  Actions options, 23
  Language options, 22
  Session options, 23
  username/password entries, 22, 25
logons for IM sessions, launching (Gaim Instant Messenger), 208
Logout options, 25-27
ls command (list), 50-51

M

mail merges for form letters, creating (Writer), 266-269
Main toolbar (OpenOffice.org), 238
Mandrake Linux, 4
manual synchronization of iFolder files, 399-400
master slides (Impress), 317
mathematical operators in formulas (Calc), 280-281
meetings (Evolution)
  invitations, responding to, 377
  invitations, RSVPs, 375
  invitations, sending, 372-375
  preferences, setting, 383-384
memory, minimum hardware requirements, 13
Menu bar (Evolution), 332

menus
- desktop icons, dragging from, 59
- GNOME desktop
  - Programs, 36-37
  - System, 36-37
- items, adding, 63-65

messages
- attachments
  - opening (Evolution), 343-344
  - saving (Evolution), 345
- column width (Evolution), 347
- composing (Evolution), 338-339
- email, deleting (Evolution), 387-389
- filter rules, creating (Evolution), 348-351
- folder organization (Evolution), 348-351
- forwarding (Evolution), 343
- junk mail filter, setting (Evolution), 351-353
- Pan News Reader
  - posting, 214
  - viewing, 214
- reading (Evolution), 341-345
- replying to (Evolution), 343
- searching (Evolution), 347
- sending, 339
  - with attachments (Evolution), 340-341
- sorting (Evolution), 345

Microsoft Office, OpenOffice.org documents, sharing with, 227-228

mkdir command (make directory), 50-52

monitors
- refresh rates, 89
- screen resolution, changing, 110-111

screensavers
- locking options, 78-79
- selecting, 76-78
- settings, configuring, 89
- video settings, configuring, 110

Month View calendar (Evolution), 383

mouse
- acceleration, configuring, 95
- buttons, configuring, 95
- click speeds, configuring, 95
- cursors, configuring, 95
- keyboard arrows, configuring for disabilities, 69
- settings, configuring, 89, 94-96

Mouse Preferences dialog box, 94-96

moving
- files (Nautilus File Manager), 136-137
- local files to iFolder, 396
- text in documents (Writer), 257

Mozilla Firefox, 174
- adware/spyware protections, 5, 9
- Back/Forward button, 177
- cookies
  - accepting, 194-195
  - deleting, 196
  - function of, 192
  - handling, 193
  - rejecting, 194-195
- Download Manager, 175
- extensions, 175
- files, downloading, 178
- GNU licensing, 6
- Google searches, 175-176
- multiple platform support, 9
- pictures, downloading, 178

Mozilla Firefox

preferences
  advanced, 175
  downloads, 175
  general, 175
  privacy, 175
  web, 175
security barriers, 174
tabbed browsing, 175
URL entry, 176
web pages
  browsing, 176-180
  browsing history, 185-186
  pop-up controls, 182-185
  printing, 180-182
  tabbed browsing, 178-180
website bookmarks
  creating, 187
  deleting, 191
  editing, 189-191
  importing/exporting, 189
  moving, 189-191
  naming, 188
  sorting, 191-192
  viewing list of, 188
Mozilla.org, Firefox browser resources, 9
MSN IM, 206
multimedia applications, Volume Control adjustments, 37
multiple calendars (Evolution), viewing, 369

N

naming sheets in spreadsheets (Calc), 289-291
Nautilus File Manager, 50, 120
  files
    accessing, 120-122
    accessing from USB memory sticks, 138-140

browsing, 129-131
copying, 136-137
deleting, 134-136
emblems, 124
moving, 136-137
opening, 129-131
recent, accessing, 137-138
saving to USB memory sticks, 138-140
searching, 131-134
folders
  adding emblems to, 128
  adding notes to, 128
  copying, 127
  creating, 126
  deleting, 128
  emblems, 124
  moving, 127
preferences
  behavior options, 125
  configuring, 122-126
  icon caption options, 125
  list columns options, 125
  preview options, 126
  view options, 124
network proxies
  Autoconfiguration URL, 117
  FTP Proxy, 117
  HTTP Proxy, 116
  manual configuration, 116
  Secure HTTP Proxy, 116
  Socks Host, 117
  system settings, configuring, 90, 114-117
network printers, deleting, 106-107
new documents, starting (OpenOffice.org), 228-230

OpenOffice.org

newsgroups (Usenet), Pan News Reader, 210
   configuring, 210-212
   messages, posting, 214
   messages, viewing, 214
   newsgroup lists, downloading, 212-213
   subscribing to, 214
NLD (Novell Linux Desktop), 3
   end-user environments, 5
   hardware requirements
      hard drive space, 13
      memory, 13
      processors, 13
      video display, 13
   installation, 15
      root account creation, 15-16
      user account creation, 15-16
      YaST (Yet Another Setup Tool), 12-13
   Novell.com documentation, 67
   SUSE Linux distribution, 4
   user accounts
      adding, 17
      editing, 17
   user migration from Windows and Macintosh systems, 3
nonsession managed applications, 112
notes
   folders, adding to (Nautilus File Manager), 128
   slide show presentations, printing (Impress), 328-329
Notes view, presentations, viewing (Impress), 321-323
Novell Evolution. *See* Evolution

Novell iFolder. *See* iFolder
Novell Linux Desktop. *See* NLD
Novell.com, NLD documentation, 67
numbers, styles, applying (Writer), 247-248

O

Object bar
   Calc (OpenOffice.org), 274
   Impress (OpenOffice.org), 302, 313-314
   Writer (OpenOffice.org), 229, 238
open source software, 4-6
OpenClipart.org website, 315
opening
   files (Nautilus File Manager), 129-131
   OpenOffice.org applications, 221-222
OpenOffice.org, 6, 220
   applications
      closing, 223
      interface, 229
      opening, 221-222
      switching between windows, 223
   available versions, 221
   Calc, 220, 274
      Formula bar, 274
      Function bar, 274
      Object bar, 274
      spreadsheets, area charts, 294
      spreadsheets, bar charts, 294
      spreadsheets, cell formatting, 285-286
      spreadsheets, cell selection, 285-286
      spreadsheets, cells, 275

spreadsheets, chart formatting, 294-297
spreadsheets, chart insertion, 294-297
spreadsheets, column insertion/deletion, 286-288
spreadsheets, columns, 274
spreadsheets, data entry, 275-278
spreadsheets, data filtering, 291-293
spreadsheets, data formatting, 278
spreadsheets, data sorting, 291-293
spreadsheets, date entry, 279
spreadsheets, formulas, 279-284
spreadsheets, functionality of, 275
spreadsheets, line charts, 294
spreadsheets, pie charts, 294
spreadsheets, printing, 297, 299
spreadsheets, row insertion/deletion, 288
spreadsheets, rows, 274
spreadsheets, scatter charts, 294
spreadsheets, sheet insertion/
deletion, 289-291
spreadsheets, size of, 274
spreadsheets, text entry, 275-278
spreadsheets, text formatting, 278
documents
   existing, opening, 232-233
   new, starting, 228-230
   saving, 230-231
   sharing with Microsoft Office users, 227-228
Draw, 220
Function bar, 229

global options
   Appearance option, 227
   Colors option, 226
   configuring, 223-227
   General option, 225
   Paths option, 226
   User Data option, 225
   View option, 226
Help system
   accessing, 233-235
   topics, bookmarking, 235
   topics, browsing, 234
Impress, 220, 302
   Function bar, 302
   Object bar, 302
   Presentation bar, 302
   presentations, animation effects, 319-321
   presentations, audio additions, 316
   presentations, creating, 303-305
   presentations, graphics additions, 315-317
   presentations, master slides, 317
   presentations, Notes view, 321-323
   presentations, Outline view, 321-323
   presentations, printing handouts for, 328-329
   presentations, saving, 306
   presentations, slide backgrounds, 313
   presentations, slide design changes, 311-313
   presentations, slide insertion, 306-307, 310

presentations, slide layout, 309

presentations, slide show execution, 327

presentations, slide show modifications, 325-326

presentations, slide show timings, 323-325

presentations, slide text, 306-308

presentations, Slides view, 321, 323

presentations, spreadsheet additions, 317

presentations, transition effects, 305, 317-318

presentations, type templates, 304

Object bar, 229

suite elements

    Calc, 8

    Database User Tools, 8

    Draw, 8

    Impress, 8

    Writer, 8

website resources, 8

Writer, 220

    documents, background colors, 254-257

    documents, borders, 254-257

    documents, column selection, 254-257

    documents, creating via AutoPilot, 240-243

    documents, exporting as PDF, 269

    documents, floating frame insertion, 263

    documents, footer insertion, 252-254

    documents, graphics insertion, 263-265

    documents, header insertion, 252-254

    documents, moving text, 257

    documents, navigating, 239-240

    documents, page number insertion, 252-254

    documents, printing, 269-270

    documents, styles, 247-252

    documents, table autoformatting, 260

    documents, table formatting, 260

    documents, table insertion, 258-260

    documents, text frame insertion, 261-263

    form letters, mail merging, 266-269

    Function bar, 238

    launching, 238

    Main toolbar, 238

    Object bar, 238

    paragraph formatting, 245-247

    text character formatting, 243-245

    toolbars, customizing, 238

    XML default file format, 221

OpenOffice.org website

    slide designs (Impress), downloading, 311

    templates (Impress), downloading, 311

operators, mathematical formulas (Calc), 280-281

Outbox (Evolution), 337

Outline view, presentations, viewing (Impress), 321-323

Outport tool, importing Outlook information to Evolution, 365

P

packages
- applications
  - installing (YaST), 167-168
  - removing (YaST), 167-168
- tar archives, installing applications from, 168-170
- updates, installing (Red Carpet), 156-158

page numbers in documents, inserting (Writer), 252-254

Page Style dialog box (Writer), document format settings, 254-257

Palm PDA devices, synchronizing, 384-387

Pan News Reader, 210
- configuring, 210-212
- messages
  - posting, 214
  - viewing, 214
- newsgroups
  - downloading, 212-213
  - subscribing, 214

paragraphs
- formatting (Writer), 245-247
- styles
  - applying (Writer), 247-248
  - creating (Writer), 250-252

partitions
- dual-boot systems, creation considerations, 14
- Linux versus Windows assignments, 13
- root, creation of, 13-14
- swap, creation of, 13-14

passwords
- log on requirements, 20
- root accounts, selection criteria, 15-16
- screensavers, lock settings, 78-79

passwords (email), 201

Patch CD Update tool (YaST), 154

patches (software), 154

PDAs, Palm types, synchronizing (Evolution), 384-387

PDF documents, exporting as (Writer), 269

performance of system processes, viewing (System Monitor), 54

permissions for files, assignment of, 128

Personal settings (GNOME desktop), 65-67
- accessibility options, 68-70

personalizing GNOME desktop
- background colors, 70-73
- wallpaper images, 70-73

Pick a Font dialog box, 74-76

pictures, downloading (Mozilla Firefox), 178

pie charts in spreadsheets (Calc), 294

playing DVDs, 11

pop-up controls in web pages (Mozilla Firefox), 182-185

POP3 servers (email), 201

positioning graphics in documents (Writer), 263-265

preferences
- Evolution, setting, 383-384
- iFolder, setting, 401-402
- Mozilla Firefox
  - advanced settings, 175
  - download settings, 175

printing

general settings, 175
privacy settings, 175
web settings, 175
Presentation bar (OpenOffice.org), Impress, 302
presentations Impress (OpenOffice.org), 220, 302
animation effects, 319-321
audio additions, 316
creating, 303-305
Function bar, 302
graphics additions, 315-317
handouts, printing, 328-329
master slides, 317
Notes view, 321, 323
Object bar, 302, 313
    drawn object tools, 314
    image formatting tools, 314
    text formatting tools, 313
Outline view, 321, 323
Presentation bar, 302
saving, 306
slide backgrounds, 313
slide design changes, 311-313
slide insertion, 306-307, 310
slide layout, modifying, 309
slide show
    execution, 327
    modifications, 325-326
    timings, 323-325
    text, 306-308
Slides view, 321, 323
spreadsheet additions, 317
transition effects, 305, 317-318
type templates, 304

Preview pane (Evolution), 333
Print dialog box, 102
number of copies option, 103
paper type option, 103
print jobs
canceling, 105
managing, 104-106
pausing, 105
Print Queue dialog box, 104-106
job cancel option, 105
paused jobs, 105
printers
adding to networks, 96
CUPS (Common UNIX Print System), 96
deleting, 106-107
documents, printing, 102-104
drivers, selecting, 101
GNOME Add a Printer utility, 96-102
HP DirectJet technology, 97
jobs
    canceling, 105
    managing, 104-106
    pausing, 105
network connection types
    CUPS (IPP), 100
    HP DirectJet, 101
    Unix (LPD), 101
    Windows (SMB), 100
settings, configuring, 89, 96-102
test pages, printing, 101
printing
documents (Writer), 269-270
help topics, 42
spreadsheets (Calc), 297-299
web pages (Mozilla Firefox), 180-182

processors, minimum hardware requirements, 13
programs, running from Run Application dialog box, 45-46
Programs menu, 36-37
  items, adding to, 63-65
proxy servers, 90
ps command (current processes), 53, 55

Q - R

quickstart icons, 33
  adding to desktop panels, 62-63
  applications, launching, 37
  removing from desktop panels, 63

ranges in spreadsheet cells (Calc), 278
reading messages (Evolution), 341, 343
recent files, accessing (Nautilus File Manager), 137-138
recently used commands, viewing, 51
recurring appointments, setting (Evolution), 372
Red Carpet
  applications
    installing, 164
    searching on subscribed channels, 162-163
    updating, 156-160
  software dependencies, 155-156
  versus YaST, 156
RedHat Linux, 4
refresh rates of monitor screens, 89
regular expressions as search tool, 134
Regular-Expressions.info website, search resources, 134
Rehearsal Slide Show Timings feature (Impress), 323-325
removing applications (YaST), 167-168

replying messages (Evolution), 343
Resolution Switcher applet, 5
Restart option, log offs, 25
Restore Backup utility, 148-149
rm command (delete file), 50
rmdir command (remove directory), 50-52
root accounts, 5
  accessing from command line (su command), 56
  NLD installations
    creation of, 15
    passwords, 15-16
root administrators, user accounts, adding, 20
root partitions, creation of, 13-14
rows in spreadsheets
  Calc (OpenOffice.org), 274
  inserting/deleting (Calc), 288
RPM (RedHat Package Manager) files, installing, 160-162
Run Application dialog box, applications, launching from, 45-46
Run Program command (System menu), 45-46

S

SAMBA protocol, 97
saving
  documents (OpenOffice.org), 230-231
  files to USB memory sticks (Nautilus File Manager), 138-140
scatter charts in spreadsheets (Calc), 294
screen resolution, changing, 110-111
screensavers
  display modes, 76-77
  energy saving settings (Display Power Management compliance), 78

slides

GNOME desktop
    locking options, 78-79
    selecting, 76-78
locking settings, 78-79
timing settings, 78

searching
    applications via subscribed channels (Red Carpet), 162-163
    contacts in Address Book (Evolution), 361
    email messages (Evolution), 347
    files in Nautilus File Manager, 131-134

security
    adware protections, 5
    Mozilla Firefox built-in barriers, 174
    software patches, 154
    spyware protections, 5
    viruses, lack of threat in Linux distributions, 5

sending messages via Gaim Instant Messenger, 209

Sent folder (Evolution), 337

servers, remote file access (iFolder), 392

session managed applications, 112

Session option (Logon Manager), 23

sessions
    gnome-session tool, 113
    log off process, 25-29
    nonsession managed applications, 112
    session managed applications, 112
    system settings
        configuring, 90, 112-114

Sessions dialog box, 112-114

Settings dialog box
    hardware options, 88-90
    system options, 88-90

shell commands, 47
Shortcut bar (Evolution), 333
Shutdown options, log offs, 25, 28-29
slide show presentations
    handouts, printing (Impress), 328-329
    modifying settings (Impress), 325-326
    rehearsing timings (Impress), 323-325
    running (Impress), 327
slides
    Impress designs, downloading (OpenOffice.org website), 311
    presentations
        animation effects (Impress), 319-321
        audio additions (Impress), 316
        backgrounds (Impress), 313
        creating (Impress), 303, 305
        design changes (Impress), 311-313
        Function bar (Impress), 302
        graphics additions (Impress), 315-317
        inserting (Impress), 306-307, 310
        layout modifications (Impress), 309
        master (Impress), 317
        Notes view (Impress), 321-323
        Object bar (Impress), 302, 313-314
        Outline view (Impress), 321-323
        Presentation bar (Impress), 302
        saving (Impress), 306
        Slides view (Impress), 321-323
        spreadsheet additions (Impress), 317

slides

text additions (Impress), 307-308
text entry (Impress), 306
transition effects (Impress), 305, 317-318
type templates (Impress), 304
presentations (Impress), 302
printing (Impress), 328-329
Slides view (Impress), 321-323
SMTP servers (email), 201
software
dependencies, Red Carpet issues, 155-156
groupware, 10
searches (Linux.org), 161
sorting
bookmarks in Mozilla Firefox, 191-192
data in spreadsheets (Calc), 291-293
sound
adding to slide presentations (Impress), 316
ALSA (Advanced Linux Sound Architecture), 107-108
settings, configuring, 89
system bell, enabling, 108
system settings, configuring, 90, 107-108
volume level, setting, 110
Sound Preferences dialog box, 108
spam message filters, setting (Evolution), 351-353
spreadsheets
Calc (OpenOffice.org), 220, 274
area charts, 294
bar charts, 294
cell formatting, 285-286

cell selection, 285-286
cells, 275
chart formatting, 294-297
chart insertion, 294-297
column insertion/deletion, 286-288
columns, 274
data entry, 275, 277-278
data formatting, 278
data, filtering, 291-293
data, sorting, 291-293
date entry, 279
Formula bar, 274
formulas, built-in functions, 282
formulas, copying, 279
formulas, creating, 280-281
formulas, Function AutoPilot, 283-284
Function bar, 274
functionality of, 275
line charts, 294
Object bar, 274
pie charts, 294
printing, 297-299
row insertion/deletion, 288
rows, 274
scatter charts, 294
sheet insertion/deletion, 289-291
size of, 274
text entry, 275-278
text formatting, 278
cells
autofill feature (Calc), 277
compute totals (Calc), 278
ranges (Calc), 278
slides, adding (Impress), 317

spyware, Mozilla Firefox browser protections, 5
standard folders, 120-122
sticky keys, accessibility settings, 68
Stored Cookies dialog box, deletion of cookies option, 196
strong passwords, root accounts selection criteria, 15-16
styles in documents, applying (Writer), 247-252
Stylist (Writer)
> documents, formatting attributes, 247-249
> paragraphs, formatting attributes, 250-252

su command (root account), 56
Subpixel Font Smoothing, 75
subscribing newsgroups (Pan News Reader), 214
subscription channels
> applications, searching (Red Carpet), 162-163
> software availability, 161

SUSE Linux, 4
swap partitions, creation of, 13-14
switching OpenOffice.org windows, 223
synchronizing
> iFolder files
>> between web server and NLD system, 398-400
>> viewing in Conflict Bin, 400
> Palm PDA devices (Evolution), 384-387

System Backup utility, backup files, creating, 148-149
system bell, enabling, 108

system commands
> date (time settings), 53
> df (free disk space), 53-54
> du (total disk space), 53-54
> free (memory stats), 53-54
> kill (terminate), 53
> ps (current processes), 53-55
> su (root account), 56

System menu, 36-37
> log off options
>> Logout, 25-27
>> Restart, 25
>> Shutdown, 25, 28-29
> Run Program command, 45-46

System Monitor, performance statistics, viewing, 54
system settings
> configuring, 88-90
> file associations, 90, 114-117
> GNOME desktop, 66
> network proxies, 90, 114-117
> sessions, 90, 112-114
> sound preferences, 90, 107-108

System Update tool (YaST), 154

T

tabbed browsing in web pages (Mozilla Firefox), 178-180
tables
> autoformatting (Writer), 260
> formatting (Writer), 260
> inserting (Writer), 258-260

tar file format (archives), 145
> installing from, 168-170

tar.gz file extension, desktop theme files, 84

tasks
    assigning (Evolution), 379-381
    creating (Evolution), 377, 379
    marking as completed (Evolution), 379
    multiple lists (Evolution), 381-382
    status of (Evolution), 379
templates, Impress, downloading (OpenOffice.org website), 311
test pages for printers, printing, 101
text
    character formatting (OpenOffice.org), 243-245
    character formatting (Writer), 243-245
    documents, moving (Writer), 257
    paragraph formatting (OpenOffice.org), 245-247
    slides, adding (Impress), 307-308
    spreadsheets
        entry of (Calc), 275-278
        formatting (Calc), 278
    styles, applying (OpenOffice.org), 247-252
text frames in documents, inserting (Writer), 261-263
Theme Preferences dialog box, 81-85
themes (GNOME desktop), 58
    adding, 82-85
    Controls subtheme, 79-80
    custom creation, 82-85
    downloading, 80
    file extension, 84
    Icons subtheme, 79-80
    selecting, 80-82
    Window Border subtheme, 79-80

time and date settings, changing, 39-41
timings of slide shows, rehearsing (Impress), 323-325
to-do lists
    assigning (Evolution), 379-381
    creating (Evolution), 377-379
    marking items as completed (Evolution), 379
    multiple lists (Evolution), 381-382
    status of (Evolution), 379
toolbars
    Evolution, 332
    OpenOffice.org, customizing, 238
tools (Accessories submenu)
    calculator, 11
    dictionary, 11
    file manager, 11
top panel as GNOME desktop element, 33
Torvalds, Linus, Linux development, 4
transition effects in presentations, setting (Impress), 305, 317-318
trash, emptying options, 125
Trash folder (Evolution), 337
troubleshooting tips, boot loading process, 22
typing breaks, enabling, 92

U

Universal Coordinated Time (UTC), 42
UNIX, AT&T Bell Labs development, 4
updating applications
    Red Carpet, 154-160
    YaST, 154
Updating Systems/Processing Transactions dialog box, 160
URLs, entering (Mozilla Firefox), 176

USB memory sticks
    accessing (Nautilus File Manager), 138-140
    saving to (Nautilus File Manager), 138-140

Usenet newsgroups, Pan News Reader, 210
    configuring, 210-212
    messages, posting, 214
    messages, viewing, 214
    newsgroup lists, downloading, 212-213
    subscribing to groups, 214

user accounts
    adding, 17
    editing, 17
    NLD installations, creation of, 15-16
    user versus administrator rights, adding, 20

User's Manual, Help Center, opening, 42-44
usernames, log on requirements, 20
users, migration from Windows and Macintosh systems, 3

V

vFolders (Evolution), 337
    creating, 353-356
    messages, viewing, 356

video display, minimum hardware requirements, 13
video settings of monitors, configuring, 110
videoconferencing (GnomeMeeting), 215-216
viewing files in iFolder, 396
virtual desktop, 33
    applications, opening, 39
    management of, 37-39
    original state, returning to, 39
    switching between (Workspace Switcher), 38-39

virtual folders (Evolution), 337
    creating, 353-356
    messages, viewing, 356

viruses, lack of threat in Linux, 5
Volume Control applet, 5
Volume Control dialog box, 37, 110
volume level, setting, 110

W

wallpaper on GNOME desktop
    changing, 70-73
    screen placement, 72

web browsers
    iFolder icon, accessing, 396-398
    Mozilla Firefox
        adware/spyware protections, 9
        multiple platform support, 9

web pages
    browsing, 176-180
        history, 185-186
    pop-up controls, 182-185
    printing, 180-182
    tabbed browsing, 178-180

websites
    bookmarks
        creating, 187
        deleting, 191
        editing, 189-191
        importing/exporting, 189
        moving, 189-191
        naming, 188
        sorting, 191-192
        viewing list of, 188

cookies
    accepting, 194-195
    deleting, 196
    function of, 192
    handling, 193
    rejecting, 194-195
GNOME.org, 7
    desktop theme downloads, 80
GNU.org, distribution licensing, 6
instant messaging tools, 206
KDE.org, 7
Linux Forum, commands listing, 51
Linux.org, software searches, 161
Mozilla.org, Firefox browser resources, 9
Novell.com, NLD documentation, 67
OpenClipart.org, 315
OpenOffice.org, 8
Regular-Expressions.info website, 134

Week View calendar (Evolution), 383
Window Border subtheme, GNOME desktop, 79-80
windows
    GNOME desktop
        preference settings, 85-86
        rolling up, 86
    OpenOffice.org, switching between, 223
    pop-up controls (Mozilla Firefox), 182-185
Windows OS, disadvantages of, 3
Windows Preferences dialog box, 86

word processors, Writer (OpenOffice.org), 220
    documents
        background colors, 254-257
        borders, 254-257
        column insertion, 254-257
        creating via AutoPilot, 240-243
        floating frame insertion, 263
        graphics insertion, 263, 265
        moving text, 257
        navigating, 239-240
        printing, 269-270
        styles, 247-252
        table autoformatting, 260
        table formatting, 260
        table insertion, 258-260
        text frame insertion, 261-263
    exporting as PDF, 269
    footer insertion, 252-254
    form letters, mail merging, 266-269
    Function bar, 238
    header insertion, 252-254
    launching, 238
    Main toolbar, 238
    Object bar, 238
    page number insertion, 252-254
    text character formatting, 243-245
    text paragraph formatting, 245-247
    toolbars, customizing, 238
Workspace Switcher, 33
    virtual desktop, switching between, 38-39
Workweek View calendar (Evolution), 383

Writer (OpenOffice.org), 220
- documents
  - background colors, 254-257
  - borders, 254-257
  - column insertion, 254-257
  - creating via AutoPilot, 240-243
  - exporting as PDF, 269
  - floating frame insertion, 263
  - footer insertion, 252-254
  - graphics insertion, 263-265
  - header insertion, 252-254
  - moving text, 257
  - navigating, 239-240
  - page number insertion, 252-254
  - printing, 269-270
  - styles, 247-252
  - table autoformatting, 260
  - table formatting, 260
  - table insertion, 258-260
  - text frame insertion, 261-263
- form letters, mail merging, 266-269
- Function bar, 238
- launching, 238
- Main toolbar, 238
- Object bar, 238
- text
  - character formatting, 243-245
  - paragraph formatting, 245-247
- toolbars, customizing, 238

Writer program (OpenOffice.org), 8

X - Y - Z

X Window System, graphical display environment, 32-33

XML (eXtensible Markup Language), 221

Yahoo! IM, 206

YaST (Yet Another Setup Tool), 12-13
- application installations
  - Install and Remove Software tool, 154
  - Patch CD Update tool, 154
  - System Update tool, 154
- applications
  - installing, 165-168
  - removing, 167-168
- autoYaST version (automated), 12-13
- date and time settings, changing, 41
- desktop preference settings, 13
- hardware configuration, 13
- NLD installations, 12-13
- user accounts
  - adding, 17
  - editing, 17
- versus Red Carpet, 156

zip file format (archives), 145

Novell Press

www.novellpress.com

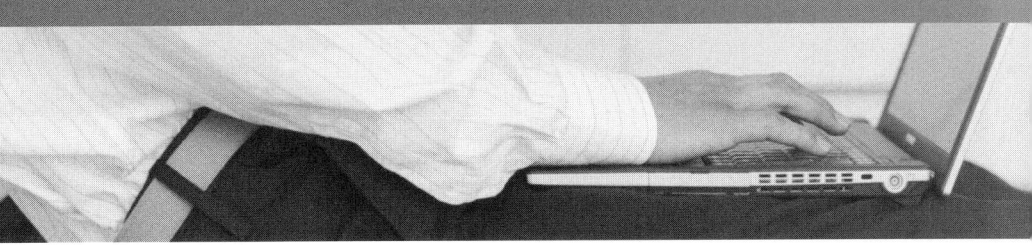

Expanding Choice
Jason Williams, Peter Clegg, and Emmett Dulaney
ISBN: 0-672-32722-8
$29.99 US

Novell Linux Desktop 9 Administrator's Handbook
Emmett Dulaney
ISBN: 0-672-32790-2
$39.99 US

Linux Kernel Development, Second Edition
Robert Love
ISBN: 0-672-32720-1

Novell Certified Linux Engineer (CLE) 9 Study Guide
Robb H. Tracy
ISBN: 0-672-32787-2

Novell Open Enterprise Server Administrator's Handbook, SUSE LINUX Edition
Jeffrey Harris
ISBN: 0-672-32749-X

SUSE LINUX Enterprise Server 9 Administrator's Handbook
Peter Kuo and Jacques Béland
ISBN: 0-672-32735-X

Novell Certified Linux Professional (CLP) Study Guide
Emmett Dulaney
ISBN: 0-672-32719-8

Novell Press is the Novell-authorized publisher of books about Novell products and Novell-related technologies. A partnership between Novell and Pearson Education, Novell Press combines the subject matter expertise of Novell employees with the editorial and marketing experience of Pearson to publish the best books about Novell products and open-source technologies on the market today.

What's On the DVD

The book's DVD includes the complete version of the Novell Linux Desktop 9.

Hardware Requirements

- Pentium II+, 266 MHz or higher, or any AMD64 or Intel EM64T processor
- 1–2 physical CPUs
- Minimum 128 MB (256 MB recommended, 64 GB maximum) physical RAM
- 800 MB available disk space
- 8 TB maximum disk space
- 800 x 600 or higher display resolution; 1024 x 768 or higher suggested

Installing Novell Linux Desktop 9

You may need to change your BIOS settings to boot directly from a DVD drive. If you are not sure if you can boot from a DVD, you should start or reboot your computer and go into the computer's BIOS setup utility. Pressing the DEL (Delete) or the F2 key usually accesses this utility while the computer is starting up. Once in the BIOS setup utility, look for a boot priority option. If your computer is capable of booting from a DVD, your DVD drive will be listed. Make sure the DVD drive has a higher boot priority than your hard drive(s) to enable booting from a DVD.

Once you have determined that you can boot from the DVD, start or reboot your machine with the disc in your DVD drive. After a few moments, you should see the installation routine. Follow the onscreen prompts to finish the installation.

NOTE

To get Service Pack 2, you can download the ISO disk images from download.novell.com or use the Red Carpet update tools to download individual packages from update.novell.com. Service Pack 2 includes the most current device drivers for the supported architectures (x86, AMD64 and EMT64).

License Agreement

By opening this package, you are also agreeing to be bound by the following agreement:

You may not copy or redistribute the entire DVD-ROM as a whole. Copying and redistribution of individual software programs on the DVD-ROM is governed by terms set by individual copyright holders.

The installer and code from the author(s) are copyrighted by the publisher and the author(s). Individual programs and other items on the DVD-ROM are copyrighted or are under an Open Source license by their various authors or other copyright holders.

This software is sold as-is without warranty of any kind, either expressed or implied, including but not limited to the implied warranties of merchantability and fitness for a particular purpose. Neither the publisher nor its dealers or distributors assumes any liability for any alleged or actual damages arising from the use of this program. (Some states do not allow for the exclusion of implied warranties, so the exclusion may not apply to you.)